הישר

OR

THE BOOK OF JASHER;

REFERRED TO IN

JOSHUA AND SECOND SAMUEL.

FAITHFULLY TRANSLATED

FROM THE ORIGINAL HEBREW INTO ENGLISH.

Published 2000
The Book Tree
Escondido, CA

NEW YORK:
PUBLISHED BY M. M. NOAH & A. S. GOULD,
AT 144 NASSAU-STREET.
1840.

The Book of Jasher
ISBN 1-58509-081-6

©2000
THE BOOK TREE
All Rights Reserved

Published by
The Book Tree
Post Office Box 724
Escondido, CA 92033

We provide controversial and educational products to help awaken the public to new ideas and information that would not be available otherwise. We carry over 1100 Books, Booklets, Audio, Video, and other products on Alchemy, Alternative Medicine, Ancient America, Ancient Astronauts, Ancient Civilizations, Ancient Mysteries, Ancient Religion and Worship, Angels, Anthropology, Anti-Gravity, Archaeology, Area 51, Assyria, Astrology, Atlantis, Babylonia, Townsend Brown, Christianity, Cold Fusion, Colloidal Silver, Comparative Religions, Crop Circles, The Dead Sea Scrolls, Early History, Electromagnetics, Electro-Gravity, Egypt, Electromagnetic Smog, Michael Faraday, Fatima, Fluoride, Free Energy, Freemasonry, Global Manipulation, The Gnostics, God, Gravity, The Great Pyramid, Gyroscopic Anti-Gravity, Healing Electromagnetics, Health Issues, Hinduism, Human Origins, Jehovah, Jesus, Jordan Maxwell, John Keely, Lemuria, Lost Cities, Lost Continents, Magick, Masonry, Mercury Poisoning, Metaphysics, Mythology, Occultism, Paganism, Pesticide Pollution, Personal Growth, The Philadelphia Experiement, Philosophy, Powerlines, Prophecy, Psychic Research, Pyramids, Rare Books, Religion, Religious Controversy, Roswell, Walter Russell, Scalar Waves, SDI, John Searle, Secret Societies, Sex Worship, Sitchin Studies, Smart Cards, Joseph Smith, Solar Power, Sovereignty, Space Travel, Spirituality, Stonehenge, Sumeria, Sun Myths, Symbolism, Tachyon Fields, Templars, Tesla, Theology, Time Travel, The Treasury, UFOs, Underground Bases, World Control, The World Grid, Zero Point Energy, and much more. Call **(800) 700-TREE** for our *FREE BOOK TREE CATALOG* or visit our website at www.thebooktree.com for more information.

INTRODUCTION

According to some sources, this book was once the original start of the Bible. Whether that was true or not, we do know that it was once contained in the Bible, being referred to in Joshua and Second Samuel. It states, "Is not this written in the Book of Jasher?" in Joshua 10:13; and "Behold, it is written in the Book of Jasher," in 2 Samuel 1:18. These references have puzzled Bible students and scholars for centuries.

Many versions of this book have appeared over the years and were proven to be forgeries. Therefore this version, which seems to be the clear and legitimate one, is often dismissed due to those many "pretenders" in the past. According to the translator (in his Preface), the reference to *Jasher* in Second Samuel is one place that authenticates this book, stating how it clears up an otherwise vague Biblical reference. At the same time he admits that some things seem to have been added to the book over the years, but that has happened to other works and, according to him, should not change the overall legitimacy found here.

Not being experts in ancient Hebrew, we can only provide this rare work to the world and let those who read it be the judges as to its legitimacy and value.

It's been claimed that the fable of creation in the Bible was compiled from this one book, in greatly altered form. Although we are not entirely sure, careful study of this book may in fact prove the claim to be true.

The story behind *The Book of Jasher* is an interesting one. The Jewish priest named Esdras, or Ezra, was among the able-bodied men taken to Babylon as prisoners after Nebuchadnezzer captured Jerusalem in 587 BC. While there, Esdras studied holy Chaldean scrolls that dealt with the Creation. He condensed these works into scrolls that later became the Pentateuch, according to some, and they were then attributed to Moses. These scrolls later became part of the library at Alexandria. Around 389 AD the custodian at the library was informed of a plot to burn it down, so quickly gathered some of the more valuable scrolls together and sent them to Arabia for safe-keeping. One of them was

The Book of Jasher. The library was indeed burned down, but *Jasher*, among only a few other valuable works, was saved.

A man named Albinus Alcuin discovered this work and did the original translation of it from the Hebrew in 800 AD. It was later suppressed but finally rediscovered in 1829, when it was once again suppressed. Only now has it reemerged and we hope, for the first time, that it will become widely available and be judged properly for its value, whatever that might be.

Paul Tice

PREFACE.

It is with pleasure that I am able to present to the American public the translation of the Book of Jasher, as referred to in *Joshua* and *Second Samuel*, which, after several years' negotiation with the owner and translator of the work in England, I have succeeded in obtaining.

There are many books named in the Old Testament, which are now classed among the missing books, or books supposed to have been lost amidst the many revolutions which have occurred in Judea. These books are not included in the Jewish Canons, and it is questionable whether there are any missing of what were considered as emanating from inspired writers ; for, when the works enumerated in the Bible could not be found after the most diligent search, the inference was, that the names applied to other books, or that they were different versions of the same work.

Thus, the *Book of the Covenant*, (Exodus xxiv. 7.) was a mere collection of the injunctions and institutions delivered by the Almighty to Moses. So it might also be said of the *Book of the Law*, (Deut. xxxi. 9.) *The Book of the wars of the Lord* (Numbers xxi. 14.) cannot be found, and is every where spoken of as one of the missing books. Dr. Lightfoot, in his Chronicles, thinks that Moses refers to a book of his own composing, written by command of God, (Exodus xvii. 14.) We think, however, that the Book of Judges is the one referred to as the *Book of the wars of the Lord ;* because, in that book we have all the exploits of the Hebrews detailed at length. We find in Chronicles and Kings a number of books

named, which are not to be found. The acts of David the King, written
in the Book of Samuel the Seer, also in the Book of Nathan the Prophet,
and also in the Book of Gad the Seer; the acts of Solomon are in the
Book of Nathan the Prophet, and also in the Book of Abijah the Shulam-
ite; the acts of Rehoboam in the Book of Shemaiah the Prophet; the acts
of Jehoshaphat in the Book of Jehu. The journals of the kings of Judah
and Israel; the three thousand and five songs, and a treatise on botany
and animated nature, by this learned king, are lost; so also are the "Acts
of Manasseh." These works, not having been found by Ezra, could not
have been inserted in the Old Testament, and consequently cannot be considered as having been written by divine inspiration. Nevertheless, it
would be assuming more than is required or necessary, to say that there
were no other books in the time of Ezra, than those considered as divinely
inspired. St. Austin says, "The penmen of the Sacred Scripture writ
some things as they are, men with historical lore and diligence : other
things they writ as prophets, by inspiration from God." We thus have a
classification of their labors, both as historians and as prophets. The ne-
gligence of the Jews in ancient days, and their constant transition from
one country to another, occasioned many losses of the sacred writings.
The Book of Deuteronomy was lost for a long time. There were many
books rejected by the Canons which are still objects of curiosity, and
venerable for their antiquity. The prayer of King Manasseh, Bel and
the Dragon, the two Books of Esdras, the Book of the Maccabees,
and the Book of Enoch, recently found and translated from the Ethiopic.
The Book of Jasher, referred to in Joshua and Second Samuel, has been
long an object of great curiosity. Some of the Hebrew writers contend
that it was the lives and acts of Abraham, Isaac, and Jacob, and other
patriarchs, who were called *Jasherim*, the Just. Dr. Lightfoot thinks it
is the Book of the Wars of God, and so the reader may think in perusing
the various battles it recounts. Grotius calls it a triumphal poem. Jose-
phus says, "That by this book are to be understood certain records kept
in some safe place on purpose, giving an account of what happened among
the Hebrews from year to year, and called Jasher, or the upright, on account of the fidelity of the annals."

It is known that such have been the curiosity and anxiety to discover this missing book, that several forgeries under that name have appeared from time to time; and the Rev. Mr. Horne, in his Introduction to the Study of the Scripture, has been at some pains to collect a history of the various fabrications of Jasher; the most remarkable of which was originally published in England, in the year 1750, by a person called Illive, and purported to be a translation from a Hebrew work of that name, found in Persia by *Alcuin*. It was republished in Bristol in the year 1829, and a copy is now in my possession. It is a miserable fabrication, occupying but sixty two and a half pages, with copious notes, making out Jasher to be one of the Judges, whereas the translation of the word is the upright, or the upright record. In the same work of Dr. Horne, a slight reference is made to the Book of Jasher, written in Rabbinical Hebrew, said to have been discovered in Jerusalem at its capture under Titus, and printed in Venice in 1613. This is the book now translated into English for the first time. Long prior to the destruction of Jerusalem, the Jews had established themselves in various parts of Spain and Italy; they traded to the bay of Gibraltar, as historians affirm, in the earliest periods of history; and Basnage mentions that in Sagunto, a town in Spain, a tombstone was discovered, bearing the following inscription in the Hebrew language: "*This is the tomb of Adoniram, an officer of King Solomon, who came to collect the tribute, and died the   day,*" &c. There can be no doubt that Spain, probably France and Italy, were tributary to Solomon. It is, however, certain, that the Jews carried with them into Spain, on their dispersion, an immense number of manuscripts and sacred rolls, where they remained many years, and were, in the eleventh century, placed in their great college at Cordova, and from thence were conveyed to Venice on the first discovery of printing. The printer's Hebrew preface to Jasher shows that it was a painful transcript from a very old and almost illegible Hebrew record, and printed by and with the consent of the great Consistory of Rabbins at Venice, who alone had the power of publishing such works from the Hebrew records as they deemed authentic. From the Venice edition of Jasher, another edition was many years subsequently published, in Lemberg, in Gallicia. Both editions, in Hebrew, are now in my possession; and the Royal Asiatic Society, having found a copy of Jasher in Calcutta, gave orders to have it translated, which order was countermanded when it was ascertained that considerable progress had been made in England in this translation. The following copy of a letter from the secretary to the translator, shows the estimate which that learned Society placed upon the work.

ROYAL ASIATIC SOCIETY HOUSE.
Grafton St., Bond St., London, Sept. 2, 1831.

DEAR SIR :

I am extremely obliged by your having favored me with the sight of Mr. Noah's letter, and in reply to your letter, mention that the Oriental Translation Committee does not consider that it has any claims on your work, and if that ever the Rev. Mr. Adams translates the Book of Jasher, it will not be in the lapse of several years. Hoping that your praiseworthy and valuable labors in that interesting work will soon, in one shape or other, be presented to the public,

I remain, Dear Sir,
Your obliged and ob't Serv't,
WM. HUTTMAN.

Whatever may have been written and published by commentators, relative to the fabrications of Jasher, I am persuaded they had no reference to this work, although this is the work slightly touched upon by Dr. Horne, as the publication in Venice, on the first discovery of printing; but of its origin and history he knew nothing beyond the rumor that it had originally been brought from Jerusalem. There are some events recorded in Jasher, that are found in the Talmud, no doubt copied from Jasher; for although we find in the Talmud, the Mishnah, and Gemarrah, many parables and fanciful tales, to effect moral and religious purposes, yet every thing that we have in Jasher we find recorded in the Bible, with this difference, that in Jasher the occurrences of the Bible are amplified and detailed at length. The celebrated philosopher, Mendelsohn, expresses a high opinion of this work. There are, nevertheless, some events which are recorded in Jasher, which may create surprise, particularly a detail of the rape of the Sabines, which, at the first glance, I was disposed to consider as an interpolation; but a little reflection satisfied me that it was an event placed in proper chronological order. Pizron, in his Revolution of Empires, or Antiquities of Nations, says, (page 164,) "It is therefore likely from what I have said, that several of the Titans, in the reign of Uranus, or, at least, in that of Saturn, staying and fixing themselves in that part of Italy which is adjacent to the Tiber and the Appenines, were afterward called Umbrians. If such were the case, as it seems it was, the settlement of the Titans in Italy was made about the time of the calling of Abraham, that is, when he left Chaldea, to-go and dwell in the land of Canaan." Page 175, "Now, if all this came to pass, it must have happened about the time Deucalion reigned in Greece, or some years after the deluge that happened under that prince." If as Pizron says, the separation of the Sabines from the Umbrians took place 1500 years before Christ, it will not be far distant from the time at which Jasher places the rape of the Sabine women, in the 91st year of the life of Abraham.

The following is the translator's preface, and with all his admitted learning and ability, he has been unable to do justice to the beauty, grandeur, and alike the simplicity of the original Hebrew. I also subjoin a translation of the Hebrew preface and a translation of the printer's preface, being all the documents in my possession.

Without giving it to the world as a work of Divine inspiration, or assuming the responsibility to say that it is not an inspired book, I have no hesitation in pronouncing it a work of great antiquity and interest, and a work that is entitled, even regarding it as a literary curiosity, to a great circulation among those who take pleasure in studying the Scriptures.

M. M. Noah.

New-York, April, 1839.

TRANSLATOR'S PREFACE.

THE age in which we live has been, and continues to be, particularly distinguished by a laudable desire in the minds of men, to inquire into the various states of knowledge, and of the arts, as they existed in times anterior to the Christian era; animated with these noble and elevated views, a considerable number of individuals, greatly distinguished for their genius and learning, have in succession turned their attention to the East—to those celebrated countries, in which the arts of civilization and the lights of science first dawned upon, enlightened, and embellished human society. The magnificent and unequalled remains of the arts in Egypt, Babylonia, Assyria, Palestine, and Persia, have, from time to time, been visited and explored; and it has been amidst these fallen monuments of human grandeur, that the adventurous and enlightened traveller has found himself amply rewarded for his laborious and hazardous undertakings; for, amidst these wrecks of human greatness, he has succeeded in gathering ample evidence, in confirmation of many of the most important truths recorded in sacred history.

Profane histories have, indeed, conveyed down to us some account of these kingdoms, and of the mighty monarchs who, during a long succession of ages, ruled over them; but the events which they relate are evidently so mixed up with exaggeration, and so adulterated with fable, that, however celebrated their authors might have been, and however fascinating may be the style of their composition, the religious and philosophic student turns from them with dissatisfaction, to the divinely authenticated annals of the Hebrews; because, it is from these alone that he can derive true information concerning the rise, the splendour, the decline, and the real causes of the ruin of those celebrated empires.

In the sacred history we are presented with the only authentic, and, of course, the only valuable information concerning the origin of the universe, —of men and all other animated creatures,—of the gradual increase of the human race,—of the flood in the year A. M. 1656, of which mighty event there are existing evidences to the present day; evidences, so universal and so ponderous, that all the ingenuity of the sceptical geologists will never be able to remove them in order to make room for their plausible hypotheses.

The ever memorable events and transactions recorded in Scripture are with many others of the most interesting nature, comprehended in the Book of Jasher; and they are all arrayed in that style of simple, unadorned majesty and precision, which so peculiarly distinguishes the genius of the Hebrew language; and this, together with other numerous internal evidences, it is presumed will go far to convince the Hebrew scholar that the book is, with the exception of some doubtful parts, a venerable monument of antiquity; and that, notwithstanding some few additions may have been made to it in comparatively modern times, it still retains sufficient to prove it a copy of the book referred to in Joshua, ch. x., and 2 Samuel, ch. i. There are not more than seven or eight words in the whole book that by construction can be derived from the Chaldean language.

The printed Hebrew copy, in the hands of the translator, is without points. During his first perusal of it, some perplexities and doubts rose up in his mind respecting its authenticity: but the more closely he studied it, the more its irresistible evidence satisfied him, that it contained a treasure of information concerning those early times, upon which the histories of other nations are either silent, or cast not a single ray of real light; and he was more especially delighted to find that the evidence of the whole of its contents went to illustrate and confirm the great and inestimable truths which are recorded in divine history, down to a few years later than the death of Joshua, at which period the book closes.

In this extraordinary book, the reader will meet with models of the most sublime virtue, devotion and magnanimity, that cannot fail to raise his admiration, and, at the same time, to excite a generous feeling of emulation to follow the glorious examples set before him.

With these preliminary observations, the translator now respectfully proceeds to lay before the readers a few remarks upon the contents of the book. The title ספר הישר is literally, "the upright or correct record;" but because the book was not known, it was therefore termed the "Book of Jasher;" this has caused some persons, who are ignorant of the Hebrew language, to suppose that Jasher was the name of a prophet, or of one of the Judges of Israel; an instance of which appears in a publication which came from the press about the middle of the last century, and which purported to have been a translation into English of the Hebrew manuscript of Jasher, found at Gazna in Persia; which translation *only* was said to have been thence brought by Alcuin. When the translator wrote to the Editor of the London Courier, in November last, he was not aware that the copy of Jasher, announced in the Bristol Gazette as an important discovery, had reference to that fictitious book, which, through the kindness of a friend, he had previously obtained a sight of, and was soon convinced that the whole book was the work of some sceptic in England, in imitation of the language of Scripture, as it was sent forth from the press without the name of printer, bookseller, editor or publisher; and it is evident that those who were concerned in getting it up, in making Jasher the name of a Judge of Israel were ignorant of the very rudiments of the language, from which they pretended to have translated it, as it is well known, even to a tyro in the Hebrew language, that the definite article, ה is never prefixed to proper names.

The important transactions which are narrated with so remarkable a brevity in the Bible, are, in Jasher, more circumstantially detailed; as in the instance of the murder of Abel by his brother Cain, a particular account is given of the disagreement which preceded it, and of the pretext which Cain sought for the commission of the crime. It appears, also, that when the divine judgment condemned him to wander upon the earth, his wife accompanied him, not to the land of *Nod*, for no such place is mentioned; but, from this book it appears that the word *Nod*, in the Scripture, has been given for the participle of the verb נדד " to move or wander about. Jasher has it thus:

ויצא קין בעת ההיא מלפני יהוה מן המקום אשר היה שם ' וילך נע
ונודד בארץ קדמת עדן הוא וכל אשר לו

" And at that time Cain went forth from the presence of the Lord, from the place where he was; and he went moving and wandering in the land at the east of Eden, he and all belonging to him."

In the passage respecting the birth of Cain and Abel, three daughters are also mentioned. According to Jasher, the art of writing appears to have been known and practised from the earliest periods; it is stated that Cainan was informed beforehand by God, of the intended destruction of mankind by the flood, which he engraved upon tablets of stone, and preserved amongst his treasures.

This book contains a more detailed account of the awful circumstances attending the commencement of the flood, and of the conduct of Noah toward the terrified multitude who had assembled about the ark, when the fatal moment had arrived, and their doom was irrevocably fixed.

A particular delineation of the life and character of Enoch is given, showing, that by his wisdom he reigned over the sons of men, continually instructing them in truth, righteousness, and a knowledge of the Most High.

Jasher informs us, that in the days of Peleg, not only the families of the human race were separated and spread abroad, but that the earth itself was divided ; and of both these facts, it may be presumed, there are sufficient existing evidences, even at this day. This book gives, also, a more detailed account of the genealogies of the descendants of Japheth, Shem, and Ham, and of the various parts of the earth which were colonized by them.

Connected with this period of the history is given an account of Nimrod ; in which is strikingly depicted the arbitrary and violent character of his conduct and government. The contested point, as to whether Nimrod was the founder of the Assyrian Empire, is here decided. The cause of the dispute amongst commentators proceeded from the word אַשׁוּר in Gen. chapter x. ver. 11, signifying either the name of a man, or the name of the land of Assyria. Jasher has it thus :

ויצא אשור בן שם הוא ובניו ובני ביתו &c. ויבנו שם ערים ארבעה '

"And Asher, the son of Shem, went forth, he and his sons, and the children of his household, &c., and they there built four cities."

Jasher clearly elucidates a number of genealogical and chronological difficulties, which occur in the Bible ; an instance is here adduced of the genealogy of Seir, the Horite, upon which the Bible is silent.

The learned commentator, Aben Ezra, remarks, שעיר לא ידענו יחוסו " Seir, his genealogy we do not know ;" and the word החרי is supposed to come from חור a noble ; but Jasher gives us the descent of Seir, (which accounts for his being called the Horite,) in the following words :

וילך שעיר בן חור בן חוי בן כנען

"And Seir, the son of Hur, the son of Hivi, the son of Canaan, went," &c. ; hence he was called the Horite, from Hur, his father.

The character of Abraham, for piety, true dignity and hospitality, appears to stand unrivalled ; but the most affecting and beautiful account in this book, is that of Abraham offering up his son Isaac. The mutual affection of the father and son, and their willing devotion and obedience to the commands of their Maker, are so exquisitely described, that the heart of him who can peruse the narrative without being deeply affected, must be callous indeed. The conduct of Sarah, as connected with this unexampled and glorious event, was altogether worthy of the wife of Abraham, and the mother of Isaac. At this time Sarah died at Kireath-arba. Her funeral is described as having been magnificent ; and it is expressly mentioned, that it was attended by Shem, the son of Noah, Eber his son, king Abimelech, together with 'Anar, Ashcol and Mamre, and other great people of the land.

In the Bible, Sarah is the only woman whose age is given at her death; but it may be interesting to the reader to know, that Jasher generally states the ages of all the women who are particularly mentioned in the course of the history.

From this book we learn that Noah and Abraham were contemporaries. How beautiful the contemplation of the meeting of these two Patriarchs, the one being a monument of God's mercy, and the other having the promise of the favour and grace of God, not only to himself, but to his seed after him. This fact might be proved from Scripture; but from the 32d verse in the 11th chapter of Genesis, most of the Christian commentators have erroneously dated the birth of Abraham 60 years later than it actually took place; as it is generally stated that he was born A. M. 2008, whereas the regular calculation in the Bible leads us to 60 years earlier, viz. 1948. The only cause of this error has been that Abraham's departure from Haran, at the age of 75, is recorded close to the description of the death of Terah, at the age of 205, in Gen. ch. xi. v. 32. Although this is the frequent manner of Scripture, to record events out of the regular order of succession, (an instance of which we find in Isaac, whose death is recorded in Gen. xxxv. 29, when we know from the calculations given us in Scripture, that Isaac's death, must have taken place when Joseph was about 29 years old; and the description given in Jasher, of Isaac's coming from Hebron to comfort Jacob upon the loss of Joseph, is beautiful,) it is of great importance, in its making a difference of 60 years in the chronology of the world.

This book gives a particular account of the instruction received by Abraham, Isaac and Jacob, from Shem and Eber, through which they became so excellent in piety and wisdom, their tutors in learning having lived to so great an age; and Shem particularly, who, being acquainted with all that was known before the flood, could therefore strengthen his precepts of virtue, the true worship of God, and the necessary dependance upon him alone, by recording the awful events which he had seen.

The history of Joseph has always been considered one of the most admirable and interesting on record. It is composed in a style of simple and artless eloquence, which touches every feeling heart. A judicious critic has observed, that he considers it a perfect composition. This history, in Jasher, enters more into detail concerning the affairs of Potiphar's wife, Zelicah; Joseph's magnificent procession through the cities of Egypt, on coming into power; the pomp with which he was attended by Pharaoh's chariots, officers, and people, when he went up to meet his father; the affecting scene which then took place, together with other remarkable incidents. This beautiful narrative might justly be entitled, the triumph of virtue and piety ; and it is presumed that few can peruse it, unmoved by sentiments of the highest admiration, mixed with the deepest feelings of sympathy. The history of the Israelites during their sojourning in Egypt, contains an account of many interesting particulars not noticed in the Bible. Toward the latter end of this period, Balaam, Job, Jannes, and Jambres, appear to have acted their respective parts in some memorable transactions.

This book clears up the reference in 2 Samuel, ch. i., by showing that David, in the commencement of his beautiful elegy on the death of Saul and Jonathan, revived an injunction given by Jacob in his dying charge to his son Judah, contained in Jasher in these words :

אך למד נא בניך קשת וכל כלי מלחמה

" But teach, I pray thee, thy children the use of the bow, and all instruments of war," &c. This goes far to prove the authenticity of the book, as it beautifully clears up what was always considered obscure.

If commentators upon the holy Scriptures have sought for illustrations in the works of Homer, Pliny, Herodotus, and other profane writers ; if they have anxiously caught at glimmerings among the absurdities of Paganism, and the obscurities of Heathen fables, the translator humbly and respectfully hopes that they will now grant a favorable reception to evidence of an entirely opposite character, which is presented in the Book of Jasher.

He does not recommend it to their notice as a work of inspiration, but as a monument of history, comparatively covered with the ivy of the remotest ages ; as a work possessing, in its language, all the characteristic simplicity of patriarchal times ; and as such, he conceives it peculiarly calculated to illustrate and confirm the sacred truths handed down to us in the Scriptures.

But in making these observations, he is far from offering it as a perfect record. Like all other ancient writings, (except the inspired volume,) it has in some respects suffered from the consuming hand of time ; and there is reason to believe that some additions have been made to it. In fine, it contains a history of the lives and memorable transactions of all the illustrious characters recorded in sacred history, from Adam down to the time of the Elders, who immediately succeeded Joshua.

TRANSLATION OF THE HEBREW PREFACE.

THIS BOOK IS THAT WHICH IS CALLED THE UPRIGHT BOOK.

IT has at this time been ascertained by us that when the holy city Jerusalem was destroyed by Titus, all the military heads went in to rob and plunder, and that amongst the officers* of Titus was one whose name was Sidrus, who went in to search, and found in Jerusalem a house of great extent, and took away all the spoils which he found there ; when he wished to go out of the house, he looked at the wall and fancied that he saw treasures there, so he broke down the wall and the building and found a cask full of various books of the Law, the Prophets, and the Hagiographa,† also books of the kings of Israel, and of the kings of other nations, as well as many other books of Israel, together with the books of the Mishnah adopted and established ; many rolls were also lying there : he also found there all sorts of provision and wine in abundance, and discovered an old man sitting there, who was reading in those books. When the officer saw this great sight he was greatly astonished, and said to the old man, why dost thou sit alone in this place, without any person remaining with thee ? So the old man answered, for many years past was I aware of this second destruction of Jerusalem, so I built this house and made for myself a balcony,‡ and I brought with me these books to read, and I brought also sufficient provision, thinking thereby to‖ save my life.

And God caused the old man to find favor in the eyes of the officer, who brought him forth with respect with all his books, and they went from city to city and from country to country until they reached Sevilia ; and the officer found that this old man was possessed of wisdom and understanding and acquainted with various kinds of science, upon discovering which he raised and honored him, was constantly in his house and was taught by him all sorts of wisdom, and they built for themselves a lofty and capacious house in the suburbs of Sevilia and placed there all those books.

This house is yet in Sevilia unto this day, and they wrote there all the events that would hereafter take place amongst the kings of the world unto the coming of our Messiah.

---

* הגמון Buxton gives this word "*episcopus*" which, besides a bishop, means also a lieu-tenant, overseer, superintendant. See Arach.

† Psalms, Proverbs, &c.

‡ אכסדרה or porch, a Talmudical word derived from the Greek. See Arach.

‖ See Jeremiah 38 2, the same expression.

And it came to pass that when God carried[*] us away with a mighty captivity by the hands of the kings of Edom, from city to city and from country to country in bitter anxiety, this book, called "The Generations of Adam" together with other books came into our hands, for they came from that house in Sevilia, and they came afterward to our city Napuli, which city is under the sway of the king of Spain, (whose glory may be exalted.) And when we saw these books, that they were books of all wisdom, we resolved in our minds to print them like all the books that came to our hands. Now this book is the best and most valuable of all, and of this book twelve copies have reached us, and we searched in them and found them all of one copy, there was no difference, nothing added and nothing deficient, nor any alteration in letters, words or events, for they were all alike as it were of one copy.

Since, therefore, we saw in this book great merit urging us to this resolve, we are determined to print it—and it is found written that this book is called the Book Jasher, because all its transactions are in that order as they had taken place in the world as regards priority and succession, for thou wilt not find in this book any postponement of events that were anterior, or priority of those that were posterior, but every thing is recorded in its place and time.

Thou wilt thus find that it relates the death of such a one at the particular time of the life of another and thus throughout. Owing to this it was called Sepher Hajashar, but it is customary to call it the Generations of Adam, the reason of which is that they call it by that with which it commences, but the chief name thereof is the book "JASHER" owing to the reasons we have assigned. Now it is found that this book is translated into Greek, entitled " *Lo libris de los divitiis,*"

It is also found written in the book of the Asmoneans which has come down to us, that in the days of Ptolemy king of Egypt, he ordered his servants to go and gather all the books of laws, and all the books of Chronicles which they could find in the world, so that he might become wise through them, and by examining them become acquainted with the subjects and events of the world, and to compile from them a book in all matters of jurisdiction regarding the affairs of life, thereby to exercise pure justice. So they went and collected for him nine hundred and sixty five books and brought to him, when he commanded them to go again and seek to complete the number of a thousand books, and they did so. After this, some of the persecutors of Israel stood up before him and said, O king, why wilt thou trouble thyself in this manner? Send to the Jews in Jerusalem that they shall bring unto thee the book of their law which was written for them from the mouth of the Lord by their Prophets, from which thou mayest become wise, and regulate all judgments and laws according to thy desire ; so the king hearkened to their words, and sent to the Jews upon this matter, who sent to him this book, for they could not give unto him the book of the Lord, for they said, we cannot give the law

---

[*] See same expression, Isaiah 22. 17.

of the Lord to a stranger. Now when this book came to the hands of
Ptolemy he read it and it pleased him greatly, and he searched therein
in his wisdom, and he examined it and found therein what he had desired,
and he neglected all the other books which they had collected for him,
and he blessed him who had advised him to this thing.

After some time the persecutors of Israel became aware of this, that
the Israelites had not sent the book of the law to the king, and they
came and said unto him, O king, the Israelites have treated thee with contempt, for they did not send to thee the book of the law which we had
mentioned to thee, but they sent to thee another book which they had in
their hands, therefore send to them that they may forward unto thee the
book of their law, for from that book thou wilt obtain thy desire much
more than from the book which they have sent to thee ; so when the king
heard their words he became exceedingly wroth against the Israelites, and
his anger burned within him until he sent again to them for them to forward to him the book of the law. Fearing that they might still continue
to scorn him, he acted prudently with them and sent to seventy of their
elders and placed them in seventy houses, that each should write the
book of the law, so that no alteration might be found in them, and the
divine spirit rested upon them, and they wrote for him seventy books and
they were all of one version, without addition or diminution. At this the
king rejoiced greatly and he honored the elders, together with all the
Jews, and he sent offerings and gifts to Jerusalem as it is written there.*
At his death, the Israelites acted cunningly with his son and took from
his treasures the book of the law, but left this book there and took it not
away, in order that every future king might know the wonders of the
Lord, blessed be his name, and that he had chosen Israel from all nations,
and that there is no God beside him.

This book is therefore in Egypt unto this day, and from that time it
became circulated throughout the earth, until it reached us in our captivity
this day in the city of Napuli, which is under the rule of the king of Spain.
Now thou wilt find in this book that some of the kings of Edom, of Chittim and the kings of Africa who were in those days, are mentioned,
although it might appear that such was not the aim or intent of this book ;
but the reason of this was to show to every person obtaining this book,
the contrast between the wars of Israel and the wars of the Gentiles, for the
conquest of Gentile kings one over the other was by accident, which is not so
in the conquest of the kings of Israel over the Gentiles, which is by a miracle
from our blessed Lord as long as the Israelites trust in his exalted name.

Now the uses of this book are many, all of which lead us to confidence
in God, (whose name be exalted,) and to our adherence unto him and his
ways.

The first use is the additional information it affords us upon the subjects of the creation of man and the deluge, recording also the years of the
twenty generations and their misdeeds ; also at what period they were

* In the book of the Asmoneans mentioned above.

B

born, and when they died, by which means, our hearts may be inclined to adhere to the Lord, when we see the mighty works which he performed in days of old.

The second use is in the additional account respecting the birth of Abraham and how it was that he cleaved to the Lord, and the transactions that took place between him and Nimrod; and thus also of the account of the builders of the tower of Babel,* how that the Lord drove them to the four corners of the earth, and how they established the countries and lands called after their names unto this day, by which means we may draw nigh to our Creator. The third use is the explanation it gives us how the patriarchs adhered to the Lord, and of their transactions which convince us of their fear of God. The fourth use is, in what it records of the affairs of Sodom and the iniquities of its people, and in what consisted their sins, as well as their punishment, by which means we may refrain from all evil doings. The fifth use is in the account of the faith of Isaac and Jacob in the Lord, and the prayers and weeping of Sarah at the binding of Isaac *for a sacrifice*, which is of great use in inclining our hearts to the service of the Lord. The sixth use is in the information it affords us upon the subject of the wars of the sons of Jacob with the people of Shechem and the seven cities of the Amorites. This will rouse our hearts to faith in our God ; for how could ten men destroy seven cities, if their hearts had not been impressed with faith in the Lord ?

The seventh use is, in the information it gives us of all the events that happened to Joseph in Egypt, with Potiphar and his wife and with the king of Egypt, for this will also rouse our hearts to the fear of the Lord, and to remove ourselves from all sin, so that it may be well with us in the latter end.

The eighth use is in the account it furnishes us of what happened to Moses in Cush and in Midian, by which we may understand the wonders of the Lord which he performs for the righteous, and that we may thereby adhere to him. The ninth use is in its recording what had happened to the Israelites in Egypt, and when the commencement of their servitude took place, and how they served the Egyptians in all manner of hard work, and to what purpose all this tended—how after this God was favorable to them through their trusting in him, and there is no doubt of this that he who reads the events of Egypt from this book on the nights of the Passover, will receive a great reward, as our Rabbins of blessed memory say, he that is occupied in relating the exit from Egypt is to be praised, in which this book is included, for this is the true narration which ought to be read after the Hagadah, for such person (reading this) may be assured that he will be greatly rewarded ; we do so this day in our captivity in the countries of Spain, after having finished reading the Hagadah, we commence reading in this book the whole affair of Egypt, from the Israelites going down to Egypt unto their exit, for in this book a person ought to

---

* Called דור הפלגה because the earth was then divided.

read. The eleventh* use is, that some of the comments of our Rabbies and of other commentators who have explained the law, thou wilt find illustrated in this book, such as the account of the messengers who met Jacob† when he came from Mesopotamia after they had gone to Esau, also the account of Gabriel who taught Joseph seventy languages, also the illustration it affords of him‡ who smote Midian in the fields of Moab, and the like. The twelfth use is, that every person lecturing in public may bring forward in his discourse, subjects from this book, which the commentators have not explained, by which means he may make an impression upon the hearts of his audience. The thirteenth use is, that all merchants and travellers, who have an opportunity to study the law, may read this book and receive their reward, for therein is the reward of the soul as well as the delight of the body, in the discovery of new matter not recorded in any other book, and by these means will man understand to know the Lord and cleave unto him.

Now because we have seen the merit of this book, and the great usefulness thereof, we have undertaken to print it without addition or diminution, and from this time we have commenced to print it in a book, that such books may be in the hands of the members of our covenant, the men of our captivity in order that it may be farther circulated throughout every generation, and every city, family and country, so that they may understand the wonders of the Lord which he performed for our ancestors, and his bounties toward them from the days of old, and that he chose us from all nations. May they who devote their hearts to the fear of the Lord, be rendered meritorious by studying therein whilst we confide in the Lord, the God of Gods, and depend upon him and seek salvation and assistance from him, in this heavenly work, and may he prosper us in the right path, and deliver us from errors, and cleanse us from secret faults, as his anointed said, "*who can understand his errors? cleanse thou me from secret faults.*"§ May God teach us the good way and direct us in a prosperous path for the sake of his mercies and kindnesses, and may he graciously fulfil the desires of our hearts, Amen, and so be his will.

* The eleventh use.—I cannot see any mention of the tenth use ; this must have been omitted. I think, before the words above, "how after this God was favourable to them through their trusting in him."

† See the latter part of ch. 31.

‡ The obscure passage in Genesis, 36. 35. in the Bible, is cleared up in Jasher, ch. 62. where it gives a long history of Hadad, the son of Bedad.

§ Psalms, 19. 12.

THE PRINTER'S PREFACE.

THE humble worm, and no man, Joseph, son to my father, the wise and highly respected in Israel, Samuel the little one, says, my witness is in heaven and my testimony is on high, the God of Gods knows, and Israel knows also, how much fatigue I have undergone, and how much trouble I have taken until I had brought to light the hidden treasures of this book; for ever since I was driven from my land, from the metropolis of Israel, the great city of wise men and scribes, the renowned city of Pasia, ever since the Lord, through my great offences, has driven me with a violent captivity, one stumbling after the other, he weakened my strength in the way, the iron entered my soul until I reached the Italian harbor, the royal city Livorno (Leghorn,) which is under the sway of our Lord the most serene Grand Duke Don Ferdinand de Media (Medici Qu?) for neither by day nor by night could I remain silent, I was continually in thought, my soul was humbled in me, and sleep was removed from mine eyes, when I reflected how energetically my father, the crown of my head, strove with his purse and labor to transcribe this book, as was his constant custom from his love of the study of the Law, to lavish money and wealth, principal and interest, for the purchase and the transcribing, for my own use,of books without end, in order that I might obtain wisdom and instruction, to comprehend the words of understanding, as all of the inhabitants of my city can testify and declare; (O God remember him favorably to rest in glory with the righteous who are in the garden of Eden, Amen! for this loss is felt only by me,) especially in the transcribing of this book it is holy for praises to the Lord, for there was never seen nor found but one, which the intelligent and pious scribe Jacob, the son of Atiyah, transcribed from a very old manuscript, the letters of which were defaced; and had it not been for the consummate ability of the above mentioned Rabbi, no other person could have made out those letters, nor have transcribed them, from their antiquity and from their having been defaced.

Now my father, of blessed memory, found favor in his eyes, to obtain this book on loan, in order that he might also get one transcribed by the hands of a certain scribe, and in the year 5373,* through my great sins, I went out of the pale of my birth place, and from my father's house, owing to the terrors of famine, pestilence and slaughter. The sword de-

* Corresponding with the year 1613.

stroyed from without, and within was the terror of pestilence and famine, on account of the battles and contentions which took place between the sons of the old king Maruccus who had died, for each lifted himself up, saying, I will reign, and they devoured the Israelites with open mouth, so that very few remained of them, even a tithe of a tithe; many families and heads of the houses of their fathers were lost and destroyed and became as naught; many books of various kinds, new and old, some in manuscript and others in print, as well as those of modern times, were mostly destroyed by fire, or were torn to pieces, which, together with their owners, lie hid under the ruins to this day. Woe to the eyes that beheld this! yet may the name of the Lord be blessed for the evil as well as for the good.

Fearing that this book might share the same fate as the others, I daily used the most persevering exertions in sending letters to some particular individuals in the city Argilia, in the city Titu, and in the city Pasia, to such as had been left, humbly beseeching them to search and inquire where might be the place of the glory of this book, and it was sought after and found to be hid in the hands of one of the individuals of the congregation, the wise and highly gifted Moses Chasan; and thanks are due to him, that upon his ascertaining my good intention to print it and to scatter it throughout all Jewish communities, he did not delay to send it, as he felt a desire for a heavenly reward for this pious act, yea, he sent it to me as a gift, may he receive a blessing from the Lord, and may his reward be perfect. Amen.

Now I in my humble station have composed a work entitled כתונת יוסף in two parts, one part containing some of the scriptural comments which I made with the gracious help of the Lord, and the second part containing fifty lectures which I delivered to a great congregation, besides a later comment containing explanations of parts of the Talmud which I met with in the course of my studies, and which I illustrated according to my humble abilities; now I am revising this work a second time in order to bring it to the press, if heaven spare my life, yet I said to my heart, to thee, O worm, and no man, does the scripture proclaim "*It is time for thee, O Lord, to work, for they have made void thy law,*" for the printing of this book of Jasher tends to the honor and glory of the Lord, for through it will the hearts of men be directed to cleave to the blessed Lord, and by the means of which they will understand the wonderful works of God, and his bounties toward our ancestors from the days of old, and how he chose us from all nations, as thou wilt see at length in the preface, wherein thou wilt perceive enumerated the great many uses, thirteen in number, which induce men to confide in the Lord and to adhere to him.

I have also found another use therein, which is, that many parts of the five books difficult of comprehension, and which the commentators have been unable to reconcile, are, by means of this book, properly understood, because it gives a detail of those parts, wherein the sacred volume is brief in its account, and relates events as they occurred; thou wilt therefore find me lifting up my hand in the margin with the words אמר הצעיר "*The humble editor says,*" by which will be understood what I have asserted ; search and thou will find many things also, which our Rabbies in their works gave in short, are brought forth more fully in this book since it is high time now to act and have a care for the glory of God's name. Since then it is proper for me at present to defer the publication of my above mentioned work until I shall first have brought to light the hidden treasures of this book and to reveal them to the world, I am confident that with the help of the Lord all Israel will exult and rejoice therein.

I have therefore put my trust in the Lord, may he remember me favorably, that I may be enabled in the next year by his help and decree to publish also my afore mentioned work.

As for me, my prayer is to him who dwells on high, may the Lord God assist me, and send me from on high his peace, favor, and faithfulness to help me, that he may lead me beside the still waters, and conduct me to the paths of righteousness for the sake of his great name, and for the sake of his law. Amen for ever and ever.

CONTENTS.

CONTENTS.

CONTENTS.

CONTENTS

CONTENTS

CONTENTS.

CERTIFICATES.

names Adam and Eve," but in the very words of the Hebrew bible, v. 2, "called their name Adam." In chap. **xx**, v. 4, the version reads thus; "and the servants of Abimelech went to Abimelech, saying," in the original it is "and the servants of Abimelech came and praised Sarah to the king, saying, &c." In v. 19, the name of Pharaoh is omitted, and occasionally the word "subjects," is substituted for "servants."

It is possible that the translator made use of a copy of some other edition which may have varied in a few words from that examined by me. The points referred to, are, on the whole, unimportant, and do not detract from the general accuracy of the translation.

I am respectfully,

Your obt. serv't.

To Messrs. Noah & Gould,   SAMUEL H. TURNER.

The following letter is from Professor Bush of New York.

New York, April 30, 1840.

Gentlemen,

I have examined portions of several chapters of the "Book of Jasher" in the original, carefully comparing with it the translation put into my hands by the publishers. The work itself is evidently composed in the purest Rabbinical Hebrew, with a large intermixture of the Biblical idiom, and I consider the translation as a whole, not only as decidedly *faithful*, but as peculiarly *happy* in retaining the air of antique simplicity which distinguishes the original, and which constitutes the matchless excellence of our English version of the Hebrew Scriptures. In a few instances I have noticed slight verbal variations from the original, similar to those adverted to by Prof. Turner, as in one case "choice of our *sepulchres*" for "choice of our *land*;" but they are of too little moment to detract from the character of *general fidelity* which I do not hesitate to assign to the translation

Very respectfully,

Yours, &c.,

To Messrs. Noah & Gould.   GEO. BUSH.

ספר הישר

OR

THE BOOK OF JASHER.

THIS IS THE BOOK OF THE GENERATIONS OF MAN WHOM GOD CREATED
UPON THE EARTH ON THE DAY WHEN THE LORD GOD MADE
HEAVEN AND EARTH.

CHAPTER I.

1. And God said let us make man in our image, after our likeness, and God created man in his own image.

2. And God formed man from the ground, and he blew into his nostrils the breath of life, and man became a living soul endowed with speech.

⁚. And the Lord said it is not good for man to be alone; I will make unto him a helpmate.

4. And the Lord caused a deep sleep to fall upon Adam, and he slept, and he took away one of his ribs, and he built flesh upon it and formed it and brought it to Adam, and Adam awoke from his sleep, and behold a woman was standing before him.

5. And he said, this is a bone of my bones and it shall be called woman, for this has been taken from man; and Adam called her name Eve, for she was the mother of all living.

6. And God blessed them and called their names Adam and Eve in the day that he created them, and the Lord God said, be fruitful and multiply and fill the earth.

7. And the Lord God took Adam and his wife, and he placed them in the garden of Eden to dress it and to keep it; and he commanded them and said unto them, from every tree of the garden you may eat, but from the tree of the knowledge of good and evil you shall not eat, for in the day that you eat thereof you shall surely die.

8. And when God had blessed and commanded them he went from them, and Adam and his wife dwelt in the garden according to the command which the Lord had commanded them.

9. And the serpent, which God had created with them in the earth, came to them to incite them to transgress the command of God which he had commanded them.

10. And the serpent enticed and persuaded the woman to eat from the tree of knowledge, and the woman hearkened to the voice of the serpent, and she transgressed the

i

word of God, and took from the tree
of the knowledge of good and evil
and she ate, and she took from it
and gave also to her husband and he
ate.

11. And Adam and his wife transgressed the command of God which
he commanded them, and God knew
it, and his anger was kindled against
them and he cursed them.

12. And the Lord God drove them
that day from the garden of Eden,
to till the ground from which they
were taken, and they went and dwelt
at the east of the garden of Eden;
and Adam knew his wife Eve and she
bore two sons and three daughters.

13. And she called the name of
the first born Cain, saying, I have
obtained a man from the Lord, and
the name of the other she called Abel,
for she said, in vanity we came into
the earth and in vanity we shall be
taken from it.

14. And the boys grew up and
their father gave them a possession
in the land; and Cain was a tiller
of the ground, and Abel a keeper of
sheep.

15. And it was at the expiration
of a few years, that they brought an
approximating offering to the Lord,
and Cain brought from the fruit of
the ground, and Abel brought from
the firstlings of his flock from the fat
thereof, and God turned and inclined
to Abel and his offering, and a fire
came down from the Lord from
heaven and consumed it.

16. And unto Cain and his offering the Lord did not turn, and he
did not incline to it, for he had
brought from the inferior fruit of the
ground before the Lord, and Cain
was jealous against his brother Abel
on account of this, and he sought a
pretext to slay him.

17. And in some time after, Cain
and Abel his brother went one day
into the field to do their work; and
they were both in the field, Cain
tilling and ploughing his ground,
and Abel feeding his flock; and the
flock passed that part which Cain
had ploughed in the ground, and it
sorely grieved Cain on this account.

18. And Cain approached his brother Abel in anger, and he said unto
him, what is there between me and
thee that thou comest to dwell and
bring thy flock to feed in my land?

19. And Abel answered his brother Cain and said unto him, what
is there between me and thee, that
thou shalt eat the flesh of my flock
and clothe *thyself* with their wool?

20. And now *therefore*, put off
the wool of my sheep *with* which
thou hast clothed *thyself*, and recom-
pense *me* for their fruit and flesh
which thou hast eaten, and when
thou shalt have done this, I will then
go from thy land as thou hast said?

21. And Cain said to his brother
Abel, surely if I slay thee this day,
who will require thy blood from me?

22. And Abel answered Cain,
saying, surely God who has made us
in the earth, he will avenge my cause,
and he will require my blood from
thee shouldst thou slay me, for the
Lord is the judge and arbiter, and it
is he who will requite man according
to his evil, and the wicked *man* according to the wickedness that he
may do upon earth.

23. And now, if thou shouldst
slay me here, surely God knoweth
thy secret *views*, and will judge thee
for the evil which thou didst declare
to do unto me this day.

24. And when Cain heard the
words which Abel his brother had
spoken, *behold* the anger of Cain

was kindled against his brother Abel for declaring this thing.

25. And Cain hastened and rose up, and took the iron *part* of his ploughing instrument, with which he suddenly smote his brother and he slew him, and Cain spilt the blood of his brother Abel upon the earth, and the blood of Abel streamed upon the earth before the flock.

26. And after this Cain repented having slain his brother, and he was sadly grieved, and he wept over him and it vexed him exceedingly.

27. And Cain rose up and dug a hole in the field, wherein he put his brother's body, and he turned the dust over it.

28. And the Lord knew what Cain had done to his brother, and the Lord appeared to Cain and said unto him, where is Abel thy brother that was with thee?

29. And Cain dissembled, and said, I do not know, am I my brother's keeper? And the Lord said unto him, what hast thou done? The voice of thy brother's blood crieth unto me from the ground where thou hast slain him.

30. For thou hast slain thy brother and hast dissembled before me, and didst imagine in thy heart that I saw thee not, nor knew all thy actions.

31. But thou didst this thing and didst slay thy brother for naught *and* because he spoke rightly to thee, and now, *therefore*, cursed be thou from the ground which opened its mouth to receive thy brother's blood from thy hand, and wherein thou didst bury him.

32. And it shall be when thou shalt till it, it shall no more give thee its strength as in the beginning, for thorns and thistles shall the ground produce, and thou shalt be moving

and wandering in the earth* until the day of thy death.

33. And at that time Cain went out from the presence of the Lord from the place where he was, and he went moving and† wandering in the land towards the east of Eden, he and all belonging to him.

34. And Cain knew his wife in those days, and she conceived and bare a son, and he called his name Enoch, *saying*, in that time the Lord began to give him rest and quiet in the earth.

35. And at that time Cain also began to build a city: and he built the city and he called the name of the city Enoch, according to the name of his son; for in those days the Lord had given him rest upon the earth, and he did not move about and wander as in the beginning.

36. And Irad was born to Enoch, and Irad begat Mechuyael and Mechuyael begat Methusael.

CHAPTER II.

1. And it was in the hundred and thirtieth year of the life of Adam upon the earth, that he again knew Eve his wife, and she conceived and bare a son in his likeness *and* in his image, and she called his name *Seth*, saying, because God has appointed

* Although we find in the 34th and 35th verses that God gave him rest, it might only have been a temporary rest; and as we are neither told in scripture nor in this book anything more relating to Cain, we cannot infer anything contrary to this declaration.

† There is no mention made of the land of Nod; the word here used is נוד the participle present of the verb נודד to wander; the last letter of those verbs whose two final letters are similar, is sometimes dropped, and it might have been נוד with one daleth, like the word used in scripture נד without the vau, which is frequently omitted.

me another seed in the place of Abel, for Cain has slain him.

2. And Seth lived one hundred and five years, and he begat a son; and Seth called the name of his son Enosh, saying, because in that time the sons of men began to multiply, and to afflict their souls and hearts by transgressing and rebelling against God.

3. And it was in the days of Enosh that the sons of men continued to rebel and transgress against God, to increase the anger of the Lord against the sons of men.

4. And the sons of men went and they served other Gods, and they forgot the Lord who had created them in the earth : and in those days the sons of men made images of brass and iron, wood and stone, and they bowed down and served them.

5. And every man made his God and they bowed down to them, and the sons of men forsook the Lord all the days of Enosh and his children ; and the anger of the Lord was kindled on account of their works and abominations which they did in the earth.

6. And the Lord caused the waters of the river Gihon to overwhelm them, and he destroyed and consumed them, and he destroyed the third part of the earth : and notwithstanding this, the sons of men did not turn from their evil ways, and their hands were yet extended to do evil in the sight of the Lord.

7. And in those days there was neither sowing nor reaping in the earth ; and there was no food for the sons of men and the famine was very great in those days.

8. And the seed which they sowed in those days in the ground became thorns, thistles and briers ; for from the days of Adam was this declaration concerning the earth, of the curse of God, which he cursed the earth, on account of the sin which Adam sinned before the Lord.

9. And it was when men continued to rebel and transgress against God, and to corrupt their ways, that the earth also became corrupt.

10. And Enosh lived ninety years and he begat Cainan ;

11. And Cainan grew up and he was forty years old, and he became wise and had knowledge and skill in all wisdom, and he reigned over all the sons of men, and he led the sons of men to wisdom and knowledge ; for Cainan was a very wise man and had understanding in all wisdom, and with his wisdom he ruled over spirits and dæmons ;

12. And Cainan knew by his wisdom that God would destroy the sons of men for having sinned upon earth, and that the Lord would in the latter days bring upon them the waters of the flood.

13. And in those days Cainan wrote upon tablets of stone, what was to take place in time to come, and he put them in his treasures.

14. And Cainan reigned over the whole earth, and he turned some of the sons of men to the service of God.

15. And when Cainan was seventy years old, he begat three sons and two daughters.

16. And these are the names of the children of Cainan ; the name of the first born Mahlallel, the second Enan, and the third Mered, and their sisters were Adah and Zillah ; these are the five children of Cainan that were born to *him*.

17. And Lamech, the son of Methusael, became related to Cainan by

marriage, and he took his two daughters for his wives, and Adah conceived and bare a son to Lamech, and she called his name Jabal.

18. And she again conceived and bare a son, and called his name Jubal; and Zillah, her sister, was barren in those days and had no offspring.

19. For in those days the sons of men began to trespass against God, and to transgress the commandments which he had commanded to Adam, to be fruitful and multiply in the earth.

20. And some of the sons of men caused their wives to drink a draught that would render them barren, in order that they might retain their figures and *whereby* their beautiful appearance might not fade.

21. And when the sons of men caused some of their wives to drink, Zillah drank with them.

22. And the child-bearing women appeared abominable in the sight of their husbands, as widows, *whilst their husbands lived,* for to the barren ones only they were attached.

23. And in the end of days and years, when Zillah became old, the Lord *opened her womb.

24. And she conceived and bare a son and she called his name Tubal Cain, saying, after I had withered away have I obtained him from the Almighty God.

25. And she conceived again and bare a daughter, and she called her name Naamah, for she said, after I had withered away have I obtained pleasure and delight.

26. And Lamech was old *and* ad-

* It cannot be supposed that they gave Zillah the drink to cause barrenness when she became old, for as it is expressed in verse twenty, it was given to those to retain their figures and whereby their beautiful appearance might not fade.

vanced in years, and his eyes were dim that he could not see, and Tubal Cain, his son, was leading him, and it was one day that Lamech went into the field and Tubal Cain his son was with him, and whilst they were walking in the field, Cain the son of Adam *advanced* towards them; for Lamech was very old and could not see much, and Tubal Cain his son was very young.

27. And Tubal Cain told his father to draw his bow, and with the arrows he smote Cain, who was yet far off, and he slew him, for he appeared to them to be an animal.

28. And the arrows entered Cain's body *although* he was distant from them, and he fell to the ground and died.

29. And the Lord requited Cain's evil according to his wickedness, which he had done to his brother Abel, according to the word of the Lord which he had spoken.

30. And it came to pass when Cain had died, that Lamech and Tubal went to see the animal which they had slain, and they saw, and behold Cain their grandfather was fallen dead upon the earth.

31. And Lamech was very much grieved at having done this, and in clapping his hands together he struck his son and caused his death.

32. And the wives of Lamech heard what Lamech had done, and they sought to kill him.

33. And the wives of Lamech hated him from that day, because he slew Cain and Tubal Cain, and the wives of Lamech separated from him, and would not hearken to him in those days.

34. And Lamech came to his wives, and he pressed them to listen to him about this matter.

35. And he said to his wives Adah and Zillah, hear my voice O wives of Lamech, attend to my words, for now you have imagined and said that I slew a man with my wounds, and a child with my stripes for *their* having done no violence, *but* surely know that I am old and greyheaded, and that my eyes are heavy through age, and I did this thing unknowingly.

36. And the wives of Lamech listened to him in this matter, and they returned to him with the advice of their father Adam, but they bore no children to him from that time, knowing that God's anger was increasing in those days against the sons of men, to destroy them with the waters of the flood for their evil doings.

37. And Mahlallel the son of Cainan lived sixty five years and he begat Jered ; and Jered lived sixty-two years and he begat Enoch.

CHAPTER III.

1. AND Enoch lived sixty-five years and he begat Methuselah ; and Enoch walked with God after having begot Methuselah, and he served the Lord, and despised the evil ways of men.

2. And the soul of Enoch was wrapped up in the instruction of the Lord, in knowledge and in understanding ; and he wisely retired from the sons of men, and secreted himself from them for many days.

3. And it was at the expiration of many years, whilst he was serving the Lord, and praying before him in *his* house, that an angel of the Lord called to him from Heaven, and he said, here am I.

4. And he said, rise, go forth from thy house and from the place where thou dost hide thyself, and appear to the sons of men, in order that thou mayst teach them the way in which they should go, and the work which they must accomplish to enter in the ways of God.

5. And Enoch rose up according to the word of the Lord, and went forth from his house, from his place and from the chamber in which he was *concealed ;* and he went to the sons of men and taught them the ways of the Lord, and at that time assembled the sons of men and acquainted them with the instruction of the Lord.

6. And he ordered it to be proclaimed in all places *where* the sons of men *dwelt,* saying, where is the man who wishes to know the ways of the Lord and good works? let him come to Enoch.

7. And all the sons of men then assembled to him, for all who desired this thing went to Enoch, and Enoch reigned over the sons of men according to the word of the Lord, and they came and bowed to him and they heard his word.

8. And the spirit of God was upon Enoch, and he taught all his men the wisdom of God and his ways, and the sons of men served the Lord all the days of Enoch, and they came to hear his wisdom.

9. And all the kings of the sons of men, both first and last, together with their princes and judges, came to Enoch when they heard of his wisdom, and they bowed down to him, and they also required of Enoch to reign over them, to which he consented.

10. And they assembled in all, one hundred and thirty kings and princes, and they made Enoch king over

them, and they were all under his power and command.

11. And Enoch taught them wisdom, knowledge, and the ways of the Lord; and he made peace amongst them, and peace was throughout the earth during the life of Enoch.

12. And Enoch reigned over the sons of men two hundred and forty-three years, and he did justice and righteousness with all his people, and he led them in the ways of the Lord.

13. And these are the generations of Enoch; Methuselah, Elisha, and Elimelech, three sons; and their sisters were Melca and Nahmah, and Methuselah lived eighty-seven years and he begat Lamech.

14. And it was in the fifty-sixth year of the life of Lamech when Adam died; nine hundred and thirty years old was he at his death, and his two sons, with Enoch and Methuselah his son, buried him with great pomp, as at the burial of kings, in the cave which God had told him.

15. And in that place all the sons of men made a great mourning and weeping on account of Adam; it has therefore become a custom among the sons of men to this day.

16. And Adam died because he ate of the tree of knowledge; he and his children after him, as the Lord God had spoken.

17. And it was in the year of Adam's death which was the two hundred and forty-third year of the reign of Enoch, in that time Enoch resolved to separate himself from the sons of men and to secrete himself as at first in order to serve the Lord.

18. And Enoch did so, but did not entirely secrete himself from them, but kept away from the sons of men three days and then went to them for one day.

19. And during the three days that he was in his chamber, he prayed to, and praised the Lord his God, and the day on which he went and appeared to his subjects he taught them the ways of the Lord, and all they asked him about the Lord he told them.

20. And he did in this manner for many years, and he afterward concealed himself for six days, and appeared to his people one day in seven; and after that once in a month, and then once in a year, until all the kings, princes and sons of men sought for him, and desired again to see the face of Enoch, and to hear his word; but they could not, as all the sons of men were greatly afraid of Enoch, and they feared to approach him on account of the Godlike awe that was seated upon his countenance; therefore no man could look at him, fearing he might be punished and die.

21. And all the kings and princes resolved to assemble the sons of men, and to come to Enoch, thinking that they might all speak to him at the time when he should come forth amongst them, and they did so.

22. And the day came when Enoch went forth and they all assembled and came to him, and Enoch spoke to them the words of the Lord and he taught them wisdom and knowledge, and they bowed down before him and they said, may the king live, may the king live!

23. And in some time after, when the kings and princes and the sons of men were speaking to Enoch, and Enoch was teaching them the ways of God, behold an angel of the Lord then called unto Enoch from heaven, and wished to bring him up to heaven to make him reign there over the sons

of God, as he had reigned over the sons of men upon earth.

&4·23. When at that time Enoch heard this he went and assembled all the inhabitants of the earth, and taught them wisdom and knowledge and gave them divine instructions, and he said to them, I have been required to ascend into heaven, I therefore do not know the day of my going.

25. And now therefore I will teach you wisdom and knowledge and will give you instruction before I leave you, how to act upon earth whereby you may live ; and he did so.

26. And he taught them wisdom and knowledge, and gave them instruction, and he reproved them, and he placed before them statutes and judgments to do upon earth, and he made peace amongst them, and he taught them everlasting life, and dwelt with them some time teaching them all these things.

27. And at that time the sons of men were with Enoch, and Enoch was speaking to them, and they lifted up their eyes and the likeness of a great horse descending from heaven, and the horse paced in the* air ;

28. And they told Enoch what they had seen, and Enoch said to them, on my account does this horse descend upon earth ; the time is come when I must go from you and I shall no more be seen by you.

29. And the horse descended at that time and stood before Enoch,

and all the sons of men that were with Enoch saw him.

30. And Enoch then again ordered a voice to be proclaimed, saying, where is the man who delighteth to know the ways of the Lord his God, let him come this day to Enoch before he is taken from us.

31. And all the sons of men assembled and came to Enoch that day ; and all the kings of the earth with their princes and counsellors remained with him that day ; and Enoch then taught the sons of men wisdom and knowledge, and *gave them* divine instruction ; and he bade them serve the Lord and walk in his ways all the days of their lives, and he continued to make peace amongst them.

32. And it was after this that he rose up and rode upon the horse ; and he went forth and all the sons of men went after him, about eight hundred thousand men ; and they went with him one day's journey.

33. And the second day he said to them, return home to your tents, why will you go ? perhaps you may die ; and some of them went from him, and those that remained went with him six day's journey ; and Enoch said to them every day, return to your tents, lest you may die ; but they were not willing to return, and they went with him.

34. And on the sixth day some of the men remained and clung to him, and they said to him, we will go with thee to the place where thou goest : as the Lord liveth, death only shall separate us.

35. And they urged so much to go with him, that he ceased speaking to them ; and they went after him and would not return ;

36. And when the kings returned

* To express the region of the atmosphere רוח is often used, as the word אויר air, met with in modern Hebrew works, is of rabbinical extraction and may be derived from אור light, by which it might have been intended to show that the air is the medium through which the rays of light become visible to us.

they caused a census to be taken, in order to know the number of remaining men that went with Enoch; and it was upon the seventh day that Enoch ascended into heaven in a whirlwind, with horses and chariots of fire.

37. And on the eighth day all the kings that had been with Enoch sent to bring back the number of men that were with Enoch, in that place from which he ascended into heaven.

38. And all those kings went to the place and they found the earth there filled with snow, and upon the snow were large stones of snow, and one said to the other, come, let us break through this snow and see, perhaps the men that remained with Enoch are dead, and are now under the stones of snow, and they searched but could not find him, for he had ascended into heaven.

CHAPTER IV.

1. And all the days that Enoch lived upon the earth, were three hundred and sixty five years.

2. And when Enoch had ascended into heaven, all the kings of the earth rose and took Methuselah his son and anointed him, and they caused him to reign over them in the place of his father.

3. And Methuselah acted uprightly in the sight of God, as his father Enoch had taught him, and he likewise during the whole of his life taught the sons of men wisdom, knowledge and the fear of God, and he did not turn from the good way either to the right or to the left.

4. But in the latter days of Methuselah, the sons of men turned from the Lord, they corrupted the earth, they robbed and plundered each other, and they rebelled against God and they transgressed, and they corrupted their ways, and would not hearken to the voice of Methuselah, but rebelled against him.

5. And the Lord was exceedingly wroth against them, and the Lord continued to destroy the seed in those days, so that there was neither sowing nor reaping in the earth.

6. For when they sowed the ground in order that they might obtain food for their support, behold, thorns and thistles were produced which they did not sow.

7. And still the sons of men did not turn from their evil ways, and their hands were still extended to do evil in the sight of God, and they provoked the Lord with their evil ways, and the Lord was very wroth, and repented that he had made man.

8. And he thought to destroy and annihilate them *and he did so.

9. In those days when Lamech the son of Methuselah was one hundred and sixty years old, Seth the son of Adam died.

10. And all the days that Seth lived, were nine hundred and twelve years, and he died.

11. And Lamech was one hundred and eighty years old when he took Ashmua, the daughter of Elishaa the son of Enoch his uncle, and she conceived.

12. And at that time the sons of men sowed the ground, and a little food was produced, yet the sons of men did not turn from their evil ways, and they trespassed and rebelled against God.

13. And the wife of Lamech conceived and bare him a son at

*Referring to what was shortly to take place; the flood.

that time, at the revolution of the year.

14. And Methuselah called his name Noah, saying, the earth was in his days at rest and free from corruption, and Lamech his father called his name *Menachem, saying, this one shall comfort us in our works and miserable toil in the earth, which God had cursed.

15. And the child grew up and was weaned, and he went in the ways of his father Methuselah, perfect and upright with God.

16. And all the sons of men departed from the ways of the Lord in those days as they multiplied upon the face of the earth with sons and daughters, and they taught one another their evil practices, and they continued sinning against the Lord.

17. And every man made unto himself a god, and they robbed and plundered every man his neighbor as well as his relative, and they corrupted the earth, and the earth was filled with violence.

18. And their judges and rulers went to the daughters of men and took their wives by force from their husbands according to their choice, and the sons of men in those days took from the cattle of the earth, the beasts of the field and the fowls of the air, and taught the mixture of animals of one species with the other, in order therewith to provoke the Lord; and God saw the whole earth and it was corrupt, for all flesh had corrupted its ways upon earth, all men and all animals.

* Menachem signifies a comforter. We have no account in scripture of his being called Menachem, although the reason why he might have had that name is given as it is here: "this one will comfort us," (Gen.) which does not so well accord with the name Noah, which means to rest.

19. And the Lord said, I will blot out man that I created from the face of the earth, yea from man to the birds of the air, together with cattle and beasts that are in the field, for I repent that I made them.

20. And all men who walked in the ways of the Lord, died in those days, before the Lord brought the evil upon man which he had declared, for this was from the Lord, that they should not see the evil which the Lord spoke of concerning the sons of men.

21. And Noah found grace in the sight of the Lord, and the Lord chose him and his children to raise up seed from them upon the face of the whole earth.

CHAPTER V.

1. And it was in the eighty fourth year of the life of Noah, that Enoch the son of Seth died; he was nine hundred and five years old at his death.

2. And in the one hundred and seventy ninth year of the life of Noah, Cainan the son of Enosh, died, and all the days of Cainan were nine hundred and ten years, and he died.

3. And in the two hundred and thirty fourth year of the life of Noah, Mahlallel the son of Cainan died, and the days of Mahlallel were eight hundred and ninety five years, and he died.

4. And Jered the son of Mahlallel died in those days, in the three hundred and thirty sixth year of the life of Noah; and all the days of Jered were nine hundred and sixty two years, and he died.

5. And all who followed the Lord died in those days, before they saw

the evil which God declared to do upon earth.

6. And after the lapse of many years, in the four hundred and eightieth year of the life of Noah, when all those men, who followed the Lord had died away from amongst the sons of men, and only *Methuselah was then left, God said unto Noah and Methuselah, saying,

7. Speak ye, and proclaim to the sons of men, saying, thus saith the Lord, return from your evil ways and forsake your works, and the Lord will repent of the evil that he declared to do to you, so that it shall not come to pass.

8. For thus saith the Lord, behold I give you a period of one hundred and twenty years; if you will turn to me and forsake your evil ways, then will I also turn away from the evil which I told you, and it shall not exist, saith the Lord.

9. And Noah and Methuseleh spoke all the words of the Lord to the sons of men, day after day, constantly speaking to them.

10. But the sons of men would not hearken to them, nor incline their ears to their words, and they were stiffnecked.

11. And the Lord granted them a period of one hundred and twenty years, saying, if they will return, then will God repent of the evil, so as not to destroy the earth.

12. And Noah the son of Lamech refrained from taking a wife in those days, to beget children, for he said, surely now God will destroy the earth, wherefore then shall I beget children?

13. And Noah was a just man, he was perfect in his generation, and the Lord chose him to raise up seed from his seed upon the face of the earth.

14. And the Lord said unto Noah, take unto thee a wife, and beget children, for I have seen thee righteous before me in this generation.

15. And thou shalt raise up seed, and thy children with thee, in the midst of the earth; and Noah went and took a wife, and he chose* Naamah the daughter of Enoch, and she was five hundred and eighty years old.

16. And Noah was four hundred and ninety eight years old, when he took Naamah for a wife.

17. And Naamah conceived and bare a son, and he called his name Japheth, saying, God has enlarged me in the earth; and she conceived again and bare a son, and he called his name Shem, saying, God has made me a remnant, to raise up *seed* in the midst of the earth.

18. And Noah was five hundred and two years old when Naamah bare Shem, and the boys grew up and went in the ways of the Lord, in all that Methuselah and Noah their father taught them.

19. And Lamech the father of Noah died in those days; yet verily he did not go with all his heart in

---

* Methuslah only was left of the good ones who did not die, besides Noah, who is mentioned in the beginning of the verse, in the 450th year of the life of Noah.

* From this it appears that the offspring of the great, pious and illustrious Enoch was reserved to be the partner of the just and upright Noah, thereby connecting the best of the family of Cain and Seth together. It was certainly a great age to contract matrimony, but it must be remembered that Noah was then getting on to five hundred years, and as he deferred marriage to this exceeding great age, he looked out for one of his own age. I suppose that Enoch's daughter intended living secluded from men, like her father, until Noah, the best of men then living, applied to her.

the ways of his father, and he died in the hundred and ninety-fifth year of the life of Noah.

20. And all the days of Lamech were seven hundred and seventy years and he died.

21. And all the sons of men who knew the Lord, died in that year before the Lord brought evil upon them; for the Lord willed them to die, so as not to behold the evil that God would bring upon their brothers and relatives, as he had so declared to do.

22. In that time, the Lord said to Noah and Methuselah, stand forth and proclaim to the sons of men all the words that I spoke to you in those days, peradventure they may turn from their evil ways, and I will then repent of the evil and will not bring it.

23. And Noah and Methuselah stood forth, and said in the ears of the sons of men, all that God had spoken concerning them.

24. But the sons of men would not hearken, neither would they incline their ears to all their declarations.

25. And it was after this that the Lord said to Noah, the end of all flesh is come before me, on account of their evil deeds, and behold I will destroy the earth.

26. And do thou take unto thee Gopher wood, and go to a certain place and make a large ark, and place it in that spot.

27. And thus shalt thou make it; three hundred cubits its length, fifty cubits broad and thirty cubits high.

28. And thou shalt make unto thee a door, open at its side, and to a cubit thou shalt finish above, and cover it within and without with pitch.

29. And behold I will bring the flood of waters upon the earth, and all flesh be destroyed, from under the heavens, all that is upon earth shall perish.

30. And thou and thy household shall go and gather two couple of all living things, male and female, and shall bring them to the ark, to raise up seed from them upon earth.

31. And gather unto thee all food that is eaten by all the animals, that there may be food for thee and for them.

32. And thou shalt choose for thy sons three maidens, from the daughters of men, and they shall be wives to thy sons.

33. And Noah rose up, and he made the ark, in the place where God had commanded him, and Noah did as God had ordered him.

34. In his five hundred and ninety fifth year Noah commenced to make the ark, and he made the ark in five years, as the Lord had commanded.

35. Then Noah took the three daughters of Eliakim, son of Methuselah, for wives for his sons, as the Lord had commanded Noah.

36. And it was at that time Methuselah the son of Enoch died; nine hundred and sixty years old was he, at his death.

CHAPTER VI.

1. At that time, after the death of Methuselah, the Lord said to Noah, go thou with thy household into the ark; behold I will gather to thee all the animals of the earth, the beasts of the field and the fowls of the air, and they shall all come and surround the ark.

2. And thou shalt go and seat thyself by the doors of the ark, and all the beasts, the animals, and the fowls, shall assemble and place themselves

before thee, and such of them as shall come and crouch before thee, shalt thou take and deliver into the hands of thy sons, who shall bring them to the ark, and all that will stand before thee thou shalt leave.

3. And the Lord brought this about on the next day, and animals, beasts and fowls came in great multitudes and surrounded the ark.

4. And Noah went and seated himself by the door of the ark, and of all flesh that crouched before him, he brought into the ark, and all that stood before him he left upon earth.

5. And a lioness came, with her two whelps, male and female, and the three crouched before Noah, and the two whelps rose up against the lioness and smote her, and made her flee from her place, and she went away, and they returned to their places, and crouched upon the earth before Noah.

6. And the lioness ran away, and stood in the place of the lions.

7. And Noah saw this, and* wondered greatly, and he rose and took the two whelps, and brought them into the ark.

8. And Noah brought into the ark from all living *creatures* that were upon earth, so that there was none left but which Noah brought into the ark.

9. Two and two came to Noah into the ark, but from the clean animals, and clean fowls, he brought seven couples, as God had commanded him.

10. And all the animals, and beasts, and fowls, were still there, and they surrounded the ark at every place,

and the rain had not descended till *seven days* after.

11. And on that day, the Lord caused the whole earth to shake, and the sun darkened, and the foundations of the world raged, and the whole earth was moved violently, and the lightning flashed, and the thunder roared, and all the fountains in the earth were broken up, such as was not known to the inhabitants *before;* and *God* did this mighty act, in order to terrify the sons of men, that there might be no more evil upon earth.

12. And still the sons of men would not return from their evil ways, and they increased the anger of the Lord at that time, and did not even direct their hearts to all this.

13. And at the end of seven days, in the six hundredth year of the life of Noah, the waters of the flood were upon the earth.

14. And all the fountains of the deep were broken up, and the windows of heaven were opened, and the rain was upon the earth forty days and forty nights.

15. And Noah and his household, and all the living creatures that were with him, came into the ark on account of the waters of the flood, and the Lord shut him in.

16. And all the sons of men that were left upon the earth, became exhausted through evil on account of the rain, for the waters were coming more violently upon the earth, and the animals and beasts were still surrounding the ark.

17. And the sons of men assembled together, about* seven hundred

---

* At the height to which even the animals of the earth had corrupted themselves, that the young whelps could so unnaturally rise up against their parent in such a time of disaster.

* It must be remembered, that according to this book, a third part of the earth had already been destroyed by the overflowing of the river Gihon. See chapter 2, verse 6.

thousand men and women, and they came unto Noah to the ark.

18. And they called to Noah, saying, open for us that we may come to thee in the ark—and wherefore shall we die ?

19. And Noah, with a loud voice, answered them from the ark, saying, have you not all rebelled against the Lord, and said that he does not exist ? and *therefore* the Lord brought upon you this evil, to destroy and cut you off from the face of the earth.

20. Is not this the thing that I spoke to you of one hundred and twenty years back, and you would not hearken to the voice of the Lord, and now do you desire to live upon earth ?

21. And they said to Noah, we are ready to return to the Lord ; only open for us that we may live and not die

22. And Noah answered them, saying, behold now that you see the trouble of your souls, you *wish* to return to the Lord ; why did you not return during these hundred and twenty years, which the Lord granted you as the determined period ?

23. But now you come and tell me this on account of the troubles of your souls, *now* also the Lord will not listen to you, neither will he give ear to you on this day, so that you will not now succeed in your wishes.

24. And the sons of men approached *in order* to break into the ark, to come in on account of the rain, for they could not bear the rain upon them.

25. And the Lord sent all the beasts and animals that stood round the ark. And the beasts overpowered them and drove them from that place, and every man went his way

and they *again* scattered themselves upon the face of the earth.

26. And the rain was still descending upon the earth, and it descended forty days and forty nights, and the waters prevailed greatly upon the earth ; and all flesh that was upon the earth or in the waters died, whether men, animals, beasts, creeping things or birds of the air, and there only remained Noah and those that were with him in the ark.

27. And the waters prevailed and they greatly increased upon the earth, and they lifted up the ark and it was raised from the earth.

28. And the ark floated upon the face of the waters, and it was tossed upon the waters so that all the living *creatures* within were turned about like pottage in the cauldron.

29. And great anxiety seized all the living creatures that were in the ark, and the ark was like to be broken.

30. And all the living *creatures* that were in the ark were terrified, and the lions roared, and the oxen lowed, and the wolves howled, and every living creature in the ark spoke and lamented in its own language, so that their voices reached to a great distance, and Noah and his sons cried and wept in their troubles; they were greatly afraid that they had reached the gates of death.

31. And Noah prayed unto the Lord, and he cried unto him on account of this, and he said, O Lord help us, for we have no strength to bear this evil that has encompassed us, for the waves of the waters have surrounded us, mischievous torrents have terrified us, the snares of death have come before us ; answer us, O Lord, answer us, light up thy countenance toward us and be gracious to us, redeem us and deliver us.

32. And the Lord hearkened to the voice of Noah, and the Lord remembered him.

33. And a wind passed over the earth, and the waters were still and the ark rested.

34. And the fountains of the deep and the windows of heaven were stopped, and the rain from heaven was restrained.

35. And the waters decreased in those days, and the ark rested upon the mountains of Ararat.

36. And Noah then opened the windows of the ark, and Noah still called out to the Lord at that time and he said, O Lord, who didst form the earth and the heavens and all that are therein, bring forth our souls from this confinement, and from the prison wherein thou hast placed us, for I am much wearied with sighing.

37. And the Lord hearkened to the voice of Noah, and said to him, when thou shalt have completed a full year thou shalt then go forth.

38. And at the revolution of the year, when a full year was completed to Noah's dwelling in the ark, the waters were dried from off the earth, and Noah put off the covering of the ark.

39. At that time, on the twenty-seventh day of the second month, the earth was dry, but Noah and his sons, and those that were with him, did not go out from the ark until the Lord told them.

40. And the day came that the Lord told them to go out, and they all went out from the ark.

41. And they went and returned every one to his way and to his place, and Noah and his sons dwelt in the land that God had told them, and they served the Lord all their days, and the Lord blessed Noah and his

sons on their going out from the ark.

42. And he said to them, be fruitful and fill all the earth; become strong and increase abundantly in the earth and multiply therein.

CHAPTER VII.

1. And these are the names of the sons of Noah : Japheth, Ham and Shem ; and children were born to them after the flood, for they had taken wives before the flood.

2. These are the sons of Japheth; Gomer, Magog, Madai, Javan, Tubal, Meshech and Tiras, seven sons.

3. And the sons of Gomer were Askinaz, Rephath and Togarmah.

4. And the sons of Magog were Elichanaf and Lubal.

5. And the children of Madai were Achon, Zeelo, Chazoni and Lot.

6. And the sons of Javan were Elisha, Tarshish, Chittim and Dudonim.

7. And the sons of Tubal were Ariphi, Kesed and Taari.

8. And the sons of Meshech were Dedon, Zaron and Shebashni.

9. And the sons of Tiras were Benib, Gera, Lupirion and Gilak ; these are the sons of Japheth according to their families, and their numbers in those days were about four hundred and sixty men.

10. And these are the sons of Ham ; Cush, Mitzraim, Phut and Canaan, four sons ; and the sons of Cush were Seba, Havilah, Sabta, Raama and Satecha, and the sons of Raama were Sheba and Dedan.

11. And the sons of Mitzraim were Lud, Anom and Pathros, Chasloth and Chaphtor.

12. And the sons of Phut were Gebul, Hadan, Benah and Adan.

13. And the sons of Canaan were Zidon, Heth, Amori, Gergashi, Hivi, Arkee, Seni, Arodi, Zimodi and Chamothi.

14. These are the sons of Ham, according to their families, and their numbers in those days were about seven hundred and thirty men.

15. And these are the sons of Shem; Elam, Ashur, Arpachshad, Lud and Aram, five sons; and the sons of Elam were Shushan, Machul and Harmon.

16. And the sons of Ashar were Mirus and Mokil, and the sons of Arpachshad were Shelach, Anar and Ashcol.

17. And the sons of Lud were Pethor and Bizayon, and the sons of Aram were Uz, Chul, Gather and Mash.

18. These are the sons of Ham, according to their families; and their numbers in those days were about three hundred men.

19. These are the generations of Shem; Shem begat Arpachshad and Arpachshad begat Shelach, and Shelach begat Eber and to Eber were born two children, the name of one was Peleg, for in his days the sons of men were divided, and in the latter days, the earth was divided.

20. And the name of the second was Yoktan, meaning that in his day the lives of the sons of men were diminished and lessened.

21. These are the sons of Yoktan; Almodad, Shelaf, Chazarmoveth, Yerach, Hadurom, Ozel, Diklah, Obal, Abimael, Sheba, Ophir, Havilah and Jobab; all these are the sons of Yoktan.

22. And Peleg his brother begat Yen, and Yen begat Serug, and Serug begat Nahor, and Nahor begat Terah, and Terah was thirty-eight years old, and he begat Haran and Nahor.

23. And Cush the son of Ham, the son of Noah, took a wife in those days, in his old age, and she bare a son, and they called his name Nimrod, saying, at that time the sons of men again began to rebel and transgress against God, and the child grew up, and his father loved him exceedingly, for he was the son of his old age.

24. And the garments of skin which God made for Adam and his wife, when they went out of the garden, were given to Cush.

25. For after the death of Adam and his wife, the garments were given to Enoch, the son of Jered, and when Enoch was taken up to God, he gave them to Methuselah, his son.

26. And at the death of Methuselah, Noah took them and brought them to the ark, and they were with him until he went out of the ark.

27. And in their going out, Ham stole those garments from Noah his father, and he took them and hid them from his brothers.

28. And when Ham begat his first born Cush, he gave him the garments in secret, and they were with Cush many days.

29. And Cush also concealed them from his sons and brothers, and when Cush had begotten Nimrod, he gave him those garments through his love for him, and Nimrod grew up, and when he was twenty years old he put on those garments.

30. And Nimrod became strong when he put on the garments, and God gave him might and strength, and he was a mighty hunter in the earth, yea, he was a mighty hunter in the field, and he hunted the ani-

mals and he built altars, and he offered upon them the animals before the Lord.

31. And Nimrod strengthened himself, and he rose up from amongst his brethren, and he fought the battles of his brethren against all their enemies round about.

32. And the Lord delivered all the enemies of his brethren in his hands, and God prospered him from time to time in his battles, and he reigned upon earth.

33. Therefore it became current in those days, when a man ushered forth those that he had trained up for battle, he would say to them, like God did to Nimrod, who was a mighty hunter in the earth, and who succeeded in the battles that prevailed against his brethren, that he delivered them from the hands of their enemies, so may God strengthen us and deliver us this day.

34. And when Nimrod was forty years old, at that time there was a war between his brethren and the children of Japheth, so that they were in the power of their enemies.

35. And Nimrod went forth at that time, and he assembled all the sons of Cush and their families, about four hundred and sixty men, and he hired also *from* some of his friends and acquaintances about eighty men, and *he* gave them their hire, and he went with them to battle, and when he was on the road, Nimrod strengthened the hearts of the people that went with him.

36. And he said to them, do not fear, neither be alarmed, for all our enemies will be delivered into our hands, and you may do with them as you please.

37. And all the men that went were about five hundred, and they

fought against their enemies, and they destroyed them, and subdued them, and Nimrod placed standing officers over them in their *respective* places.

38. And he took some of their children as security, and they were all servants to Nimrod and to his brethren, and Nimrod and all the people that were with him turned homeward.

39. And when Nimrod had joyfully returned from battle, after having conquered his enemies, all his brethren, together with those who knew him before, assembled to make him king over them, and they placed the regal crown upon his head.

40. And he set over his subjects and people, princes, judges and rulers, as is the custom amongst kings.

41. And he placed Terah the son of Nahor the prince of his host, and he dignified him and elevated him above all his princes.

42. And whilst he was reigning according to his heart's desire, after having conquered all his enemies around, he advised with his counsellors to build a city for his palace, and they did so.

43. And they found a large valley opposite to the east, and they built him a large and extensive city, and Nimrod called the name of the city that he built Shinar, for the Lord had vehemently shaken his enemies and destroyed them.

44. And Nimrod dwelt in Shinar, and he reigned securely, and he fought with his enemies and he subdued them, and he prospered in all his battles, and his kingdom became very great.

45. And all nations and tongues heard of his fame, and they gathered

themselves* to him, and they bowed down to the earth, and they brought him offerings, and he became their lord and king, and they all dwelt with him in the city of Shinar, and Nimrod reigned in the earth over all the sons of Noah, and they were all under his power and counsel.

46. And all the earth was of one tongue and words of union, but Nimrod did not go in the ways of the Lord, and he was more wicked than all the men that were before him, from the days of the flood until those days.

47. And he made Gods of wood and stone, and he bowed down to them, and he rebelled against the Lord, and taught all his subjects and the people of the earth his wicked ways; and Mardon his son was more wicked than his father.

48. And every one that heard of the acts of Mardon the son of Nimrod would say, concerning him, from the wicked goeth forth wickedness; therefore it became a proverb in the whole earth, saying, from the wicked goeth forth wickedness, and it was current in the words of men from that time to this.

---

* According to Jasher, (and, I believe, Dr. Clarke gives the same opinion of some Christian commentators,) an inference can be drawn that there was a partial separation of mankind long before the affair at Babel, as the confusion of languages did not take place till about 340 years after the flood, being the end of Peleg's life, or the 48th year of the life of Abraham; and having shown that the date of Abraham's birth should be A. M. 1948 instead of 2008, it will follow that the confusion of Babel took place A. M. 1996. I have no doubt that a separation took place before then, until they were reunited under the dominion of Nimrod. Owing to this separation, and their numerous increase, their having no regular form of government, and particularly their petty wars among each other, their first language would branch out into many variations, but still near enough to the original to be understood by each other, and sufficiently altered to be called different tongues; and as a number of families might, by co-operating together, be called a petty nation, so would some alteration in their speech, or tongue, be sufficient to distinguish them. Jasher tells us, that when Nimrod was 40 years old, there was war between his brethren and the children of Japheth; (see verse 34;) and that they were under the power of their enemies; that with a few people, (of the children of Cush only,) he made war, and subdued them; and that they all came to dwell with him in Shinar. I have frequently had to remark that the word *all* must not in the Hebrew be taken in that latitude, as it would in the modern languages. When a united number is intended to be expressed, the word *all* is used as in verse 35, when "Nimrod assembled all the sons of Cush, and their families, about four hundred and sixty men," by this is meant that *all those assembled* of the families of Cush were four hundred and sixty men. Sufficient examples will be found in Jasher as well as in scripture, where כל must be understood in this sense. I therefore understand in this verse, not that all mankind came to live in Shinar, but that all those that did come, resided in Shinar. And if, owing to their former separation into petty nations, they must have adopted various dialects sufficient to distinguish them, as Jasher tells us that "all nations and tongues heard his fame," so when they were reunited, and become under one government, not from choice, but from compulsion, then they became again of one lip and words of union; for thus would I translate ודברים אחדים, commonly translated, *and one speech*, which is the literal translation, meaning that after their cessation from war and petty broils, they again spoke in *one lip and words of union*, in opposition to *separate dialects and words of strife*. This inference of a former separation will explain that part of the speech of the builders of Babel, "we will build a tower, &c., &c., lest we be scattered upon the face of the earth," alluding to their former dissensions, by which means they had originally separated, and become scattered, but wishing to unite in idolatry, and raise an amazing tower, they hoped it would be the means of uniting the whole race of mankind under their impious standard. It seems that the families of Cush, Mitzraim, Phut and Canaan were the chief instigators to this impious act, and that out of all the families then existing, not of Ham only, but the impious of all the families that assembled to the task, were 600,000 men; and they chose a valley at two days' distance from Shinar, say twenty miles. I have no doubt the numbers of the human race were very considerable at that time, as it was 340 years after the flood, and there was plenty of time for the propagation of men to three or four millions of inhabitants.

49. And Terah the son of Nahor, prince of Nimrod's host, was in those days very great in the sight of the king and his subjects, and the king and princes loved him, and they elevated him very high.

50. And Terah* took a wife, and her name was Amthelo the daughter of Cornebo; and the wife of Terah conceived and bare him a son in those days.

51. Terah was seventy years old when he begat him, and Terah called the name of his son that was born to him† Abram, because the king had raised him in those days, and dignified him above all his princes that were with him.

CHAPTER VIII.

1. And it was in the night that Abram was born, that all the servants of Terah, and all the wise men of Nimrod, and his conjurors came and ate and drank in the house of Terah, and they rejoiced with him on that night.

2. And when all the wise men and conjurors went out from the house of Terah, they lifted up their eyes toward heaven that night *to look* at the stars, and they saw, and behold one very large star came from the east and ran in the heavens, and he swallowed up the four stars from the four sides of the heavens.

* By this it seems he had another wife who bare Abram, different from her who bare Haran and Nahor. See verse 22.

† אברם From this it seems that Abram was called so, not because *he* was a mighty father, but because Terah was a mighty father in the court of Nimrod, and therefore God changed his name to Abraham, appropriating to him in a much more extensive sense, the meaning which Terah applied to himself.

3. And all the wise men of the king and his conjurors were astonished at the sight, and the sages understood this matter, and they knew its import.

4. And they said to each other, this only *betokens* the child that has been born to Terah this night, who will grow up and be fruitful, and multiply, and possess all the earth, he and his children for ever, and he and his seed will slay great kings, and inherit their lands.

5. And the wise men and conjurors went home that night, and in the morning all *these* wise men and conjurors rose up early, and assembled in an appointed house.

6. And they spoke and said to each other, behold the sight that we saw last night is hidden from the king, it has not been made known to him.

7. And should this thing get known to the king in the latter days, he will say to us, why have you concealed this matter from me, and then we shall all suffer death; *therefore*, now let us go and tell the king the sight which we saw, and the interpretation thereof, and we shall *then remain* clear.

8. And they did so, and they all went to the king and bowed down to him to the ground, and they said, may the king live, may the king live.

9. We heard that a son was born to Terah the son of Nahor, the prince of thy host, and we yesternight came to his house, and we ate and drank and rejoiced with him that night.

10. And when thy servants went out from the house of Terah, to go to our respective homes to abide there for the night, we lifted up our eyes to heaven, and we saw a great star coming from the east, and the same star ran with great speed, and

swallowed up four great stars, from the four sides of the heavens.

11. And thy servants were astonished at the sight which we saw, and were greatly terrified, and we made our judgment upon the sight, and knew by our wisdom the proper interpretation thereof, that this thing applies to the child that is born to Terah, who will grow up and multiply greatly, and become powerful, and kill all the kings of the earth, and inherit all their lands, he and his seed forever.

12. And now our lord *and* king, behold we have truly acquainted thee with what we have seen concerning this child.

13. If it seemeth good to the king to give his father value for this child, we will slay him before he shall grow up and increase in the land, and his evil increase against us, that we and our children perish through his evil.

14. And the king heard their words and they seemed good in his sight, and he sent and called for Terah, and Terah came before the king.

15. And the king said to Terah, I have been told that a son was yesternight born to thee, and after this manner was observed in the heavens at his birth.

16. And now *therefore* give me the child, that we may slay him before his evil springs up against us, and I will give thee for his value, thy house full of silver and gold.

17. And Terah answered the king and said to him ; my Lord *and* king, I have heard thy words, and thy servant shall do all that his king desireth.

18. But my lord *and* king, I will tell thee what happened to me yesternight, that I may see what advice the king will give his servant, and then I will answer the king upon what he has *just* spoken ; and the king said, speak.

19. And Terah said to the king, Ayon, son of Mored, came to me yesternight, saying,

20. Give unto me the great and beautiful horse that the king gave thee, and I will give thee silver and gold, and straw and provender for its value ; and I said to him, wait till I see the king concerning thy words, *and* behold whatever the king saith, that will I do.

21. And now my lord *and* king, behold I have made this thing known to thee, and the advice which my king will give unto his servant, that will I follow.

22. And the king heard the words of Terah, and his anger was kindled and he considered him in the light of a fool.

23. And the king answered Terah, and he said to him, art thou so silly, ignorant, or deficient in understanding, to do this thing, to give thy beautiful horse for silver and gold or even for straw and provender ?

24. Art thou *so* short of silver and gold, that thou shouldest do this thing, because thou canst not obtain straw and provender to feed thy horse ? and what is silver and gold to thee, or straw and provender, that thou shouldst give away that fine horse which I gave thee, like which there is none to be had on the whole earth ?

25. And the king left off speaking, and Terah answered the king, saying, like unto this has the king spoken to his servant ;

26. I beseech thee, my lord and king, what is this which thou didst say unto me, saying, give thy son that we may slay him, and I will

give thee silver and gold for his value; what shall I do with silver and gold after the death of my son? who shall inherit me? *surely* then at my death, the silver and gold will return to my king who gave it.

27. And when the king heard the words of Terah, and the parable which he brought concerning the king, it grieved him greatly and he was vexed at this thing, and his anger burned within him.

28. And Terah saw that the anger of the king was kindled against him, and he answered the king, saying, all that I have is in the king's power; whatever the king desireth to do to his servant, that let him do, *yea,* even my son, he is in the king's power, without value in exchange, he and his two brothers that are older than he.

29. And the king said to Terah, no, but I will purchase thy younger son for a price.

30. And Terah answered the king, saying, I beseech thee my lord and king to let thy servant speak a word before thee, and let the king hear the word of his servant, and Terah said, let my king give me three days time till I consider this matter within myself, and *consult* with my family concerning the words of my king; and he pressed the king greatly *to agree* to this.

31. And the king hearkened to Terah, and he did so and he gave him three days time, and Terah went out from the king's presence, and he came home to his family and spoke to them all the words of the king; and the people were greatly afraid.

32. And it was in the third day that the king sent to Terah, saying, send me thy son for a price as I spoke to thee; and shouldst thou not do this, I will send and slay all thou hast in thy house, so that thou shalt not even have a dog remaining.

33. And Terah hastened, (as the thing was urgent from the king), and he took a child from one of his servants, which his handmaid had born to him that day, and Terah brought the child to the king and received value for him.

34. And the Lord was with Terah in this matter, that Nimrod might not cause Abram's death, and the king took the child from Terah and with all his might dashed his head to the ground, for he thought it had been Abram; and this was concealed from him from that day, and it was forgotten by the king, as it was the will of Providence not to suffer Abram's death.

35. And Terah took Abram his son secretly, together with his mother and nurse, and he concealed them in a cave, and he brought them their provisions monthly.

36. And the Lord was with Abram in the cave and he grew up, and Abram was in the cave ten years, and the king and his princes, soothsayers and sages, thought that the king had killed Abram.

CHAPTER IX.

1. AND Haran, the son of Terah, Abram's oldest brother, took a wife in those days.

2. Haran was thirty-nine years old when he took her; and the wife of Haran conceived and bare a son, and he called his name Lot.

3. And she conceived again and bare a daughter, and she called her name Milca; and she again conceived and bare a daughter, and she called her name Sarai.

4. Haran was forty-two years old when he begat Sarai, which was in the tenth year of the life of Abram; and in those days Abram and his mother and nurse went out from the cave, as the king and his subjects had forgotten the affair of Abram.

5. And when Abram came out from the cave, he went to Noah and his son Shem, and he remained with them to learn the instruction of the Lord and his ways, and no man knew *where* Abram *was*, and Abram served Noah and Shem his son for a long time.

6. And Abram was in Noah's house thirty-nine years, and Abram knew the Lord from three years old, and he went in the ways of the Lord until the day of his death, as Noah and his son Shem had taught him; and all the sons of the earth in those days greatly transgressed against the Lord, and they rebelled against him and they served other gods, and they forgot the Lord who had created them in the earth; and the inhabitants of the earth made unto themselves, at that time, every man his God; gods of wood and stone which could neither speak, hear, nor deliver, and the sons of men served them and they became their gods.

7. And the king and all his servants, and Terah with all his household were then the first of those that served *gods* of wood and stone.

8. And Terah had twelve gods of large size, made of wood and stone, after the twelve months *of the year*, and he served each one monthly, and every month Terah would bring his *meat* offering and drink offering to his gods; thus did Terah all the days.

9. And all that generation were wicked in the sight of the Lord, and they thus made every man his god, but they forsook the Lord who had created them.

10. And there was not a man found in those days in the whole earth, who knew the Lord (for they served each man his *own* God) except Noah and his household, and all *those* who were under his counsel knew the Lord in those days.

11. And Abram the son of Terah was waxing *great in those days in the house of Noah, and no man knew it, and the Lord was with him.

12. And the Lord gave Abram an understanding heart, and he knew all the works of that generation were vain, and that all their gods were vain and were of no avail.

13. And Abram saw the sun *shining* upon the earth, and Abram said unto himself surely now this sun that shines upon the earth is God, and him will I serve.

14. And Abram served the sun in that day and he prayed to him, and when evening came the sun set as usual, and Abram said within himself, surely this cannot be God?

15. And Abram still continued to speak within himself, who is he who made the heavens and the earth? who created upon earth? where is he?

16. And night darkened over him, and he lifted up his eyes toward the west, north, south and east, and he saw that the sun had vanished from the earth, and the day became dark.

17. And Abram saw the stars and moon before him, and he said, surely this is the God who created the whole earth as well as man, and behold these his servants are gods around him; and Abram served the moon and prayed to it all that night.

* In divine truths, as is explained in the next verse.

18. And in the morning when it was light and the sun shone upon the earth as usual, Abram saw all the things that the Lord God had made upon earth.

19. And Abram said unto himself, surely these are not gods that made the earth and all mankind, but *these are* the servants of God; and Abram remained in the house of Noah and there knew the Lord and his ways, and he served the Lord all the days of his life, and all that generation forgot the Lord, and served other gods of wood and stone, and rebelled all their days.

20. And king Nimrod reigned securely, and all the earth was under his control, and all the earth was of one tongue and words of union.

21. And all the princes of Nimrod and his great men took counsel together; Phut, Mitzraim, Cush and Canaan with their families, and they said to each other, come let us build ourselves a city and in it a strong tower, and its top reaching heaven, and we will make ourselves famed, so that we may reign upon the whole world, in order that the evil of our enemies may cease from us, that we may reign mightily over them, and that we may not become scattered over the earth on account of their wars.

22. And they all went before the king, and they told the king these words, and the king agreed with them in this affair, and he did so.

23. And all the families assembled *consisting* of about six hundred thousand men, and they went to seek an extensive piece of ground to build the city and the tower, and they sought in the whole earth and they found none like one valley at the east of the land of Shinar, about two days' walk, and they journeyed there and they dwelt there.

24. And they began to make bricks and burn fires to build the city and the tower that they had imagined to *complete*.

25. And the building of the tower was unto them a transgression and a sin, and they began to build it, and whilst they were building against the Lord God of heaven, they imagined in their hearts to war against him and to ascend into heaven.

26. And all these people and all the families divided themselves in three parts; the first said we will ascend into heaven and fight against him; the second said, we will ascend to heaven and place our own gods there and serve them; and the third *part* said, we will ascend to heaven and smite him with bows and spears; and God knew all their works and all their evil thoughts, and he saw the city and the tower which they were building.

27. And when they were building they built themselves a great city and a very high and strong tower; and on account of its height the mortar and bricks did not reach the builders in their ascent to it, until those who went up had completed a full year, and after that, they reached to the builders and gave them the mortar and bricks; thus was it done daily.

28. And behold these ascended and others descended the whole day; and if a brick should fall from their hands and get broken, they would all weep over it, and if a man fell and died, none of them would look at him.

29. And the Lord knew their thoughts, and it came to pass when they were building they cast the arrows toward the heavens, and all the arrows fell upon them filled with

blood, and when they saw them they said to each other, surely we have slain all those that are in heaven.

30. For this was from the Lord in order to cause them to err, and in order to destroy them from off the face of the ground.

31. And they built the tower and the city, and they did this thing daily until many days and years were elapsed.

32. And God said to the seventy angels who stood foremost before him, *to* those who were near to him, saying, come let us descend and confuse their tongues, that one man shall not understand the language of his neighbor, and they did so unto them.

33. And from that day following, they forgot each man his neighbor's tongue, and they could not understand to speak in one tongue, and when the builder took from the hands of his neighbor lime or stone which he did not order, the builder would cast it away and throw it upon his neighbor, that he would die.

34. And they did so many days, and they killed many of them in this manner.

35. And the Lord smote the three divisions that were there, and he punished them according to their works and designs ; those who said, we will ascend to heaven and serve our Gods, became *like apes and elephants ; and those who said, we will smite the heaven with arrows, the Lord killed them, one man through the hand of his neighbor ;

*A long note I have upon this, as it might be translated, "and they became apes and elephants," this being the example of the work in the hands of Mr. Adam of Calcutta, sent to me by the royal Asiatic society, to see if it were like mine. The words are "and his heart died within him, and he became" (not a stone) but " like unto a stone," as it is rightly translated in the English Bible.

and the third *division* of those who said, we will ascend to heaven and fight against him, the Lord scattered them throughout the earth.

36. And those who were left amongst them, when they knew and understood the evil which was coming upon them, they forsook the building, and they also became scattered upon the face of the whole earth.

37. And they ceased building the city and the tower ; therefore he called that place Babel, for there the Lord confounded the language of the whole earth ; behold it *was* at the east of the land of Shinar.

38. And *as* to the tower which the sons of men built, the earth opened its mouth and swallowed up *one* third part thereof, and a fire also descended from heaven and burned another third, and the other third is left to this day, and it is of that part which was aloft. and its circumference is *three days' walk.

39. And many of the sons of men died in that tower, a people without number.

CHAPTER X.

1. And Peleg the son of Eber died in those days, in the forty-eighth year of the life of Abram son of Terah, and all the days of Terah were two hundred and thirty nine years.

* This cannot be the tower that Herodotus saw, though it might be erected on the same spot ; reckoning a day's walk 10 miles, as is supposed by the best Christian commentators, its circumference will be 30 miles. This will not appear so very astonishing when it is considered that six hundred thousand men were employed in erecting it, and, as Jasher tells, they were many years engaged in this infamous work , and it will not exceed credibility, when it is remembered that the wall of China is 1500 miles in length.

2. And when the Lord had scattered the sons of men on account of their sin at the tower, *behold* they spread forth into many divisions, and all the sons of men were dispersed into the four corners of the earth.

3. And all the families became each according to its language, its land, or its city.

4. And the sons of men built many cities according to their families, in all the places where they went, and throughout the earth where the Lord had scattered them.

5. And some of them built cities in places from which they were *afterward* extirpated, and they called these cities after their own names, or the names of their children, or after their *particular* occurrences.

6. And the sons of Japheth the son of Noah went and built themselves cities in the places where they were scattered, and they called all their cities after their names, and the sons of Japheth were divided upon the face of the earth into many divisions and languages.

7. And these are the sons of Japheth according to their families, Gomer, Magog, Medai, Javan, Tubal, Meshech and Tiras ; these are the children of Japheth according to their generations.

8. And the children of Gomer, according to their cities, were the Francum who dwelt in the land of Franza by the river Franza by the river Senah.

9. And the children of Rephath are the Bartonim, who dwell in the land of Bartonia by the river Ledah which empties its waters in the great *sea Gihon, that is, oceanus.

---

* This is the same as the river Gihon mentioned in ch. 5, which overflowed and destroyed part of the earth. In the Hebrew ים sea, and נהר river are frequently put for each other.

10. And the children of Tugarma are ten families, and these are their names ; Buzar, Parzunac, Balgar, Elicanum, Ragbib, Tarki, Bid, Zebuc, Ongal and Tilmaz ; all these spread and rested in the North and built themselves cities.

11. And they called their cities after their *own* names, those are they who abide by the rivers Hithlah and Italac unto *this* day.

12. But *the families* of Angoli, Balgar and Parzunac, they dwell by the great river Dubnee ; and the names of their cities are also according to their own names.

13. And the children of Javan are the Javanim who dwell in the land of Makdonia, and *the children* of Madai are the Orelum that dwell in the land of Curson, and the children of Tubal are those that dwell in the land of Tuskanah by the river Pashiah.

14. And the children of Meshech are the Shibashni and *the children* of Tiras are Rushash, Cushni, and Ongolis ; all these went and built themselves cities ; those are the cities that are situate by the sea Jabus by the river Cura, which empties itself in the river Tragan.

15. And the children of Elishah are the Almanim, and they also went and built themselves cities ; those are the cities situate between the mountains of Job and Shibathmo ; and of them were the people of Lumbardi who dwell opposite the mountains of Job and Shibathmo, and they conquered the land of Italia and remained there unto this day.

16. And the children of Chittim are the Romim who dwell in the valley of Canopia by the river Tibreu.

17. And the children of Dudonim

are those who dwell in the cities of the sea Gihon in the land of Bordna.

18. These are the families of the children of Japheth according to their cities and languages, when they were scattered after the tower, and they called their cities after their names and occurrences; and these are the names of all their cities according to their families, which they built in those days after the tower.

19. And the children of Ham were Cush, Mitzraim, Phut and Canaan according to their generation and cities.

20. All these went and built themselves cities as they found *fit places for them*, and they called their cities after the names of their fathers Cush, Mitzraim, Phut and Canaan.

21. And the children of Mitzraim are the Ludim, Anamim, Lehabim, Naphtuchim, Pathrusim, Casluchim and Caphturim, seven families.

22. All these dwell by the river Sihor, that is the brook of Egypt, and they built themselves cities and called them after their own names.

23. And the children of Pathros and Casloch intermarried together, and from them went forth the Pelishtim, the Azathim, and the Gerarim, the Githim and the Ekronim, in all five families; these also built themselves cities, and they called their cities after the names of their fathers unto this day.

24. And the children of Canaan also built themselves cities, and they called their cities after their names, eleven cities and others without number.

25. And four men from the family of Ham went to the land of the plain; these are the names of the four men, Sodom, Gomorrah, Admah and Zeboyim.

26. And these men built themselves four cities in the land of the plain, and they called the names of their cities after their own names.

27. And they and their children and all belonging to them dwelt in those cities, and they were fruitful and multiplied greatly and dwelt peaceably.

28. And Seir the son of Hur, son of Hivi, son of Canaan, went and found a valley opposite to Mount Paran, and he built a city there, and he and his seven sons and his household dwelt there, and he called the city which he built Seir, according to his name; that is the land of Seir unto this day.

29. These are the families of the children of Ham, according to their languages and cities, when they were scattered to their countries after the tower.

30. And some of the children of Shem son of Noah, father of all the children of Eber, also went and built themselves cities in the places wherein they were scattered, and they called their cities after their names.

31. And the sons of Shem were Elam, Ashur, Arpachshad, Lud and Aram, and they built themselves cities and called the names of all their cities after their names.

32. And Ashur son of Shem and his children and household went forth at that time, a very large *body of them*, and they went to a distant land that they found, and they met with a very extensive valley in the land that they went to, and they built themselves four cities, and they called them after their own names and occurrences.

33. And these are the names of the cities which the children of Ash-

ur built, Ninevah, Resen, Calach
and Rehobother; and the children
of Ashur dwell there unto this day.

34. And the children of Aram also
went and built themselves a city, and
they called the name of the city Uz
after their eldest brother, and they
dwelt therein; that is the land of
Uz to this day.

35. And in the second year after
the tower a man from the house of
Ashur, whose name was Bela, went
from the land of Ninevah to sojourn
with his household wherever he
could find a *place;* and they came
until opposite the cities of the plain
against Sodom, and they dwelt there.

36. And the man rose up and
built there a small city, and called
its name Bela after his name; that
is the land of Zoar unto this day.

37. And these are the families of
the children of Shem according to
their language and cities, *after* they
were scattered upon the earth after
the tower.

38. And every kingdom, city and
family of the families of the children of Noah built themselves many
cities after this.

39. And they established govern-
ments in all their cities, in order to
be regulated by their orders; so did
all the families of the children of
Noah forever.

CHAPTER XI.

1. AND Nimrod son of Cush was
still in the land of Shinar, and he
reigned over it and dwelt there, and
he built cities in the land of Shinar.

2. And these are the names of
the four cities which he built, and
he called their names after the occurrences that happened to them in
the building of the tower.

3. And he called the first Babel,
saying, because the Lord there confounded the language of the whole
earth; and the name of the second
he called *Erech, because from there
God dispersed them.

4. And the third he called †Eched,
saying, there was a great battle at
that place; and the fourth he called
Calnah, because his princes and
mighty men were consumed there,
and they vexed the Lord, they rebelled and transgressed against him.

5. And when Nimrod had built
these cities in the land of Shinar, he
placed in them the remainder of
his people, his princes and his mighty
men that were left in his kingdom.

6. And Nimrod dwelt in Babel,
and he there renewed his reign over
the rest of his subjects, and he
reigned securely, and the subjects
and princes of Nimrod called his
name Amraphel, saying that at the
tower his princes and men fell
through his means.

7. And notwithstanding this, Nimrod did not return to the Lord, and
he continued in wickedness and
teaching wickedness to the sons of
men; and Mardon his son was
worse than his father, and continued
to add to the abominations of his
father.

8. And he caused the sons of men
to sin, therefore it is said, from the
wicked goeth forth wickedness.

9. At that time there was war between the families of the children
of Ham, as they were dwelling in
the cities which they had built.

10. And Chedorlaomer, king of
Elam, went away from the families of

* ארך like ויאריכו הברים, as Kimchi explains
it, that they drew them out.
† אכד is a term for battle, from כידורי אש,
sparks of fire.

the children of Ham, and he fought with them and he subdued them, and he went to the five cities of the plain and he fought against them and he subdued them, and they were under his control.

11. And they served him twelve years, and they gave him a yearly tax.

12. At that time died Nahor, son of Serug, in the forty ninth year of the life of Abram son of Terah.

13. And in the fiftieth year of the life of Abram son of Terah, Abram came forth from the house of Noah, and went to his father's house.

14. And Abram knew the Lord, and he went in his ways and instructions, and the Lord his God was with him.

15. And Terah his father was in those days still captain of the host of king Nimrod, and he still followed strange gods.

16. And Abram came to his father's house and saw twelve gods standing there in their temples, and the anger of Abram was kindled when he saw these images in his father's house.

17. And Abram said, as the Lord liveth these images shall not remain in my father's house; so shall the Lord who created me do unto me if in three days' time I do not break them all.

18. And Abram went from them, and his anger burned within him. And Abram hastened and went from the chamber to his father's outer court, and he found his father sitting in the court, and all his servants with him, and Abram came and sat before him.

19. And Abram asked his father, saying, Father, tell me where is God who created heaven and earth, and all the sons of men upon earth, and who created thee and me. And Te-rah answered his son Abram and said, behold those who created us are all with us in the house.

20. And Abram said to his father, my lord shew them to me I pray thee; and Terah brought Abram into the chamber of the inner court, and Abram saw, and behold the whole room was full of gods of wood and stone, twelve great images and others less than they without number.

21. And Terah said to his son, behold these are they which made all thou seest upon earth, and which created me and thee, and all mankind.

22. And Terah bowed down to his gods, and he *then* went away from them, and Abram his son went away with him.

23. And when Abram had gone from them he went to his mother and sat before *her*, and he said to his mother, behold, my father has shown me those who made heaven and earth, and all the sons of men.

24. Now therefore hasten and fetch a kid from the flock, and make of it savoury meat, that I may bring it to my father's gods as an offering for them to eat; perhaps I may thereby become acceptable to them.

25. And his mother did so, and she fetched a kid, and made savoury meat thereof, and brought it to Abram, and Abram took the savoury meat from his mother and brought it before his father's gods, and he drew nigh to them that *they* might eat; and Terah his father did not know of it.

26. And Abram saw on the day when he was sitting amongst them that they had no voice, no hearing, no motion, and not one of them *could* stretch forth his hand to eat.

27. And Abram mocked them,

and said, surely the savoury meat that I prepared has not pleased them, or *perhaps* it was too little for them, *and* for that reason they would not eat ; therefore to-morrow I will prepare fresh savoury meat, better and more plentiful than this, *in order* that I may see the result.

28. And it was on the next day that Abram directed his mother concerning the savoury meat, and his mother rose and fetched three fine kids from the flock, and she made of them some excellent savoury meat, such as her son was fond of, and she gave it to her son Abram ; and Terah his father did not know of it.

29. And Abram took the savoury meat from his mother, and brought it before his father's gods into the chamber; and he came nigh unto them that they might eat, and he placed it before them, and Abram sat before them all day,* thinking perhaps they might eat.

30. And Abram viewed them, and behold they had neither voice nor hearing, nor did one of them stretch forth his hand to the meat to eat.

31. And in the evening of that day in that house Abram was clothed with the spirit of God.

32. And he called out and said, wo unto my father and this wicked

* This is continued in the same beautiful strain of irony as the whole ; his first visit to the idols with the first dish, his troubling his mother to make fresh delicacies, fearing the first was not good enough, and then his sitting there all day watching them if they would eat, were all to afford him materials for making a noble and forcible appeal to his father, to show him that he exerted his best efforts to please his gods ; that he attended twice upon them to try their appetites with the most relishing dishes, and that he did not do this in haste, but that he had watched them the whole day to see of what his gods were capable. This strain of irony is not much inferior to that where Elisha calls on the worshippers of Baal.

generation, whose hearts are all inclined to vanity, who serve these idols of wood and stone which can neither eat, smell, hear nor speak, who have mouths without speech, eyes without sight, ears without hearing, hands without feeling, and legs which cannot move ; like them are those that made them and that trust in them.

33. And when Abram saw all these things his anger was kindled against his father, and he hastened and took a hatchet in his hand, and came unto the chamber of the gods, and he broke all his father's gods.

34. And when he had done breaking the images, he placed the hatchet in the hand of the great god which was there before them, and he went out; and Terah his father came home, for he had heard at the door the sound of the striking of the hatchet ; so Terah came into the house to know what this was about.

35. And Terah, having heard the noise of the hatchet in the room of images, ran to the room to the images, and he met Abram going out.

36. And Terah entered the room and found all the idols fallen down and broken, and the hatchet in the hand of the largest, which was not broken, and the savoury meat which Abram his son had made was still before them.

37. And *when* Terah saw this his anger was greatly kindled, and he hastened and went from the room to Abram.

38. And he found Abram his son still sitting in the house ; and he said to him, what is this work thou hast done to my gods ?

39. And Abram answered Terah his father and he said, not so my lord, for I brought savoury meat

before them, and when I came nigh to them with the meat that *they* might eat, they *all at once* stretched forth their hands to eat before the great one had put forth his hand to eat.

40. And the large one saw their works that they did before him, and his anger was violently kindled against them, and he went and took the hatchet that was in the house and came. to them and broke them all, and behold the hatchet is yet in his hand as thou seest.

41. And Terah's anger was kindled against his son Abram, when he spoke this; and Terah said to Abram his son in his anger, what is this tale that thou hast told? Thou speakest lies to me.

42. Is there in these gods spirit, soul or power to do all thou hast told me? Are they not wood and stone, and have I not *myself* made them, and canst thou speak such lies, saying that the large god that was with them smote them? It is thou that didst place the hatchet in his hands, and then sayest he smote them all.

43. And Abram answered his father and said to him, and how canst thou *then* serve these idols in whom there is no power to do any thing? Can those idols in which thou trustest deliver thee? can they hear thy prayers when thou callest upon them? can they deliver thee .from the hands of thy enemies, or will they fight thy battles for thee against thy enemies, that thou shouldst serve wood and stone which can neither speak nor hear?

44. And now *surely* it is not good for thee nor for the sons of men that are connected with thee, to do these things; are you so silly, so foolish or so short of understanding that you will serve wood and stone, and do after this manner?

45. And forget the Lord God who made heaven and earth, and who created you in the earth, and *thereby* bring a great evil upon your souls in this matter by serving stone and wood?

46. Did not our fathers in days of old sin in this manner, and the Lord God of the universe brought the waters of the flood upon them and destroyed the whole earth?

47. And how can you continue to do this and serve gods of wood and stone, who cannot hear, or speak, or deliver you from oppression, thereby bringing down the anger of the God of the universe upon you?

48. Now *therefore* my father refrain from this, and bring not evil upon thy soul and the souls of thy household.

49. And Abram hastened and sprang from before his father, and took the hatchet from his father's largest idol, with which Abram broke it and ran away.

50. And Terah, seeing all that Abram had done, hastened to go from his house, and he went to the king and he came before Nimrod and stood before him, and he bowed down to the king; and the king said, what dost thou want?

51. And he said, I beseech thee my lord, to hear me—now fifty years back a child was born to me, and thus has he done to my gods and thus has he spoken; and now therefore, my lord *and* king, send *for him* that he may come before thee, and judge him according to the law, that we may be delivered from his evil.

52. And the king sent three men of his servants, and they went and brought Abram before the king.

And Nimrod and all his princes and servants were that day sitting before him, and Terah sat also before them.

53. And the king said to Abram, what is this that thou hast done to thy father and to his gods? And Abram answered the king in the words that he spoke to his father, and he said, the large god that was with them in the house did to them what thou hast heard.

54. And the king said to Abram, had they power to speak and eat and do as thou hast said? And Abram answered the king, saying, and if there be no power in them why dost thou serve them and cause the sons of men to err through thy follies?

55. Dost thou imagine that they can deliver thee or do any thing small or great, that thou shouldst serve them? And why wilt thou not serve the God of the whole universe, who created thee and in whose power it is to kill and to keep alive?

56. O foolish, simple, and ignorant king, woe unto thee forever.

57. I thought thou wouldst teach thy servants the upright way, but thou hast not done this, but hast filled the whole earth with thy sins and the sins of thy people who have followed thy ways.

58. Dost thou not know, or hast thou not heard, that this evil which thou doest, our ancestors sinned therein in days of old, and the eternal God brought the waters of the flood upon them and destroyed them all, and also destroyed the whole earth on their account? And wilt thou and thy people rise up now and do like unto this work, in order to bring down the anger of the Lord God of the universe, and to bring evil upon thee and the whole earth?

59. Now *therefore* put away this evil deed which *thou doest, and serve the God of the universe, as thy soul is in his hands, and *then* it will be well with thee.

60. And if thy wicked heart will not hearken to my words to cause thee to forsake thy evil ways and to serve the eternal God, *then* wilt thou die in shame in the latter days, thou, thy people and all who are connected with thee, hearing thy words or walking in thy evil ways.

61. And when Abram had ceased speaking before the king and princes, Abram lifted up his eyes to the heavens, and he said, the Lord seeth all the wicked and he will judge them.

CHAPTER XII.

1. And when the king heard the words of Abram he ordered him to be put into prison; and Abram was ten days in prison.

2. And at the end of those days the king ordered that all the kings, princes and governors of different provinces and the sages should come before him, and they sat before him, and Abram was still in the house of confinement.

3. And the king said to the princes and sages, have you heard what Abram the son of Terah has done to his father? Thus has he done to him, and I ordered him to be brought before me, *and* thus has he spoken; his heart did not misgive him, neither did he stir *in my presence,* and behold now he is confined in the prison.

4. And therefore decide what judg-

* I have here continued the singular pronoun in order to keep up the chain of the narrative, though the Hebrew has the transition to the plural, as including Nimrod's men.

ment is due to this man who reviled the king ; who spoke and did all the things that you heard.

5. And they all answered the king, saying, the man who revileth the king should be hanged upon a tree ; but having done all the things that he said, and having despised our gods, he must therefore be burned to *death*, for this is the law in this matter.

6. If it pleaseth the king to do this, let him order his servants to kindle a fire *both* night and day in thy brick furnace, and then we will cast this man into it. And the king did so, and he commanded his servants that they should prepare a fire for three days and three nights in the king's furnace, that is in Casdim ; and the king ordered them to take Abram from prison and bring him *out* to be burned.

7. And all the king's servants, princes, lords, governors and judges, and all the inhabitants of the land, about nine hundred thousand men, stood opposite the furnace to see Abram.

8. And all the women and little ones crowded upon the roofs and towers to see *what was doing* with Abram, and they all stood together at a distance ; and there was not a man left that did not come on that day to behold the scene.

9. And when Abram was come, the conjurors of the king and the sages saw Abram, and they cried out to the king, saying, our sovereign lord, surely this is the man whom we know to have been the child at whose birth the great star swallowed the four stars, which we declared to the king now fifty years since.

10. And behold now his father has also transgressed thy command, and

mocked thee by bringing thee another child, which thou didst kill.

11. And when the king heard their words he was exceedingly wroth, and he ordered Terah to be brought before him.

12. And the king said, hast thou heard what the conjurors have spoken ? Now tell me truly, how didst thou ; and if thou shalt speak truth thou shalt be acquitted.

13. And seeing that the king's anger was so much kindled, Terah said to the king, my lord *and* king, thou hast heard the truth and what the sages have spoken is right. And the king said, how couldst thou do this thing, to transgress my orders and to give me a child that thou didst not beget, and to take value for him ?

14. And Terah answered the king, because my tender feelings were excited for my son, at that time, and I took a son of my handmaid, and I brought him to the king.

15. And the king said, who advised thee *to* this ? Tell me, do not hide aught from me, and *then* thou shalt not die.

16. And Terah was greatly terrified in the king's presence, and he said to the king, it was Haran *my* eldest son who advised me to this ; and Haran was in those days that Abram was born, two and thirty years old.

17. But Haran did not advise his father to anything, for Terah said this to the king in order *to* deliver his soul from the king, for he feared greatly ; and the king said to Terah, Haran thy son who advised thee to this shall die through fire with Abram ; for the sentence of death is upon him for having rebelled against the king's desire in doing this thing.

18. And Haran at that time felt

inclined *to follow the ways* of Abram, but he kept it within himself.

19. And Haran said in his heart, behold now the king has seized Abram on account of these things which Abram did, and it shall come to pass, that if Abram prevail over the king I will follow him, but if the king prevail I will go after the king.

20. And when Terah had spoken this to the king concerning Haran his son, the king ordered Haran to be seized with Abram.

21. And they brought them both, Abram and Haran his brother, to cast them into the fire; and all the inhabitants of the land and the king's servants and princes and all the women and little ones were there, standing that day over them.

22. And the king's servants took Abram and his brother, and they stripped them of all their clothes excepting their lower garments which were upon them.

23. And they bound their hands and feet with linen cords, and the servants of the king lifted them up and cast them both into the furnace.*

24. And the Lord loved Abram and he had compassion over him, and the Lord came down and delivered Abram from the fire and he was not burned.

25. But all the cords with which they bound him were burned, while Abram remained and walked about in the fire.

26. And Haran died when they had cast him into the fire, and he was burned to ashes, for his heart was not perfect with the Lord; and those men who cast him into the

fire, the flame of the fire spread over them, and they were burned; and twelve men of them died.

27. And Abram walked in the midst of the fire three days and three nights, and all the servants of the king saw him walking in the fire, and they came and told the king, saying, behold we have seen Abram walking about in the midst of the fire, and *even* the lower garments which are upon him are not burned, but the cord with which he was bound is burned.

28. And when the king heard their words his heart fainted and he would not believe them; so he sent other faithful princes to see this matter, and they went and saw *it* and told *it* to the king; and the king rose to go and see *it*, and he saw Abram walking to and fro in the midst of the fire, and he saw Haran's body burned, and the king wondered greatly.

29. And the king ordered Abram to be taken out from the fire; and his servants approached to take him out and they could not, for the fire was round about and the flame ascending toward them from the furnace.

30. And the king's servants fled from it, and the king rebuked them, saying, make haste and bring Abram out of the fire that you shall not die.

31. And the servants of the king *again* approached to bring Abram out, and the flames came upon them and burned their faces so that eight of them died.

32. And when the king saw that his servants could not approach the fire lest they should be burned, the king called to Abram, O servant of the God who is in heaven, go forth from amidst the fire and come hither before me; and Abram hearkened

* This is noticed in the Talmud. The Rechabites have this tradition, and we also find it recorded in the Koran that Abram was thrown into a fiery furnace by Nimrod.

to the voice of the king, and he went forth from the fire and came and stood before the king.

33. And when Abram came out the king and all his servants saw Abram coming before the king, with his lower garments upon him, for they were not burned, but the cord with which he was bound was burned.

34. And the king said to Abram, how is it that thou wast not burned in the fire?

35. And Abram said to the king, the God of heaven and earth in whom I trust and who has all in his power, he delivered me from the fire into which thou didst cast me.

36. And Haran the brother of Abram was burned to ashes, and they sought for his body and they found it consumed.

37. And Haran was eighty-two years old when he died in the fire of Casdim. And the king, princes and inhabitants of the land, seeing that Abram was delivered from the fire, they came and bowed down to Abram.

38. And Abram said to them, do not bow down to me but bow down to the God of the world who made you, and serve him and go in his ways for it is he who delivered me from out of this fire, and it is he who created the souls and spirits of all men, and formed man in his mother's womb, and brought him forth into the world, and it is he who will deliver those who trust in him from all pain.

39. And this thing seemed very wonderful in the eyes of the king and princes, that Abram was saved from the fire and that Haran was burned; and the king gave Abram many presents and he gave him his two head servants from the king's house; the name of one was Oni and the name of the other was Eliezer.

40. And all the kings, princes and servants gave Abram many gifts of silver and gold and pearl, and the king and his princes sent him away, and he went in peace.

41. And Abram went forth from the king in peace, and many of the king's servants followed him, and about three hundred men joined him.

42. And Abram returned on that day and went to his father's house, he and the men that followed him, and Abram served the Lord his God all the days of his life, and he walked in his ways and *followed* his law.

43. And from that day forward Abram inclined the hearts of the sons of men to serve the Lord.

44. And at that time Nahor and Abram took unto themselves wives, the daughters of their brother Haran; the wife of Nahor *was* Milca and the name of Abram's wife was Sarai. And Sarai wife of Abram was barren; she had no offspring in those days.

45. And at the expiration of two years from Abram's going out of the fire, that is in the fifty second year of his life, *behold* king Nimrod sat in Babel upon the throne, and the king fell asleep and dreamed that he was standing with his troops and hosts in a valley opposite the king's furnace.

46. And he lifted up his eyes and saw a man in the likeness of Abram coming forth from the furnace, and that he came and stood before the king with his drawn sword, and then sprang to the king with his sword, when the king fled from the man, for he was afraid; and while he

was running, the man threw an egg upon the king's head, and the egg became a great river.

47. And the king dreamed that all his troops sank in that river and died, and the king took flight with three men who were before him and he escaped.

48. And the king looked at these men and they were clothed in princely dresses as the garments of kings, and had the appearance and majesty of kings.

49. And while they were running, the river again turned to an egg before the king, and there came forth from the egg a young bird which came before the king, and flew at his head and plucked out the king's eye.

50. And the king was grieved at the sight, and he awoke out of his sleep and his spirit was agitated, and he felt a great terror.

51. And in the morning the king rose from his couch in fear, and he ordered all the wise men and magicians to come before him, when the king related his dream to them.

52. And a wise servant of the king, whose name was Anuki, answered the king, saying, this is nothing else but the evil of Abram and his seed which will spring up against my lord and king in the latter days.

53. And behold the day will come when Abram and his seed and the children of his household will war with my king, and they will smite all the king's hosts and his troops.

54. And as to what thou hast said concerning three men which thou didst see like unto thyself, and which did escape, this *means* that only thou wilt escape with three kings from the kings of the earth who will be with thee in battle.

55. And that which thou sawest of the river which turned to an egg as at first, and the young bird plucking out thine eye, this *means* nothing else but the seed of Abram which will slay the king in latter days.

56. This is my king's dream, and this is its interpretation, and the dream is true, and the interpretation which thy servant has given thee is right.

57. Now therefore my king, surely thou knowest that it is now fifty-two years since thy sages saw this at the birth of Abram, and if my king will suffer Abram to live in the earth it will be to the injury of my lord *and* king, for all the days that Abram liveth neither thou nor thy kingdom will be established, for this was known formerly at his birth; and why will not my king slay him, that his evil may be kept from thee in latter days?

58. And Nimrod hearkened to the voice of Anuki, and he sent some of his servants in secret to go and seize Abram, and bring him before the king to suffer death.

59. And Eliezer, Abram's servant whom the king had given him, was at that time in the presence of the king, and he heard what Anuki had advised the king, and what the king had said to cause Abram's death.

60. And Eliezer said to Abram, hasten, rise up and save thy soul, that thou mayest not die through the hands of the king, for thus did he see in a dream concerning thee, and thus did Anuki interpret it, and thus *also* did Anuki advise the king concerning thee.

61. And Abram hearkened to the voice of Eliezer, and Abram hastened and ran for safety to the house of Noah and his son, Shem, and he

concealed himself there and found a place of safety; and the king's servants came to Abram's house to seek him, but they could not find him, and they searched throughout the country and he was not to be found, and they went and searched in every direction and he was not *to be met with.*

62. And when the king's servants could not find Abram they returned to the king, but the king's anger against Abram was stilled, as they did not find him, and the king drove from his mind this matter concerning Abram.

63. And Abram was concealed in Noah's house for one month until the king had forgotten this matter, but Abram was still afraid of the king; and Terah came to see Abram his son secretly in the house of Noah, and Terah was very great in the eyes of the king.

64. And Abram said to his father, dost thou not know that the king thinketh to slay me, and to annihilate my name from the earth by the advice of his wicked counsellors?

65. Now whom hast thou here and what hast thou in this land? Arise, let us go together to the land of Canaan, that we may be delivered from his hand, lest thou perish also through him in the latter days.

66. Dost thou not know *or* hast thou not heard, that it is not through love that Nimrod giveth thee all this honour, but it is *only* for his benefit that he bestoweth all this good upon thee?

67. And if he do unto thee greater good than this, surely these are only vanities of the world, for wealth and riches cannot avail in the day of wrath and anger.

68. Now *therefore* hearken to my voice, and let us arise and go to the land of Canaan, *out of the* reach of injury from Nimrod; and serve *thou* the Lord who created thee in the earth and it will be well with thee; and cast away all the vain *things* which thou pursuest.

69. And Abram ceased to speak, when Noah and his son Shem answered Terah, saying, true is the word which Abram hath said unto thee.

70. And Terah hearkened to the voice of his son Abram, and Terah did all that Abram said, for this was from the Lord, that the king should not cause Abram's death.

CHAPTER XIII.

1. And Terah took his son Abram and his grandson Lot, the son of Haran, and Sarai his daughter-in-law, the wife of his son Abram, and all the souls of his household and went with them from Ur Casdim to go to the land of Canaan. And when they came as far as the land of Haran they remained there, for it was exceeding good land for pasture, and of *sufficient* extent for those who accompanied them.

2. And the people of the land of Haran saw that Abram was good and upright with God and men, and that the Lord his God was with him, and some of the people of the land of Haran came and joined Abram, and he taught them the instruction of the Lord and his ways; and these men remained with Abram in his house and they adhered to him.

3. And Abram remained in the land three years, and at the expiration of three years the Lord appeared to Abram and said to him; I am the Lord who brought thee forth from

Ur Casdim, and delivered thee from the hands of all thine enemies.

4. And now *therefore* if thou wilt hearken to my voice and keep my commandments, my statutes and my laws, *then* will I cause thy enemies to fall before thee, and I will multiply thy seed like the stars of heaven, and I will send my blessing upon all the works of thy hands, and thou shalt lack nothing.

5. Arise now, take thy wife and all belonging to thee and go to the land of Canaan and remain there, and I will there be unto thee for a God, and I will bless thee. And Abram rose and took his wife and all belonging to him, and he went to the land of Canaan as the Lord had told him; and Abram was fifty years old when he went from Haran.

6. And Abram came to the land of Canaan and dwelt in the midst of the city, and he there pitched his tent amongst the children of Canaan, inhabitants of the land.

7. And the Lord appeared to Abram when he came to the land of Canaan, and said to him, this is the land which I gave unto thee and to thy seed after thee forever, and I will make thy seed like the stars of heaven, and I will give unto thy seed for an inheritance all the lands which thou seest.

8. And Abram built an altar in the place where God had spoken to him, and Abram there called upon the name of the Lord.

9. At that time, at the end of three years of Abram's dwelling in the land of Canaan, in that year Noah died, which was the fifty-eighth year of the life of Abram; and all the days that Noah lived were nine hundred and fifty years and he died.

10. And Abram dwelt in the land of Canaan, he, his wife, and all belonging to him, and all those that accompanied him, together with those that joined him from the people of the land; but Nabor, Abram's brother, and Terah his father, and Lot the son of Haran and all belonging to them dwelt in Haran.

11. In the fifth year of Abram's dwelling in the land of Canaan the people of Sodom and Gomorrah and all the cities of the plain revolted from the power of Chedorlaomer, king of Elam; for all the kings of the cities of the plain had served Chedorlaomer for twelve years, and given him a yearly tax, but in those days in the thirteenth year, they rebelled against him.

12. And in the tenth year of Abram's dwelling in the land of Canaan there was war between Nimrod king of Shinar and Chedorlaomer king of Elam, and Nimrod came to fight with Chedorlaomer *and* to subdue him.

13. For Chedorlaomer was at that time one of the princes of the hosts of Nimrod, and when all the people at the tower were dispersed and those that remained were *also* scattered upon the face of the earth, Chedorlaomer went to the land of Elam and reigned over it and rebelled against his Lord.

14. And in those days when Nimrod saw that the cities of the plain had rebelled, he came with pride and anger to war with Chedorlaomer, and Nimrod assembled all his princes and subjects, about seven hundred thousand men, and went against Chedorlaomer, and Chedorlaomer went out to meet him with five thousand men, and they prepared for battle in the valley of Babel which is between Elam and Shinar.

15. And all those kings fought

there, and Nimrod and his people were smitten before the people of Chedorlaomer, and there fell from Nimrod's men about six hundred thousand, and Mardon the king's son fell amongst them.

16. And Nimrod fled and returned in shame and disgrace to his land, and he was under subjection to Chedorlaomer for a long time, and Chedorlaomer returned to his land and sent princes of his host to the kings that *dwelt* around him, to Arioch king of Elasar, and to Tidal king of Goyim, and made a covenant with them, and they were all obedient to his commands.

17. And it was in the fifteenth year of Abram's dwelling in the land of *Canaan, which* is the seventieth year of the life of Abram, and the Lord appeared to Abram in that year and he said to him, I am the Lord who brought thee out from Ur Casdim to give thee this land for an inheritance.

18. Now *therefore* walk before me and be perfect and keep my commands, for to thee and to thy seed I will give this land for an inheritance, from the river Mitzraim unto the great river Euphrates.

19. And thou shalt come to thy fathers in peace and in good age, and the fourth generation shall return here in this land and shall inherit it forever; and Abram built an altar, and he called upon the name of the Lord who appeared to him, and he brought up sacrifices upon the altar to the Lord.

20. At that time Abram returned and went to Haran to see his father and mother, and his father's household, and Abram and his wife and all belonging to him returned to Haran, and Abram dwelt in Haran five years.

21. And many of the people of Haran, about seventy two men, followed Abram and Abram taught them the instruction of the Lord and his ways, and he taught them to know the Lord.

22. In those days the Lord appeared to Abram in Haran, and he said to him, behold, I spoke unto thee these twenty years back saying,

23. Go forth from thy land, from thy birth-place and from thy father's house, to the land which I have shown thee to give it to thee and to thy children, for there in that land will I bless thee, and make thee a great nation, and make thy name great, and in thee shall the families of the earth be blessed.

24. Now *therefore* arise, go forth from this place, thou, thy wife, and all belonging to thee, also every one born in thy house and all the souls thou hast made in Haran, and bring *them* out with thee from here, and rise to return to the land of Canaan.

25. And Abram arose and took his wife Sarai and all belonging to him, and all that were born to him in his house and the souls which they had made in Haran, and they came out to go to the land of Canaan.

26. And Abram went and returned to the land of Canaan, according to the word of the Lord. And Lot the son of his brother Haran went with him, and Abram was seventy five years old when he went forth from Haran to return to the land of Canaan.

27. And he came to the land of Canaan according to the word of the Lord to Abram, and he pitched his tent and he dwelt in the plain of Mamre, and with him was Lot his brother's son, and all belonging to him.

28. And the Lord again appeared to Abram and said, to thy seed will I give this land; and he there built an altar to the Lord who appeared to him, which is still to this day in the plains of Mamre.

CHAPTER XIV.

1. In those days there was in the land of Shinar a wise man who had understanding in all wisdom, and of a beautiful appearance, but he was poor and indigent; his name was Rikayon and he was hard set to support himself.

2. And he resolved to go to Egypt, to Oswiris the son of Anom king of Egypt, to show the king his wisdom; for perhaps he might find grace in his sight, to raise him up and give him maintenance; and Rikayon did so.

3. And when Rikayon came to Egypt he asked the inhabitants of Egypt concerning the king, and the inhabitants of Egypt told him the custom of the king of Egypt, for it was then the custom of the king of Egypt that he went from his royal palace and was seen abroad only one day *in* the year, and after that the king would return to his palace to remain there.

4. And on the day when the king went forth he passed judgment in the land, and every one having a suit came before the king that day to obtain his request.

5. And when Rikayon heard of the custom in Egypt and that he could not come into the presence of the king, he grieved greatly and was very sorrowful.

6. And in the evening Rikayon went out and found a house in ruins, *formerly* a bake house in Egypt, and he abided there all night in bitterness of soul and *pinched* with hunger, and sleep was removed from his eyes.

7. And Rikayon considered within himself what he should do in the town until the king made his appearance, and how he might maintain himself there.

8. And he rose in the morning and walked about, and met in his way those who sold vegetables and *various sorts* of seed with which they supplied the inhabitants.

9. And Rikayon wished to do the same in order to get a maintenance in the city, but he was unacquainted with the custom of the people, and he was like a blind man among them.

10. And he went and obtained vegetables to sell them for his support, and the rabble assembled about him and ridiculed him, and took his vegetables from him and left him nothing.

11. And he rose up from there in bitterness of soul, and went sighing to the bake house in which he had remained *all the night before*, and he slept there the second night.

12. And on that night *again* he reasoned within himself how he could save himself from *starvation*, and he devised a scheme how to act.

13. And he rose up in the morning and acted ingeniously, and went and hired thirty strong men of the rabble, carrying their war instruments in their hands, and he led them to the top of the Egyptian sepulchre, and he placed them there.

14. And he commanded them, saying, thus saith the king, strengthen yourselves and be valiant men, and let no man be buried here until two hundred pieces of silver be given, and then he may be buried,

and those men did according to the order of Rikayon to the people of Egypt the whole of that year.

15. And in eight months time Rikayon and his men gathered great riches of silver and gold, and Rikayon took a great quantity of horses and other animals, and he hired more men, and he gave them horses and they *remained* with him.

16. And when the year came round, at the time the king went forth into the town, all the inhabitants of Egypt assembled together to speak to him concerning the work of Rikayon and his men.

17. And the king went forth on the appointed day, and all the Egyptians came before him and cried unto him, saying,

18. May the king live forever. What is this thing thou doest in the town to thy servants, not to suffer a dead body to be buried until *so much* silver and gold be given? Was there *ever* the like unto this done in the whole earth, from the days of former kings *yea* even from the days of Adam, unto this day, that the dead should not be buried only for a *set* price?

19 We know it to be the custom of kings to take a yearly tax from the living, but thou dost not only do this, but from the dead also thou exactest a tax day by day.

20. Now, O king, we can no more bear this, for the whole city is ruined on this account, and dost thou not know it?

21. And when the king heard all that they had spoken he was very wroth, and his anger burned within him at this affair, for he had known nothing of it.

22. And the king said, who and where is he that dares to do this wicked thing in my land without my command? Surely you will tell me.

23. And they told him all the works of Rikayon and his men, and the king's anger was aroused, and he ordered Rikayon and his men to be brought before him.

24. And Rikayon took about a thousand children, sons and daughters, and clothed them in silk and embroidery, and he set them upon horses and sent them to the king by means of his men, and he also took a great quantity of silver and gold and precious stones, and a strong and beautiful horse, as a present for the king, with which he came before the king and bowed down to the earth before him; and the king, his servants and all the inhabitants of Egypt wondered at the work of Rikayon, and they saw his riches and the present that he had brought to the king.

25. And it greatly pleased the king and he wondered at it; and when Rikayon sat before him the king asked him concerning all his works, and Rikayon spoke all his words wisely before the king, his servants and all the inhabitants of Egypt.

26. And when the king heard the words of Rikayon and his wisdom, Rikayon found grace *in his sight,* and he met with grace and kindness from all the servants of the king and from all the inhabitants of Egypt, on account of his wisdom and excellent speeches, and from that time they loved him exceedingly.

2̶7̶6. And the king answered and said to Rikayon, thy name shall no more be called Rikayon but Pharaoh* shall be thy name, since thou

* Pharaoh from פרע, to get paid, to exact.

didst exact a tax from the dead ; and he called his name Pharaoh,

28. And the king and his subjects loved Rikayon for his wisdom, and they consulted with all the inhabitants of Egypt to make him prefect under the king.

29. And all the inhabitants of Egypt and *its* wise men did so, and it was made a law in Egypt.

30. And they made Rikayon Pharaoh, prefect under Oswiris king of Egypt, and Rikayon Pharaoh governed over Egypt, daily administering justice to the whole city, but Oswiris the king would judge the *people of the* land one day in the year, when he went out to make his appearance.

31. And Rikayon Pharaoh cunningly usurped the government of Egypt, and he exacted a tax from all the inhabitants of Egypt.

32. And all the inhabitants of Egypt greatly loved Rikayon Pharaoh, and they made a decree to call every king that should reign over them and their seed in Egypt, Pharaoh.

33. Therefore all the kings that reigned in Egypt from that time forward were called Pharaoh unto this day.

CHAPTER XV.

1. And in that year there was a heavy famine throughout the land of Canaan, and the inhabitants of the land could not remain on account of the famine for it was very grievous.

2. And Abram and all belonging to him rose and went down to Egypt on account of the famine, and when they were at the brook Mitzraim they remained there some time to rest from *the fatigue* of the road.

3. And Abram and Sarai were walking at the border of the brook Mitzraim, and Abram beheld his wife Sarai that she was very beautiful.

4. And Abram said to his wife Sarai, since God has created thee with such a beautiful countenance, I am afraid of the Egyptians lest they should slay me and take thee away, for the fear of God is not in *these* places.

5 Surely then thou shalt do this, say thou art my sister to all that may ask thee, in order that it may be well with me, and that we may live and not be put to death.

6. And Abram commanded *the same* to all those that came with him to Egypt on account of the famine ; also his nephew Lot he commanded, saying, if the Egyptians ask thee concerning Sarai say she is the sister of Abram.

7. And yet with all these orders Abram did not put confidence in them, but he took Sarai and placed her in a chest and concealed it amongst their vessels, for Abram was greatly concerned about Sarai on account of the wickedness of the Egyptians.

8. And Abram and all belonging to him rose up from the brook Mitzraim and came to Egypt ; and they had *scarcely* entered the gates of the city when the guards stood up to them, saying, give tythe to the king from what you have, and then you may come into the town ; and Abram and those that were with him did so.

9. And Abram with the people that were with him came to Egypt, and when they came they brought the chest in which Sarai was concealed, and the Egyptians saw the chest.

10. And the king's servants approached Abram, saying, what hast

thou here in this chest which we have not seen? Now open thou the chest and give tythe to the king of all that it contains.

11. And Abram said, this chest I will not open, *but* all you demand upon it I will give. And Pharaoh's officers answered Abram, saying, it is a chest of precious stones, give us the tenth *thereof*.

12. Abram said, all that you desire I will give, but you must not open the chest.

13. And the king's officers pressed Abram, and they reached the chest and opened it with force, and they saw, and behold a beautiful woman was in the chest.

14. And when the officers of the king beheld Sarai they were struck with admiration at her beauty, and all the princes and servants of Pharaoh assembled to see Sarai, for she was very beautiful. And the king's officers ran and told Pharaoh all that they had seen, and they praised Sarai to the king; and Pharaoh ordered her to be brought, and the woman came before the king.

15. And Pharaoh beheld Sarai and she pleased him exceedingly, and he was struck with her beauty, and the king rejoiced greatly on her account, and made presents to those who brought him the tidings concerning her.

16. And the woman was then brought to Pharaoh's house, and Abram grieved on account of his wife, and he prayed to the Lord to deliver her from the hands of Pharaoh.

17. And Sarai also prayed at that time and said, O Lord God thou didst tell my Lord Abram to go from his land and from his father's house to the land of Canaan, and thou didst

promise to do well with him if he would perform thy commands; now behold we have done that which thou didst command us, and we left our land and our families, and we went to a strange land and to a people whom we have not known before.

18. And we came to this land to avoid the famine, and this evil accident has befallen me; now therefore O Lord God deliver us and save us from the hand of this oppressor, and do well with me for the sake of thy mercy.

19. And the Lord hearkened to the voice of Sarai, and the Lord sent an angel to deliver Sarai from the power of Pharaoh.

20. And the king came and sat before Sarai, and behold an angel of the Lord was standing over them, and he appeared to Sarai and said to her, do not fear for the Lord has heard thy prayer.

21. And the king approached Sarai and said to her, what is that man to thee who brought thee hither? and she said, he is my brother.

22. And the king said, it is *incumbent* upon us to make him great, to elevate him and to do unto him all the good which thou shalt command us; and at that time the king sent to Abram silver and gold and precious stones in abundance, together with cattle, men servants and maid servants; and the king ordered Abram to be brought, and he sat in the court of the king's house, and the king greatly exalted Abram on that night.

23. And the king approached to speak to Sarai, and he reached out his hand to touch her, when the angel smote him heavily, and he was terrified and he refrained from reaching to her.

24. And when the king came near

to Sarai, the angel smote him to the ground, and acted thus to him the whole night, and the king was terrified.

25. And the angel on that night smote heavily all the servants of the king, and his whole household, on account of Sarai, and there was a great lamentation that night amongst the people of Pharaoh's house.

26. And Pharaoh, seeing the evil that befel him, said, surely on account of this woman has this thing happened to me, and he removed himself at *some distance* from her and spoke pleasing words* to her.

27. And the king said to Sarai, tell me I pray thee concerning the man with whom thou camest here ; and Sarai said this man is my husband, and I said to thee that he was my brother for I was afraid, lest thou shouldst put him to death through wickedness.

28. And the king kept away from Sarai, and the plagues of the angel of the Lord ceased from him and his household ; and Pharaoh knew that he was smitten on account of Sarai, and the king was greatly astonished at this.

29. And in the morning the king called for Abram and said *to him,* what is this thou hast done to me ? Why didst thou say, she is my sister, *owing to which* I took her unto me for a wife, and this heavy plague has *therefore* come upon me and my household.

30. Now therefore here is thy wife, take *her* and go from our land lest we all die on her account. And Pha-

* Hebrew, spoke good words to her heart, meaning that he endeavored to gain her heart or confidence, by good words and modest conduct, to tell him what Abram was really akin to her, whereby he might discover the cause of the angel smiting him and his people.

raoh took more cattle, men servants and maid servants, and silver and gold, to give to Abram, and he returned unto him Sarai his wife.

31. And the king took a maiden whom he begat by his concubines, and he gave her to Sarai for a handmaid.

32. And the king said to his daughter, it is better for thee my daughter to be a handmaid in this man's house than to be a mistress in my house, after we have beheld the evil that befel us on account of this woman.

33. And Abram arose, and he and all belonging to him went away from Egypt ; and Pharaoh ordered some of his men to accompany him and all that *went* with him.

34. And Abram returned to the land of Canaan, to the place where he had made the altar, where he at first had pitched his tent.

35. And Lot the son of Haran, Abram's brother, had a heavy *stock* of cattle, flocks and herds and tents, for the Lord was bountiful to them on account of Abram.

36. And when Abram was dwelling in the land the herdsmen of Lot quarrelled with the herdsmen of Abram, for their property was too great for them to remain together in the land, and the land could not bear them on account of their cattle.

37. And when Abram's herdsmen went to feed *their flock* they would not go into the fields of the people of the land, but the cattle of Lot's herdsmen did otherwise, for they were suffered to feed in the fields of the people of the land.

38. And the people of the land saw this occurrence daily, and they came to Abram and quarrelled with him on account of Lot's herdsmen.

39. And Abram said to Lot, what

is this thou art doing to me, to make me despicable to the inhabitants of the land, that thou orderest thy herdsmen to feed thy cattle in the fields of other *people*? Dost thou not know that I am a stranger in this land amongst the children of Canaan, and why wilt thou do this unto me?

40. And Abram quarrelled daily with Lot on account of this, but Lot would not listen to Abram, and he continued to do the same and the inhabitants of the land came and told Abram.

41. And Abram said unto Lot, how long wilt thou be to me for a stumbling block with the inhabitants of the land? Now I beseech thee let there be no more quarrelling between us, for we are kinsmen.

42. But I pray thee separate from me, go and choose a place where thou mayst dwell with thy cattle and all belonging to thee, but keep thyself at a distance from me, thou and thy household.

43. And be not afraid in going from me, for if any one do an injury to thee, let me know and I will avenge thy cause from him, only remove from me.

44. And when Abram had spoken all these words to Lot, then Lot arose and lifted up his eyes toward the plain of Jordan.

45. And he saw that the whole of this place was well watered, and good for man as well as affording pasture for the cattle.

46. And Lot went from Abram to that place, and he there pitched his tent and he dwelt in Sodom, and they were separated from each other.

47. And Abram dwelt in the plain of Mamre, which is in Hebron, and he pitched his tent there, and Abram remained in that place many years.

CHAPTER XVI.

1. At that time Chedorlaomer king of Elam sent to all the neighboring kings, to Nimrod king of Shinar who was then under his power, and to Tidal king of Goyim, and to Arioch king of Elasar, with whom he made a covenant, saying, come up to me and assist me, that we may smite all the towns of Sodom and its inhabitants, for they have rebelled against me these thirteen years.

2. And these four kings went up with all their camps, about eight hundred thousand men, and they went as they were, and smote every man they found in their road.

3. And the five kings of Sodom and Gomorrah, Shinab king of Admah, Shemeber king of Zeboyim, Bera king of Sodom, Bersha king of Gomorrah, and Bela king of Zoar, went out to meet them, and they all joined together in the valley of Siddim.

4. And these nine kings made war in the valley of Siddim; and the kings of Sodom and Gomorrah were smitten before the kings of Elam.

5. And the valley of Siddim was full of lime-pits and the kings of Elam pursued the kings of Sodom, and the kings of Sodom with their camps fled and fell into the lime-pits, and all that remained went to the mountain for safety, and the five kings of Elam came after them and pursued them to the gates of Sodom, and they took all that there was in Sodom.

6. And they plundered all the cities of Sodom and Gomorrah, and they also took Lot, Abram's brother's son, and his property, and they

seized all the goods of the cities of Sodom, and they went away; and Unic, Abram's servant, who was in the battle, saw *this*, and told Abram all that the kings had done to the cities of Sodom, and that Lot was taken captive by them.

7. And Abram heard this, and he rose up with about three hundred and eighteen men that were with him, and he that night pursued these kings and smote them, and they all fell before Abram and his men, and there was none remaining but the four kings who fled, and they went each his *own* road.

8. And Abram recovered all the property of Sodom, and he also recovered Lot and his property, his wives and little ones and all belonging to him, so that Lot lacked nothing.

9. And when he returned from smiting these kings, he and his men passed the valley of Siddim where the kings had made war together.

10. And Bera king of Sodom, and the rest of his men that were with him, went out from the lime-pits into which they had fallen, to meet Abram and his men.

11. And Adonizedek king of Jerusalem, the same was Shem, went out with his men to meet Abram and his people, with bread and wine, and they remained together in the valley of Melech.

12. And Adonizedek blessed Abram, and Abram gave him a tenth from all that he had brought from the spoil of his enemies, for Adonizedek was a priest before God.

13. And all the kings of Sodom and Gomorrah who were there, with their servants, approached Abram and begged of him to return them their servants whom he had made captive, and to take unto himself all the property.

14. And Abram answered the kings of Sodom, saying, as the Lord liveth who created heaven and earth, and who redeemed my soul from all affliction, and who delivered me this day from my enemies, and gave them into my hand, I will not take any thing belonging to you, that you may not boast to-morrow, saying, Abram became rich from our property that he saved.

15. For the Lord my God in whom I trust said unto me, thou shalt lack nothing, for I will bless thee in all the works of thy hands.

16. And now therefore behold, here is all belonging to you, take it and go; as the Lord liveth I will not take from you from a *living* soul down to a shoe tie or thread, excepting the *expense* of the food of those who went out with me to battle, as also the portions of the men who went with me, Anar, Ashcol and Mamre, they and their men, as well as those also who had remained to watch the baggage, they shall take their portion of the spoil.

17. And the kings of Sodom gave Abram according to all that he had said, and they pressed him to take of whatever he chose, but he would not.

18. And he sent away the kings of Sodom and the remainder of their men, and he gave them orders about Lot, and they went to their respective places.

19. And Lot, his brother's son, he also sent away with his property, and he* went with them. and Lot returned to his home, to Sodom, and Abram and his people returned to their home to the plains of Mamre which is in Hebron.

* Lot went with the kings.

20. At that time the Lord again appeared to Abram in Hebron, and he said to him, do not fear, thy reward is very great before me, for I will not leave thee, until I shall have multiplied thee, and blessed thee and made thy seed like the stars in heaven, which cannot be measured nor numbered.

21. And I will give unto thy seed all these lands that thou seest with thine eyes, to them will I give them for an inheritance forever, only be strong and do not fear, walk before me and be perfect.

22. And in the seventy eighth year of the life of Abram, in that year died Reu the son of Peleg, and all the days of Reu were two hundred and thirty nine years, and he died.

23. And Sarai the daughter of Haran, Abram's wife, was still barren in those days, she did not bear to Abram either son or daughter.

24. And when she saw that she bare no *children* she took her handmaid Hagar, whom Pharaoh had given her, and she gave her to Abram her husband for a wife.

25. For Hagar learned all the ways of Sarai as Sarai taught her, she was not in any way deficient in following her good ways.

26. And Sarai said to Abram, behold *here is* my handmaid Hagar, go to her that she may bring forth upon my knees, that I may also obtain children through her.

27. And at the end of ten years of Abram's dwelling in the land of Canaan, which is the eighty fifth year of Abram's life, Sarai gave Hagar unto him.

28. And Abram hearkened to the voice of his wife Sarai, and he took his handmaid Hagar and Abram came to her and she conceived.

29. And when Hagar saw that she had conceived she rejoiced greatly, and her mistress was despised in her eyes, and she said within herself, this can only be that I am better before God than Sarai my mistress, for all the days that my mistress has been with my lord, she did not conceive, but me the Lord has caused in so short a time to conceive by him.

30. And when Sarai saw that Hagar had conceived by Abram, Sarai was jealous of her handmaid, and Sarai said within herself, this is surely nothing else but that she must be better than I *am*.

31. And Sarai said unto Abram, my wrong be upon thee, for at the time when thou didst pray before the Lord for children why didst thou not pray on my account, that the Lord should give me seed from thee?

32. And when I speak to Hagar in thy presence, she despiseth my words, because, she has conceived, and thou wilt say nothing to her; may the Lord judge between me and thee for what thou hast done to me.

33. And Abram said to Sarai, behold thy handmaid is in thy hand, do unto her as it may seem good in thy eyes; and Sarai afflicted her, and Hagar fled from her to the wilderness.

34. And an angel of the Lord found her in the place where she had fled, by a well, and he said to her, do not fear, for I will multiply thy seed, for thou shalt bear a son and thou shalt call his name Ishmael; now *then* return to Sarai thy mistress and submit thyself under her hands.

35. And Hagar called the place of that well Beer-lahai-roi, it is between Kadesh and the wilderness of Bered.

36. And Hagar at that time returned to her master's house, and at the end of days Hagar bare a son to Abram, and Abram called his name Ishmael ; and Abram was eighty-six years old when he begat him.

CHAPTER XVII.

1. And in those days, in the ninety-first year of the life of Abram, the children of Chittim made war with the children of Tubal, for when the Lord had scattered the sons of men upon the face of the earth, the children of Chittim went and embodied themselves in the plain of Canopia, and they built themselves cities there and dwelt by the river Tibreu.

2. And the children of Tubal dwelt in Tuscanah, and their boundaries reached the river Tibreu, and the children of Tubal built a city in Tuscanah, and they called the name Sabinah, after the name of Sabinah son of Tubal their father, and they dwelt there unto this day.

3. And it was at that time the children of Chittim made war with the children of Tubal, and the children of Tubal were smitten before the children of Chittim, and the children of Chittim caused three hundred and seventy men to fall from the children of Tubal.

4. And at that time the children of Tubal swore to the children of Chittim, saying, you shall not intermarry amongst us, and no man shall give his daughter to any of the sons of Chittim.

5. For all the daughters of Tubal were in those days fair, for no women were then found in the whole earth so fair as the daughters of Tubal.

6. And all who delighted in the beauty of women went to the daughters of Tubal and took wives from them, and the sons of men, kings and princes, who greatly delighted in the beauty of women, took *wives* in those days from the daughters of Tubal.

7. And at the end of three years after the children of Tubal had sworn to the children of Chittim not to give them their daughters for wives, about twenty men of the children of Chittim went to take some of the daughters of Tubal, but they found none.

8. For the children of Tubal kept their oaths not to intermarry with them, and they would not break their oaths.

9. And in the days of harvest the children of Tubal went into their fields to get in their harvest, when the young men of Chittim assembled and went to the city of Sabinah, and each man took a young woman from the daughters of Tubal, and they came to their cities.

10. And the children of Tubal heard *of it* and they went to make war with them, and they could not prevail over them, for the mountain was exceedingly high from them, and when they saw they could not prevail over them they returned to their land.

11. And at the revolution of the year the children of Tubal went and hired about ten thousand men from those cities that were near them, and they went to war with the children of Chittim.

12. And the children of Tubal went to war with the children of Chittim, to destroy their land and to distress them, and in this *engagement* the children of Tubal prevailed over the children of Chittim, and the children of Chittim, seeing that they were greatly distressed, lifted up the children which they had had by the

daughters of Tubal, upon the wall which had been built, to be before the eyes of the children of Tubal.

13. And the children of Chittim said to them, have you come to make war with your own sons and daughters, and have we not been *considered* your flesh and bones from that time till now?

14. And when the children of Tubal heard this they ceased to make war with the children of Chittim, and they went away.

15. And they returned to their cities, and the children of Chittim at that time assembled and built two cities by the sea, and they called one Purtu and the other Ariza.

16. And Abram the son of Terah was then ninety-nine years old.

17. At that time the Lord appeared to him and he said to him, I will make my covenant between me and thee, and I will greatly multiply thy seed, and this is the covenant which I make between me and thee, that every male child be circumcised, thou and thy seed after thee.

18. At eight days old shall it be circumcised, and this covenant shall be in your flesh for an everlasting covenant.

19. And now *therefore* thy name shall no more be called Abram but Abraham, and thy wife shall no more be called Sarai but Sarah.

20. For I will bless you *both*, and I will multiply your seed after you that you shall become a great nation, and kings shall come forth from you.

CHAPTER XVIII.

1. And Abraham rose and did all that God had ordered him, and he took the men of his household and those bought with his money, and he circumcised them as the Lord had commanded him.

2. And there was not one left whom he did not circumcise, and Abraham and his son Ishmael were circumcised in the flesh of their foreskin; thirteen years old was Ishmael when he was circumcised in the flesh of his foreskin.

3. And in the third day Abraham went out of his tent and sat at the door to enjoy the heat of the sun, during the pain of his flesh.

4. And the Lord appeared to him in the plain of Mamre, and sent three of his ministering angels to* visit him, and he was sitting at the door of the tent, and he lifted up his eyes and saw, and lo, three men were coming from a distance, and he rose up and ran to meet them, and he bowed down to them and brought them into his house.

5. And he said to them, if now I have found favor in your sight, turn in and eat a morsel of bread; and he pressed them, and they turned in and he gave them water and they washed their feet, and he placed them under a tree at the door of the tent.

6. And Abraham ran and took a calf, tender and good, and he hastened to kill it, and gave it to his servant Eliezer to dress.

7. And Abraham came to Sarah into the tent, and he said to her, make ready quickly three measures of fine meal, knead it and make cakes to cover the pot containing the meat, and she did so.

8. And Abraham hastened and brought before them butter and milk, beef and mutton, and gave it before them to eat before the flesh of the calf was sufficiently done, and they did eat.

Hebrew לבקר, to seek or inquire after him.

9. And when they had done eating, one of them said to him, I will return to thee according to the time of life, and Sarah thy wife shall have a son.

10. And the men afterward departed and went their ways, to the places to which they were sent.

11. In those days all the people of Sodom and Gomorrah, and of the whole five cities, were exceedingly wicked and sinful against the Lord, and they provoked the Lord with their abominations, and they strengthened in acting abominably and scornfully before the Lord, and their wickedness and crimes were in those days great before the Lord.

12. And they had in their land a very extensive valley, about half a day's walk, and in it there were fountains of water and a great deal of herbage surrounding the water.

13. And all the people of Sodom and Gomorrah went there four times in the year, with their wives and children and all belonging to them, and they rejoiced there with timbrels and dances.

14. And in the time of rejoicing they would all rise and lay hold of their neighbors' wives, and some, the virgin daughters of their neighbors, and they enjoyed them, and each man saw his wife and daughter in the hands of his neighbor and did not say a word.

15. And they did so from morning to night, and they afterward returned home each man to his house and each woman to her tent; so they always did four times in the year.

16. Also when a stranger came into their cities and brought goods which he had purchased with a view to dispose of there, the people of these cities would assemble, men, women and children, young and old, and go to the man and take his goods by force, giving a little to each man until there was an end to all the goods of the owner which he had brought into the land.

17. And if the owner of the goods quarreled with them, saying, what is this work which you have done to me, then they would approach to him one by one, and each would show him the little which he took and taunt him, saying, I only took that little which thou didst give me; and when he heard this from them all, he would arise and go from them in sorrow and bitterness of soul, when they would all arise and go after him, and drive him out of the city with great noise and tumult.

18. And there was a man from the country of Elam who was leisurely going on the road, seated upon his ass, which carried a fine mantle of divers colors, and the mantle was bound with a cord upon the ass.

19. And the man was on his journey passing through the street of Sodom when the sun set in the evening, and he remained there in order to abide during the night, but no one would let him into his house; and at that time there was in Sodom a wicked and mischievous man, one skilful to do evil, and his name was Hedad.

20. And he lifted up his eyes and saw the traveller in the street of the city, and he came to him and said, whence comest thou and whither dost thou go?

21. And the man said to him, I am travelling from Hebron to Elam where I belong, and as I passed the sun set and no one would suffer me

4

to enter his house, though I had bread and water and also straw and provender for my ass, and am short of nothing.

22. And Hedad answered and said to him, all that thou shalt want shall be supplied by me, but in the street thou shalt not abide all night.

23. And Hedad brought him to his house, and he took off the mantle from the ass with the cord, and brought them to his house, and he gave the ass straw and provender whilst the traveller ate and drank in Hedad's house, and he abided there that night.

24. And in the morning the traveller rose up early to continue his journey, when Hedad said to him, wait, comfort thy heart with a morsel of bread and then go, and the man did so; and he remained with him, and they both ate and drank together during the day, when the man rose up to go.

25. And Hedad said to him, behold now the day is declining, thou hadst better remain all night that thy heart may be comforted; and he pressed him so that he tarried there all night, and on the second day he rose up early to go away, when Hedad pressed him, saying, comfort thy heart with a morsel of bread and then go; and he remained and ate with him also the second day, and *then* the man rose up to continue his journey.

26. And Hedad said to him, behold now the day is declining, remain with me to comfort thy heart and in the morning rise up early and go thy way.

27. And the man would not remain, but rose and saddled his ass, and whilst he was saddling his ass the wife of Hedad said to *her hus-*

band, behold this man has remained with us for two days eating and drinking and he has given us nothing, and now shall he go away from us without giving any thing? and Hedad said to her, be silent.

28. And the man saddled his ass to go, and he asked Hedad to give him the cord and mantle to tie it upon the ass.

29. And Hedad said to him, what sayest thou? and he said to him, that thou my lord shalt give me the cord and the mantle made with divers colors which thou didst conceal with thee in thy house to take care of it.

30. And Hedad answered the man, saying, this is the interpretation of thy dream, the cord which thou didst see, *means that* thy life will be lengthened out like a cord, and having seen the mantle colored with all sorts of colors, means that thou shalt have a vineyard in which thou wilt plant trees of all fruits.

31. And the traveller answered, saying, not so my lord, for I was awake when I gave thee the cord and also a mantle woven with different colors, which thou didst take off the ass to put them by *for me;* and Hedad answered and said, surely I have told thee the interpretation of thy dream and it is *a* good *dream,* and this is the interpretation thereof.

32. Now the sons of men give me four pieces of silver, which is my charge for interpreting dreams, and of thee only I require three pieces of silver.

33. And the man was provoked at the words of Hedad, and he cried bitterly, and he brought Hedad to Serak judge of Sodom.

34. And the man laid his cause before Serak the judge, when Hedad

replied, saying, it is not so, but thus the matter stands; and the judge said to the traveller, this man Hedad telleth thee truth, for he is famed in the cities for the accurate interpretation of dreams.

35. And the man cried at the word of the judge, and he said, not so my Lord, for it was in the day that I gave him the cord and mantle which was upon the ass, in order to put them by in his house; and they both disputed before the judge, the one saying thus the matter was, and the other declaring otherwise.

36. And Hedad said to the man, give me four pieces of silver that I charge for my interpretations of dreams; I will not make any allowance; and give me the expense of the four meals that thou didst eat in my house.

37. And the man said to Hedad, truly I will pay thee for what I ate in thy house, only give me the cord and mantle which thou didst conceal in thy house.

38. And Hedad replied before the judge and said to the man, did I not tell thee the interpretation of thy dream? the cord means that thy days shall be prolonged like a cord, and the mantle, that thou wilt have a vineyard in which thou wilt plant all kinds of fruit trees.

39. This is the proper interpretation of thy dream, now give me the four pieces of silver that I require as a compensation, for I will make thee no allowance.

40. And the man cried at the words of Hedad and they both quarreled before the judge, and the judge gave orders to his servants, who drove them rashly from the house.

41. And they went away quarreling from the judge, when the people of Sodom heard them, and they gathered about them and they exclaimed against the stranger, and they drove him rashly from the city.

42. And the man continued his journey upon his ass with bitterness of soul, lamenting and weeping.

43. And whilst he was going along he wept at what had happened to him in the corrupt city of Sodom.

CHAPTER XIX.

1. And the cities of Sodom had four judges to four cities, and these were their names, Serak in the city of Sodom, Sharkad in Gomorrah, Zabnac in Admah, and Menon in Zeboyim.

2. And Eliezer Abraham's servant applied to them *different* names, and he converted Serak to *Shakra, Sharkad to Shakrura, Zabnac to Kezobim, and Menon to Matzlodin.

3. And by desire of their four judges the people of Sodom and Gomorrah had beds erected in the streets of the cities, and if a man came to these places they laid hold of him and brought him to one of their beds, and by force made him to lie in them.

4. And as he lay down, three men would stand at his head and three at his feet, and measure him by the *length* of the bed, and if the man was less than the bed these six men would stretch him at each end, and when he cried out to them they would not answer him.

5. And if he was longer than the bed then they would draw together the two sides of the bed at each end,

*שׁקרא אשׁקרורא כוזבים are different names for falsehood. Eliezer made these puns upon their names to show that falsehood formed the foundation of their decisions.

until the man had reached the gates of death.

6. And if he *continued* to cry out to them, they would answer him, saying, thus shall it be done to a man that cometh into our land.

7. And when men heard all these things that the people of the cities of Sodom did, they refrained from coming there.

8. And when a poor man came to their land they would give him silver and gold, and cause a proclamation in the whole city not to give him a morsel of bread to eat, and if the stranger should remain there some days, and die from hunger, not having been able to obtain a morsel of bread, then at his death all the people of the city would come and take their silver and gold which they had given to him.

9. And those that could recognize the silver or gold which they had given him took it back, and at his death they *also* stripped him of his garments, and they would fight about them, and he that prevailed over his neighbor took them.

10. They would after that carry him and bury him under *some of the* shrubs in the deserts; so they did all the days to any one that came to them and died in their land.

11. And in the course of time Sarah sent Eliezer to Sodom, to see Lot and inquire after his welfare.

12. And Eliezer went to Sodom, and he met a man of Sodom fighting with a stranger, and the man of Sodom stripped the poor man of all his clothes and went away.

13. And this poor man cried to Eliezer and supplicated his favor on account of what the man of Sodom had done to him.

14. And he said to him, why dost thou act thus to the poor man who came to thy land?

15. And the man of Sodom answered Eliezer, saying, is this man thy brother, or have the people of Sodom made thee a judge this day, that thou speakest about this man?

16. And Eliezer strove with the man of Sodom on account of the poor man, and when Eliezer approached to recover the poor man's clothes from the man of Sodom, he hastened and with a stone smote Eliezer in the forehead.

17. And the blood flowed copiously from Eliezer's forehead, and when the man saw the blood he caught hold of Eliezer, saying, give me my hire for having rid thee of this bad blood that was in thy forehead, for such is the custom and the law in our land.

18. And Eliezer said to him, thou hast wounded me and *requirest me* to pay thee thy hire; and Eliezer would not hearken to the words of the man of Sodom.

19. And the man laid hold of Eliezer and brought him to Shakra the judge of Sodom for judgment.

20. And the man spoke to the judge, saying, I beseech thee my lord, thus has this man done, for I smote him with a stone that the blood flowed from his forehead, and he is unwilling to give me my hire.

21. And the judge said to Eliezer, this man speaketh truth to thee, give him his hire, for this is the custom in our land; and Eliezer heard the words of the judge and he lifted up a stone and smote the judge, and the stone struck on his forehead and the blood flowed copiously from the forehead of the judge, and Eliezer said, if this then is the custom in your land give thou unto this man what I should

have given him, for this has been thy decision, thou didst decree it.

22. And Eliezer left the man of Sodom with the judge, and he went away.

23. And when the kings of Elam had made war with the kings of Sodom, the kings of Elam captured all the property of Sodom, and they took Lot captive, with his property, and when it was told to Abraham he went and made war with the kings of Elam, and he recovered from their hands all the property of Lot as well as the property of Sodom.

24. At that time the wife of Lot bare him a daughter, and he called her name Paltith, saying, because God had delivered him and his whole household from the kings of Elam; and Paltith daughter of Lot grew up, and one of the men of Sodom took her for a wife.

25. And a poor man came into the city to seek a maintenance, and he remained in the city some days, and all the people of Sodom caused a proclamation of their custom not to give this man a morsel of bread to eat, until he dropped dead upon the earth, and they did so.

26. And Paltith the daughter of Lot saw this man lying in the streets *starved* with hunger, and no one would give him any thing to keep him alive, and he was just upon the point of death.

27. And her soul was filled with pity on account of the man, and she fed him secretly with bread for many days, and the soul of this man was revived.

28. For when she went forth to fetch water she would put the bread in the water pitcher, and when she came to the place where the poor man was, she took the bread from the pitcher and gave it him to eat; so she did many days.

29. And all the people of Sodom and Gomorrah wondered how this man could bear starvation for so many days.

30. And they said to each other, this can only be that he eats and drinks, for no man can bear starvation for so many days or live as this man has, without even his countenance changing; and three men concealed themselves in a place where the poor man was stationed, to know who it was that brought him bread to eat.

31. And Paltith daughter of Lot went forth that day to fetch water, and she put bread into her pitcher of water, and she went to draw water by the poor man's place, and she took out the bread from the pitcher and gave it to the poor man and he ate *it*.

32. And the three men saw what Paltith did to the poor man, and they said *to her*, it is thou then who hast supported him, and therefore has he not starved, nor changed in appearance, nor died like the rest.

33. And the three men went out of the place in which they were concealed, and they seized Paltith and the bread which was in the poor man's hand.

34. And they took Paltith and brought her before their judges, and they said to them, thus did she do, and it is she who supplied the poor man with bread, therefore did he not die all this time; now therefore declare to us the punishment due to this woman for having transgressed our law.

35. And the people of Sodom and Gomorrah assembled and kindled a fire in the street of the city, and they

took the woman and cast her into the fire and she was burned to ashes.

36. And in the city of Admah there was a woman to whom they did the like.

37. For a traveller came into the city of Admah to abide *there* all night, *with the intention* of going home in the morning, and he sat opposite the door of the house of the young woman's father, to remain there, as the sun had set when *he had reached* that place; and the young woman saw him sitting by the door of the house.

38. And he asked her for a drink of water and she said to him, who art thou? and he said to her I was this day going on the road, and *reached* here when the sun set, so I will abide here all night, and in the morning I will arise early and continue my journey.

39. And the young woman went into the house and fetched the man bread and water to eat and drink.

40. And *this* affair became known to the people of Admah, and they assembled and brought the young woman before the judges, that they should judge her for this act.

41. And the judge said the judgment of death *must pass* upon this woman because she transgressed our law, and this *therefore* is the decision concerning her.

42. And the people of those cities assembled and brought out the young woman, and anointed her with honey from head to foot, as the judge had decreed, and they placed her before a swarm of bees which were then in their hives, and the bees flew upon her and stung her that her whole body was swelled.

43. And the young woman cried out on account of the bees, but no one took notice of her or pitied her, and her cries ascended to heaven.

44. And the Lord was provoked at this and at all the works of the cities of Sodom, for they had abundance of food and had tranquility amongst them, and still would not sustain the poor and the needy, and in those days their evil doings and sins became great before the Lord.

45. And the Lord sent for two of the angels that had come to Abraham's house, to destroy Sodom and its cities.

46. And the angels rose up from the door of Abraham's tent, after they had eaten and drunk, and they reached Sodom in the evening, and Lot was then sitting in the gate of Sodom; and when he saw them he rose to meet them and he bowed down to the ground.

47. And he pressed them greatly and brought them into his house, and he gave them victuals which they ate, and they abided all night in his house.

48. And the angels said to Lot, arise, go forth from this place, thou and all belonging to thee, lest thou be consumed in the iniquity of this city, for the Lord will destroy this place.

49. And the angels laid hold upon the hand of Lot and upon the hand of his wife, and upon the hands of his children, and all belonging to him, and they brought him forth and set him without the cities.

50. And they said to Lot, escape for thy life, and he fled and all belonging to him.

51. Then the Lord rained upon Sodom and upon Gomorrah and upon all these cities brimstone and fire from the Lord out of heaven.

52. And he overthrew these cities,

all the plain and all the inhabitants of the cities, and that which grew upon the ground ; and Ado the wife of Lot looked back to see the destruction of the cities, for her compassion was moved on account of her daughters who remained in Sodom, for they did not go with her.

53. And when she looked back she became a pillar of salt, and it is yet in that place unto this day.

54. And the oxen which stood in that place daily licked up the salt to the extremities of their feet, and in the morning it would spring forth afresh, and they again licked it up unto this day.

55. And Lot and two of his daughters that remained with him fled and escaped to the cave of Adullam, and they remained there for some time.

56. And Abraham rose up early in the morning to see what had been done to the cities of Sodom ; and he looked and beheld the smoke of the cities going up like the smoke of a furnace.

57. And Lot and his two daughters remained in the cave, and they made their father drink wine, and they lay with him, for they said there was no man upon earth that could raise up seed from them, for they thought that the whole earth was destroyed.

58. And they both lay with their father, and they conceived and bare sons, and the first born called the name of her son Moab, saying, from my father did I conceive him ; he is the father of the Moabites unto this day.

59. And the younger also called her son Benami ; he is the father of the children of Ammon unto this day.

60. And after this Lot and his two daughters went away from there, and he dwelt on the other side of the Jordan with his two daughters and their sons, and the sons of Lot grew up, and they went and took themselves wives from the land of Canaan, and they begat children and they were fruitful and multiplied.

CHAPTER XX.

1. And at that time Abraham journeyed from the plain of Mamre, and he went to the land of the Philistines, and he dwelt in Gerar ; it was in the twenty-fifth year of Abraham's being in the land of Canaan, and the hundreth year of the life of Abraham, that he came to Gerar in the land of the Philistines.

2. And when they entered the land he said to Sarah his wife, say thou art my sister, to any one that shall ask thee, in order that we may escape the evil of the inhabitants of the land.

3. And as Abraham was dwelling in the land of the Philistines, the servants of Abimelech, king of the Philistines, saw that Sarah was exceedingly beautiful, and they asked Abraham concerning her, and he said, she is my sister.

4. And the servants of Abimelech went to Abimelech, saying, a man from the land of Canaan is come to dwell in the land, and he has a sister that is exceeding fair.

5. And Abimelech heard the words of his servants who praised Sarah to him, and Abimelech sent his officers, and they brought Sarah to the king.

6. And Sarah came to the house of Abimelech, and the king saw that Sarah was beautiful, and she pleased him exceedingly.

7. And he approached her and said to her, what is that man to thee with whom thou didst come to our land? and Sarah answered and said he is my brother, and we came from the land of Canaan to dwell wherever we could find *a place*.

8. And Abimelech said to Sarah, behold my land is before thee, place thy brother in any part of this land that pleases thee, and it will be our duty to exalt and elevate him above all the people of the land since he is thy brother.

9. And Abimelech sent for Abraham, and Abraham came to Abimelech.

10. And Abimelech said to Abraham, behold I have given orders that thou shalt be honored as thou desirest on account of thy sister Sarah.

11. And Abraham went forth from the king, and the king's present followed him.

12. As at evening time, before men lie down to *rest*, the king was sitting upon his throne, and a deep sleep fell upon him, and he lay upon the throne and slept till morning.

13. And he dreamed that an angel of the Lord came to him with a drawn sword in his hand, and the angel stood over Abimelech, and wished to slay him with the sword, and the king was terrified in his dream, and said to the angel, in what have I sinned against thee that thou comest to slay me with thy sword?

14. And the angel answered and said to Abimelech, behold thou diest on account of the woman which thou didst yesternight bring to thy house, for she is a married woman, the wife of Abraham who came to thy house; now therefore return that man his wife, for she is his wife; and shouldst thou not return her, know that thou

wilt surely die, thou and all belonging to thee.

15. And on that night there was a great outcry in the land of the Philistines, and the inhabitants of the land saw the figure of a man standing with a drawn sword in his hand, and he smote the inhabitants of the land with the sword, *yea* he continued to smite them.

16. And the angel of the Lord smote the whole land of the Philistines on that night, and there was a great confusion on that night and on the following morning.

17. And every womb was closed, and all their issues, and the hand of the Lord was upon them on account of Sarah, wife of Abraham, whom Abimelech had taken.

18. And in the morning Abimelech rose with terror and confusion and with a great dread, and he sent and had his servants called in, and he related his dream to them, and the people were greatly afraid.

19. And one man standing amongst the servants of the king answered the king, saying, O sovereign king, restore this woman to her husband, for he is her husband, for the like happened to the king of Egypt when this man came to Egypt.

20. And he said concerning his wife, she is my sister, for such is his manner of doing when he cometh to dwell in the land in which he is a stranger.

21. And Pharaoh sent and took this woman for a wife, and the Lord brought upon him grievous plagues until he returned the woman to her husband.

22. Now therefore, O sovereign king, know what happened yesternight to the whole land, for there was a very great consternation and great

pain and lamentation, and we know that this was on account of the woman which thou didst take.

23. Now therefore, restore this woman to her husband, lest it should befall us as it did to Pharaoh king of Egypt and his subjects, and that we may not die ; and Abimelech hastened and called and had Sarah called for, and she came before him, and he had Abraham called for, and he came before him.

24. And Abimelech said to them, what is this work you have been doing in saying you are brother and sister, and I took this woman for a wife ?

25. And Abraham said, because I thought I should suffer death on account of my wife ; and Abimelech took flocks and herds, and men servants and maid servants, and a thousand *pieces* of silver, and he gave them to Abraham, and he returned Sarah to him.

26. And Abimelech said to Abraham, behold the whole land is before thee, dwell in it wherever thou shalt choose.

27. And Abraham and Sarah his wife went forth from the king's presence with honor and respect, and they dwelt in the land, *even* in Gerar.

28. And all the inhabitants of the land of the Philistines and the king's servants were still in pain, through the plague which the angel had inflicted upon them the whole night on account of Sarah.

29. And Abimelech sent for Abraham, saying, pray now for thy servants to the Lord thy God, that he may put away this mortality from amongst us.

30. And Abraham prayed on account of Abimelech and his subjects, and the Lord heard the prayer of Abraham, and he healed Abimelech and all his subjects.

CHAPTER XXI.

1. And it was at that time at the end of a year and four months of Abraham's dwelling in the land of the Philistines in Gerar, that God visited Sarah, and the Lord remembered her, and she conceived and bare a son to Abraham.

2. And Abraham called the name of the son which was born to him, which Sarah bare to him, Isaac.

3. And Abraham circumcised his son Isaac at eight days old, as God had commanded Abraham to do unto his seed after him ; and Abraham was one hundred, and Sarah ninety years old, when Isaac was born to them.

4. And the child grew up and he was weaned, and Abraham made a great feast upon the day that Isaac was weaned.

5. And Shem and Eber and all the great *people* of the land, and Abimelech king of the Philistines, and his servants, and Phicol the captain of his host, came to eat and drink and rejoice at the feast which Abraham made upon the day of his son Isaac's being weaned.

6. Also Terah, the father of Abraham, and Nahor his brother, came from Haran, they and all belonging to them, for they greatly rejoiced on hearing that a son had been born to Sarah.

7. And they came to Abraham, and they ate and drank at the feast which Abraham made upon the day of Isaac's being weaned.

8. And Terah and Nahor rejoiced with Abraham, and they remained

with him many days in the land of the Philistines.

9. At that time Serug the son of Reu died, in the first year of the birth of Isaac son of Abraham.

10. And all the days of Serug were two hundred and thirty-nine years, and he died.

11. And Ishmael the son of Abraham was grown up in those days; he was fourteen years old when Sarah bare Isaac to Abraham.

12. And God was with Ishmael the son of Abraham, and he grew up and he learned the use of the bow and became an archer.

13. And when Isaac was five years old he was sitting with Ishmael at the door of the tent.

14. And Ishmael came to Isaac and seated himself opposite to him, and he took the bow and drew it and put the arrow in it, and intended to slay Isaac.

15. And Sarah saw the act which Ishmael desired to do to her son Isaac, and it grieved her exceedingly on account of her son, and she sent for Abraham and said to him, cast out this bondwoman and her son, for her son shall not be heir with my son, for thus did he seek to do unto him this day.

16. And Abraham hearkened to the voice of Sarah, and he rose up early in the morning, and he took twelve loaves and a bottle of water which he gave to Hagar, and sent her away with her son, and Hagar went with her son to the wilderness, and they dwelt in the wilderness of Paran with the inhabitants of the wilderness, and Ishmael was an archer, and he dwelt in the wilderness a long time.

17. And he and his mother afterward went to the land of Egypt, and they dwelt there, and Hagar took a wife for her son from Egypt, and her name was Meribah.

18. And the wife of Ishmael conceived and bare four sons and two daughters, and Ishmael and his mother and his wife and children afterward went and returned to the wilderness.

19. And they made themselves tents in the wilderness, in which they dwelt, and they continued to travel and *then* to rest monthly and yearly.

20. And God gave Ishmael flocks and herds and tents on account of Abraham his father, and the man increased in cattle.

21. And Ishmael dwelt in deserts and in tents, travelling and resting for a long time, and he did not see the face of his father.

22. And in some time after, Abraham said to Sarah his wife, I will go and see my son Ishmael, for I have a desire to see him, for I have not seen him for a long time.

23. And Abraham rode upon one of his camels to the wilderness to seek his son Ishmael, for he heard that he was dwelling in a tent in the wilderness with all belonging to him.

24. And Abraham went to the wilderness, and he reached the tent of Ishmael about noon, and he asked after Ishmael, and he found the wife of Ishmael sitting in the tent with her children, and Ishmael her husband and his mother were not with them.

25. And Abraham asked the wife of Ishmael, saying, where has Ishmael gone? and she said, he has gone to the field to hunt, and Abraham was still mounted upon the camel, for he would not get off to the ground as he had sworn to his wife Sarah that he would not get off from the camel.

26. And Abraham said to Ishmael's wife, my daughter give me a little water that I may drink, for I am fatigued from the journey.

27. And Ishmael's wife answered and said to Abraham, we have neither water nor bread, and she *continued* sitting in the tent and did not notice Abraham, neither did she ask him who he was.

28. But she was beating her children in the tent, and she was cursing them, and she also cursed her husband Ishmael and reproached him, and Abraham heard the words of Ishmael's wife to her children, and he was very angry and displeased.

29. And Abraham called to the woman to come out to him from the tent, and the woman came and stood opposite to Abraham, for Abraham was still mounted upon the camel.

30. And Abraham said to Ishmael's wife, when thy husband Ishmael returneth home say these words to him.

31. A very old man from the land of the Philistines came hither to seek thee, and thus was his appearance and figure; I did not ask him who he was, and seeing thou wast not here he spoke unto me and said, when Ishmael they husband returneth tell him thus did this man say, when thou comest home put away this nail of the tent which thou hast placed here, and place another nail in its stead.

32. And Abraham finished his instructions to the woman, and he turned and went off on the camel homeward.

33. And after that Ishmael come from the chase, he and his mother, and returned to the tent, and his wife spoke these words to him.

34. A very old man from the land of the Philistines came to seek thee, and thus was his appearance and figure; I did not ask him who he was, and seeing thou wast not at home he said to me, when they husband cometh home tell him, thus saith the old man, put away the nail of the tent which thou hast placed here and place another nail in its stead.

35. And Ishmael heard the words of his wife, and he knew that it was his father, and that his wife did not honor him.

36. And Ishmael understood his father's words that he had spoken to his wife, and Ishmael hearkened to the voice of his father, and Ishmael cast off that woman and she went away.

37. And Ishmael afterward went to the land of Canaan, and he took another wife and he brought her to his tent to the place where he then dwelt.

38. And at the end of three years Abraham said, I will go again and see Ishmael my son, for I have not seen him for a long time.

39. And he rode upon his camel and went to the wilderness, and he reached the tent of Ishmael about noon.

40. And he asked after Ishmael, and his wife came out of the tent and she said, he is not here my lord, for he has gone to hunt in the fields, and to feed the camels, and the woman said to Abraham, turn in my lord into the tent and eat a morsel of bread, for thy soul must be wearied on account of the journey.

41. And Abraham said to her, I will not stop for I am in haste to continue my journey, but give me a little water to drink, for I have

thirst; and the woman hastened and ran into the tent and she brought out water and bread to Abraham, which she placed before him and she urged him to eat, and he ate and drank and his heart was comforted and he blessed his son Ishmael.

42. And he finished his meal and he blessed the Lord, and he said to Ishmael's wife, when Ishmael cometh *home* say these words to *him;*

43. A very old man from the land of the Philistines came hither and asked after thee, and thou wast not *here,* and I *brought* him out bread and water and he ate and drank and his heart was comforted.

44. And he spoke these words to me; when Ishmael thy husband cometh home, say unto him, the nail of the tent which thou hast is very good, do not put it away from the tent.

45. And Abraham finished commanding the woman, and he rode off to his home to the land of the Philistines; and when Ishmael came to his tent his wife went forth to meet him with joy and a cheerful heart.

46. And she said to him, an old man came here from the land of the Philistines and thus was his appearance, and he asked after thee and thou wast not here, so I brought out bread and water, and he ate and drank and his heart was comforted.

47. And he spoke these words to me; when Ishmael thy husband cometh home say to him, the nail of the tent which thou hast is very good, do not put it away from the tent.

48. And Ishmael knew that it was his father, and that his wife had honored him, and the Lord blessed Ishmael.

CHAPTER XXII.

1. And Ishmael then rose up and took his wife and his children and his cattle and all belonging to him, and he journeyed from there and he went to his father in the land of the Philistines.

2. And Abraham related to Ishmael his son the transaction with the first wife that Ishmael took, according to what she did.

3. And Ishmael and his children dwelt with Abraham many days in *that* land, and Abraham dwelt in the land of the Philistines a long time.

4. And the days increased and reached twenty six years, and after that Abraham with his servants and all belonging to him went from the land of the Philistines and removed to a great distance, and they came near to Hebron, and they remained there, and the servants of Abraham dug wells of water, and Abraham and all belonging to him dwelt by the water, and the servants of Abimelech king of the Philistines heard the report that Abraham's servants had dug wells of water in the borders of the land.

5. And they came and quarreled with the servants of Abraham, and they robbed them of the great well which they had dug.

6. And Abimelech king of the Philistines heard of this affair, and he with Phicol the captain of his host and twenty of his men came to Abraham, and Abimelech spoke to Abraham concerning his servants, and Abraham rebuked Abimelech concerning the well of which his servants had robbed him.

7. And Abimelech said to Abraham, as the Lord liveth who created the whole earth I did not hear of the

act which my servants did unto thy servants until this day.

8. And Abraham took seven ewe lambs and gave them to Abimelech, saying, take *these* I pray thee from my hands that it may be a testimony for me that I dug this well.

9. And Abimelech took the seven ewe lambs which Abraham had given to him, for he had also given him cattle and herds in abundance, and Abimelech swore to Abraham concerning the well, therefore he called that well Beersheba, for there they both swore concerning it.

10. And they both made a covenant in Beersheba, and Abimelech rose up with Phicol the captain of his host and all his men, and they returned to the land of the Philistines, and Abraham and all belonging to him dwelt in Beersheba and he was in that land a long time.

11. And Abraham planted a large grove in Beersheba, and he made to it four gates facing the four sides of the earth, and he planted a vineyard in it, so that if a traveller came to Abraham he entered any gate which was in his road, and remained there and ate and drank and satisfied himself and then departed.

12 For the house of Abraham was always open to the sons of men that passed and repassed, who came daily to eat and drink in the house of Abraham.

13. And any man who had hunger and came to Abraham's house, Abraham would give him bread that he might eat and drink and be satisfied, and any one that came naked to his house he would clothe with garments as he might choose, and give him silver and gold and make known to him the Lord who had created him

in the earth; this did Abraham all his life.*

14. And Abraham and his children and all belonging to him dwelt in Beersheba, and he pitched his tent as far as Hebron.

15. And Abraham's brother Nahor and his father and all belonging to them dwelt in Haran, for they did not come with Abraham to the land of Canaan.

16. And children were born to Nahor which Milca the daughter of Haran, and sister to Sarah, Abraham's wife, bare to him.

17. And these are the names of those that were born to him, Uz, Buz, Kemuel, Kesed, Chazo, Pildash, Tidlaf, and Bethuel, *being* eight sons, these are the children of Milca which she bare to Nahor Abraham's brother.

18. And Nahor had a concubine and her name was Reumah, and she also bare to Nahor, Zebach, Gachash, Tachash and Maacha, *being* four sons.

19. And the children that were born to Nahor were twelve sons besides his daughters, and they also had children born to them in Haran.

20. And the children of Uz the first born of Nahor were Abi, Cheref, Gadin, Melus, and Deborah their sister.

21. And the sons of Buz were Berachel, Naamath, Sheva and Madonu.

22. And the sons of Kemuel were Aram and Rechob.

23. And the sons of Kesed were Anamlech, Meshai, Benon and Yifi; and the sons of Chazo were Pildash, Mechi and Opher.

24. And the sons of Pildash were Arud, Chamum, Mered and Moloch.

* Hebrew, all the days.

25. And the sons of Yidlaf were Mushan, Cushan and Mutzi.

26. And the children of Bethuel were Sechar, Laban and their sister Rebecca.

27. These are the families of the children of Nahor, that were born to them in Haran; and Aram the son of Kemuel and Rechob his brother went away from Haran, and they found a valley in the land by the river Euphrates.

28. And they built a city there, and they called the name of the city after the name of Pethor the son of Aram, that is Aram Naherayim* unto this day.

29. And the children of Kesed also went to dwell where they could find a *place*, and they went and they found a valley opposite to the land of Shinar, and they dwelt there.

30. And they there built themselves a city, and they called the name of the city Kesed after the name of their father, that is the land Kasdim† unto this day, and the Kasdim dwelt in that land and they were fruitful and multiplied exceedingly

31. And Terah father of Nahor and Abraham went and took another wife in his old age, and her name was Pelilah, and she conceived and bare him a son and he called his name Zoba.

32. And Terah lived twenty five years after he begat Zoba.

33. And Terah died in that year, that is in the thirty fifth year of the birth of Isaac son of Abraham.

34. And the days of Terah were two hundred and five years, and he was buried in Haran.

35. And Zoba the son of Terah

* Mesopotamia.
† Chaldea.

lived thirty years and he begat Aram, Achlis and Merik.

36. And Aram son of Zoba son of Terah, had three wives and he begat twelve sons and three daughters; and the Lord gave to Aram the son of Zoba, riches and possessions, and abundance of cattle, and flocks and herds, and the man increased greatly.

37. And Aram the son of Zoba and his brother and all his household journeyed from Haran, and they went to dwell where they should find a *place*, for their property was too great to remain in Haran; for they could not stop in Haran together with their brethren the children of Nahor.

38. And Aram the son of Zoba went with his brethren, and they found a valley at a distance toward the eastern country and they dwelt there.

39. And they also built a city there, and they called the name thereof Aram, after the name of their eldest brother; that is Aram Zoba to this day.

40. And Isaac the son of Abraham was growing up in those days, and Abraham his father taught him the way of the Lord to know the Lord, and the Lord was with him.

41. And when Isaac was thirty seven years old, Ishmael his brother was going about with him in the tent.

42. And Ishmael boasted of himself to Isaac, saying, I was thirteen years old when the Lord spoke to my father to circumcise us, and I did *according to* the word of the Lord which he spoke to my father, and I gave my soul unto the Lord, and I did not transgress his word which he commanded my father.

43. And Isaac answered Ishmael, saying, why dost thou boast to me about this, about a little bit of thy flesh which thou didst take from thy body, concerning which the Lord commanded thee?

44. As the Lord liveth, the God of my father Abraham, if the Lord should say unto my father, take now thy son Isaac and bring him up an offering before me, I would not refrain but I would joyfully accede to it.

45. And the Lord heard the word that Isaac spoke to Ishmael, and it seemed good in the sight of the Lord, and he thought to try Abraham in this matter.

46. And the day arrived when the sons of God came and placed *themselves* before the Lord, and Satan also came with the sons of God before the Lord.

47. And the Lord said unto Satan, whence comest thou? and Satan answered the Lord and said, from going to and fro in the earth, and from walking up and down in it.

48. And the Lord said to Satan, what is thy word to me concerning all the children of the earth? and Satan answered the Lord and said, I have seen all the children of the earth who serve thee and remember thee when they require anything from thee.

49. And when thou givest them the thing which they require from thee, they *sit at their ease*, and forsake thee and they remember thee no more.

50. Hast thou seen Abraham the son of Terah, who at first had no children, and he served thee and erected altars to thee wherever he came, and he brought up offerings upon them, and he proclaimed thy name continually to all the children of the earth.

51. And now that his son Isaac is born to him, he has forsaken thee, he has made a great feast for all the inhabitants of the land, and the Lord he has forgotten.

52. For amidst all that he has done he brought thee no offering; neither burnt offering nor peace offering, neither ox, lamb nor goat of all that he killed on the day that his son was weaned.

53. Even from the time of his son's birth till now, being thirty-seven years, he built no altar before thee, nor brought up any offering to thee, for he saw that thou didst give what he requested before thee, and he *therefore* forsook thee.

54. And the Lord said to Satan, hast thou *thus* considered my servant Abraham? for *there* is none like him upon earth, a perfect and an upright man before me, one that feareth God and avoideth evil; as I live, were I to say unto him, bring up Isaac thy son before me, he would not withhold him from me, much more if I told him to bring up a burnt offering before me from his flocks or herds.

55. And Satan answered the Lord and said, speak then now unto Abraham as thou hast said, and *thou wilt see* whether he will not this day transgress and cast aside thy words.

CHAPTER XXIII.

1. At that time the word of the Lord *came* to Abraham, and he said unto him, Abraham, and he said here I am.

2. And he said to him, take now thy son, thine only *son* whom thou lovest, even Isaac, and go to the land of Moriah, and offer him there for a

burnt offering upon one of the mountains which shall be shown to thee, for there wilt *thou see* a cloud and the glory of the Lord.

3. And Abraham said within himself, how shall I separate my son Isaac from Sarah his mother, in order to bring him up for a burnt offering before the Lord?

4. And Abraham came into the tent, and he sat before Sarah his wife, and he spoke these words to her.

5. My son Isaac is grown up and he has not for some time studied the service of his God, now to-morrow I will go and bring him to Shem, and Eber his son, and there he will learn the ways of the Lord, for they will teach him to know the Lord as well as to know that when he prayeth continually before the Lord, he will answer him, *therefore* there he will know the way of serving the Lord his God.

6. And Sarah said, thou hast spoken well, go my lord and do unto him as thou hast said, but remove him not at a *great* distance from me, neither let him remain there too long, for my soul is bound within his soul.

7. And Abraham said unto Sarah, my daughter, let us pray to the Lord our God that he may do good with us.

8. And Sarah took her son Isaac and he abided all that night with her, and she kissed and embraced him, and gave him instructions till morning.

9. And she said to him, O my son how can my soul separate itself from thee? And she still kissed him and embraced him, and she gave Abraham instructions concerning him.

10. And Sarah said to Abraham, O my lord, I pray thee take heed of thy son, and place thine eyes over him, for I have no other son nor daughter but him.

11. O forsake him not. If he be hungry give him bread, and if he be thirsty give him water to drink ; do not let him go on foot, neither let him sit in the sun.

12. Neither let him go by himself in the road, neither force him from whatever he may desire, but do unto him as he may say to thee.

13. And Sarah wept bitterly the whole night on account of Isaac, and she gave him instructions till morning.

14. And in the morning Sarah selected a very fine and beautiful garment from *those* garments which she had in the house, that Abimelech had given to her.

15. And she dressed Isaac her son therewith, and she put a turban upon his head, and she enclosed a precious stone in the top of the turban, and she gave them provision for the road, and they went forth, and Isaac went with his father Abraham, and some of their servants accompanied them to see them off the road.

16. And Sarah went out with them, and she accompanied them upon the road to see them off, and they said to her, return to the tent.

17. And when Sarah heard the words of her son Isaac she wept bitterly, and Abraham her husband wept with her, and their son wept with them a great weeping; also those who went with them wept greatly.

18. And Sarah caught hold of her son Isaac, and she held him in her arms, and she embraced him and continued to weep with him, and Sarah said, who knoweth if after this day I shall ever see thee again?

19. And they still wept *together,*

Abraham, Sarah and Isaac and all those that accompanied them on the road wept with them, and Sarah afterward turned away from her son, weeping bitterly, and all her men servants and maid servants returned with her to the tent.

20. And Abraham went with Isaac his son to bring him up as an offering before the Lord, as he had commanded him.

21. And Abraham took two of his young men with him, Ishmael the son of Hagar and Eliezer his servant, and they went together with them, and whilst they were walking in the road the young men spoke these words to themselves.

22. And Ishmael said to Eliezer, now my father Abraham is going with Isaac to bring him up for a burnt offering to the Lord, as he commanded him.

23. Now when he returneth he will give unto me all that he possesses, to inherit after him, for I am his first born.

24. And Eliezer answered Ishmael and said, surely Abraham did cast thee away with thy mother, and swear that thou shouldst not inherit any thing of all he possesses, and to whom will he give all that he has, with all his treasures, but unto *me* his servant, who has been faithful in his house, who has served him night and day, and has done all that he desired me? to me will he bequeath at his death all that he possesses.

25. And whilst Abraham was proceeding with his son Isaac along the road, Satan came and appeared to Abraham in the figure of a very aged man, humble and of contrite spirit, and he approached Abraham and said to him, art thou silly or brutish,

5

that thou goest to do this thing this day to thine only son?

26. For God gave thee a son in thy latter days, in thy old age, and wilt thou go and slaughter him this day because he committed no violence, and wilt thou cause the soul of thine only son to perish from the earth?

27. Dost thou not know and understand that this thing cannot be from the Lord? for the Lord cannot do unto man such evil upon earth to say *to him*, go slaughter thy child.

28. And Abraham heard this and knew that it was the word of Satan who endeavored to draw him aside from the way of the Lord, but Abraham would not hearken to the voice of Satan, and Abraham rebuked him so that he went away.

29. And Satan returned and came to Isaac; and he appeared unto Isaac in the figure of a young man, comely and well favoured.

30. And he approached Isaac and said unto him, dost thou not know and understand that thy old silly father bringeth thee to the slaughter this day for nought?

31. Now therefore, my son, do not listen nor attend to him, for he is a silly old man, and let not thy precious soul and beautiful figure be lost from the earth.

32. And Isaac heard this, and said unto Abraham, hast thou heard, my father, that which this man has spoken? *even* thus has he spoken.

33. And Abraham answered his son Isaac and said to him, take heed of him and do not listen to his words, nor attend to him, for he is Satan endeavoring to draw us aside this day from the commands of God.

34. And Abraham still rebuked Satan, and Satan went from them,

and seeing he could not prevail over them he hid himself from them, and he went and passed before them in the road; and he transformed himself to a large brook of water in the road, and Abraham and Isaac and his two young men reached that place, and they saw a brook large and powerful as the mighty waters.

35. And they entered the brook and passed through it, and the waters *at first* reached their legs.

36. And they went deeper in the brook and the waters reached up to their necks, and they were all terrified on account of the water; and whilst they were going over the brook Abraham recognized that place, and he knew that there was no water there before.

37. And Abraham said to his son Isaac, I know this place in which there was no brook nor water, now therefore it is this Satan who does all this to us, to draw us aside this day from the commands of God.

38. And Abraham rebuked him and said unto him, the Lord rebuke thee, O Satan, begone from us for we go by the commands of God.

39. And Satan was terrified at the voice of Abraham, and he went away from them, and the place again became dry land as it was at first.

40. And Abraham went with Isaac toward the place that God had told him.

41. And on the third day Abraham lifted up his eyes and saw the place at a distance which God had told him of.

42. And a pillar of fire appeared to him *that reached* from the earth to heaven, and a cloud of glory upon the mountain, and the glory of the Lord was seen in the cloud.

43. And Abraham said to Isaac, my son dost thou see in that mountain, which we perceive at a distance, that which I see upon it?

44. And Isaac answered and said unto his father, I see and lo a pillar of fire and a cloud, and the glory of the Lord is seen upon the cloud.

45. And Abraham knew that his son Isaac was accepted before the Lord for a burnt offering.

46. And Abraham said unto Eliezer and unto Ishmael his son, do you also see that which we see upon the mountain *which is* at a distance?

47. And they answered and said, we see nothing more than like the *other* mountains of the earth. And Abraham knew that they were not accepted before the Lord to go with them, and Abraham said to them, abide ye here with the ass whilst I and Isaac my son will go to yonder mount and worship there before the Lord and then return to you.

48. And Eliezer and Ishmael remained in that place, as Abraham had commanded.

49. And Abraham took wood for a burnt offering and placed it upon his son Isaac, and he took the fire and the knife, and they both went to that place.

50. And when they were going along Isaac said to his father, behold, I see here the fire and wood, and where *then* is the lamb *that is to be* the burnt offering before the Lord?

51. And Abraham answered his son Isaac, saying, the Lord has made choice of thee my son, to be a perfect burnt offering instead of the lamb.

52. And Isaac said unto his father, I will do all that the Lord spoke

to thee with joy and cheerfulness of heart.

53. And Abraham again said unto Isaac his son, is there in thy heart any thought or counsel concerning this, which is not proper? tell me my son, I pray thee, O my son conceal it not from me.

54. And Isaac answered his father Abraham and said unto him, O my father, as the Lord liveth and as thy soul liveth there is nothing in my heart to cause me to *deviate* either to the right or to the left from the word that he has spoken to thee.

55. Neither limb nor muscle has moved or stirred at this, nor is there in my heart any thought or evil counsel concerning this.

56. But I am of joyful and cheerful heart in this matter, *and* I say, blessed is the Lord who has this day chosen me to be a burnt offering before him.

57. And Abraham greatly rejoiced at the words of Isaac, and they went on and came together to that place that the Lord had spoken of.

58. And Abraham approached to build the altar in that place, and Abraham was weeping, and Isaac took stones and mortar until they had finished building the altar.

59. And Abraham took the wood and placed it in order upon the altar which he had built.

60. And he took his son Isaac and bound him in order to place him upon the wood which was upon the altar, to slay him for a burnt offering before the Lord.

61. And Isaac said to his father, bind me securely and then place me upon the altar lest I should turn and move, and break loose from the force of the knife upon my flesh and *thereby*

profane the burnt offering; and Abraham did so.

62. And Isaac still said to his father, O my father, when thou shalt have slain me and burnt me for an offering, take with thee that which shall remain of my ashes to bring to Sarah my mother, and say to her, this is the sweet smelling savor of Isaac; but do not tell her this if she should sit near a well or upon any high place, lest she should cast her soul after me and die.

63. And Abraham heard the words of Isaac, and he lifted up his voice and wept when Isaac spake these words; and Abraham's tears gushed down upon Isaac his son, and Isaac wept bitterly, and he said to his father, hasten *thou*, O my father, and do with me the will of the Lord our God as he has commanded thee.

64. And the hearts of Abraham and Isaac rejoiced at this thing which the Lord had commanded them; but the eye wept bitterly whilst the heart rejoiced.

65. And Abraham bound his son Isaac, and placed him on the altar upon the wood, and Isaac stretched forth his neck upon the altar before his father, and Abraham stretched forth his hand to take the knife to slay his son as a burnt offering before the Lord.

66. At that time the angels of mercy came before the Lord and spake to him concerning Isaac, saying,

67. O Lord, thou art a merciful and compassionate king over all that thou hast created in heaven and in earth, and thou supportest them all; give therefore ransom and redemption instead of thy servant Isaac, and pity and have compassion upon Abra-

ham and upon Isaac his son, who are this day performing thy commands.

68. Hast thou seen, O Lord, how Isaac the son of Abraham thy servant is bound down to the slaughter like an animal? now therefore let thy pity be roused for them, O Lord.

69. At that time the Lord appeared unto Abraham, and called to him from heaven, and said unto him, lay not thine hand upon the lad, neither do thou any thing unto him, for now I know that thou fearest God in performing this act, and in not withholding thy son, thine only *son*, from me.

70. And Abraham lifted up his eyes and saw, and behold, a ram was caught in a thicket by his horns; that was the ram which the Lord God had created in the earth in the day that he made earth and heaven.

71. For the Lord had prepared this ram from that day, to be a burnt offering instead of Isaac.

72. And this ram was advancing to Abraham when Satan caught hold of him and entangled his horns in the thicket, that he might not advance to Abraham, in order that Abraham might slay his son.

73. And Abraham, seeing the ram advancing to him and Satan withholding him, fetched him and brought him before the altar, and he loosened his son Isaac from his binding, and he put the ram in his stead, and Abraham killed the ram upon the altar, and brought it up as an offering in the place of his son Isaac.

74. And Abraham sprinkled *some* of the blood of the ram upon the altar, and he exclaimed and said, this is in the place of my son, and may this be considered this day as the blood of my son before the Lord.

75. And all that Abraham did on this occasion by the altar, he would exclaim and say, this is in the room of my son, and may it this day be considered before the Lord in the place of my son; and Abraham finished the whole of the service by the altar, and the service was accepted before the Lord, and was accounted as *if it had been* Isaac; and the Lord blessed Abraham and his seed on that day.

76. And Satan went to Sarah, and he appeared to her in the figure of an old man very humble and meek, and Abraham was yet engaged in the burnt offering before the Lord.

77. And he said unto her, dost thou not know all the work that Abraham has made with thine only son this day? for he took Isaac and built an altar and killed him, and brought him up as a sacrifice upon the altar, and Isaac cried and wept before his father, but he looked not at him, neither did he have compassion over him.

78. And Satan repeated these words, and he went away from her, and Sarah heard all the words of Satan, and she imagined him to be an old man from amongst the sons of men who had been with her son, and had come and told her these things.

79. And Sarah lifted up her voice and wept and cried out bitterly on account of her son; and she threw herself upon the ground and she cast dust upon her head, and she said, O my son, Isaac my son, O that I had this day died instead of thee. And she continued to weep and said, it grieves me for thee, O my son, my son Isaac, O that I had died this day in thy stead.

80. And she still continued to weep, and said, it grieves me for thee after that I have reared thee and

have brought thee up ; *now* my joy is turned into mourning over thee, I that had a longing for thee, and cried and prayed *to God* till I bare thee at ninety years old ; and now hast thou served this day for the knife and the fire, to be made an offering.

81. But I console myself with thee my son, in its being the word of the Lord, for thou didst perform the command of thy God : for who can transgress the word of our God, in whose hands is the soul of every living creature ?

82. Thou art just O Lord our God, for all thy works are good and righteous ; for I also am rejoiced with thy word which thou didst command, and whilst mine eye weepeth bitterly *my* heart rejoiceth.

83. And Sarah laid her head upon the bosom of one of her handmaids, and she became as still as a stone.

84. She afterward rose up and went about making inquiries till she came to Hebron, and she inquired of all those whom she met walking in the road, and no one could tell her what had happened to her son.

85. And she came with her maid servants and men servants to Kireath Arba, which is Hebron, and she asked concerning her son, and she remained there whilst she sent some of her servants to seek where Abraham had gone with Isaac ; they went to seek him in the house of Shem and Eber, and they could not find him, and they sought throughout the land and he was not there.

86. And behold, Satan came to Sarah in the shape of an old man, and he came and stood before her, and he said unto her, I spoke falsely unto thee, for Abraham did not kill his son and he is not dead ; and when she heard the word her joy was so exceedingly violent on account of her son, that her soul went out through joy ; she died and was gathered to her people.

87. And when Abraham had finished his service he returned with his son Isaac to his young men, and they rose up and went together to Beersheba, and they came home.

88. And Abraham sought for Sarah, and could not find her, and he made inquiries concerning her, and they said unto him, she went as far as Hebron to seek you both where you had gone, for thus was she informed.

89. And Abraham and Isaac went to her to Hebron, and when they found that she was dead they lifted up their voices and wept bitterly over her; and Isaac fell upon his mother's face and wept over her, and he said, O my mother, my mother, how hast thou left me, and where hast thou gone ? O how, how hast thou left me !

90. And Abraham and Isaac wept greatly and all their servants wept with them on account of Sarah, and they mourned over her a great and heavy mourning.

CHAPTER XXIV.

1. And the life of Sarah was one hundred and twenty seven years, and Sarah died; and Abraham rose up from before his dead to seek a burial place to bury his wife Sarah ; and he went and spoke to the children of Heth, the inhabitants of the land, saying,

2. I am a stranger and a sojourner with you in your land ; give me a possession of a burial place in your land, that I may bury my dead from before me.

3. And the children of Heth said unto Abraham, behold the land is before thee, in the choice of our sepulchres bury thy dead, for no man shall withhold thee from burying thy dead.

4. And Abraham said unto them, if you are agreeable to this go and intreat for me to Ephron, the son of Zochar, requesting that he may give me the cave of Machpelah, which is in the end of his field, and I will purchase it of him for whatever he desire for it.

5. And Ephron dwelt among the children of Heth, and they went and called for him, and he came before Abraham, and Ephron said unto Abraham, behold all thou requirest thy servant will do; and Abraham said, no, but I will buy the cave and the field which thou hast for value, *in order that it may be* for a possession of a burial place for ever.

6. And Ephron answered and said, behold the field and the cave are before thee, give whatever thou desirest; and Abraham said, only at full value will I buy it from thy hand, and from the hands of those that go in at the gate of thy city, and from the hand of thy seed for ever.

7. And Ephron and all his brethren heard this, and Abraham weighed to Ephron four hundred shekels of silver in the hands of Ephron and in the hands of all his brethren; and Abraham wrote this transaction, and he wrote *it* and testified it with four witnesses.

8. And these are the names of the witnesses, Amigal son of Abishna the Hittite, Adichorom son of Ashunach the Hivite, Abdon son of Achiram the Gomerite, Bakdil the son of Abudish the Zidonite.

9. And Abraham took the book of the purchase, and placed it in his treasures, and these are the words that Abraham wrote in the book, namely.

10. That the cave and the field Abraham bought from Ephron the Hittite, and *from* his seed, and *from* those that go out of his city, and *from* their seed for ever, are *to be* a a purchase to Abraham and to his seed and to those that go forth from his loins, for a possession of a burial place for ever; and he put a signet to it and testified it *with* witnesses.

11. And the field and the cave that was in it and all that place were made sure unto Abraham and unto his seed after him, from the children of Heth; behold it is before Mamre in Hebron, which is in the land of Canaan.

12. And after this Abraham buried his wife Sarah there, and that place and all its boundary became to Abraham and unto his seed for a possession of a burial place.

13. And Abraham buried Sarah with pomp as *observed* at the *interment of kings*, and she was buried in very fine and beautiful garments.

14. And at her bier was Shem, his sons Eber and Abimelech, together with Anar, Ashcol and Mamre, and all the grandees of the land followed her bier.

15. And the days of Sarah were one hundred and twenty seven years and she died, and Abraham made a great and heavy mourning, and he performed the *rites* of mourning for seven days.

16. And all the inhabitants of the land comforted Abraham and Isaac his son on account of Sarah.

17. And when the days of their mourning passed by Abraham sent away his son Isaac, and he went to

the house of Shem and Eber, to learn the ways of the Lord and his instructions, and Abraham remained there three years.

18. At that time Abraham rose up with all his servants, and they went and returned homeward to Beersheba, and Abraham and all his servants remained in Beersheba.

19. And at the revolution of the year Abimelech king of the Philistines died in that year; he was one hundred and ninety three years old at his death; and Abraham went with his people to the land of the Philistines, and they comforted the whole household and all his servants, and he then turned and went home.

20. And it was after the death of Abimelech that the people of Gerar took Benmalich his son, and he was *only* twelve years old, and they made him king· in the place of his father.

21. And they called his name Abimelech after the name of his father, for thus was it their custom to do in Gerar, and Abimelech reigned instead of Abimelech his father, and he sat upon his throne.

22. And Lot the son Haran also died in those days, in the thirty ninth year of the life of Isaac, and all the days that Lot lived were one hundred and forty years and he died.

23. And these are the children of Lot, that were born to him by his daughters; the name of the first born was Moab, and the name of the second was Benami.

24. And the two sons of Lot went and took themselves wives from the land of Canaan, and they bare children to them, and the children of Moab were Ed, Mayon, Tarsus, and Kanvil, four sons, these are fathers to the children of Moab unto this day.

25. And all the families of the children of Lot went to dwell wherever they should light upon, for they were fruitful and increased abundantly.

26. And they went and built themselves cities in the land where they dwelt, and they called the names of the cities which they built after their *own* names.

27. And Nahor the son of Terah, brother to Abraham, died in those days in the fortieth year of the life of Isaac, and all the days of Nahor were one hundred and seventy two years and he died and was buried in Haran.

28. And when Abraham heard that his brother was dead he grieved sadly, and he mourned over his brother many days.

29. And Abraham called for Eliezer his head servant, to give him orders concerning his house, and he came and stood before him.

30. And Abraham said to him, behold I am old, I do not know the day of my death; for I am advanced in days; now therefore rise up, go forth and do not take a wife for my son from this place and from this land, from the daughters of the Canaanites amongst whom we dwell.

31. But go to my land and to my birth place, and take from thence a wife for my son, and the Lord God of Heaven and earth who took me from my father's house and brought me to this place, and said unto me, to thy seed will I give this land for an inheritance for ever, he will send his angel before thee and prosper thy way, that thou mayest obtain a wife for my son from my family and from my father's house.

32. And the servant answered his master Abraham and said, behold I

go to thy birth place and to thy father's house, and take a wife for thy son from there ; but if the woman be not willing to follow me to this land, shall I take thy son back to the land of thy birth place ?

33. And Abraham said unto him, take heed that thou bring not my son hither again, for the Lord before whom I have walked he will send his angel before thee and prosper thy way.

34. And Eliezer did as Abraham ordered him, and Eliezer swore unto Abraham his master upon this matter ; and Eliezer rose up and took ten camels of the camels of his master, and ten men from his master's servants with him, and they rose up and went to Haran, the city of Abraham and Nahor, in order to fetch a wife for Isaac the son of Abraham ; and whilst they were gone Abraham sent to the house of Shem and Eber, and they brought from thence his son Isaac.

35. And Isaac came home to his father's house to Beersheba, whilst Eliezer and his men came to Haran ; and they stopped in the city by the watering *place*, and he made his camels to kneel down by the water and they remained there.

36. And Eliezer, Abraham's servant, prayed and said, O God of Abraham my master ; send me I pray thee good speed this day and show kindness unto my master, that thou shalt appoint this day a wife for my master's son from his family.

37. And the Lord hearkened to the voice of Eliezer, for the sake of his servant Abraham, and he happened to meet with the daughter of Bethuel, the son of Milcah, the wife of Nahor, brother to Abraham, and Eliezer came to her house.

38. And Eliezer related to them all his concerns, and that he was Abraham's servant, and they greatly rejoiced at him.

39. And they all blessed the Lord who brought this thing about, and they gave him Rebecca, the daughter of Bethuel, for a wife for Isaac.

40. And the young woman was of very comely appearance, she was a virgin, and Rebecca was ten years old in those days.

41. And Bethuel and Laban and his children made a feast on that night, and Eliezer and his men came and ate and drank and rejoiced there on that night.

42. And Eliezer rose up in the morning, he and the men that were with him, and he called to the whole household of Bethuel, saying, send me away that I may go to my master ; and they rose up and sent away Rebecca and her nurse Deborah, the daughter of Uz, and they gave her silver and gold, men servants and maid servants, and they blessed her.

43. And they sent Eliezer away with his men ; and the servants took Rebecca, and he went and returned to his master to the land of Canaan.

44. And Isaac took Rebecca and she became his wife, and he brought her into the tent.

45. And Isaac was forty years old when he took Rebecca, the daughter of his uncle Bethuel, for a wife.

CHAPTER XXV.

1. And it was at that time that Abraham again took a wife in his old age, and her name was Keturah, from the land of Canaan.

2. And she bare unto him Zimran, Yokshan, Medan, Midian, Yishbak and Shuach, *being* six sons.

And the children of Zemran were Abihen, Molich and Marim.

3. And the sons of Yokshan were Sheba and Dedan, and the sons of Medan were Amida, Joab, Gochi, Elisha and Nothach; and the sons of Midian were Ephah, Epher, Chanoch, Abida and Eldaah.

4. And the sons of Yishbak were Makiro, Beyodua and Tator.

5. And the sons of Shuach were Bildad, Mamdad, Munan and Meban; all these are the families of the children of Keturah the Canaanitish woman which she bare unto Abraham the Hebrew.

6. And Abraham sent all these away, and he gave them gifts, and they went away from his son Isaac to dwell wherever they should find a *place*.

7. And all these went to the mountain at the east, and they built themselves six cities in which they dwelt unto this day.

8. But the children of Sheba and Dedan, children of Yokshan, with their children, did not dwell with their brethren in their cities, and they journeyed and encamped in the countries and wildernesses unto this day.

9. And the children of Midian, son of Abraham, went to the east of the land of Cush, and they there found a large valley in the eastern country, and they remained *there* and built a city, and they dwelt therein; that is the land of Midian unto *this* day.

10. And Midian dwelt in the city which he built, he and his five sons and all belonging to him.

11. And these are the names of the sons of Midian according to their names in their cities, Ephah, Epher, Chanoch, Abida and Eldaah.

12. And the sons of Ephah were Methach, Meshar, Avi and Tzanua, and the sons of Epher were Ephron, Zur, Alirun and Medin, and the sons of Chanoch were Reuel, Rekem, Azi, Alyoshub and Alad.

13. And the sons of Abida were Chur, Melud, Keruy, Molchi; and the sons of Eldaah were Miker, and Reba, and Malchiyah and Gabol; these are the names of the Midianites according to their families; and afterward the families of Midian spread throughout the land of Midian.

14. And these are the generations of Ishmael the son of Abraham, whom Hagar, Sarah's handmaid, bare unto Abraham.

15. And Ishmael took a wife from the land of Egypt, and her name was Ribah, the same is Meribah.

16. And Ribah bare unto Ishmael Nebayoth, Kedar, Adbeel, Mibsam and their sister Bosmath.

17. And Ishmael cast away his wife Ribah, and she went from him and returned to Egypt to the house of her father, and she dwelt there, for she had been very bad in the sight of Ishmael, and in the sight of his father Abraham.

18. And Ishmael afterward took a wife from the land of Canaan, and her name was Malchuth, and she bare unto him Nishma, Dumah, Masa, Chadad, Tema, Yetur, Naphish and Kedma.

19. These are the sons of Ishmael, and these are their names, *being* twelve princes according to their nations; and the families of Ishmael afterward spread forth, and Ishmael took his children and all the property that he had gained, together with the souls of his household and all belonging to him, and they went to dwell where they should find a place.

20. And they went and dwelt near

the wilderness of Paran, and their dwelling was from Havilah unto Shur, that is before Egypt as thou comest toward Assyria.

21. And Ishmael and his sons dwelt in the land, and they had children born to them, and they were fruitful and increased abundantly.

22. And these are the names of the sons of Nebayoth the first born of Ishmael; Mend, Send, and Mayon; and the sons of Kedar were Alyon, Kezem, Chamad and Eli.

23. And the sons of Adbeel were Chamad and Jabin; and the sons of Mibsam were Obadiah, Ebedmelech and Yeush; these are the families of the children of Ribah the wife of Ishmael.

24. And the sons of Mishma the son of Ishmael were Shamua, Zecaryon and Obed; and the sons of Dumah were Kezed, Eli, Machmad* and Amed.

25. And the sons of Masa were Melon, Mula and Ebidadon; and the sons of Chadad were Azur, Minzar and Ebedmelech; and the sons of Tema were Seir, Sadon and Yakol.

26. And the sons of Yetur were Merith, Yaish, Alyo, and Pachoth; and the sons of Naphish were Ebed-Tamed, Abiyasaph and Mir; and the sons of Kedma were Calip, Tachti, and Omir; these were the children of Malchuth the wife of Ishmael according to their families.

27. All these are the families of Ishmael according to their generations, and they dwelt in those lands wherein they had built themselves cities unto this day.

28. And Rebecca the daughter of Bethuel, the wife of Abraham's son Isaac, was barren in those days, she had no offspring; and Isaac dwelt

* This is generally called Mohammed.

with his father in the land of Canaan; and the Lord was with Isaac; and Arpachshad the son of Shem the son of Noah died in those days, in the forty eighth year of the life of Isaac, and all the days that Arpachshad lived were four hundred and thirty eight years, and he died.

CHAPTER XXVI.

1. And in the fifty ninth year of the life of Isaac the son of Abraham, Rebecca · his wife was still barren in those days.

2. And Rebecca said unto Isaac, truly I have heard, my lord, that thy mother Sarah was barren in her days · until my lord Abraham, thy father, prayed for her and she conceived by him.

3. Now therefore stand up, pray thou also to God and he will hear thy prayer and remember us through his mercies.

4. And Isaac answered his wife Rebecca, saying, Abraham has already prayed for me to God to multiply his seed, now therefore this barrenness must proceed to us from thee.

5. And Rebecca said unto him, but arise now thou also and pray, that the Lord may hear thy prayer and grant me children, and Isaac hearkened to the words of his wife, and Isaac and his wife rose up and went to the land of Moriah to pray there and to seek the Lord, and when they had reached that place Isaac stood up and prayed to the Lord on account of his wife because she was barren.

6. And Isaac said, O Lord God of heaven and earth, whose goodness and mercies fill the earth, thou who didst take my father from his

father's house and from his birth place, and didst bring him unto this land, and didst say unto him, to thy seed will I give the land, and thou didst promise him and didst declare unto him, I will multiply thy seed as the stars of heaven and as the sand of the sea, now may thy words be verified which thou didst speak unto my father.

7. For thou art the Lord our God, our eyes are toward thee to give i s seed of men, as thou didst promise us, for thou art the Lord our God and our eyes *are directed* toward thee *only.*

8. And the Lord heard the prayer of Isaac the son of Abraham, and the Lord was intreated of him and Rebecca his wife conceived.

9. And in about seven months *after* the children struggled together within her, and it pained her greatly that she was wearied on account of them, and she said to all the women who were then in the land, did such a thing happen to you as it has to me ? and they said unto her, no.

10. And she said unto them, why am I alone in this amongst all the women that were upon earth ? and she went to the land of Moriah to seek the Lord on account of this ; and she went to Shem and Eber his son to make inquiries of them in this matter, and that they should seek the Lord in this thing respecting her.

11. And she also asked Abraham to seek and inquire of the Lord about all that had befallen her.

12. And they all inquired of the Lord concerning this matter, and they brought her word from the Lord and told her, two children are in thy womb, and two nations shall rise from them ; and one nation shall be

stronger than the other, and the greater shall serve the younger.

13. And when her days to be delivered were completed, she knelt down, and behold there were twins in her womb, as the Lord had spoken to her.

14. And the first came out red all over like a hairy garment, and all the *people of the land* called his name Esau, saying, that this one was made complete from the womb.

15. And after that came his brother, and his hand took hold of Esau's heel, therefore they called his name Jacob.

16. And Isaac, the son of Abraham, was sixty years old when he begat them.

17. And the boys grew up to their fifteenth year, and they came amongst the *society* of men. Esau was a designing and deceitful man, and an expert hunter in the field, and Jacob was a man perfect and wise, dwelling in tents, feeding flocks and learning the instructions of the Lord and the commands of his father and mother.

18. And Isaac and the children of his household dwelt with his father Abraham in the land of Canaan, as God had commanded them.

19. And Ishmael the son of Abraham went with his children and all belonging to them, and they returned there to the land of Havilah, and they dwelt there.

20. And all the children of Abraham's concubines went to dwell in the land of the east, for Abraham had sent them away from his son, and had given them presents, and they went away.

21. And Abraham gave all that he had to his son Isaac, and he also gave him all his treasures.

22. And he commanded him, say-

ing, dost thou not know and under-stand the Lord is God in heaven and in earth, and there is no other beside him?

23. And it was he who took me from my father's house, and from my birth-place, and gave me all the delights upon earth; who delivered me from the counsel of the wicked, for in him did I trust.

24. And he brought me to this place, and he delivered me from Ur Casdim; and he said unto me, to thy seed will I give all these lands, and they shall inherit them when they keep my commandments, my statutes and my judgments that I have commanded thee, and which I shall command them.

25. Now therefore my son, hearken to my voice, and keep the commandments of the Lord thy God, which I commanded thee, do not turn from the right way either to the right or to the left, in order that it may be well with thee and thy children after thee forever.

26. And remember the wonderful works of the Lord, and his kindness that he has shown toward us, in having delivered us from the hands of our enemies, and the Lord our God caused them to fall into our hands; and now therefore keep all that I have commanded thee, and turn not away from the commandments of thy God, and serve none beside him, in order that it may be well with thee and thy seed after thee.

27. And teach thou thy children and thy seed the instructions of the Lord and his commandments, and teach them the upright way in which they should go, in order that it may be well with them forever.

28. And Isaac answered his father and said unto him, that which my

Lord has commanded *that* will I do, and I will not depart from the commands of the Lord my God, I will keep all that he commanded me; and Abraham blessed his son Isaac, and also his children; and Abraham taught Jacob the instruction of the Lord and his ways.

29. And it was at that time that Abraham died, in the fifteenth year of the life of Jacob and Esau, the sons of Isaac, and all the days of Abraham were one hundred and seventy-five years, and he died and was gathered to his people in good old age, old and satisfied with days, and Isaac and Ishmael his sons buried him.

30. And when the inhabitants of Canaan heard that Abraham was dead, they all came with their kings and princes and all their men to bury Abraham.

31. And all the inhabitants of the land of Haran, and all the families of the house of Abraham, and all the princes and grandees, and the sons of Abraham by the concubines, all came when they heard of Abraham's death, and they requited Abraham's kindness, and comforted Isaac his son, and they buried Abraham in the cave which he bought from Ephron the Hittite and his children, for the possession of a burial place.

32. And all the inhabitants of Canaan, and all those who had known Abraham, wept for Abraham a whole year, and men and women mourned over him.

33. And all the little children, and all the inhabitants of the land wept on account of Abraham, for Abraham had been good to them all, and because he had been upright with God and men.

34. And there arose not *a man*

who feared God like unto Abraham, for he had feared his God from his youth, and had served the Lord, and had gone in all his ways during his life, from his childhood to the day of his death.

35. And the Lord was with him and delivered him from the counsel of Nimrod and his people, and when he made war with the four kings of Elam he conquered them.

36. And he brought all the children of the earth to the service of God, and he taught them the ways of the Lord, and caused them to know the Lord.

37. And he formed a grove and he planted a vineyard therein, and he had always prepared in his tent meat and drink to those that passed through the land, that they might satisfy themselves in his house.

38. And the Lord God delivered the whole earth on account of Abraham.

39. And it was after the death of Abraham that God blessed his son Isaac and his children, and the Lord was with Isaac as he had been with his father Abraham, for Isaac kept all the commandments of the Lord as Abraham his father had commanded him; he did not turn to the right or to the left from the right path which his father had commanded him.

CHAPTER XXVII.

1. And Esau at that time, after the death of Abraham, frequently went in the field to hunt.

2. And Nimrod king of Babel, the same was Amraphel, also frequently went with his mighty men to hunt in the field, and to walk about with his men in the cool of the day.

3. And Nimrod was observing Esau all the days, for a jealousy was formed in the heart of Nimrod against Esau all the days.

4. And on a certain day Esau went in the field to hunt, and he found Nimrod walking in the wilderness with his two men.

5. And all his mighty men and his people were with him in the wilderness, but they removed at a distance from him, and they went from him in different directions to hunt, and Esau concealed himself for Nimrod, and he lurked for him in the wilderness.

6. And Nimrod and his men that were with him did not know him, and Nimrod and his men frequently walked about in the field at the cool of the day, and to know where his men were hunting in the field.

7. And Nimrod and two of his men that were with him came to the place where they were, when Esau started suddenly from his lurking place, and drew his sword, and hastened and ran to Nimrod and cut off his head.

8. And Esau fought a desperate fight with the two men that were with Nimrod, and when they called out to him, Esau turned to them and smote them to death with his sword.

9. And all the mighty men of Nimrod, who had *left him* to go to the wilderness, heard the cry at a distance, and they knew the voices of those two men, and they ran to know the cause of it, when they found their king and the two men that were with him lying dead in the wilderness.

10. And when Esau saw the mighty men of Nimrod coming at a distance, he fled, and *thereby* escaped; and Esau took the valuable garments of Nimrod, which Nimrod's

father had bequeathed to Nimrod, and with which Nimrod prevailed over the whole land, and he ran and concealed them in his house.

11. And Esau took those garments and ran into the city on account of Nimrod's men, and he came unto his father's house wearied and exhausted from fight, and he was ready to die through grief when he approached his brother Jacob and sat before him.

12. And he said unto his brother Jacob, behold I shall die this day, and wherefore then do I want the birthright? And Jacob acted wisely with Esau in this matter, and Esau sold his birthright to Jacob, for it was so *brought about* by the Lord.

13. And Esau's portion in the cave of the field of Machpelah, which Abraham had bought from the children of Heth for the possession of a burial ground, Esau also sold to Jacob, and Jacob bought all this from his brother Esau for value *given*.

14. And Jacob wrote the whole of this in a book, and he testified the same with witnesses, and he sealed it, and the book remained in the hands of Jacob.

15. And when Nimrod the son of Cush died, his men lifted him up and brought him in consternation, and buried him in his city, and all the days that Nimrod lived were two hundred and fifteen years and he died.

16. And the days that Nimrod reigned upon the people of the land were one hundred and eighty-five years; and Nimrod died by the sword of Esau in shame and contempt, and the seed of Abraham caused his death as he had seen in his dream.

17. And at the death of Nimrod his kingdom became divided into many divisions, and all those parts that Nimrod reigned over were restored to the respective kings of the land, who recovered them after the death of Nimrod, and all the people of the house of Nimrod were for a long time enslaved to all the other kings of the land.

CHAPTER XXVIII.

1. And in those days, after the death of Abraham, in that year the Lord brought a heavy famine in the land, and whilst the famine was *raging* in the land of Canaan, Isaac rose up to go down to Egypt on account of the famine, as his father Abraham had done.

2. And the Lord appeared that night to Isaac and he said to him, do not go down to Egypt *but* rise and go to Gerar, to Abimelech king of the Philistines, and remain there till the famine shall cease.

3. And Isaac rose up and went to Gerar, as the Lord commanded him, and he remained there a full year.

4. And when Isaac came to Gerar, the people of the land saw that Rebecca his wife was of a beautiful appearance, and the people of Gerar asked Isaac concerning his wife, and he said, she is my sister, for he was afraid to say *she was* his wife lest the people of the land should slay him on account of her.

5. And the princes of Abimelech went and praised the woman to the king, but he answered them not, neither did he attend to their words.

6. But he heard them say that Isaac declared her to be his sister, so the king reserved this within himself.

7. And when Isaac had remained three months in the land, Abimelech looked out at the window, and he

saw, and behold Isaac was sporting with Rebecca his wife, for Isaac dwelt in the outer house belonging to the king, so that the house of Isaac was opposite the house of the king.

8. And the king said unto Isaac, what is this thou hast done to us in saying of thy wife, she is my sister? how *easily* might one of the great men of the people have lain with her, and thou wouldst *then* have brought guilt upon us.

9. And Isaac said unto Abimelech, because I was afraid lest I die on account of my wife, therefore I said, she is my sister.

10. At that time Abimelech gave orders to all his princes and great men, and they took Isaac and Rebecca his wife and brought them before the king.

11. And the king commanded that they should dress them in princely garments, and make them ride through the streets of the city, and proclaim before them throughout the land, saying, this is the man and this is his wife; whoever toucheth this man or his wife shall surely die. And Isaac returned with his wife to the king's house, and the Lord was with Isaac and he continued to wax great and lacked nothing.

12. And the Lord caused Isaac to *find* favor in the sight of Abimelech, and in the sight of all his subjects, and Abimelech acted well with Isaac, for Abimelech remembered the oath and the covenant that existed between his father and Abraham.

13. And Abimelech said unto Isaac, behold the whole earth is before thee; dwell wherever it may seem good in thy sight until thou shalt return to thy land; and Abimelech gave Isaac fields and vineyards and the best part of the land of Gerar, to sow and reap and eat the fruits of the ground until the days of the famine should have passed by.

14. And Isaac sowed in that land, and received a hundred-fold in the same year, and the Lord blessed him.

15. And the man waxed great, and he had possession of flocks and possession of herds and great store of servants.

16. And when the days of the famine had passed away the Lord appeared to Isaac and said unto him, rise up, go forth from this place and return to thy land, to the land of Canaan; and Isaac rose up and returned to Hebron which is in the land of Canaan, he and all belonging to him as the Lord commanded him.

17. And after this Shelach the son of Arpachshad died in that year, which is the eighteenth year of the lives of Jacob and Esau; and all the days that Shelach lived were four hundred and thirty-three years and he died.

18. At that time Isaac sent his younger son Jacob to the house of Shem and Eber, and he learned the instructions of the Lord, and Jacob remained in the house of Shem and Eber for thirty-two years, and Esau his brother did not go, for he was not willing to go, and he remained in his father's house in the land of Canaan.

19. And Esau was continually hunting in the fields to bring home what he could get, so did Esau all the days.

20. And Esau was a designing and deceitful man, one who hunted after the hearts of men and *invei-

* The literal meaning of the Hebrew is, "he stole their minds," a beautiful figure in the original to express deceit, falsehood and fraud.

gled them, and Esau was a valiant man in the field, and in the course of time went as usual to hunt; and he came as far as the field of Seir, the same is Edom.

21. And he remained in the land of Seir hunting in the field a year and four months.

22. And Esau there saw in the land of Seir the daughter of a man of Canaan, and her name was Jehudith, the daughter of Beeri, son of Epher, from the families of Heth the son of Canaan.

23. And Esau took her for a wife, and he came unto her; forty years old was Esau when he took her, and he brought her to Hebron the land of his father's dwelling place, and he dwelt there.

24. And it came to pass in those days, in the hundred and tenth year of the life of Isaac, that is *in* the fiftieth year of the life of Jacob, in that year died Shem the son of Noah; Shem was six hundred years old at his death.

25. And when Shem died Jacob returned to his father to Hebron which is in the land of Canaan.

26. And in the fifty-sixth year of the life of Jacob, people came from Haran, and Rebecca was told concerning her brother Laban the son of Bethuel.

27. For the wife of Laban was barren in those days, and bare *no children*, and also all his handmaids bare none to him.

28. And the Lord afterward remembered Adinah the wife of Laban, and she conceived and bare twin daughters, and Laban called the names of his daughters, the name of the elder Leah, and the name of the younger Rachel.

29. And those people came and told these things to Rebecca, and Rebecca rejoiced greatly that the Lord had visited her brother and that he had got children.

CHAPTER XXIX.

1. And Isaac the son of Abraham became old and advanced in days, and his eyes became heavy through age; they were dim and could not see.

2. At that time Isaac called unto Esau his son, saying, get I pray thee thy weapons, thy quiver and thy bow, rise up and go forth into the field and get me some venison, and make me savory meat and bring *it* to me, that I may eat in order that I may bless thee before my death, as I have *now* become old and greyheaded.

3. And Esau did so; and he took his weapon and went forth into the field to hunt *for* venison, as usual, to bring to his father as he had ordered him, so that he might bless him.

4. And Rebecca heard all the words that Isaac had spoken unto Esau, and she hastened and called her son Jacob, saying, thus did thy father speak unto thy brother Esau, and thus did I hear, now therefore hasten thou and make that which I shall tell thee.

5. Rise up and go, I pray thee, to the flock and fetch me two fine kids of the goats, and I will get the savory meat for thy father, and thou shalt bring the savory meat that he may eat before thy brother shall have come from the chase, in order that thy father may bless thee.

6. And Jacob hastened and did as his mother had commanded him, and he made the savory meat and brought

it before his father before Esau had come from his chase.

7. And Isaac said unto Jacob, who art thou, my son? And he said I am thy first born Esau, I have done as thou didst order me, now therefore rise up I pray thee, and eat of my hunt, in order that thy soul may bless me as thou didst speak unto me.

8. And Isaac rose up and he ate and he drank, and his heart was comforted, and he blessed Jacob, and Jacob went away from his father; and *as soon* as Isaac had blessed Jacob and he had gone away from him, behold Esau came from his hunt from the field, and he also made savory meat and brought it to his father to eat *thereof* and to bless him.

9. And Isaac said unto Esau, and who was he that has taken venison and brought it me before thou camest and whom I did bless? And Esau knew that his brother Jacob had done this, and the anger of Esau was kindled against his brother Jacob that he had acted thus toward him.

10. And Esau said, is he not rightly called Jacob? for he has supplanted me twice, he took away my birth right and now he has taken away my blessing; and Esau wept greatly; and when Isaac heard the voice of his son Esau weeping, Isaac said unto Esau, what can I do my son, thy brother came with subtlety and took away thy blessing; and Esau hated his brother Jacob on account of the blessing that his father had given him, and his anger was greatly roused *against him*.

11. And Jacob was very much afraid of his brother Esau, and he rose up and fled to the house of Eber the son of Shem, and he concealed

himself there on account of his brother, and Jacob was sixty three years old when he went forth from the land of Canaan from Hebron, and Jacob was concealed in Eber's house fourteen years on account of his brother Esau, and he there continued to learn the ways of the Lord and his commandments.

12. And when Esau saw that Jacob had fled and escaped from him, and that Jacob had cunningly obtained the blessing, then Esau grieved exceedingly, and he was also vexed at his father and mother; and he also rose up and took his wife and went away from his father and mother to the land of Seir, and he dwelt there; and Esau saw there a woman from amongst the daughters of Heth whose name was Bosmath, the daughter of Elon the Hittite, and he took her for a wife in addition to his *first* wife, and Esau called her name Adah, saying the blessing had in that time passed from him.

13. And Esau dwelt in the land of Seir six months without seeing his father and mother, and afterward Esau took his wives and rose up and returned to the land of Canaan, and Esau placed his two wives in his father's house in Hebron.

14. And the wives of Esau vexed and provoked Isaac and Rebecca with their works, for they walked not in the ways of the Lord, but served their father's gods of wood and stone as their father had taught them, and they were more wicked than their father.

15. And they went according to the evil desires of their hearts, and they sacrificed and burnt incense to the Baalim, and Isaac and Rebecca became weary of them.

16. And Rebecca said, I am

6

weary of my life because of the daughters of Heth; if Jacob take a wife of the daughters of Heth, such as these *which are* of the daughters of the land, what *good then* is life unto me?

17. And in those days Adah the wife of Esau conceived and bare him a son, and Esau called the name of the son that was born unto him Eliphaz, and Esau was sixty five years old when she bare him.

18. And Ishmael the son of Abraham died in those days, in the sixty fourth year of the life of Jacob, and all the days that Ishmael lived were one hundred and thirty seven years and he died.

19. And when Isaac heard that Ishmael was dead he mourned for him, and Isaac lamented over him many days.

20. And at the end of fourteen years of Jacob's residing in the house of Eber, Jacob desired to see his father and mother, and Jacob came to the house of his father and mother to Hebron, and Esau had in those days forgotten what Jacob had done to him in having taken the blessing from him in those days.

21. And when Esau saw Jacob coming to his father and mother he remembered what Jacob had done to him, and he was greatly incensed against him and he sought to slay him.

22. And Isaac the son of Abraham was old *and* advanced in days, and Esau said, now my father's time is drawing nigh that he must die, and when he shall die I will slay my brother Jacob.

23. And this was told to Rebecca, and she hastened and sent and called for Jacob her son, and she said unto him, arise go and flee to Haran to my brother Laban and remain there for some time, until thy brother's anger be turned from thee and then shalt thou come back.

24. And Isaac called unto Jacob and said unto him, take not a wife from the daughters of Canaan, for thus did our father Abraham command us according to the word of the Lord which he had commanded him, saying, unto thy seed will I give this land; if thy children keep my covenant that I have made with thee, then will I also perform to thy children that which I have spoken unto thee and I will not forsake them.

25. Now therefore my son hearken to my voice, to all that I shall command *thee,* and refrain from taking a wife from amongst the daughters of Canaan; arise, go to Haran to the house of Bethuel thy mother's father, and take unto thee a wife from there from the daughters of Laban thy mother's brother.

26. Therefore take heed lest thou shouldst forget the Lord thy God and all his ways in the land to which thou goest, and shouldst get connected with the people of the land and pursue vanity and forsake the Lord thy God.

27. But when thou comest to the land serve there the Lord, do not turn to the right or to the left from the way which I commanded thee and which thou didst learn.

28. And may the Almighty God grant thee favor *in the sight* of the people of the earth, that thou mayest there take a wife according to thy choice; one who is good and upright in the ways of the Lord.

29. And may God give unto thee and thy seed the blessing of thy father Abraham, and make thee fruitful and multiply thee, and may-

est thou become a multitude of people in the land whither thou goest, and may God cause thee to return to this land, the land of thy father's dwelling, with children and with great riches, with joy and with pleasure.

30. And Isaac finished commanding Jacob and blessing him, and he gave him many gifts, together with silver and gold, and he sent him away; and Jacob hearkened to his father and mother; he kissed them and arose and went to Padanaram, and Jacob was seventy seven years old when he went out from the land of Canaan from Beersheba.

31. And when Jacob went away to go to Haran Esau called unto his son Eliphaz, and secretly spoke unto him, saying, now hasten, take thy sword in thy hand and pursue Jacob and pass before him in the road, and lurk for him, and slay him with thy sword in one of the mountains, and take all belonging to him and come back.

32. And Eliphaz the son of Esau was an active man and expert with the bow as his father had taught him, and he was a noted hunter in the field and a valiant man.

33. And Eliphaz did as his father had commanded him, and Eliphaz was at that time thirteen years old, and Eliphaz rose up and went and took ten of his mother's brothers with him and pursued Jacob.

34. And he closely followed Jacob, and he lurked for him in the border of the land of Canaan opposite to the city of Shechem.

35. And Jacob saw Eliphaz and his men pursuing him, and Jacob stood still in the place in which he was going, in order to know what this was, for he did not know the

thing; and Eliphaz drew his sword and he went on advancing, he and his men, toward Jacob; and Jacob said unto them, what is *to do* with you that you have come hither, and what *meaneth it* that you pursue with your swords.

36. And Eliphaz came near to Jacob and he answered and said unto him, thus did my father command me, and now therefore I will not deviate from the orders which my father gave me; and when Jacob saw that Esau had spoken to Eliphaz to employ force Jacob then approached and supplicated Eliphaz and his men, saying *to him*,

37. Behold all that I have and which my father and mother gave unto me, that take unto thee and go from me and do not slay me, and may this thing be accounted unto thee a righteousness.

38. And the Lord caused Jacob to find favor in the sight of Eliphaz the son of Esau, and his men, and they hearkened to the voice of Jacob, and they did not put him to death, and Eliphaz and his men took all belonging to Jacob together with the silver and gold that he had brought with him from Beersheba; they left him nothing.

39. And Eliphaz and his men went away from him and they returned to Esau to Beersheba, and they told him all that had occurred to them with Jacob, and they gave him all that they had taken from Jacob.

40. And Esau was indignant at Eliphaz his son, and at his men that were with him, because they had not put Jacob to death.

41. And they answered and said unto Esau, because Jacob supplicated us in this matter not to slay him.

our pity was excited toward him, and we took all belonging to him and brought it *unto thee ;* and Esau took all the silver and gold which Eliphaz had taken from Jacob and he put them by in his house.

42. At that time when Esau saw that Isaac had blessed Jacob, and had commanded him, saying, thou shalt not take a wife from *amongst* the daughters of Canaan, and that the daughters of Canaan were bad in the sight of Isaac and Rebecca,

43. Then he went to the house of Ishmael his uncle, and in addition to his *other* wives he took Machlath the daughter of Ishmael, the sister of Nebayoth, for a wife.

CHAPTER XXX.

1. And Jacob went forth continuing his road to Haran, and he came as far as mount Moriah, and he tarried there all night near the city of Luz; and the Lord appeared there unto Jacob on that night, and he said unto him, I am the Lord God of Abraham and the God of Isaac thy father; the land upon which thou liest I will give unto thee and thy seed.

2. And behold I am with thee and will keep thee wherever thou goest, and I will multiply thy seed as the stars of Heaven, and I will cause all thine enemies to fall before thee; and when they shall make war with thee they shall not prevail over thee, and I will bring thee again unto this land with joy, with children, and with great riches.

3. And Jacob awoke from his sleep and he rejoiced greatly at the vision which he had seen; and he called the name of that place Bethel.

4. And Jacob rose up from that place quite rejoiced, and when he walked his feet felt light to him for joy, and he went from there to the land of the children of the East, and he returned to Haran and he sat by the shepherd's well.

5. And he there found some men going from Haran to feed their flock, and Jacob made inquiries of them, and they said, we are from Haran.

6. And he said unto them, do you know Laban the son of Nahor ? and they said we know *him* and behold his daughter Rachel is coming along to feed her father's flock.

7. Whilst he was yet speaking with them, Rachel the daughter of Laban came to feed her father's sheep, for she was a shepherdess.

8. And when Jacob saw Rachel the daughter of Laban his mother's brother, he ran and kissed her, and lifted up his voice and wept.

9. And Jacob told Rachel that he was the son of Rebecca her father's sister, and Rachel ran and told her father, and Jacob continued to cry because he had nothing* with him to bring to the house of Laban.

10. And when Laban heard that his sister's son Jacob had come, he ran and kissed him and embraced him and brought him into the house and gave him bread, and he ate.

11. And Jacob related to Laban what his brother Esau had done to him, and what his son Eliphaz had done to him in the road.

12. And Jacob resided in Laban's house for one month, and Jacob ate and drank in the house of Laban, and afterward Laban said unto Jacob, tell me what shall be thy wages, for how canst thou serve me for nought?

13. And Laban had no sons but

* Having been robbed on the road by Eliphaz, the son of Esau.

only daughters, and his *other* wives and handmaids were still barren in those days; and these are the names of Laban's daughters which his wife Adinah had borne unto him; the name of the elder was Leah and the name of the younger was Rachel; and Leah was tender-eyed, but Rachel was beautiful and well favored, and Jacob loved her.

14. And Jacob said unto Laban, I will serve thee seven years for Rachel thy younger daughter; and Laban consented to this and Jacob served Laban seven years for his daughter Rachel.

15. And in the second year of Jacob's dwelling in Haran, that is in the seventy-ninth year of the life of Jacob, in that year died Eber the son of Selah, he was four hundred and sixty-four years old at his death.

16. And when Jacob heard that Eber was dead he grieved exceedingly, and he lamented and mourned over him many days.

17. And in the third year of Jacob's dwelling in Haran, Bosmath, the daughter of Ishmael, the wife of Esau, bare unto him a son, and Esau called his name Reuel.

18. And in the fourth year of Jacob's residence in the house of Laban, the Lord visited Laban and remembered him on account of Jacob, and sons were born unto him, and his first born was Beor, his second was Alib, and the third was Chorash.

19. And the Lord gave Laban riches and honor, sons and daughters, and the man increased greatly on account of Jacob.

20. And Jacob in those days served Laban in all manner of work, in the house and in the field, and the blessing of the Lord was in all that belonged to Laban in the house and in the field.

21. And in the fifth year died Jehudith, the daughter of Beeri, the wife of Esau, in the land of Canaan, and she had no sons but daughters *only.*

22. And these are the names of her daughters which she bare to Esau, the name of the elder was Marzith, and the name of the younger was Puith.

23. And when Jehudith died, Esau rose up and went to Seir to hunt in the field, as usual, and Esau dwelt in the land of Seir for a long time.

24. And in the sixth year Esau took for a wife, in addition to his *other* wives, Ahlibamah, the daughter of Zebeon the Hivite, and Esau brought her to the land of Canaan.

25. And Ahlibamah conceived and bare unto Esau three sons, Yeush, Yaalan and Korah.

26. And in those days, in the land of Canaan, there was a quarrel between the herdsmen of Esau and the herdsmen of the inhabitants of the land of Canaan, for Esau's cattle and goods were too abundant for him to remain in the land of Canaan, in his father's house, and the land of Canaan could not bear him on account of his cattle.

27. And when Esau saw that his quarrelling increased with the inhabitants of the land of Canaan, he rose up and took his wives and his sons and his daughters, and all belonging to him, and the cattle which he possessed, and all his property that he had acquired in the land of Canaan, and he went away from the inhabitants of the land to the land of Seir, and Esau and all belonging to him dwelt in the land of Seir.

28. But from time to time Esau

would go and see his father and mother in the land of Canaan, and Esau intermarried with the Horites, and he gave his daughters to the sons of Seir, the Horite.

29. And he gave his elder daughter Marzith to Anah, the son of Zebeon, his wife's brother, and Puith he gave to Azar, the son of Bilhan the Horite; and Esau dwelt in the mountain, he and his children, and they were fruitful and multiplied.

CHAPTER XXXI.

1. And in the seventh year, Jacob's service which he served Laban was completed, and Jacob said unto Laban, give me my wife, for the days of my service are fulfilled; and Laban did so, and Laban and Jacob assembled all the people of that place and they made a feast.

2. And in the evening Laban came to the house, and afterward Jacob came there with the people of the feast, and Laban extinguished all the lights that were there in the house.

3. And Jacob said unto Laban, wherefore dost thou do this thing unto us? and Laban answered, such is our custom to act in this land.

4. And afterward Laban took his daughter Leah, and he brought her to Jacob, and he came to her and Jacob did not know that she was Leah.

5. And Laban gave his daughter Leah his maid Zilpah for a handmaid.

6. And all the people at the feast knew what Laban had done to Jacob, but they did not tell the thing to Jacob.

7. And all the neighbors came that night to Jacob's house, and they ate and drank and rejoiced, and played before Leah upon timbrels, and with dances,* and they responded before Jacob, Heleah, Heleah.†

8. And Jacob heard their words but did not understand their meaning, but he thought such might be their custom in this land.

9. And the neighbors spoke these words before Jacob during the night, and all the lights that were in the house Laban had that night extinguished.

10. And in the morning, when daylight appeared, Jacob turned to his wife and he saw, and behold it was Leah that had been lying in his bosom, and Jacob said, behold now I know what the neighbors said last night, Heleah they said, and I knew it not.

11. And Jacob called unto Laban, and said unto him, what is this that thou didst unto me? Surely I served thee for Rachel, and why didst thou deceive me and didst give me Leah?

12. And Laban answered Jacob, saying, not so is it done in our place to give the younger before the elder; now therefore if thou desirest to take her sister likewise, take her unto thee for the service which thou wilt serve me for another seven years.

13. And Jacob did so, and he also took Rachel for a wife, and he served Laban seven years more, and Jacob also came to Rachel, and he loved Rachel more than Leah, and Laban gave her his maid Bilhah for a handmaid.

14. And when the Lord saw that Leah was hated, the Lord opened her womb, and she conceived and bare Jacob four sons in those days.

* מחול is commonly translated a dance, but it seems by this book that it must have been a sort of musical instrument.
† Composed of two Hebrew words, היא לאה He Leah, i. e., she is Leah.

15. And these are their names, Reuben, Simeon, Levi, and Judah, and she afterward left bearing.

16. And at that time Rachel was barren, and she had no offspring, and Rachel envied her sister Leah, and when Rachel saw that she bare no children to Jacob, she took her handmaid Bilhah, and she bare Jacob two sons, Dan and Naphtali.

17. And when Leah saw that she had left bearing, she also took her handmaid Zilpah, and she gave her to Jacob for a wife, and Jacob also came to Zilpah, and she also bare Jacob two sons, Gad and Asher.

18. And Leah again conceived and bare Jacob in those days two sons and one daughter, and these are their names, Issachar, Zebulon, and their sister Dinah.

19. And Rachel was still barren in those days, and Rachel prayed unto the Lord at that time, and she said, O Lord God remember me and visit me, I beseech thee, for now my husband will cast me off, for I have borne him no children.

20. Now O Lord God, hear my supplication before thee, and see my affliction, and give me children like one of the handmaids, that I may no more bear my reproach.

21. And God heard *her* and opened her womb, and Rachel conceived and bare a son, and she said the Lord has taken away my reproach, and she called his name Joseph, saying, may the Lord add to me another son ; and Jacob was ninety one years old when she bare him.

22. At that time Jacob's mother Rebecca sent her nurse Deborah the daughter of Uz, and two of Isaac's servants unto Jacob.

23. And they came to Jacob to Haran and they said unto him, Re-becca has sent us to thee that thou shalt return to thy father's house to the land of Canaan ; and Jacob hearkened unto them in this which his mother had spoken.

24. At that time, the other seven years which Jacob served Laban for Rachel were completed, and it was at the end of fourteen years that he had dwelt in Haran that Jacob said unto Laban, give *me* my wives and send me away, that I may go to my land, for behold my mother did send unto me from the land of Canaan that I should return to my father's house.

25. And Laban said unto him, not so I pray thee ; if I have found favor in thy sight do not leave me ; appoint me thy wages and I will give them, and remain with me.

26. And Jacob said unto him, this is what thou shalt give me for wages, that I shall this day pass through all thy flock and take away from them every lamb that is speckled and spotted and such as are brown amongst the sheep, and amongst the goats, and if thou wilt do this thing for me I will return *and* feed thy flock and keep *them* as at first.

27. And Laban did so, and Laban removed from his flock all that Jacob had said and gave *them* to him.

28. And Jacob placed all that he had removed from Laban's flock in the hands of his sons, and Jacob was feeding the remainder of Laban's flock.

29. And when the servants of Isaac which he had sent unto Jacob saw that Jacob would not then return with them to the land of Canaan to his father, they *then* went away from him, and they returned home to the land of Canaan.

30. And Deborah remained with Jacob in Haran, and she did not return with the servants of Isaac to the land of Canaan, and Deborah resided with Jacob's wives and children in Haran.

31. And Jacob served Laban six years longer, and when the sheep brought forth, Jacob removed from them such as were speckled and spotted, as he had determined with Laban, and Jacob did so at Laban's for six years, and the man increased abundantly and he had cattle and maid servants, and men servants, camels and asses.

32. And Jacob had two hundred drove of cattle, and his cattle were of large size and of beautiful appearance and were very productive, and all the families of the sons of men desired to get some of the cattle of Jacob, for they were exceedingly prosperous.

33. And many of the sons of men came to procure some of Jacob's flock, and Jacob gave them a sheep for a man servant or a maid servant or for an ass or a camel, or whatever Jacob desired from them they gave him.

34. And Jacob obtained riches and honor and possessions by means of these transactions with the sons of men, and the children of Laban envied him of this honor.

35. And in the course of time he heard the words of Laban's sons, saying, Jacob has taken away all that was our father's, and of that which was our father's has he acquired all this glory.

36. And Jacob beheld the countenance of Laban and of his children, and behold it was not toward him in those days as it had been before.

37 And the Lord appeared to Jacob at the expiration of the six years, and said unto him, arise go forth out of this land, and return to the land of thy birth place and will be with thee.

38. And Jacob rose up at that time and he mounted his children and wives and all belonging to him upon camels, and he went forth to go to the land of Canaan to his father Isaac.

39. And Laban did not know that Jacob had gone from him, for Laban had been that day sheep shearing.

40. And Rachel stole her father's images, and she took them and she concealed them upon the camel upon which she sat, and she went on.

41. And this is the manner of the images; in taking a man who is the first born and slaying him and taking the hair off his head, then taking salt and salting the head and anointing it in oil, then taking a small tablet of copper or a tablet of gold and writing the name upon it, and placing the tablet under his tongue, and taking the head with the tablet under the tongue and putting it in the house, and lighting up lights before it and bowing down to it.

42. And at the time when they bow down to it, it speaketh to them in all matters that they ask of it, through the power of the name which is written in it.

43. And some make them in the figures of men, of gold and silver, and go to them in times known to them, and the figures receive the influence of the stars, and tell them future things, and in this manner were the images which Rachel stole from her father.

44. And Rachel stole those images which were her father's, in

order that Laban might not know through them where Jacob had gone.

45. And Laban came home and he asked concerning Jacob and his household, and he was not. to be found, and Laban sought his images to know where Jacob had gone, and could not find *them*, and he went to some other images, and he inquired of them and they told him that Jacob had fled from him to his father's to the land of Canaan.

46. And Laban then rose up and he took his brothers and all his servants, and he went forth and pursued Jacob, and he overtook him in mount Gilead.

47. And Laban said unto Jacob, what is this thou hast done to me to flee and deceive* me, and lead my daughters and their children as captives taken by the sword?

48. And thou didst not suffer me to kiss them and send them away with joy, and thou didst steal my gods and didst go away.

49. And Jacob answered Laban, saying, because I was afraid lest thou wouldst take thy daughters by force from me ; and *now* with whomsoever thou findest thy gods he shall die.

50. And Laban searched for the images and he examined in all Jacob's tents and furniture, but could not find them.

51. And Laban said unto Jacob, we will make a covenant together and it shall be a testimony between me and thee ; if thou shalt afflict my daughters, or shalt take other wives besides my daughters, even God shall be a witness between me and thee in this matter.

52. And they took stones and made a heap, and Laban said, this

* Hebrew, steal my heart.

heap is a witness between me and thee, therefore he called the name thereof Gilead.

53. And Jacob and Laban offered sacrifice upon the mount, and they ate there by the heap, and they tarried in the mount all night, and Laban rose up early in the morning, and he wept with his daughters and he kissed them, and he returned unto his place.

54. And he hastened and sent off his son Beor, who was seventeen years old, with Abichorof the son of Uz, the son of Nahor, and with them were ten men.

55. And they hastened and went and passed on the road before Jacob, and they came by another road to the land of Seir.

56. And they came unto Esau and said unto him, thus saith thy brother and relative, thy mother's brother Laban, the son of Bethuel, saying,

57. Hast thou heard what Jacob thy brother has done unto me, who first came to me naked and bare, and I went to meet him, and brought him to my house with honor, and I made him great, and I gave him my two daughters for wives and also two of my maids.

58. And God blessed him on my account, and he increased abundantly, and had sons, daughters and maid servants.

59. He has also an immense stock of flocks and herds, camels and asses, also silver and gold in abundance ; and when he saw that his wealth increased, he left me whilst I went to shear my sheep, and he rose up and fled in secrecy.

60. And he lifted his wives and children upon camels, and he led away all his cattle and property

which he acquired in my land, and he lifted up his countenance to go to his father Isaac to the land of Canaan.

61. And he did not suffer me to kiss my daughters and their children, and he led my daughters as captives taken by the sword, and he also stole my gods and he fled.

62. And now I have left him in the mountain of the brook of Jabuk, him and all belonging to him; he lacketh nothing.

63. If it be thy wish to go to him, go *then* and there wilt thou find him, and thou canst do unto him as thy soul desireth; and Laban's messengers came and told Esau all these things.

64. And Esau heard all the words of Laban's messengers, and his anger was greatly kindled against Jacob, and he remembered his hatred and his anger burned within him.

65. And Esau hastened and took his children and servants and the souls of his household, *being* sixty men, and he went and assembled all the children of Seir the Horite and their people, being three hundred and forty men, and took all this number of four hundred men with drawn swords, and he went unto Jacob to smite him.

66. And Esau divided this number into several parts, and he took the sixty men of his children and servants and the souls of his household as one head, and gave them in care of Eliphaz his eldest son.

67. And the remaining heads he gave to the care of the six sons of Seir the Horite, and he placed every man over his generations and children.

68 And the whole of this camp went as it was, and Esau went amongst them toward Jacob, and he conducted them with speed.

69. And Laban's messengers departed from Esau and went to the land of Canaan, and they came to the house of Rebecca the mother of Jacob and Esau.

70. And they told her, saying, behold thy son Esau has gone against his brother Jacob with four hundred men, for he heard that he was coming, and he is gone to make war with him, and to smite him and to take all that he has.

71. And Rebecca hastened and sent seventy two men from the servants of Isaac to meet Jacob on the road; for she said, peradventure, Esau may make war in the road when he meets him.

72. And these messengers went on the road to meet Jacob, and they met him in the road of the brook on the opposite side of the brook Jabuk, and Jacob said when he saw them, this camp is destined to me from God, and Jacob called the name of that place Machnayim.

73. And Jacob knew all his father's people, and he kissed them and embraced them and came with them, and Jacob asked them concerning his father and mother, and they said, they were well.*

74. And these messengers said unto Jacob, Rebecca thy mother has sent us to thee, saying, I have heard, my son, that thy brother Esau has gone forth against thee on the road with men from the children of Seir the Horite.

75. And therefore, my son, hearken to my voice and see with thy counsel what thou wilt do, and when he cometh up to thee, supplicate him, and do not speak rashly to him, and

* Hebrew, peace.

give him a present from what thou possessest, and from what God has favored thee with.

76. And when he asketh thee concerning thy affairs, conceal nothing from him, perhaps he may turn from his anger against thee and thou wilt thereby save thy soul, thou and all belonging to thee, for it is thy duty to honor him, for he is thy elder brother.

77. And when Jacob heard the words of his mother which the messengers had spoken to him, Jacob lifted up his voice and wept bitterly, and did as his mother then commanded him.

CHAPTER XXXII.

1. And at that time Jacob sent messengers to his brother Esau toward the land of Seir, and he spoke to him words of supplication.

2. And he commanded them, saying, thus shall ye say to my lord, to Esau, thus saith thy servant Jacob, let not my lord imagine that my father's blessing with which he did bless me has proved beneficial to me.

3. For I have been these twenty years with Laban, and he deceived me and changed my wages ten times, as it has all been already told unto my lord.

4. And I served him in his house very laboriously, and God afterward saw my affliction, my labor and the work of my hands, and he caused me to find grace and favor in his sight.

5. And I afterward through God's great mercy and kindness acquired oxen and asses and cattle, and men servants and maid servants.

6. And now I am coming to my land and my home to my father and mother, who are in the land of Canaan; and I have sent to let my lord know all this in order to find favor in the sight of my lord, so that he may not imagine that I have *of myself* obtained wealth, or that the blessing with which my father blessed me has benefited me.

7. And those messengers went to Esau, and found him on the borders of the land of Edom going toward Jacob, and four hundred men of the children of Seir the Horite were standing with drawn swords.

8. And the messengers of Jacob told Esau all the words that Jacob had spoken to them concerning Esau.

9. And Esau answered them with pride and contempt, and said unto them, surely I have heard and truly it has been told unto me what Jacob has done to Laban, who exalted him in his house and gave him his daughters for wives, and he begat sons and daughters, and abundantly increased in wealth and riches in Laban's house through his means.

10. And when he saw that his wealth was abundant and his riches great he fled with all belonging to him, from Laban's house, and he led Laban's daughters away from the face of their father, as captives taken by the sword, without telling him of it.

11. And not only to Laban has Jacob done thus but also unto me has he done so, and has twice supplanted me, and shall I be silent?

12. Now *therefore* I have this day come with my camps to meet him, and I will do unto him according to the desire of my heart.

13. And the messengers returned and came to Jacob and said unto him, we came to thy brother, to

Esau, and we told him all thy words, and thus has he answered us, and behold he cometh to meet thee with four hundred men.

14. Now then know and see what thou shalt do, and pray before God to deliver thee from him.

15. And when he heard the words of his brother which he had spoken to the messengers of Jacob, Jacob was greatly afraid and he was distressed.

16. And Jacob prayed to the Lord his God, and he said, O Lord God of my fathers, Abraham and Isaac, thou didst say unto me when I went away from my father's house, saying.

17. I am the Lord God of thy father Abraham and the God of Isaac, unto thee do I give this land and thy seed after thee, and I will make thy seed as the stars of heaven, and thou shalt spread forth to the four sides of heaven, and in thee and in thy seed shall all the families of the earth be blessed.

18. And thou didst establish thy words, and didst give unto me riches and children and cattle, as the utmost wishes of my heart didst thou give unto thy servant; thou didst give unto me all that I asked from thee, *so that* I lacked nothing.

19. And thou didst afterward say unto me, return to thy parents and to thy birth place and I will still do well with thee.

20. And now that I have come, and thou didst deliver me from Laban, I shall fall in the hands of Esau who will slay me, *yea, together with* the mothers of my children.

21. Now therefore O Lord God deliver me, I pray thee, also from the hands of my brother Esau, for I am greatly afraid of him.

22. And if there is no righteousness in me, do it for the sake of Abraham and my father Isaac.

23. For I know that through kindness and mercy have I acquired this wealth; now therefore I beseech thee to deliver me this day with thy kindness and to answer me.

24. And Jacob ceased praying to the Lord, and he divided the people that were with him with the flocks and cattle into two camps, and he gave the half to the care of Damesek, the son of Eliezer Abraham's servant, for a camp, with his children, and the other half he gave to the care of his brother Elianus the son of Eliezer, to be for a camp with his children.

25. And he commanded them, saying, keep yourselves at a distance with your camps, and do not come too near each other, and if Esau come to one camp and slay it, the other camp at a distance from it will escape him.

26. And Jacob tarried there that night, and during the whole night he gave his servants instructions concerning the forces and his children.

27. And the Lord heard the prayer of Jacob on that day, and the Lord then delivered Jacob from the hands of his brother Esau.

28. And the Lord sent three angels of the angels of heaven, and they went before Esau and came to him.

29. And these angels appeared unto Esau and his people as two thousand men, riding upon horses furnished with all sorts of war instruments, and they appeared in the sight of Esau and all his men to be divided into four camps, with four chiefs to them.

30. And one camp went on and

they found Esau coming with four hundred men toward his brother Jacob, and this camp ran toward Esau and his people and terrified them, and Esau fell off the horse in alarm, and all his men separated from him in that place, for they were greatly afraid.

31. And the whole of the camp shouted after them when they fled from Esau, and all the warlike men answered, saying,

32. Surely we are the servants of Jacob *who is* the servant of God, and who *then* can stand against us? And Esau said unto them, O then, my lord and brother Jacob is your lord, whom I have not seen for these twenty years, and now that I have this day come to see him, do you treat me in this manner?

33. And the angels answered him, saying, as the Lord liveth, were not Jacob of whom thou spokest thy brother, we had not left one remaining from thee and thy people, but *only* on account of Jacob we will do nothing to them.

34. And this camp passed from Esau and his men and it went away, and Esau and his men had gone from them about a league when the second camp came toward him with all sorts of weapons, and they also did unto Esau and his men as the first camp had done to them.

35. And when they had left it to go on, behold the third camp came toward him and they were *all* terrified, and Esau fell off the horse, and the whole camp cried out, and said, surely we are the servants of Jacob, *who is* the servant of God, and who can stand against us?

36. And Esau again answered them, saying, O then, Jacob my lord and your lord is my brother, and for

twenty years I have not seen his countenance, and hearing this day that he was coming, I went this day to meet him, and do you treat me in this manner?

37. And they answered him, and said unto him, as the Lord liveth, were not Jacob thy brother as thou didst say, we had not left a remnant from thee and thy men, but on account of Jacob of whom thou spokest being thy brother, we will not meddle with thee or thy men.

38. And the third camp also passed from them, and he still continued his road with his men toward Jacob, when the fourth camp came toward him, and they also did unto him and his men as the others had done.

39. And when Esau beheld the evil* which the four angels had done to him and to his men, he became greatly afraid of his brother Jacob, and he went to meet him in peace.

40. And Esau concealed his hatred against Jacob, because he was afraid of his life on account of his brother Jacob, and because he imagined that the four camps that he had lighted upon were Jacob's servants.

41. And Jacob tarried that night with his servants in their camps, and he resolved with his servants to give unto Esau a present from all that he had with him, and from all his property; and Jacob rose up in the morning, he and his men, and they chose from amongst the cattle a present for Esau.

42. And this is the amount of the present which Jacob chose from his flock to give unto his brother Esau; and he selected two hundred and forty

*Although they did no actual injury to them, they caused great alarm and confusion to Esau and his people; this is the evil alluded to.

head from the flocks, and he selected from the camels and asses thirty each, and of the herds he chose fifty kine.

43. And he put them all in ten droves, and he placed each sort by itself, and he delivered them into the hands of ten of his servants, each drove by itself.

44. And he commanded them, and said unto them, keep yourselves at a distance from each other, and put a space between the droves, and when Esau and those who are with him shall meet you and ask you, saying, whose are you, and whither do you go, and to whom belongeth all this before you, you shall say unto them, we are the servants of Jacob, and we come to meet Esau in peace, and behold Jacob cometh behind us.

45. And that which is before us is a present sent from Jacob to his brother Esau.

46. And if they shall say unto you, why doth he delay behind you, from coming to meet his brother and to see his face, *then* you shall say unto them, surely he cometh joyfully behind us to meet his brother, for he said, I will appease him with the present that goeth to him, and after this I will see his face, peradventure he will accept of me.

47. So the whole present passed on in the hands of his servants, and went before him on that day, and he lodged that night with his camps by the border of the brook of Jabuk, and he rose up in the midst of the night, and he took his wives and his maid servants, and all belonging to him, and he that night passed them over the ford Jabuk.

48. And when he had passed all belonging to him over the brook, Jacob was left by himself, and a man met him, and he wrestled with him that night until the breaking of the day, and the hollow of Jacob's thigh was out of joint through wrestling with him.

49. And at the break of day the man left Jacob there, and he blessed him and went away, and Jacob passed the brook at the break of day, and he halted upon his thigh.

50. And the sun rose upon him when he had passed the brook, and he came up to the place of his cattle and children.

51. And they went on till midday, and whilst they were going the present was passing on before them.

52. And Jacob lifted up his eyes and looked, and behold Esau was at a distance, coming along with many men, *about* four hundred, and Jacob was greatly afraid of his brother.

53. And Jacob hastened and divided his children unto his wives and his handmaids, and his daughter Dinah he put in a chest, and delivered her into the hands of his servants.

54. And he passed before his children and wives to meet his brother, and he bowed down to the ground, yea he bowed down seven times until he approached his brother, and God caused Jacob to find grace and favor in the sight of Esau and his men, for God had heard the prayer of Jacob.

55. And the fear of Jacob and his terror fell upon his brother Esau, for Esau was greatly afraid of Jacob for what the angels of God had done to Esau, and Esau's anger against Jacob was turned into kindness.

56. And when Esau saw Jacob running toward him, he also ran toward him and he embraced him, and he fell upon his neck, and they kissed and they wept.

57. And God put fear and kindness toward Jacob in the hearts of the men that came with Esau, and they also kissed Jacob and embraced him.

58. And also Eliphaz, the son of Esau, with his four brothers, sons of Esau, wept with Jacob, and they kissed him and embraced him, for the fear of Jacob had fallen upon them all.

59. And Esau lifted up his eyes and saw the women with their offspring, the children of Jacob, walking behind Jacob and bowing along the road to Esau.

60. And Esau said unto Jacob, who are these with thee my brother? are they thy children or thy servants? and Jacob answered Esau and said, they are my children which God hath graciously given to thy servant.

61. And whilst Jacob was speaking to Esau and his men, Esau beheld the whole camp, and he said unto Jacob, whence didst thou get the whole of the camp that I met yesternight? and Jacob said, to find favor in the sight of my Lord, it is that which God graciously gave to thy servant.

62. And the present came before Esau, and Jacob pressed Esau, saying, take I pray thee the present that I have brought to my lord, and Esau said, wherefore is this my purpose? keep that which thou hast unto thyself.

63. And Jacob said, it is incumbent upon me to give all this, since I have seen thy face, that thou still livest in peace.

64. And Esau refused to take the present, and Jacob said unto him, I beseech thee my lord, if now I have found favor in thy sight, then receive my present at my hand, for I have therefore seen thy face, as though I had seen a god-like face, because thou wast pleased with me.

65. And Esau took the present, and Jacob also gave unto Esau silver and gold and bdellium, for he pressed him so much that he took them.

66. And Esau divided the cattle that was in the camp, and he gave the half to the men who had come with him, for they had come on hire, and the other half he delivered unto the hands of his children.

67. And the silver and gold and bdellium he gave in the hands of Eliphaz his eldest son, and Esau said unto Jacob, let us remain with thee, and we will go slowly along with thee until thou comest to my place with me, that we may dwell there together.

68. And Jacob answered his brother and said, I would do as my lord speaketh unto me, but my lord knoweth that the children are tender, and the flocks and herds with their young who are with me, go but slowly, for if they went swiftly they would all die, for thou knowest their burdens and their fatigue.

69. Therefore let my lord pass on before his servant, and I will go on slowly for the sake of the children and the flock, until I come to my lord's place to Seir.

70. And Esau said unto Jacob, I will place with thee some of the people that are with me to take care of thee in the road, and to bear thy fatigue and burden, and he said, what needeth it my lord, if I may find grace in thy sight?

71. Behold I will come unto thee to Seir to dwell there together as thou hast spoken, go thou then with thy people for I will follow thee.

72. And Jacob said this to Esau

in order to remove Esau and his men from him, so that Jacob might afterward go to his father's house to the land of Canaan.

73. And Esau hearkened to the voice of Jacob, and Esau returned with the four hundred men that were with him on their road to Seir, and Jacob and all belonging to him went that day as far as the extremity of the land of Canaan in its borders, and he remained there some time.

CHAPTER XXXIII.

1. And in some time after Jacob went away from the borders of the land, and he came to the land of Shalem, that is the city of Shechem, which is in the land of Canaan, and he rested in front of the city.

2. And he bought a parcel of the field which was there, from the children of Hamor the people of the land, for five shekels.

3. And Jacob there built himself a house, and he pitched his tent there, and he made booths for his cattle, therefore he called the name of that place Succoth.

4. And Jacob remained in Succoth a year and six months.

5. At that time some of the women of the inhabitants of the land went to the city of Shechem to dance and rejoice with the daughters of the people of the city, and when they went forth then Rachel and Leah the wives of Jacob with their families also went to behold the rejoicing of the daughters of the city.

6. And Dinah the daughter of Jacob also went along with them and saw the daughters of the city, and they remained there before these daughters whilst all the people of the city were standing by them to behold their rejoicings, and all the great people of the city were there.

7. And Shechem the son of Hamor the prince of the land was *also* standing there to see *them.*

8. And Shechem beheld Dinah the daughter of Jacob sitting with her mother before the daughters of the city, and the damsel pleased him greatly, and he there asked his friends and his people, saying, whose daughter is that sitting amongst the women, whom I do not know in this city?

9. And they said unto him, surely this is the daughter of Jacob the son of Isaac the Hebrew, who has dwelt in this city for some time, and when it was reported that the daughters of the land were going forth to rejoice she went with her mother and maid servants to sit amongst them as thou seest.

10. And Shechem beheld Dinah the daughter of Jacob, and when he looked at her his soul became fixed upon Dinah.

11. And he sent and had her taken by force, and Dinah came to the house of Shechem and he seized her forcibly and lay with her and humbled* her, and he loved her exceedingly and placed her in his house.

12. And they came and told the thing unto Jacob, and when Jacob heard that Shechem had defiled his daughter Dinah, Jacob sent twelve of his servants to fetch Dinah from the house of Shechem, and they went and came to the house of Shechem to take away Dinah from there.

13. And when they came Shechem went out to them with his men and

* Translated in the Bible, "and he defiled her." Genesis, ch. 34, v. 2.

drove them from his house, and he would not suffer them to come before Dinah, but Shechem was sitting with Dinah kissing and embracing her before their eyes.

14. And the servants of Jacob came back and told him, saying, when we came, he and his men drove us away, and thus did Shechem do unto Dinah before our eyes.

15. And Jacob knew moreover that Shechem had defiled his daughter, but he said nothing, and his sons were feeding his cattle in the field, and Jacob remained silent till their return.

16. And before his sons came home Jacob sent two maidens from his servants' daughters to take care of Dinah in the house of Shechem, and to remain with her, and Shechem sent three of his friends to his father Hamor the son of Chiddekem, the son of Pered, saying, get me this damsel for a wife.

17. And Hamor the son of Chiddekem the Hivite came to the house of Shechem his son, and he sat before him, and Hamor said unto his son, Shechem, is there then no woman amongst the daughters of thy people that thou wilt take an Hebrew woman who is not of thy people?

18. And Shechem said to him, her *only* must thou get for me, for she is delightful in my sight; and Hamor did according to the word of his son, for he was greatly beloved by him.

19. And Hamor went forth to Jacob to commune with him concerning this matter, and when he had gone from the house of his son Shechem, before he came to Jacob to speak unto him, behold the sons of Jacob had come from the field, as soon as they heard the thing that Shechem the son of Hamor had done.

20. And the men were very much grieved concerning their sister, and they all came home fired with anger, before the time of gathering in their cattle.

21. And they came and sat before their father and they spoke unto him kindled with wrath, saying, surely death is due to this man and to his household, because the Lord God of the whole earth commanded Noah and his children that man shall never rob, nor commit adultery; now behold Shechem has *both* ravaged and committed fornication with our sister, and not one of all the people of the city spoke a word to him.

22. Surely thou knowest and understandest that the judgment of death is due to Shechem, and to his father, and to the whole city on account of the thing which he has done.

23. And whilst they were speaking before their father in this matter, behold Hamor the father of Shechem came to speak to Jacob the words of his son concerning Dinah, and he sat before Jacob and before his sons.

24. And Hamor spoke unto them, saying, the soul of my son Shechem longeth for your daughter; I pray you give her unto him for a wife and intermarry with us; give us your daughters and we will give you *our daughters*, and you shall dwell with us in our land and we will be as one people in the land.

25. For our land is very extensive, so dwell ye and trade therein and get possessions in it, and do therein as you desire, and no one shall *prevent you* by saying a word to you.

26. And Hamor ceased speaking

7

unto Jacob and his sons, and behold
Shechem his son had come after
him, and he sat before them.

27. And Shechem spoke before
Jacob and his sons, saying, may I
find favor in your sight that you will
give me your daughter, and whatever you say unto me that will I do
for her.

28. Ask me for abundance of
dowry and gift, and I will give it,
and whatever you shall say unto me
that will I do, and whoever he be
that will rebel against your orders,
he shall die; only give me the damsel
for a wife.

29. And Simeon and Levi answered Hamor and Shechem his son deceitfully, saying, all you have spoken
unto us we will do for you.

30. And behold our sister is in
your house, but keep away from her
until we send to our father Isaac
concerning this matter, for we can
do nothing without his consent.

31. For he knoweth the ways of
our father Abraham, and whatever
he sayeth unto us we will tell you,
we will conceal nothing from you.

32. And Simeon and Levi spoke
this unto Shechem and his father in
order to find a pretext, and to seek
counsel what was to be done to Shechem and to his city in this matter.

33. And when Shechem and his
father heard the words of Simeon
and Levi, it seemed good in their
sight, and Shechem and his father
came forth to go home.

34. And when they had gone, the
sons of Jacob said unto their father,
saying, behold, we know that death
is due to these wicked ones and to
their city, because they transgressed
that which God had commanded unto Noah and his children and his
seed after them.

35. And also because Shechem
did this thing to our sister Dinah
in defiling her, for such vileness
shall never be done amongst us.

36. Now therefore know and see
what you will do, and seek counsel
and pretext what is to be done to
them, in order to kill all the inhabitants of this city.

37. And Simeon said to them,
here is a proper advice for you; tell
them to circumcise every male
amongst them as we are circumcised, and if they do not wish to do
this, we shall take our daughter from
them and go away.

38. And if they consent to do this
and will do it, then when they are
sunk down with pain, we will attack
them with our swords, as upon one
who is quiet and peaceable, and we
will slay every male person amongst
them.

39. And Simeon's advice pleased
them, and Simeon and Levi resolved
to do unto them as it was proposed.

40. And on the next morning Shechem and Hamor his father came
again unto Jacob and his sons, to
speak concerning Dinah, and to hear
what answer the sons of Jacob would
give to their words.

41. And the sons of Jacob spoke
deceitfully to them, saying, we told
our father Isaac all your words, and
your words pleased him.

42. But he spoke unto us, saying,
thus did Abraham his father command him from God the Lord of the
whole earth, that any man who is not
of his descendants that should wish
to take one of his daughters, shall
cause every male belonging to him
to be circumcised, as we are circumcised, and then we may give him our
daughter for a wife.

43. Now we have made known to

you all our ways that our father spoke unto us, for we cannot do this of which you spoke unto us, to give our daughter to an uncircumcised man, for it is a disgrace to us.

44. But herein will we consent to you, to give you our daughter, and we will *also* take unto ourselves your daughters, and will dwell amongst you and be one people as you have spoken, if you will hearken to us, and consent to be like us, to circumcise every male belonging to you, as we are circumcised.

45. And if you will not hearken unto us, to have every male circumcised as we are circumcised, as we have commanded, then we will come to you, and take our daughter from you and go away.

46. And Shechem and his father Hamor heard the words of the sons of Jacob, and the thing pleased them exceedingly, and Shechem and his father Hamor hastened to do the wishes of the sons of Jacob, for Shechem was very fond of Dinah, and his soul was rivetted to her.

47. And Shechem and his father Hamor hastened to the gate of the city, and they assembled all the men of their city and spoke unto them the words of the sons of Jacob, saying,

48. We came to these men, the sons of Jacob, and we spoke unto them concerning their daughter, and these men will consent to do according to our wishes, and behold our land is of great extent for them, and they will dwell in it, and trade in it, and we shall be one people; we will take their daughters, and our daughters we will give unto them for wives.

49. But only on this *condition* will these men consent to do this thing; that every male amongst us be circumcised as they are circumcised, as their God commanded them, and when we shall have done according to their instructions to be circumcised, then will they dwell amongst us, together with their cattle and possessions, and we shall be as one people with them.

50. And when all the men of the city heard the words of Shechem and his father Hamor, then all the men of their city were agreeable to this proposal, and they obeyed to be circumcised, for Shechem and his father Hamor were greatly esteemed by them, being the princes of the land.

51. And on the next day, Shechem and Hamor his father rose up early in the morning, and they assembled all the men of their city into the middle of the city, and they called for the sons of Jacob, who circumcised every male belonging to them on that day and the next.

52. And they circumcised Shechem and Hamor his father, and the five brothers of Shechem, and then every one rose up and went home, for this thing was from the Lord against the city of Shechem, and from the Lord was Simeon's counsel in this matter, in order that the Lord might deliver the city of Shechem into the hands of Jacob's two sons.

CHAPTER XXXIV.

1. And the number of all the males that were circumcised, were six hundred and forty-five men, and two hundred and forty-six children.

2. But Chiddekem, son of Pered, the father of Hamor, and his six brothers, would not listen unto Shechem and his father Hamor, and they

would not be circumcised, for the proposal of the sons of Jacob was loathsome in their sight, and their anger was greatly roused at this, that the people of the city had not hearkened to them.

3. And in the evening of the second day, they found eight small children who had not been circumcised, for their mothers had concealed them from Shechem and his father Hamor, and from the men of the city.

4. And Shechem and his father Hamor sent to have them brought before them to be circumcised, when Chiddekem and his six brothers sprang at them with their swords, and sought to slay them.

5. And they sought to slay also Shechem and his father Hamor, and they sought to slay Dinah with them, on account of this matter.

6. And they said unto them, what is this thing that you have done? are there no women amongst the daughters of your brethren the Canaanites, that you wish to take unto yourselves daughters of the Hebrews, whom ye knew not before, and will do this act which your fathers never commanded you?

7. Do you imagine that you will succeed through this act which you have done? and what will you answer in this affair to your brethren the Canaanites, who will come to-morrow and ask you concerning this thing?

8. And if your act shall not appear just and good in their sight, what will you do for your lives, and we for our lives, in your not having hearkened to our voices?

9. And if the inhabitants of the land and all your brethren the children of Ham, shall hear of your act, saying,

10. On account of a Hebrew woman did Shechem and Hamor his father, and all the inhabitants of their city, do that with which they had been unacquainted and which their ancestors never commanded them, where then will you fly or where conceal your shame, all your days before your brethren, the inhabitants of the land of Canaan?

11. Now therefore we cannot bear up against this thing which you have done, neither can we be burthened with this yoke upon us, which our ancestors did not command us.

12. Behold to-morrow we will go and assemble all our brethren the Canaanitish brethren who dwell in the land, and we will all come and smite you and all those who trust in you, that there shall not be a remnant left from you or them.

13. And when Hamor and his son Shechem and all the people of the city heard the words of Chiddekem and his brothers, they were terribly afraid of their lives at their words, and they repented of what they had done.

14. And Shechem and his father Hamor answered their father Chiddekem and his brethren, and they said unto them, all the words which you spoke unto us are true.

15. Now do not say, nor imagine in your hearts that on account of the love of the Hebrews we did this thing that our ancestors did not command us.

16. But because we saw that it was not their intention and desire to accede to our wishes concerning their daughter as to *our* taking her, except on this condition, so we hearkened to their voices and did this act which you saw, in order to obtain our desire from them.

17. And when we shall have ob-

tained our request from them, we will .hen return to them and do unto them that which you say unto us.

18. We beseech you *then* to wait and tarry until our flesh shall be healed and we *again* become strong, and we will then go together against them, and do unto them that which is in your hearts and in ours.

19. And Dinah the daughter of Jacob heard all these words which Chiddekem and his brothers had spoken, and what Hamor and his son Shechem and the people of their city had answered them.

20. And she hastened and sent one of her maidens, that her father had sent to take care of her in the house of Shechem, to Jacob her father and to her brethern, saying:

21. Thus did Chiddekem and his brothers advise concerning you, and thus did Hamor and Shechem and the people of the city answer them.

22. And when Jacob heard these words he was filled with wrath, and he was indignant at them, and his anger was kindled against them.

23. And Simeon and Levi swore and said, as the Lord liveth, the God of the whole earth, by this time to-morrow, there shall not be a remnant left in the whole city.

24. And twenty young men had concealed themselves who were not circumcised, and these young men fought against Simeon and Levi, and Simeon and Levi killed eighteen of them, and two fled from them and escaped to some lime pits that were in the city, and Simeon and Levi sought for them, but could not find them.

25. And Simeon and Levi continued to go about in the city, and they killed all the people of the city at the edge of the sword, and they left none remaining.

26. And there was a great consternation in the midst of the city, and the cry of the people of the city ascended to heaven, and all the women and children cried aloud.

27. And Simeon and Levi slew all the city; they left not a male remaining in the whole city.

28. And they slew Hamor and Shechem his son at the edge of the sword, and they brought away Dinah from the house of Shechem and they went from there.

29. And the sons of Jacob went and returned, and came upon the slain, and spoiled all their property which was in the city and the field.

30. And whilst they were taking the spoil, three hundred men stood up and threw dust at them and struck them with stones, when Simeon turned to them and he slew them all with the edge of the sword, and Simeon turned before Levi, and came into the city.

31. And they took away their sheep and their oxen and their cattle, and also the remainder of the women and little ones, and they led all these away, and they opened a gate and went out and came unto their father Jacob with vigor.

32. And when Jacob saw all that they had done to the city, and saw the spoil that they took from them, Jacob was very angry at them, and Jacob said unto them, what is this that you have done to me? behold I obtained rest amongst the Canaanitish inhabitants of the land, and none of them meddled with me.

33. And now you have done to make me obnoxious to the inhabitants of the land, amongst the Canaanites and the Perizzites, and I am but of a small number, and they will all assemble against me and slay

me when they hear of your work with their brethren, and I and my household will be destroyed.

34. And Simeon and Levi and all their brothers with them answered their father Jacob and said unto him, behold we live in the land, and shall Shechem do this to our sister? why art thou silent at all that Shechem has done? and shall he deal with our sister as with a harlot in the streets?

35. And the number of women whom Simeon and Levi took captives from the city of Shechem, whom they did not slay, was eighty-five who had not known man.

36. And amongst them was a young damsel of beautiful appearance and well favored, whose name was Bunah, and Simeon took her for a wife, and the number of the males which they took captives and did not slay, was forty-seven men, and the rest they slew.

37. And all the young men and women that Simeon and Levi had taken captives from the city of Shechem, were servants to the sons of Jacob and to their children after them, until the day of the sons of Jacob going forth from the land of Egypt.

38. And when Simeon and Levi had gone forth from the city, the two young men that were left, who had concealed themselves in the city, and did not die amongst the people of the city, rose up, and these young men went into the city and walked about in it, and found the city desolate without a man, and only women weeping, and these young men cried out and said, behold, this is the evil which the sons of Jacob the Hebrew did to this city in their having this day destroyed one of the Canaanitish cities, and were not afraid of their lives of all the land of Canaan.

39. And these men left the city and went to the city of Tapnach, and they came there and told the inhabitants of Tapnach all that had befallen them, and all that the sons of Jacob had done to the city of Shechem.

40. And the information reached Jashub king of Tapnach, and he sent men to the city of Shechem to see those young men, for the king did not believe them in this account, saying, how could two men lay waste such a large town as Shechem?

41. And the messengers of Jashub came back and told him, saying, we came unto the city, and it is destroyed, there is not a man there; only weeping women; neither is any flock or cattle there, for all that was in the city the sons of Jacob took away.

42. And Jashub wondered at this, saying, how could two men do this thing, to destroy so large a city, and not one man able to stand against them?

43. For the like has not been from the days of Nimrod, and not even from the remotest time, has the like taken place; and Jashub, king of Tapnach, said to his people, be courageous and we will go and fight against these Hebrews, and do unto them as they did unto the city, and we will avenge the cause of the people of the city.

44. And Jashub, king of Tapnach, consulted with his counsellors about this matter, and his advisers said unto him, alone thou wilt not prevail over the Hebrews, for they must be powerful to do this work to the whole city.

45. If two of them laid waste the whole city, and no one stood against them, surely if thou wilt go against them, they will all rise against us and destroy us likewise.

46. But *if thou wilt* send to all the kings that surround us, and let them come together, then we will go with them and fight against the sons of Jacob; then wilt thou prevail against them.

47. And Jashub heard the words of his counsellors, and their words pleased him and his people, and he did so; and Jashub king of Tapnach sent to all the kings of the Amorites that surrounded Shechem and Tapnach, saying,

48. Go up with me and assist me, and we will smite Jacob the Hebrew and all his sons, and destroy them from the earth, for thus did he do to the city of Shechem, and do you not know of it?

49. And all the kings of the Amorites heard the evil that the sons of Jacob had done to the city of Shechem, and they were greatly astonished at them.

50. And the seven kings of the Amorites assembled with all their armies, about ten thousand men with drawn swords, and they came to fight against the sons of Jacob; and Jacob heard that the kings of the Amorites had assembled to fight against his sons, and Jacob was greatly afraid, and it distressed him.

51. And Jacob exclaimed against Simeon and Levi, saying, what is this act that you did? why have you injured me, to bring against me all the children of Canaan to destroy me and my household? for I was at rest, even I and my household, and you have done this thing to me, and provoked the inhabitants of the land against me by your proceedings.

52. And Judah answered his father, saying, was it for nought my brothers Simeon and Levi killed all the inhabitants of Shechem? Surely

it was because Shechem had humbled our sister, and transgressed the command of our God to Noah and his children, for Shechem took our sister away by force, and committed adultery *with her*.

53. And Shechem did all this evil and not one of the inhabitants of his city interfered with him, to say, why wilt thou do this? surely for this my brothers went and smote the city, and the Lord delivered it into their hands, because its inhabitants had transgressed the commands of our God. Is it then for nought that they have done all this?

54. And now why art thou afraid or distressed, and why art thou displeased at my brothers, and why is thine anger kindled against them?

55. Surely our God who delivered into their hand the city of Shechem and its people, he will also deliver into our hands all the Canaanitish kings who are coming against us, and we will do unto them as my brothers did unto Shechem.

56. Now be tranquil about them and cast away thy fears, but trust in the Lord our God, and pray unto him to assist us and deliver us, and deliver our enemies into our hands.

57. And Judah called to one of his father's servants, go now and see where those kings, who are coming against us, are situated with their armies.

58. And the servant went and looked far off, and went up opposite mount Sihon, and saw all the camps of the kings standing in the fields, and he returned to Judah and said, behold the kings are situated in the field with all their camps, a people exceedingly numerous, like unto the sand upon the sea shore.

59. And Judah said unto Simeon

and Levi, and unto all his brothers, strengthen yourselves and be sons of valour, for the Lord our God is with us ; do not fear them.

60. Stand forth each man, girt with his weapons of war, his bow and his sword, and we will go and fight against these uncircumcised *men ;* the Lord is our God, he will save us.

61. And they rose up, and each girt on his weapons of war great and small, eleven sons of Jacob, and all the servants of Jacob with them.

62. And all the servants of Isaac who were with Isaac in Hebron, all came to them equipped in all sorts of war instruments, and the sons of Jacob and their servants, *being* one hundred and twelve men, went toward these kings, and Jacob also went with them.

63. And the sons of Jacob sent unto their father Isaac the son of Abraham to Hebron, *the same is* Kireath-arba, saying,

64. Pray we beseech thee for us unto the Lord our God, to protect us from the hands of the Canaanites who are coming against us, and to deliver them into our hands.

65. And Isaac the son of Abraham prayed unto the Lord for his sons, and he said, O Lord God, thou didst promise my father, saying, I will multiply thy seed as the stars of heaven, and thou didst also promise me, and establish thou thy word, now that the kings of Canaan are coming together, to make war with my children because they committed no violence.

66. Now therefore O Lord God, God of the whole earth, pervert I pray thee the counsel of these kings that they may not fight against my sons.

67. And impress the hearts of these kings and their people with the terror of my sons, and bring down their pride, and that they may turn away from my sons.

68. And with thy strong hand and outstretched arm deliver my sons and their servants from them, for power and might are in thy hands to do all this.

69. And the sons of Jacob and their servants went toward these kings, and they trusted in the Lord their God, and whilst they were going, Jacob their father also prayed unto the Lord and said, O Lord God, powerful and exalted God, who hast reigned from days of old, from thence till now *and* forever ;

70. Thou art he who stirreth up wars and causeth them to cease, in thy hand are power and might to exalt and to bring down ; O may my prayer be acceptable *before thee* that thou mayest turn to me with thy mercies, to impress the hearts of these kings and their people with the terror of my sons, and terrify them and their camps, and with thy great kindness deliver all those that trust in thee, for it is thou who canst bring people under us and *reduce* nations under our power.

CHAPTER XXXV.

1. And all the kings of the Amorites came and took their stand in the field to consult with their counsellors what was to be done with the sons of Jacob, for they were still afraid of them, saying, *behold,* two of them slew the whole of the city of Shechem.

2. And the Lord heard the prayers of Isaac and Jacob, and he filled the hearts of all these kings advisers

with great fear and terror, that they unanimously exclaimed,

3. Are you silly this day, *or is* there no understanding in you, that you will fight with the Hebrews, and why will you take a delight in your own destruction this day?

4. Behold two of them came to the city of Shechem without fear or terror, and they killed all the inhabitants of the city, that no man stood up against them, and how will you be able to fight with them all?

5. Surely you know that their God is exceedingly fond of them, and has done mighty things for them, such as have not been done from days of old, and amongst all the gods of nations, there is none can do like unto his mighty *deeds*.

6. Surely he delivered their father Abraham, the Hebrew, from the hand of Nimrod, and from the hand of all his people who had many times sought to slay him.

7. He delivered him also from the fire in which king Nimrod had cast him, and his God delivered him from it.

8. And who else can do the like? surely it was Abraham who slew the five kings of Elam, when they had touched his brother's son who in those days dwelt in Sodom.

9. And took his servant that was faithful in his house and a few of his men, and they pursued the kings of Elam in one night and killed them, and restored to his brother's son all his property which they had taken from him.

10. And surely you know the God of these Hebrews is much delighted with them, and they are also delighted with him, for they know that he delivered them from all their enemies.

11. And behold through his love toward his God, Abraham took his only and precious son and intended to bring him up as a burnt offering to his God, and had it not been for God who prevented him from doing this, he would then have done it through his love to his God.

12. And God saw all his works, and swore unto him, and promised him that he would deliver his sons and all his seed from every trouble that would befall them, because he had done this thing, and through his love to his God stifled his compassion for his child.

13. And have you not heard what their God did to Pharaoh king of Egypt, and to Abimelech king of Gerar, through taking Abraham's wife, who said of her she is my sister, lest they might slay him on account of her, and think of taking her for a wife? and God did unto them and their people all that you heard of.

14. And behold, we ourselves saw with our eyes that Esau, the brother of Jacob, came to him with four hundred men, with the intention of slaying him, for he called to mind that he had taken away from him his father's blessing.

15. And he went to meet him when he came from Syria, to smite the mother with the children, and who delivered him from his hands but his God in whom he trusted? he delivered him from the hand of his brother and also from the hands of his enemies, *and* surely he *again* will protect them.

16. Who does not know that it was their God who inspired them with strength to do to the town of Shechem the evil which you heard of?

17. Could it then be with their own strength that two men could destroy such a large city as Shechem had it not been for their God in whom they trusted? he said and did unto them all this to slay the inhabitants of the city in their city.

18. And can you then prevail over them who have come forth together from your city to fight with the whole of them, even if a thousand times as many more should come to your assistance.

19. Surely you know and understand that you do not come to fight with them, but you come to war with their God who made choice of them, and you have therefore all come this day to be destroyed.

20. Now therefore refrain from this evil which you are endeavoring to bring upon yourselves, and it will be better for you not to go to battle with them, although they are but few in numbers, because their God is with them.

21. And when the kings of the Amorites heard all the words of their advisers, their hearts were filled with terror, and they were afraid of the sons of Jacob and would not fight against them.

22. And they inclined their ears to the words of their advisers, and they listened to all their words, and the words of the counsellors greatly pleased the kings, and they did so.

23. And the kings turned and refrained from the sons of Jacob, for they durst not approach them to *make* war *with them*, for they were greatly afraid of them, and their hearts melted within them from their fear of them.

24. For this proceeded from the Lord to them, for he heard the prayers of his servants Isaac and Jacob,

for they trusted in him; and all these kings returned with their camps on that day, each to his own city, and they did not at that time fight with the sons of Jacob.

25. And the sons of Jacob kept their station that day till evening opposite mount Sihon, and seeing that these kings did not come to. fight against them, the sons of Jacob returned home.

CHAPTER XXXVI

1. At that time the Lord appeared unto Jacob saying, arise, go to Bethel and remain there, and make there an altar to the Lord who appeareth unto thee, who delivered thee and all thy sons from affliction.

2. And Jacob rose up with his sons and all belonging to him, and they went and came to Bethel according to the word of the Lord.

3. And Jacob was ninety nine years old when he went up to Bethel, and Jacob and his sons and all the people that were with him, remained in Bethel in Luz, and he there built an altar to the Lord who appeared unto him, and Jacob and his sons remained in Bethel six months.

4. At that time died Deborah the daughter of Uz, the nurse of Rebecca, who had been with Jacob; and Jacob buried her beneath Bethel under an oak that was there.

5. And Rebecca the daughter of Bethuel, the mother of Jacob, also died at that time in Hebron, the same is Kireath-arba, and she was buried in the cave of Machpelah which Abraham had bought from the children of Heth.

6. And the life of Rebecca was one hundred and thirty three years, and she died and when Jacob heard

that his mother Rebecca was dead he wept bitterly for his mother, and made a great mourning for her, and for Deborah her nurse beneath the oak, and he called the name of that place Allon-bachuth.

7. And Laban the Syrian died in those days, for God smote him because he transgressed the covenant that existed between him and Jacob.

8. And Jacob was a hundred years old when the Lord appeared unto him, and blessed him and called his name Israel, and Rachel the wife of Jacob conceived in those days.

9. And at that time Jacob and all belonging to him journeyed from Bethel to go to his father's house, to Hebron.

10. And whilst they were going on the road, and there was yet but a little way to come to Ephrath, Rachel bare a son and she had hard labour and she died.

11. And Jacob buried her in the way to Ephrath, which is Bethlehem, and he set a pillar upon her grave, *which is there* unto this day; and the days of Rachel were forty five years and she died.

12. And Jacob called the name of his son that was born to him, which Rachel bare unto him, Benjamin, for he was born to him in the land on the right hand.

13. And it was after the death of Rachel, that Jacob pitched his tent in the tent of her hand maid Bilhah.

14. And Reuben was jealous for his mother Leah on account of this, and he was filled with anger, and he rose up in his anger and went and entered the tent of Bilhah and he thence removed his father's bed.

15. At that time the portion of birth right, together with the kingly and priestly offices, was removed from the sons of Reuben, for he had profaned his father's bed, and the birthright was given unto Joseph, the kingly office to Judah, and the priesthood unto Levi, because Reuben had defiled his father's bed.

16. And these are the generations of Jacob who were born to him in Padan-aram, and the sons of Jacob were twelve.

17. The sons of Leah *were* Reuben the first born, and Simeon, Levi, Judah, Issachar, Zebulun, and their sister Dinah; and the sons of Rachel were Joseph and Benjamin.

18. The sons of Zilpah, Leah's handmaid, *were* Gad and Asher, and the sons of Bilhah, Rachel's handmaid, were Dan and Naphtali; these are the sons of Jacob which were born to him in Padan-aram.

19. And Jacob and his sons and all belonging to him journeyed and came to Mamre, *which is* Kircath-arba, that is in Hebron, where Abraham and Isaac sojourned, and Jacob with his sons and all belonging to him, dwelled with his father in Hebron.

20. And his brother Esau and his sons, and all belonging to him went to the land of Seir and dwelt there, and had possessions in the land of Seir, and the children of Esau were fruitful and multiplied exceedingly in the land of Seir.

21. And these are the generations of Esau that were born to him in the land of Canaan, and the sons of Esau were five.

22. And Adah bare to Esau his first born Eliphaz, and she also bare to him Reuel, and Ahlibamah bare to him Jeush, Yaalam and Korah.

23. These are the children of Esau who were born to him in the land of Canaan; and the sons of Eliphaz

the son of Esau were Teman, Omar, Zepho, Gatam, Kenaz and Amalex, and the sons of Reuel were Nachath, Zerach, Shamah and Mizzah.

24. And the sons of Jeush were Timnah, Alvah, Jetheth; and the sons of Yaalam were Alah, Phinor and Kenaz.

25. And the sons of Korah were Teman, Mibzar, Magdiel and Eram; these are the families of the sons of Esau according to their dukedoms in the land of Seir.

26. And these are the names of the sons of Seir the Horite, inhabitants of the land of Seir, Lotan, Shobal, Zibean, Anah, Dishan, Ezer and Dishon, being seven sons.

27. And the children of Lotan were Hori, Heman and their sister Timna, that is Timna who came to Jacob and his sons, and they would not give ear to her, and she went and became a concubine to Eliphaz the son of Esau, and she bare to him Amalek.

28. And the sons of Shobal were Alvan, Manahath, Ebal, Shepho, and Onam, and the sons of Zibeon were Ajah, and Anah, this *was that* Anah who found the Yemim in the wilderness when he fed the asses of Zibeon his father.

29. And whilst he was feeding his father's asses he led them to the wilderness at different times to feed them.

30. And there was a day that he brought them to one of the deserts on the sea shore, opposite the wilderness of the people, and whilst he was feeding them, behold a very heavy storm came from the other side of the sea and rested upon the asses that were feeding there, and they all stood still.

31. And afterward about one hundred and twenty great and terrible animals came out from the wilderness at the other side of the sea, and they all came to the place where the asses were, and they placed themselves there.

32. And those animals, from their middle downward, were in the shape of the children of men, and from their middle upward, some had the likeness of bears, and some the likeness of the keephas, with tails behind them from between their shoulders reaching down to the earth, like the tails of the ducheephath, and these animals came and mounted and rode upon these asses, and led them away, and they went away unto this day.

33. And one of these animals approached Anah and smote him with his tail, and then fled from that place.

34. And when he saw this work he was exceedingly afraid of his life, and he fled and escaped to the city.

35. And he related to his sons and brothers all that had happened to him, and many men went to seek the asses but could not find them, and Anah and his brothers went no more to that place from that day following, for they were greatly afraid of their lives.

36. And the children of Anah the son of Seir, were Dishon and his sister Ahlibamah, and the children of Dishon were Hemdan, Eshban, Ithran and Cheran, and the children of Ezer were Bilhan, Zaavan, and Akan, and the children of Dishan were Uz and Aran.

37. These are the families of the children of Seir the Horite, according to their dukedoms in the land of Seir.

38. And Esau and his children dwelt in the land of Seir the Horite, the inhabitant of the land, and they

had possessions in it and were fruitful and multiplied exceedingly, and Jacob and his children and all belonging to them, dwelt with their father Isaac in the land of Canaan as the Lord had commanded Abraham their father.

CHAPTER XXXVII.

1. And in the one hundred and fifth year of the life of Jacob, that is the ninth year of Jacob's dwelling with his children in the land of Canaan, he came from Padan-aram.

2. And in those days Jacob journeyed with his children from Hebron, and they went and returned to the city of Shechem, they and all belonging to them, and they dwelt there, for the children of Jacob obtained good and fat pasture *land* for their cattle in the city of Shechem, the city of Shechem having then been rebuilt, and there were in it about three hundred men and women.

3. And Jacob and his children and all belonging to him dwelt in the part of the field which Jacob had bought from Hamor the father of Shechem, when he came from Padan-aram before Simeon and Levi had smitten the city.

4. And all those kings of the Canaanites and Amorites that surrounded the city of Shechem, heard that the sons of Jacob had again come to Shechem and dwelt there.

5. And they said, shall the sons of Jacob the Hebrew again come to the city and dwell therein, after that they have smitten its inhabitants and driven them out? shall they now return and also drive out those who are dwelling in the city or slay them?

6. And all the kings of Canaan again assembled, and they came together to make war with Jacob and his sons.

7. And Jashub king of Tapnach sent also to all his neighboring kings, to Elan king of Gaash, and to Ihari king of Shiloh, and to Parathon king of Chazar, and to Susi king of Sarton, and to Laban king of Beth-horan, and to Shabir king of Othnaymah, saying,

8. Come up to me and assist me, and let us smite Jacob the Hebrew and his sons, and all belonging to him, for they are again come to Shechem to possess it and to slay its inhabitants as before;

9. And all these kings assembled together and came with all their camps, a people exceedingly plentiful like the sand upon the sea shore, and they were all opposite to Tapnach.

10. And Jashub king of Tapnach went forth to them with all his army, and he encamped with them opposite to Tapnach without the city, and all these kings they divided into seven divisions, being seven camps against the sons of Jacob.

11. And they sent a declaration* to Jacob and his son, saying, come you all forth to us that we may have an interview together in the plain, and revenge the cause of the men of Shechem whom you slew in their city, and you will now again return to the city of Shechem and dwell therein, and slay its inhabitants as before.

12. And the sons of Jacob heard this and their anger was kindled exceedingly at the words of the kings of Canaan, and ten of the sons of Jacob hastened and rose up, and each of them girt on his weapons of war; and there were one hundred

* Hebrew, a book or record.

and two of their servants with them equipped in battle array.

13. And all these men the sons of Jacob with their servants went toward these kings, and Jacob their father was with them, and they all stood upon the heap of Shechem.

14. And Jacob prayed to the Lord for his sons, and he spread forth his hands to the Lord, and he said, O God, thou art an Almighty God, thou art our father, thou didst form us and we are the works of thine hands; I pray thee deliver my sons through thy mercy from the hand of their enemies, who are this day coming to fight with them, and save them from their hand, for in thy hand is power and might, to save the few from the many.

15. And give unto my sons, thy servants, strength of heart and might to fight with their enemies, to subdue them, and make their enemies fall before them, and let not my sons and their servants die through the hands of the children of Canaan,

16. But if it seemeth good in thine eyes to take away the lives of my sons and their servants, take them in thy great mercy through the hand of thy ministers,* that they may not perish this day by the hands of the kings of the Amorites.

17. And when Jacob ceased praying to the Lord the earth shook from its place, and the sun darkened, and all these kings were terrified and a great consternation seized them.

18. And the Lord hearkened to the prayer of Jacob, and the Lord impressed the hearts of all the kings and their hosts with the terror and awe of the sons of Jacob.

19. For the Lord caused them to hear the voice of chariots, and the

* Angels or messengers.

voice of mighty horses from the sons of Jacob, and the voice of a great army accompanying them.

20. And these kings were seized with great terror at the sons of Jacob, and whilst they were standing in their quarters, behold the sons of Jacob advanced upon them, with one hundred and twelve men, with a great and tremendous shouting.

21. And when the kings saw the sons of Jacob advancing toward them, they were still more panic struck, and they were inclined to retreat˙ from before the sons of Jacob as at first, and not to fight with them.

22. But they did not retreat, saying, it would be a disgrace to us thus twice to retreat from before the Hebrews.

23. And the sons of Jacob came near and advanced against all these kings and their armies, and they saw, and behold it was a very mighty people, *numerous* as the sand of the sea.

24. And the sons of Jacob called unto the Lord and said, help us O Lord, help us and answer us, for we trust in thee, and let us not die by the hands of these uncircumcised men, who this day have come against us.

25. And the sons of Jacob girt on their weapons of war, and they took in their hands each man his shield and his javelin, and they approached to battle.

26. And Judah, the son of Jacob, ran first before his brethren, and ten of his servants with him, and he went toward these kings.

27. And Jashub, king of Tapnach, also came forth first with his army before Judah, and Judah saw Jashub and his army coming toward him, and Judah's wrath was kindled, and

his anger burned within him, and he approached to battle *in which* Judah ventured his life.*

28. And Jashub and all his army were advancing toward Judah, and he was riding upon a very strong and powerful horse, and Jashub was a very valiant man, and covered with iron and brass from head to foot.

29. And whilst he was upon the horse, he shot arrows with both hands from before and behind, as was his manner in all his battles, and he never missed the place to which he aimed his arrows.

30. And when Jashub came to fight with Judah, and was darting many arrows against Judah, the Lord bound the hand of Jashub, and all the arrows that he shot rebounded upon his *own* men.

31. And notwithstanding this, Jashub kept advancing toward Judah, to challenge him with the arrows, but the distance between them was about thirty cubits, and when Judah saw Jashub darting forth his arrows against him, he ran to him with his wrath-excited might.

32. And Judah took up a large stone from the ground, and its weight was sixty shekels, and Judah ran toward Jashub, and with the stone struck him on his shield, that Jashub was stunned with the blow, and fell off from his horse to the ground.

33. And the shield burst asunder out of the hand of Jashub, and through the force of the blow sprang to *the distance* of about fifteen cubits, and the shield fell before the second camp.

34. And the kings that came with Jashub saw at a distance the strength of Judah, the son of Jacob, and what

* The literal translation of this is, " and Judah gave his soul to die."

he had done to Jashub, and they were terribly afraid of Judah.

35. And they assembled near Jashub's camp, *seeing* his confusion, and Judah drew his sword and smote forty-two men of the camp of Jashub, and the whole of Jashub's camp fled before Judah, and no man stood against him, and they left Jashub and fled from him, and Jashub was still prostrate upon the ground.

36. And Jashub seeing that all the men of his camp had fled from him, hastened and rose up with terror against Judah, and stood upon his legs opposite Judah.

37. And Jashub had a single combat with Judah, placing shield toward shield, and Jashub's men all fled, for they were greatly afraid of Judah.

38. And Jashub took his spear in his hand to strike Judah upon his head, but Judah had quickly placed his shield to his head against Jashub's spear, *so* that the shield of Judah received the blow from Jashub's spear, and the shield was split in two.

39. And when Judah saw that his shield was split, he hastily drew his sword and smote Jashub at his ancles, and cut off his feet that Jashub fell upon the ground, and the spear fell from his hand.

40. And Judah hastily picked up Jashub's spear, with which he severed his head and cast it next to his feet.

41. And when the sons of Jacob saw what Judah had done to Jashub, they all ran into the ranks of the other kings, and the sons of Jacob fought with the army of Jashub, and the armies of all the kings that were there.

42. And the sons of Jacob caused fifteen thousand of their men to fall, and they smote them as if smiting at

gourds, and the rest fled for their lives.

43. And Judah was still standing by the body of Jashub, and stripped Jashub of his coat of mail.

44. And Judah also took off the iron and brass that was about Jashub, and behold nine men of the captains of Jashub came alone to fight against Judah.

45. And Judah hastened and took up a stone from the ground, and with it smote one *of them* upon the head, and his skull was fractured, and the body also fell from the horse to the ground.

46. And the eight captains that remained, seeing the strength of Judah, were greatly afraid and they fled, and Judah with his ten men pursued them, and they overtook them and slew them.

47. And the sons of Jacob were still smiting the armies of the kings, and they slew many of them, but those kings daringly kept their stand with their captains, and did not retreat from their places, and they exclaimed against *those* of their armies that fled from before the sons of Jacob, but none would listen to them, for they were afraid of their lives lest they should die.

48. And all the sons of Jacob, after having smitten the armies of the kings, returned and came before Judah, and Judah was still slaying the eight captains of Jashub, and stripping off their garments.

49. And Levi saw Elon, king of Gaash, advancing toward him, with his fourteen captains to smite him, but Levi did not know it *for certain.*

50. And Elon with his captains approached nearer, and Levi looked back and saw that battle was given him in the rear, and Levi ran with twelve of his servants, and they went and slew Elon and his captains with the edge of the sword.

CHAPTER XXXVIII.

1. And Ihuri king of Shiloh came up to assist Elon, and he approached Jacob, when Jacob drew his bow that was in his hand and with an arrow struck Ihuri which caused his death.

2. And when Ihuri king of Shiloh was dead, the four remaining kings fled from their station with the rest of the captains, and they endeavored to retreat, saying, we have no more strength with the Hebrews after their having killed the three kings and their captains who were more powerful than we are.

3. And when the sons of Jacob saw that the remaining kings had removed from their station, they pursued them, and Jacob also came from the heap of Shechem from the place where he was standing, and they went after the kings and they approached them with their servants.

4. And the kings and the captains with the rest of their armies, seeing that the sons of Jacob approached them, were afraid of their lives and fled till they reached the city of Chazar.

5. And the sons of Jacob pursued them to the gate of the city of Chazar, and they smote a great smiting amongst the kings and their armies, about four thousand men, and whilst they were smiting the army of the kings Jacob was occupied with his bow confining himself to smiting the kings, and he slew them all.

6. And he slew Parathon king of Chazar at the gate of the city of Chazar, and he afterward smote Susi

king of Sarton, and Laban king of Bethchorin, and Shabir king of Machnaymah, and he slew them all with arrows, an arrow to each of them, and they died.

7. And the sons of Jacob seeing that all the kings were dead and that they were broken up and retreating, continued to carry on the battle with the armies of the kings opposite the gate of Chazar, and they still smote about four hundred of their men.

8. And three men of the servants of Jacob fell in that battle, and when Judah saw that three of his servants had died, it grieved him greatly, and his anger burned within him against the Amorites.

9. And all the men that remained of the armies of the kings were greatly afraid of their lives, and they ran and broke the gate of the walls of the city of Chazar, and they all entered the city for safety.

10. And they concealed themselves in the midst of the city of Chazar, for the city of Chazar was very large and extensive, and when all these armies had entered the city, the sons of Jacob ran after them to the city.

11. And four mighty men, experienced in battle, went forth from the city and stood against the entrance of the city, with drawn swords and spears in their hands, and they placed themselves opposite the sons of Jacob, and would not suffer them to enter the city.

12. And Naphtali ran and came between them and with his sword smote two of them, and cut off their heads at one *stroke*.

13. And he turned to the other two, and behold they had fled, and he pursued them, overtook them, smote them and slew them.

14. And the sons of Jacob came to the city and saw, and behold there was another wall to the city, and they sought for the gate of the wall and could not find it, and Judah sprang upon the top of the wall, and Simeon and Levi followed him and they all three descended from the wall into the city.

15. And Simeon and Levi slew all the men who ran for safety into the city, and also the inhabitants of the city with their wives and little ones, they slew with the edge of the sword, and the cries of the city ascended up to heaven.

16. And Dan and Naphtali sprang upon the wall to see what *caused* the noise of lamentation, for the sons of Jacob felt anxious about their brothers, and they heard the inhabitants of the city speaking with weeping and supplications, saying, take all that we possess in the city and go away, only do not put us to death.

17. And when Judah, Simeon and Levi, had ceased smiting the inhabitants of the city, they ascended the wall and called to Dan and Naphtali, who were upon the wall, and to the rest of their brothers, and Simeon and Levi informed them of the entrance into the city, and all the sons of Jacob came to fetch the spoil.

18. And the sons of Jacob took the spoil of the city of Chazar, the flocks and herds, and the property, and they took all that could be captured and went away that day from the city.

19. And on the next day the sons of Jacob went to Sarton, for they heard that the men of Sarton who had remained in the city were assembling to fight with them for having slain their king, and Sarton was a very high and fortified city, and it

had a deep rampart surrounding the city.

20. And the pillar of the rampart was about fifty cubits and its breadth forty cubits, and there was no place for a man to enter the city on account of the rampart, and the sons of Jacob saw the rampart of the city and they sought an entrance in it but could not find it.

21. For the entrance to the city was at the rear, and every man that wished to come into the city came by that road and went round the whole city, and he afterward entered the city.

22. And the sons of Jacob seeing they could not find the way into the city, their anger was kindled greatly, and the inhabitants of the city seeing that the sons of Jacob were coming to them were greatly afraid of them, for they had heard of their strength and what they had done to Chazar.

23. And the inhabitants of the city of Sarton could not go out toward the sons of Jacob after having assembled in the city to fight against them, *lest* they might thereby get into the city, but when they saw that they were coming toward them, they were greatly afraid of them, for they had heard of their strength and what they had done to Chazar.

24. So the inhabitants of Sarton speedily took away the bridge of the road of the city, from its place, before the sons of Jacob came, and they brought it into the city.

25. And the sons of Jacob came and sought the way into the city, and could not find *it*, and the inhabitants of the city went up to the top of the wall, and saw, and behold the sons of Jacob were seeking an entrance into the city.

26. And the inhabitants of the city reproached the sons of Jacob from the top of the wall, and they cursed them, and the sons of Jacob heard the reproaches and they were greatly incensed, and their anger burned within them.

27. And the sons of Jacob were provoked at them, and they all rose and sprang over the rampart with the force of their strength, and through their might passed the forty cubits' breadth of the rampart.

28. And when they had passed the rampart they stood under the wall of the city, and they found all the gates of the city enclosed with iron doors.

29. And the sons of Jacob came near to break open the doors of the gates of the city, and the inhabitants did not let them, for from the top of the wall they were casting stones and arrows upon them.

30. And the number of the people that were upon the wall was about four hundred men, and when the sons of Jacob saw that the men of the city would not let them open the gates of the city, they sprang and ascended the top of the wall, and Judah went up first to the east part of the city.

31. And Gad and Asher went up after him to the west corner of the city, and Simeon and Levi to the north, and Dan and Reuben to the south.

32. And the men who were on the top of the wall, the inhabitants of the city, seeing that the sons of Jacob were coming up to them, they all fled from the wall, descended into the city, and concealed themselves in the midst of the city.

33. And Issachar and Naphtali that remained under the wall ap-

proached and broke the gates of the city, and kindled a fire at the gates of the city, that the iron melted, and all the sons of Jacob came into the city, they and all their men, and they fought with the inhabitants of the city of Sarton, and smote them with the edge of the sword, and no man stood up before them.

34. And about two hundred men fled from the city, and they all went and hid themselves in a certain tower in the city, and Judah pursued them to the tower and he broke down the tower, which fell upon the men, and they all died.

35. And the sons of Jacob went up the road of the roof of that tower, and they saw, and behold there was another strong and high tower at a distance in the city, and the top of it reached to heaven,* and the sons of Jacob hastened and descended, and went with all their men to that tower, and found it filled with about three hundred men, women and little ones.

36. And the sons of Jacob smote a great smiting amongst those men in the tower, and they ran away and fled from them.

37. And Simeon and Levi pursued them, when twelve mighty and valiant men came out to them from the place where they had concealed themselves.

38. And those twelve men maintained a strong battle against Simeon and Levi, and Simeon and Levi could not prevail over them, and those valiant men broke the shields of Simeon and Levi, and one of them struck at Levi's head with his sword, when Levi hastily placed his hand to his head, for he was afraid of the

* This is a figurative expression in the Hebrew, to express an exceeding great height.

sword, and the sword struck Levi's hand, and it wanted but little to the hand of Levi being cut off.

39. And Levi seized the sword of the valiant man in his hand, and took it forcibly from the man, and with it he struck at the head of the powerful man, and he severed his head.

40. And eleven men approached to fight with Levi, for they saw that one of them was killed, and the sons of Jacob fought, but the sons of Jacob could not prevail over them, for those men were very powerful.

41. And the sons of Jacob seeing that they could not prevail over them, Simeon gave a loud and tremendous shriek, and the eleven powerful men were stunned at the voice of Simeon's shrieking.

42. And Judah at a distance knew the voice of Simeon's shouting, and Naphtali and Judah ran with their shields to Simeon and Levi, and found them fighting with those powerful men, unable to prevail over them as their shields were broken.

43. And Naphtali saw that the shields of Simeon and Levi were broken, and he took two shields from his servants and brought them to Simeon and Levi.

44. And Simeon, Levi and Judah on that day fought *all* three against the eleven mighty men until the time of sunset, but they could not prevail over them.

45. And this was told unto Jacob, and he was sorely grieved, and he prayed unto the Lord, and he and Naphtali his son went against these mighty men.

46. And Jacob approached and drew his bow, and came nigh unto the mighty men, and slew three of their men with the bow, and the remaining eight turned back, and be-

hold, the war waged against them in the front and rear, and they were greatly afraid of their lives, and could not stand before the sons of Jacob, and they fled from before them.

47. And in their flight they met Dan and Asher coming toward them, and they suddenly fell upon them, and fought with them, and slew two of them, and Judah and his brothers pursued them, and smote the remainder of them, and slew them.

48. And all the sons of Jacob returned and walked about the city, searching if they could find any men, and they found about twenty young men in a cave in the city, and Gad and Asher smote them all, and Dan and Naphtali lighted upon the rest of the men who had fled and escaped from the second tower, and they smote them all.

49. And the sons of Jacob smote all the inhabitants of the city of Sarton, but the women and little ones they left in the city and did not slay them.

50. And all the inhabitants of the city of Sarton were powerful men, one of them would pursue a thousand, and two *of them* would not flee from ten thousand of the rest of men.

51. And the sons of Jacob slew all the inhabitants of the city of Sarton with the edge of the sword, that no man stood up against them, and they left the women in the city.

52. And the sons of Jacob took all the spoil of the city, and captured what they desired, and they took flocks and herds and property from the city, and the sons of Jacob did unto Sarton and its inhabitants as they had done to Chazar and its inhabitants, and they turned and went away.

CHAPTER XXXIX.

1. And when the sons of Jacob went from the city of Sarton, they had gone about two hundred cubits when they met the inhabitants of Tapnach coming toward them, for they went out to fight with them, because they had smitten the king of Tapnach and all his men.

2. So all that remained in the city of Tapnach come out to fight with the sons of Jacob, and they thought to retake from them the booty and the spoil which they had captured from Chazar and Sarton.

3. And the rest of the men of Tapnach fought with the sons of Jacob in that place, and the sons of Jacob smote them, and they fled before them, and they pursued them to the city of Arbelan, and they all fell before the sons of Jacob.

4. And the sons of Jacob returned and came to Tapnach, to take away the spoil of Tapnach, and when they came to Tapnach they heard that the people of Arbelan had gone out to meet them to save the spoil of their brethren, and the sons of Jacob left ten of their men in Tapnach to plunder the city, and they went out toward the people of Arbelan.

5. And the men of Arbelan went out with their wives to fight with the sons of Jacob, for their wives were experienced in battle, and they went out, about four hundred men and women.

6. And all the sons of Jacob shouted with a loud voice, and they all ran toward the inhabitants of Arbelan, and with a great and tremendous voice.

7. And the inhabitants of Arbelan heard the noise of the shouting of the sons of Jacob, and their roaring like

the noise of lions and like the roaring of the sea and its waves.

8. And fear and terror possessed their hearts on account of the sons of Jacob, and they were terribly afraid of them, and they retreated and fled before them into the city, and the sons of Jacob pursued them to the gate of the city, and they came upon them in the city.

9. And the sons of Jacob fought with them in the city, and all their women were *engaged* in slinging against the sons of Jacob, and the combat was very severe amongst them *the whole* of that day till evening.

10. And the sons of Jacob could not prevail over them, and the sons of Jacob had almost perished in that battle, and the sons of Jacob cried unto the Lord and greatly gained strength toward evening, and the sons of Jacob smote all the inhabitants of Arbelan by the edge of the sword, men, women and little ones.

11. And also the remainder of the people who had fled from Sarton, the sons of Jacob smote them in Arbelan, and the sons of Jacob did unto Arbelan and Tapnach as they had done to Chazar and Sarton, and when the women saw that all their men were dead, they went upon the roofs of the city and smote the sons of Jacob by *showering down* stones like rain.

12. And the sons of Jacob hastened and came into the city and seized all the women and smote them with the edge of the sword, and the sons of Jacob captured all the spoil and booty, flocks and herds and cattle.

13. And the sons of Jacob did unto Machnaymah as they had done to Tapnach, to Chazar and to Shiloh, and they turned from there and went away.

14. And on the fifth day the sons of Jacob heard that the people of Gaash had gathered against them to battle, because they had slain their king and their captains, for there had been fourteen captains in the city of Gaash, and the sons of Jacob had slain them all *in the first battle*.

15. And the sons of Jacob that day girt on their weapons of war, and they marched to battle against the inhabitants of Gaash, and in Gaash there was a strong and mighty people of the people of the Amorites, and Gaash was the strongest and best fortified city of all the cities of the Amorites, and it had three walls.

16. And the sons of Jacob came to Gaash and they found the gates of the city locked, and about five hundred men standing at the top of the outermost wall, and a people numerous as the sand upon the sea shore were in ambush for the sons of Jacob from without the city at the rear thereof.

17. And the sons of Jacob approached to open the gates of the city, and whilst they were drawing nigh, behold those who were in ambush at the rear of the city came *forth* from their places and surrounded the sons of Jacob.

18. And the sons of Jacob were enclosed between the people of Gaash, and the battle was both to their front and rear, and all the men that were upon the wall, were casting from the wall upon them, arrows and stones.

19. And Judah, seeing that the men of Gaash were getting too heavy for them, gave a most piercing and tremendous shriek and all the men of Gaash were terrified at the voice of Judah's cry, and men fell from the wall at *his* powerful shriek, and all

those that were from without and within the city were greatly afraid of their lives.

20. And the sons of Jacob still came nigh to break the doors of the city, when the men of Gaash threw stones and arrows upon them from the top of the wall, and made them flee from the gate.

21. And the sons of Jacob returned against the men of Gaash who were with them from without the city, and they smote them terribly, as striking against gourds, and they could not stand against the sons of Jacob, for fright and terror had seized them at the shriek of Judah.

22. And the sons of Jacob slew all those men *who were* from without the city, and the sons of Jacob still drew nigh to effect an entrance into the city, and to fight under the city walls, but they could not for all the inhabitants of Gaash who remained in the city had surrounded the walls of Gaash in every direction, so that the sons of Jacob were unable to approach the city to fight with them.

23. And as the sons of Jacob came nigh to one corner to fight under the wall, the inhabitants of Gaash threw arrows and stones upon them like *showers* of rain, and they fled from under the wall.

24. And the people of Gaash who were upon the wall, seeing that the sons of Jacob could not prevail over them from under the wall, reproached the sons of Jacob in these words; saying,

25. What is the matter with you in the battle that you cannot prevail? can you then do unto the mighty city of Gaash and its inhabitants as you did to the cities of the Amorites that were not so powerful? Surely to those weak ones amongst us you did those things, and slew them in the entrance of the city, for they had no strength when they were terrified at the sound of your shouting.

26. And will you now *then* be able to fight in this place? Surely here you will all die, and we will avenge the cause of those cities that you have laid waste.

27. And the inhabitants of Gaash greatly reproached the sons of Jacob and reviled* them with their gods, and continued to cast arrows and stones upon them from the wall.

28. And Judah and his brothers heard the words of the inhabitants of Gaash and their anger was greatly roused, and Judah was jealous of his God in this matter, and he called out and said, O Lord, help, send help to us and our brothers.

29. And he ran at a distance with all his might, with his drawn sword in his hand, and he sprang from the earth and by dint of his strength, mounted the wall, and his sword fell from his hand.

30. And Judah shouted upon the wall, and all the men that were upon the wall were terrified, and some of them fell from the wall into the city and died, and those who were yet upon the wall, when they saw Judah's strength, they were greatly afraid and fled for their lives into the city for safety.

31. And some were emboldened to fight with Judah upon the wall, and they came nigh to slay him when they saw there was no sword in Judah's hand, and they thought of

* They reviled the God of the sons of Jacob, as inferred from the next verse, " and Judah was jealous of his God," as יקללהם באלהיהם might bear the translation, and they reviled or cursed them by their own gods, or using the names of their idols in their execrations.

casting him from the wall to his brothers, and twenty men of the city came up to assist them, and they surrounded Judah and they all shouted over him, and approached him with drawn swords, and they terrified Judah, and Judah cried out to his brothers from the wall.

32. And Jacob and his sons drew the bow from under the wall, and smote three of the men that were upon the top of the wall, and Judah continued to cry and he exclaimed, O Lord help us, O Lord deliver us, and he cried out with a loud voice upon the wall, and the cry was heard at a great distance.

33. And after *this* cry he again repeated to shout, and all the men who surrounded Judah on the top of the wall were terrified, and they each threw his sword from his hand at the sound of Judah's shouting and his tremor, and fled.

34. And Judah took the swords which had fallen from their hands, and Judah fought with them and slew twenty of their men upon the wall.

35. And about eighty men and women still ascended the wall from the city and they all surrounded Judah, and the Lord impressed the fear of Judah in their hearts, that they were unable to approach him.

36. And Jacob and all who were with him drew the bow from under the wall, and they slew ten men upon the wall, and they fell below the wall, before Jacob and his sons.

37. And the people upon the wall seeing that twenty of their men had fallen, they still ran toward Judah with drawn swords, but they could not approach him for they were greatly terrified at Judah's strength.

38. And one of their mighty men whose name was Arud approached to strike Judah upon the head with his sword, when Judah hastily put his shield to his head, and the sword hit the shield, and it was split in two.

39. And this mighty man after he had struck Judah ran for his life, at the fear of Judah, and his feet slipped upon the wall and he fell amongst the sons of Jacob *who were* below the wall, and the sons of Jacob smote him and slew him.

40. And Judah's head pained him from the blow of the powerful man, and Judah had nearly died from it.

41. And Judah cried out upon the wall owing to the pain *produced* by the blow, when Dan heard him, and his anger burned within him, and he also rose up and went at a distance and ran and sprang from the earth and mounted the wall with his wrath excited strength.

42. And when Dan came upon the wall near unto Judah all the men upon the wall fled, who had stood against Judah, and they went up to the second wall, and they threw arrows and stones upon Dan and Judah from the second wall, and endeavored to drive them from the wall.

43. And the arrows and stones struck Dan and Judah, and they had nearly been killed upon the wall, and wherever Dan and Judah fled upon the wall, they were attacked with arrows and stones from the second wall.

44. And Jacob and his sons were still at the entrance of the city below the first wall, and they were not able to draw their bow against the inhabitants of the city, as they could not be seen by them, being upon the second wall.

45. And Dan and Judah when they could *no longer* bear the stones and arrows that fell upon them from the

second wall, they both sprang upon the second wall near the people of the city, and when the people of the city who were upon the second wall saw that Dan and Judah had come to them upon the second wall, they all cried out and descended below between the walls.

46. And Jacob and his sons heard the noise of the shouting from the people of the city, and they were still at the entrance of the city, and they were anxious about Dan and Judah who were not seen by them, they being upon the second wall.

47. And Naphtali went up with his wrath excited might and sprang upon the first wall to see what caused the noise of shouting which they had heard in the city, and Issachar and Zebulun drew nigh to break the doors of the city, and they opened the gates of the city and came into the city.

48. And Naphtali leaped from the first wall to the second, and came to assist his brothers, and the inhabitants of Gaash who were upon the wall, seeing that Naphtali was the third who had come up to assist his brothers, they all fled and descended into the city, and Jacob and his sons and all their young men came into the city to them.

49. And Judah and Dan and Naphtali descended from the wall into the city and pursued the inhabitants of the city, and Simeon and Levi were from without the city and knew not that the gate was opened, and they went up from there to the wall and came down to their brothers into the city.

50. And the inhabitants of the city had all descended into the city, and the sons of Jacob came to them in different directions and the battle waged against them from the front and the rear, and the sons of Jacob smote them terribly and slew about twenty thousand of them men and women, not one of them could stand up against the sons of Jacob.

51. And the blood *flowed* plentifully in the city, and it was like a brook of water, and the blood flowed like a brook to the outer part of the city, and reached the desert of Bethchorin.

52. And the people of Bethchorin saw at a distance the blood flowing from the city of Gaash, and about seventy men from amongst them ran to see the blood, and they came to the place where the blood was.

53. And they followed the track of the blood and came to the wall of the city of Gaash, and they saw the blood issue from the city, and they heard the voice of crying from the inhabitants of Gaash, for it ascended unto heaven, and the blood was continuing to flow abundantly like a brook of water.

54. And all the sons of Jacob were still smiting the inhabitants of Gaash, and *were engaged* in slaying them till evening, about twenty thousand men and women, and the people of Chorin said, surely this is the work of the Hebrews, for they are still carrying on war in all the cities of the Amorites.

55. And those people hastened and ran to Bethchorin, and each took his weapons of war, and they cried out to all the inhabitants of Bethchorin, who also girt on their weapons of war to go and fight with the sons of Jacob.

56. And when the sons of Jacob had done smiting the inhabitants of Gaash, they walked about the city to strip all the slain, and coming in the innermost part of the city and farther

on they met three very powerful men, and there was no sword in their hand.

57. And the sons of Jacob came up to the place *where they were*, and the powerful men ran away, and one of them had taken Zebulun, who he saw was a young lad and of short stature, and with his might dashed him to the ground.

58. And Jacob ran to him with his sword and Jacob smote him below his loins with the sword, and cut him in two, and the body fell upon Zebulun.

59. And the second one approached and seized Jacob to fell him to the ground, and Jacob turned to him and shouted to him, whilst Simeon and Levi ran and smote him on the hips with the sword and felled him to the ground.

60. And the powerful man rose up from the ground with wrath-excited might, and Judah came to him before he had gained his footing, and struck him upon the head with the sword, and his head was split and he died.

61. And the third powerful man, seeing that his companions were killed, ran from before the sons of Jacob, and the sons of Jacob pursued him in the city; and whilst the powerful man was fleeing he found one of the swords of the inhabitants of the city, and he picked it up and turned to the sons of Jacob and fought them with that sword.

62. And the powerful man ran to Judah to strike him upon the head with the sword, and there was no shield in the hand of Judah; and whilst he *was aiming* to strike him, Naphtali hastily took his shield and put it to Judah's head, and the sword of the powerful man hit the shield of Naphtali and Judah escaped the sword.

63. And Simeon and Levi ran upon the powerful man with their swords and struck at him forcibly with their swords, and the two swords entered the body of the powerful man and divided it in two, length-wise.

64 And the sons of Jacob smote the three mighty men at that time, together with all the inhabitants of Gaash, and the day was about to decline.

65. And the sons of Jacob walked about Gaash and took all the spoil of the city, even the little ones and women they did not suffer to live, and the sons of Jacob did unto Gaash as they had done to Sarton and Shiloh.

CHAPTER XL.

1. And the sons of Jacob led away all the spoil of Gaash, and went out of the city by night.

2. They were going out marching toward the castle of Bethchorin, and the inhabitants of Bethchorin were going to the castle to meet them, and on that night the sons of Jacob fought with the inhabitants of Bethchorin, in the castle of Bethchorin.

3. And all the inhabitants of Bethchorin were mighty men, one of them would not flee from before a thousand men, and they fought on that night upon the castle, and their shouts were heard on that night from afar, and the earth quaked at their shouting.

4. And all the sons of Jacob were afraid of those men, as they were not accustomed to right in the dark, and they were greatly confounded, and the sons of Jacob cried unto the

Lord, saying, give help to us O Lord, deliver us that we may not die by the hands of these uncircumcised men.

5. And the Lord hearkened to the voice of the sons of Jacob, and the Lord caused great terror and confusion to seize the people of Bethchorin, and they fought amongst themselves the one with the other in the darkness of night, and smote each other in great numbers.

6. And the sons of Jacob, knowing that the Lord had brought a spirit of perverseness amongst those men, and that they fought each man with his neighbor, went forth from among the bands of the people of Bethchorin and went as far as the descent of the castle of Bethchorin, and farther, and they tarried there securely with their young men on that night.

7. And the people of Bethchorin fought the whole night, one man with his brother, and the other with his neighbor, and they cried out in every direction upon the castle, and their cry was heard at a distance, and the whole earth shook at their voice, for they were powerful above all the people of the earth.

8. And all the inhabitants of the cities of the Canaanites, the Hittites, the Amorites, the Hivites and all the kings of Canaan, and also those who were on the other side of the Jordan, heard the noise of the shouting on that night.

9. And they said, surely these are the battles of the Hebrews who are fighting against the seven cities; who came nigh unto them, and who can stand against those Hebrews?

10. And all the inhabitants of the cities of the Canaanites, and all those who were on the other side of the Jordan, were greatly afraid of the sons of Jacob, for they said, behold the same will be done to us as was done to those cities, for who can stand against their mighty strength?

11. And the cries of the Chorinites were very great on that night, and continued to increase, and they smote each other till morning, and numbers of them were killed.

12. And the morning appeared, and all the sons of Jacob rose up at day break and went up to the castle, and they smote those who remained of the Chorinites in a terrible manner, and they were all killed in the castle.

13. And the sixth day appeared, and all the inhabitants of Canaan saw at a distance all the people of Bethchorin lying dead in the castle of Bethchorin, and strewed about as the carcasses of lambs and goats.

14. And the sons of Jacob led all the spoil which they had captured from Gaash and went to Bethchorin, and they found the city full of people like the sand of the sea, and they fought with them, and the sons of Jacob smote *them* there till evening time.

15. And the sons of Jacob did unto Bethchorin as they had done to Gaash and Tapnach, and as they had done to Chazar, to Sarton and to Shiloh.

16. And the sons of Jacob took with them the spoil of Bethchorin and all the spoil of the cities, and on that day they went home to Shechem.

17. And the sons of Jacob came home to the city of Shechem, and they remained without the city, and they then rested there from the war, and tarried there all night.

18. And all their servants together with all the spoil that they had taken

from the cities, they left without the city, and they did not enter the city, for they said, peradventure there may be yet more fighting against us, and they may come to besiege us in Shechem.

19. And Jacob and his sons and their servants remained on that and the next day in the portion of the field which Jacob had purchased from Hamor for five shekels, and all that they had captured was with them.

20. And all the booty which the sons of Jacob had captured, was in the portion of the field, immense as the sand upon the sea shore.

21. And the inhabitants of the land observed them from afar, and all the inhabitants of the land were afraid of the sons of Jacob who had done this thing, for no king from the days of old had ever done the like.

22. And the seven kings of the Canaanites resolved to make peace with the sons of Jacob, for they were greatly afraid of their lives, on account of the sons of Jacob.

23. And on that day, being the seventh day, Japhia king of Hebron sent secretly to the king of Ai, and to the king of Gibeon, and to the king of Shalem, and to the king of Adulam, and to the king of Lachish, and to the king of Chazar, and to all the Canaanitish kings who were under their subjection, saying,

24. Go up with me, and come to me that we may go to the sons of Jacob, and I will make peace with them, and form a treaty *with them,* lest all your lands be destroyed by the swords of the sons of Jacob, as they did to Shechem and the cities around it, as you have heard and seen.

25. And when you come to me, do not come with many men, but let every king bring his three head captains, and every captain bring three of his officers.

26. And come all of you to Hebron, and we will go together to the sons of Jacob, and supplicate them that they shall form a treaty of peace with us.

27. And all those kings did as the king of Hebron had sent to them, for they were all under his counsel and command, and all the kings of Canaan assembled to go to the sons of Jacob, to make peace with them; and the sons of Jacob returned and went to the portion of the field that was in Shechem, for they did not put confidence in the kings of the land.

28. And the sons of Jacob returned and remained in the portion of the field ten days, and no one came to make war with them.

29. And when the sons of Jacob saw that there was no appearance of war, they all assembled and went to the city of Shechem, and the sons of Jacob remained in Shechem.

30. And at the expiration of forty days, all the kings of the Amorites assembled from all their places and came to Hebron, to Japhia, king of Hebron.

31. And the number of kings that came to Hebron, to make peace with the sons of Jacob, was twenty-one kings, and the number of captains that came with them was sixty-nine, and their men were one hundred and eighty-nine, and all these kings and their men rested by mount Hebron.

32. And the king of Hebron went out with his three captains and nine men, and these kings resolved to go to the sons of Jacob to make peace.

33. And they said unto the king of Hebron, go thou before us with thy men, and speak for us unto the

sons of Jacob, and we will come after thee and confirm thy words, and
the king of Hebron did so.

34. And the sons of Jacob heard
that all the kings of Canaan had gathered together and rested in Hebron,
and the sons of Jacob sent four of
their servants as spies, saying, go
and spy these kings, and search and
examine their men whether they are
few or many, and if they are but few
in number, number them all and
come back.

35. And the servants of Jacob
went secretly to these kings, and did
as the sons of Jacob had commanded
them, and on that day they came
back to the sons of Jacob, and said
unto them, we came unto those kings,
and they are but few in number, and
we numbered them all, and behold,
they were two hundred and eighty-
eight, kings and men.

36. And the sons of Jacob said,
they are but few in number, *therefore* we will not all go out to them ;
and in the morning the sons of Jacob
rose up and chose sixty-two of their
men, and ten of the sons of Jacob
went with them ; and they girt on
their weapons of war, for they said,
they are coming to make war with
us, for they knew not that they were
coming to make peace with them.

37. And the sons of Jacob went
with their servants to the gate of Shechem, toward those kings, and their
father Jacob was with them.

38. And when they had come forth,
behold, the king of Hebron and his
three captains and nine men with
him were coming along the road
against the sons of Jacob, and the
sons of Jacob lifted up their eyes,
and saw at a distance *Japhia*, king
of Hebron, with his captains, coming
toward them, and the sons of Jacob

took their stand at the place of the
gate of Shechem, and did not proceed.

39. And the king of Hebron continued to advance, he and his captains, until he came nigh to the sons
of Jacob, and he and his captains
bowed down to them to the ground,
and the king of Hebron sat with his
captains before Jacob and his sons.

40. And the sons of Jacob said
unto him, what has befallen thee, O
king of Hebron ? why hast thou come
to us this day ? what dost thou require from us ? and the king of Hebron said unto Jacob, I beseech thee
my lord, all the kings of the Canaanites have this day come to make
peace with you.

41. And the sons of Jacob heard
the words of the king of Hebron,
and they would not consent to his
proposals, for the sons of Jacob had
no faith in him, for they imagined
that the king of Hebron had spoken
deceitfully to them.

42. And the king of Hebron knew
from the words of the sons of Jacob,
that they did not believe his words,
and the king of Hebron approached
nearer to Jacob, and said unto him,
I beseech thee my lord *to be assured*
that all these kings have come to you
on peaceable terms, for they have
not come with all their men, neither
did they bring their weapons of war
with them, for they have come to
seek peace from my lord and his
sons.

43. And the sons of Jacob answered the king of Hebron, saying, send
thou to all these kings, and if thou
speakest truth unto us, let them each
come singly before us, and if they
come unto us unarmed, we shall then
know that they seek peace from us.

44. And Japhia, king of Hebron,

sent one of his men to the kings, and they all came before the sons of Jacob, and bowed down to them to the ground, and these kings sat before Jacob and his sons, and they spoke unto them, saying,

45. We have heard all that you did unto the kings of the Amorites with your sword and exceedingly mighty arm, so that no man could stand up before you, and we were afraid of you for the sake of our lives, lest it should befall us as it did to them.

46. So we have come unto you to form a treaty of peace between us, and now therefore contract with us a covenant of peace and truth, that you will not meddle with us, inasmuch as we have not meddled with you.

47. And the sons of Jacob knew that they had really come to seek peace from them, and the sons of Jacob listened to them, and formed a covenant with them.

48. And the sons of Jacob swore unto them that they would not meddle with them, and all the kings of the Canaanites swore also to them, and the sons of Jacob made them tributary from that day forward.

49. And after this all the captains of these kings came with their men before Jacob, with presents in their hands for Jacob and his sons, and they bowed down to him to the ground.

50. And these kings *then* urged the sons of Jacob and begged of them to return all that spoil they had captured from. the seven cities of the Amorites, and the sons of Jacob did so, and they returned all that they had captured, the women, the little ones, the cattle and all the spoil which they had taken, and they sent them off, and they went away each to his city.

51. And all these kings again bowed down to the sons of Jacob, and they sent or brought them many gifts in those days, and the sons of Jacob sent off these kings and their men, and they went peaceably away from them to their cities, and the sons of Jacob also returned to their home, to Shechem.

52. And there was peace from that day forward between the sons of Jacob and the kings of the Canaanites, until the children of Israel came to inherit the land of Canaan.

CHAPTER XLI.

1. And at the revolution of the year the sons of Jacob journeyed from Shechem, and they came to Hebron, to their father Isaac, and they dwelt there, but their flocks and herds they fed daily in Shechem, for there was there in those days good and fat pasture, and Jacob and his sons and all their household dwelt in the valley of Hebron.

2. And it was in those days, in that year, being the hundred and sixth year of the life of Jacob, in the tenth year of Jacob's coming from Padan-aram, that Leah the wife of Jacob died ; she was fifty one years old when she died in Hebron.

3. And Jacob and his sons buried her in the cave of the field of Machpelah, which is in Hebron, which Abraham had bought from the children of Heth, for the possession of a burial place.

4. And the sons of Jacob dwelt with their father in the valley of Hebron, and all the inhabitants of the land knew their strength, and their fame *went* throughout the land.

5. And Joseph the son of Jacob,

and his brother Benjamin, the sons of Rachel the wife of Jacob, were yet young in those days, and did not go out with their brethren during their battles in all the cities of the Amorites.

6. And when Joseph saw the strength of his brethren, and their greatness, he praised them and extolled them, but he ranked himself greater than them, and extolled himself above them ; and Jacob, his father, also loved him more than any of his sons, for he was a son of his old age, and through his love toward him, he made him a coat of many colors.

7. And when Joseph saw that his father loved him more than his brethren, he continued to exalt himself above his brethren, and he brought unto his father evil reports concerning them.

8. And the sons of Jacob seeing the whole of Joseph's conduct toward them, and that their father loved him more than any of them, they hated him and could not speak peaceably to him all the days.

9. And Joseph was seventeen years old, and he was still magnifying himself above his brethren, and thought of raising himself above them.

10. At that time he dreamed a dream, and he came unto his brothers and told them his dream, and he said unto them, I dreamed a dream, and behold we were all binding sheaves in the field, and my sheaf rose and placed itself upon the ground and your sheaves surrounded it and bowed down to it.

11. And his brethren answered him and said unto him, what meaneth this dream that thou didst dream ? dost thou imagine in thy heart to reign or rule over us ?

12. And he still came, and told the thing to his father Jacob, and Jacob kissed Joseph when he heard these words from his mouth, and Jacob blessed Joseph.

13. And when the sons of Jacob saw that their father had blessed Joseph and had kissed him, and that he loved him exceedingly, they became jealous of him and hated him the more.

14. And after this Joseph dreamed another dream and related the dream to his father in the presence of his brethren, and Joseph said unto his father and brethren, behold I have again dreamed a dream, and behold the sun and the moon and the eleven stars bowed down to me.

15. And his father heard the words of Joseph and his dream, and seeing that his brethren hated Joseph on account of this matter, Jacob *therefore* rebuked Joseph before his brethren on account of this thing, saying, what meaneth this dream which thou hast dreamed, and this magnifying thyself before thy brethren who are older than thou *art* ?

16. Dost thou imagine in thy heart that I and thy mother and thy eleven brethren will come and bow down to thee, that thou speakest these things?

17. And his brethren were jealous of him on account of his words and dreams, and they continued to hate him, and Jacob reserved the dreams in his heart.

18. And the sons of Jacob went one day to feed their father's flock in Shechem, for they were still* herdsmen in those days ; and whilst the sons of Jacob were that day feeding

* He repeats this to contrast their pastoral employment now, with the battles which they had just been engaged in.

in Shechem they delayed, and the time of gathering in the cattle was passed, and they had not arrived.

19. And Jacob saw that his sons were delayed in Shechem, and Jacob said within himself, peradventure the people of Shechem have risen up to fight against them, therefore they have delayed coming this day.

20. And Jacob called Joseph his son, and commanded him, saying, behold thy brethren are feeding in Shechem this day, and behold they have not yet come back ; go now therefore and see where they are, and bring me word back concerning the welfare of thy brethren and the welfare of the flock.

21. And Jacob sent his son Joseph to the valley of Hebron, and Joseph came for his brothers to Shechem, and could not find them, and Joseph went about the field which was near Shechem, to see where his brothers had turned, and he missed his road in the wilderness, and knew not which way he should go.

22. And an angel of the Lord found him wandering in the road toward the field, and Joseph said unto the angel of the Lord, I seek my brethren ; hast thou not heard where they are feeding ? and the angel of the Lord said unto Joseph, I saw thy brethren feeding here, and I heard them say they would go to feed in Dothan.

23. And Joseph hearkened to the voice of the angel of the Lord, and he went to his brethren in Dothan and he found them in Dothan feeding the flock.

24. And Joseph advanced to his brethren, and before he had come nigh unto them, they had resolved to slay him.

25. And Simeon said to his brethren, behold the man of dreams is coming unto us this day, and now therefore come and let us kill him and cast him in one of the pits that are in the wilderness, and when his father shall seek him from us, we will say an evil beast has devoured him.

26. And Reuben heard the words of his brethren concerning Joseph, and he said unto them, you should not do this thing, for how can we look up to our father Jacob ? Cast him into this pit to die there, but stretch not forth a hand upon him to spill his blood ; and Reuben said this, in order to deliver him from their hand, to bring him back to his father.

27. And when Joseph came to his brethren he sat before them, and they rose upon him and seized him and smote him to the earth, and stripped the coat of many colors which he had on.

28. And they took him and cast him into a pit, and in the pit there was no water, but serpents and scorpions. And Joseph was afraid of the serpents and scorpions that were in the pit. And Joseph cried out with a loud voice, and the Lord hid the serpents and scorpions in the sides of the pit, and they did no harm unto Joseph.

29. And Joseph called out from the pit to his brethren and said unto them, what have I done unto you, and in what have I sinned ? why do you not fear the Lord concerning me ? am I not of your bones and flesh, and is not Jacob your father, my father ? why do you do this thing unto me this day, and how will you be able to look up to our father Jacob?

30. And he continued to cry out and call unto his brethren from the pit, and he said, O Judah, Simeon

and Levi my brethren, lift me up from the place of darkness in which you have placed me, and come this day to have compassion on me, ye children of the Lord, and sons of Jacob my father. And if I have sinned unto you, are you not the sons of Abraham, Isaac and Jacob? if they saw an orphan they had compassion over him, or one that was hungry they gave him bread to eat, or one that was thirsty they gave him water to drink, or one that was naked they covered him with garments!

31. And how then will you withhold your pity from your brother, for I am of your flesh and bones, and if I have sinned unto you, surely you will do this on account of my father!

32. And Joseph spoke these words from the pit, and his brethren would not listen to him, nor incline ears to the words of Joseph, and Joseph was crying and weeping in the pit.

33. And Joseph said, O that my father knew, this day, the act which my brothers have done unto me, and the words which they have *this* day spoken unto me.

34. And all his brethren heard his cries and weeping in the pit, and his brethren went and removed themselves from the pit, so that they might not hear the cries of Joseph and his weeping in the pit.

CHAPTER XLII.

1. And they went and sat on the opposite side, about the distance of a bow-shot, and they sat there to eat bread, and whilst they were eating, they held counsel together what was to be done with him, whether to slay him or to bring him back to his father.

2. They were holding the coun-sel, when they lifted up their eyes, and saw, and behold there was a company of Ishmaelites coming at a distance by the road of Gilead, going down to Egypt.

3. And Judah said unto them, what gain will it be to us if we slay our brother? peradventure God will require him from us; this *then* is the counsel proposed concerning him, which you shall do unto him; behold this company of Ishmaelites going down to Egypt.

4. Now therefore, come let us dispose of him to them, and let not our hand be upon him, and they will lead him along with them, and he will be lost amongst the people of the land, and we will not put him to death with our *own* hands. And the proposal pleased his brethren and they did according to the word of Judah.

5. And whilst they were discoursing about this matter, and before the company of Ishmaelites had come up to them, seven trading men of Midian passed by them, and as they passed they were thirsty, and they lifted up their eyes and saw the pit in which Joseph was immured, and they looked, and behold every species of bird was upon him.

6. And these Midianites ran to the pit to drink water, for they thought that it contained water, and on coming before the pit they heard the voice of Joseph crying and weeping in the pit, and they looked down into the pit, and they saw and behold there was a youth of comely appearance and well favored.

7. And they called unto him and said, who art thou and who brought thee hither, and who placed thee in this pit, in the wilderness? and they all assisted to raise up Joseph and they drew him out, and brought him

up from the pit, and took him and went away on their journey and passed by his brethren.

8. And these said unto them, why do you do this, to take our servant from us and to go away? surely we placed this youth in the pit because he rebelled against us, and you come and bring him up and lead him away; now then give us back our servant.

9. And the Midianites answered and said unto the sons of Jacob, is this your servant, or does this *man* attend you? peradventure you are all his servants, for he is more comely and well favored than any of you, and why do you all speak falsely unto us?

10. Now therefore we will not listen to your words, nor attend to you, for we found the youth in the pit in the wilderness, and we took him; we will *therefore* go on.

11. And all the sons of Jacob approached them and rose up to them and said unto them, give us back our servant, and why will you all die by the edge of the sword? And the Midianites cried out against them, and they drew their swords, and approached to fight with the sons of Jacob.

12. And behold Simeon rose up from his seat against them, and sprang upon the ground and drew his sword and approached the Midianites and he gave a terrible shout before them, so that his shouting was heard at a distance, and the earth shook at Simeon's shouting.

13. And the Midianites were terrified on account of Simeon and the noise of his shouting, and they fell upon their faces, and were excessively alarmed.

14. And Simeon said unto them, verily I am Simeon the son of Jacob the Hebrew, who have, only with my brother, destroyed the city of Shechem and the cities of the Amorites; so shall God moreover do unto me, that if all your brethren the people of Midian, and also the kings of Canaan, were to come with you, they could not fight against me.

15. Now therefore give us back the youth whom you have taken, lest I give your flesh to the birds of the skies and the beasts of the earth.

16. And the Midianites were more afraid of Simeon, and they approached the sons of Jacob with terror and fright, and with pathetic words, saying,

17. Surely you have said that the young man is your servant, and that he rebelled against you, *and* therefore you placed him in the pit; what then will you do with a servant who rebels against his master? Now *therefore* sell him unto us, and we will give you all that you require for him; and the Lord was pleased to do this in order that the sons of Jacob should not slay their brother.

18. And the Midianites saw that Joseph was of a comely appearance and well-favored; they desired him in their hearts and were urgent to purchase him from his brethren.

19. And the sons of Jacob hearkened to the Midianites and they sold their brother Joseph to them for twenty *pieces* of silver, and Reuben their brother was not with them, and the Midianites took Joseph and continued their journey to Gilead.

20. They were going along the road, and the Midianites repented of what they had done, in having purchased the young man, and one said to the other, what is this thing that we have done, in taking this

9

youth from the Hebrews, who is of comely appearance and well favored.

21. Perhaps this *youth* is stolen from the land of the Hebrews, and why *then* have we done this thing? and if he should be sought for and found in our hands we shall die through him.

22. Now surely hardy and powerful men have sold him to us, the strength of one of whom you saw this day; perhaps they stole him from his land with their might and with their powerful arm, and have therefore sold him to us for the small value which we gave unto them.

23. And whilst they were thus discoursing together, they looked, and behold the company of Ishmaelites which was coming at first, *and* which the sons of Jacob saw, was advancing toward the Midianites, and the Midianites said to each other, come let us sell this youth to the company of Ishmaelites who are coming toward us, and we will take for him the little that we gave for him, and we will be delivered from his evil.

24. And they did so, and they reached the Ishmaelites, and the Midianites sold Joseph to the Ishmaelites for twenty *pieces* of silver which they had given for him to his brethren.

25. And the Midianites went on their road to Gilead, and the Ishmaelites took Joseph and they let him ride upon *one* of the camels, and they were leading him to Egypt.

26. And Joseph heard that the Ishmaelites were proceeding to Egypt, and Joseph lamented and wept at this thing that he was to be so far removed from the land of Canaan, from his father, and he wept bitterly whilst he was riding upon the camel, and one of their men observed him, and made him go down from the camel and walk on foot, and notwithstanding this Joseph *continued* to cry and weep, and he said, O my father, my father.

27. And one of the Ishmaelites rose up and smote Joseph upon the cheek, and still he continued to weep; and Joseph was fatigued in the road, and was unable to proceed on account of the bitterness of his soul, and they all smote him and afflicted him in the road, and they terrified him in order that he might cease from weeping.

28. And the Lord saw the affliction of Joseph and his trouble, and the Lord brought down upon those men darkness and confusion, and the hand of every one that smote him became withered.

29. And they said to each other, what is this thing that God has done to us in the road? and they knew not that this befel them on account of Joseph. And the men proceeded on the road, and they passed along the road of Ephrath where Rachel was buried.

30. And Joseph reached his mother's grave, and Joseph hastened and ran to his mother's grave, and fell upon the grave and wept.

31. And Joseph cried aloud upon his mother's grave, and he said, O my mother, my mother, O thou who didst give me birth, awake now, and rise and see thy son, how he has been sold for a slave, and no one to pity him.

32. O rise and see thy son, weep with me on account of my troubles, and see the heart of my brethren.

33. Arouse my mother, arouse, awake from thy sleep for me, and direct thy battles against my brethren. O how have they stripped

me of my coat, and sold me already twice for a slave, and separated me from my father, and there is no one to pity me.

34. Arouse and lay thy* cause against them before God, and see whom God will justify in the judgment, and whom he will condemn.

35. Rise O my mother, rise, awake from thy sleep and see my father how his soul is with me this day, and comfort him and ease his heart.

36. And Joseph continued to speak these words, and Joseph cried aloud and wept bitterly upon his mother's grave; and he ceased speaking, and from bitterness of heart he became still as a stone upon the grave.

37. And Joseph heard a voice speaking to him from beneath the ground, which answered him with bitterness of heart, and with a voice of weeping and praying in these words;

38. My son, my son Joseph, I have heard the voice of thy weeping and the voice of thy lamentation; I have seen thy tears; I know thy troubles, my son, and it grieves me for thy sake, and abundant grief is added to my grief.

39. Now *therefore* my son, Joseph my son, hope to the Lord, and wait for him and do not fear, for the Lord is with thee, he will deliver thee from all trouble.

40. Rise my son, go down unto Egypt with thy masters, and do not fear, for the Lord is with thee, my son. And she continued to speak like unto these words unto Joseph, and she was still.

* Hebrew, טענותיך thy pleadings; this word is not found to have this meaning in scripture, but it is used in the Chaldee, though I have no doubt it is a Hebrew root טען to goad, as in Genesis, ch. 45, v. 17. To plead or argue, therefore, bears an affinity to the Hebrew טען to goad.

41. And Joseph heard this, and he wondered greatly at this, and he continued to weep; and after this one of the Ishmaelites observed him crying and weeping upon the grave, and his anger was kindled against him, and he drove him from there, and he smote him and cursed him.

42. And Joseph said unto the men, may I find grace in your sight to take me back to my father's house, and he will give you abundance of riches.

43. And they answered him, saying, art thou not a slave, and where is thy father? and if thou hadst a father thou wouldst not already twice have been sold for a slave for so little value; and their anger was still roused against him, and they continued to smite him and to chastise him, and Joseph wept bitterly.

44. And the Lord saw Joseph's affliction, and the Lord again smote these men, and chastised them, and the Lord caused darkness to *envelope* them upon the earth, and the lightning flashed and the thunder roared, and the earth shook at the voice of the thunder and of the mighty wind, and the men were terrified and knew not where they should go.

45. And the beasts and camels stood still, and they led them, but they would not go, they smote them, and they crouched upon the ground; and the men said to each other, what is this that God has done to us? what are our transgressions, and what are our sins that this thing has thus befallen us?

46. And one *of them* answered and said unto them, perhaps on account of the sin of afflicting this slave has this thing happened this day to us; now *therefore* implore him strongly to forgive us, and then we shall know on whose account this

evil befalleth us; and if God shall have compassion over us, then we shall know that all this cometh to us on account of the sin of afflicting this slave.

47. And the men did so, and they supplicated Joseph and pressed him to forgive them; and they said, we have sinned to the Lord and to thee, now *therefore* vouchsafe to request of thy God that he shall put away this death from amongst us, for we have sinned to him.

48. And Joseph did according to their words, and the Lord hearkened to Joseph, and the Lord put away the plague which he had inflicted upon those men on account of Joseph, and the beasts rose up from the ground and they conducted them, and they went on, and the raging storm abated and the earth became tranquilized, and the men proceeded on their journey to go down to Egypt, and the men knew that this evil had befallen them on account of Joseph.

49. And they said to each other, behold we know that it was on account of his affliction that this evil befel us; now *therefore* why shall we bring this death upon our souls? Let us hold counsel what to do to this slave.

50. And one answered and said, surely he told us to bring him back to his father; now *therefore* come, let us take him back and we will go to the place that he will tell *us*, and take from his family the price that we gave for him and we will then go away.

51. And one answered *again* and said, behold this counsel is very good, but we cannot do so for the way is very far from us, and we cannot go out of our road.

52. And one *more* answered and said unto them, this is the counsel to be adopted, we will not swerve from it; behold we are this day going to Egypt, and when we shall have come to Egypt, we will sell him there at a high price, and we will be delivered from his evil.

53. And this thing pleased the men and they did so, and they continued their journey to Egypt with Joseph.

CHAPTER XLIII.

1. And when the sons of Jacob had sold their brother Joseph to the Midianites, their hearts were smitten on account of him, and they repented of their acts, and they sought for him to bring him back, but could not find him.

2. And Reuben returned to the pit in which Joseph *had been put*, in order to lift him out, *and* restore him to his father, and Reuben stood by the pit, and he heard not a word, and he called out Joseph! Joseph! and no one answered nor uttered a word.

3. And Reuben said, Joseph has died through fright, or some serpent has caused his death: and Reuben descended into the pit, and he searched for Joseph and could not find him in the pit, and he came out *again*.

4. And Reuben tore his garments and he said, the child is not *there*, and how shall I reconcile my father about him if he be dead? and he went to his brethren and found them grieving on account of Joseph, and counselling together how to reconcile their father about him, and Reuben said unto his brethren, I came to the pit and behold Joseph was not there, what *then* shall we say unto our father, for my father will only seek the lad from me.

5. And his brethren answered him saying, thus and thus we did, and our hearts afterward smote us on account of this act, and we *now* sit to seek a pretext how we shall reconcile our father to it.

6. And Reuben said unto them, what is this you have done to bring down the grey hairs of our father in sorrow to the grave? the thing is not good, that you have done.

7. And Reuben sat with them, and they all rose up and swore to each other not to tell this thing unto Jacob, and they all said, the man who will tell this to our father or his household, or who will report this to any of the children of the land, we will all rise up against him and slay him with the sword.

8. And the sons of Jacob feared each other in this matter, from the youngest to the oldest, and no one spoke a word, and they concealed the thing in their hearts.

9. And they afterward sat down to determine and invent something to say unto their father Jacob concerning all these things.

10. And Issachar said unto them, here is an advice for you if it seem good in your eyes to do this thing, take the coat which *belongeth* to Joseph and tear it, and kill a kid of the goats and dip it in its blood.

11. And send it to our father and when he seeth it he will say an evil beast has devoured him, therefore tear ye his coat and behold his blood will be upon his coat, and by your doing this we shall be free of our father's murmurings.

12. And Issachar's advice pleased them, and they hearkened unto him and they did according to the word of Issachar which he had counselled them.

13. And they hastened and took Joseph's coat and tore it, and they killed a kid of the goats and dipped the coat in the blood of the kid, and *then* trampled it in the dust, and they sent the coat to their father Jacob by the hand of Naphtali, and they commanded him to say these words.

14. We had gathered in the cattle and had come as far as the road to Shechem and farther, when we found this coat upon the road in the wilderness dipped in blood and in dust; now *therefore* know whether it be thy son's coat or not.

15. And Naphtali went and he came unto his father and he gave him the coat, and he spoke unto him all the words which his brethren had commanded him.

16. And Jacob saw Joseph's coat and he knew it and he fell upon his face to the ground, and became as still as a stone, and he afterward rose up and cried out with a loud and weeping voice and he said, it is the coat of my son Joseph!

17. And Jacob hastened and sent one of his servants to his sons, who went to them and found them coming along the road with the flock.

18. And the sons of Jacob came to their father about evening, and behold their garments were torn and dust was upon their heads, and they found their father crying out and weeping with a loud voice.

19. And Jacob said unto his sons, tell me truly what evil have you this day suddenly brought upon me? and they answered their father Jacob, saying, we were coming along this day after the flock had been gathered in, and we came as far as the city of Shechem by the road in the wilderness, and we found this coat filled with blood upon the ground, and we

knew it and we sent unto thee if thou couldst know it.

20. And Jacob heard the words of his sons and he cried out with a loud voice, and he said *it is* the coat of my son, an evil beast has devoured him ; Joseph is rent in pieces, for I sent him this day to see whether it was well with you and well with the flocks and to bring me word again from you, and he went as I commanded him, and this has happened to him this day whilst I thought my son was with you.

21. And the sons of Jacob answered and said, he did not come to us, neither have we seen him from the time of our going out from thee until now.

22. And when Jacob heard their words he again cried out aloud and he rose up and tore his garments, and he put sackcloth upon his loins, and he wept bitterly and he mourned and lifted up his voice in weeping and exclaimed and said these words,

23. Joseph my son, O my son Joseph, I sent thee this day after the welfare of thy brethren, and behold thou hast been torn in pieces; through my hand has this happened to my son.

24. It gieves me for thee Joseph my son, it grieves me for thee ; how sweet wast thou to me during life, and now how exceedingly bitter is thy death to me.

25. O that I had died in thy stead Joseph my son, for it grieves me sadly for thee my son. O my son, my son, Joseph my son, where art thou, and where hast thou been drawn? arouse, arouse from thy place, and come and see my grief for thee, O my son Joseph.

26. Come now and number the tears gushing from my eyes down my cheeks, and bring them up before the Lord, that his anger may turn from me.

27. O Joseph my son how didst thou fall, by the hand of one by whom no one had fallen from the beginning of the world unto this day ; for thou hast been put to death by the smiting of an enemy, inflicted with cruelty, but surely I know that this has happened to thee, on account of the multitude of my sins.

28. Arouse now and see how bitter is my trouble for thee my son, although I did not rear thee, nor fashion thee, nor give thee breath and soul, but it was God who formed thee and built thy bones and covered them with flesh, and breathed in thy nostrils the breath of life, and *then* he gave thee unto me.

29. Now truly God who gave thee unto me, he has taken thee from me, and such *then* has befallen thee this day, and all the works of God are good.

30. And Jacob continued to speak like unto these words concerning Joseph, and he wept bitterly ; he fell to the ground and became still.

31. And all the sons of Jacob seeing their father's trouble, they repented of what they had done, and they also wept bitterly.

32. And Judah rose up and lifted his father's head from the ground, and placed it upon his lap, and he wiped his father's tears from his cheeks, and Judah wept an exceeding great weeping, whilst his father's head was *reclining* upon his lap, still as a stone.

33. And the sons of Jacob saw their father's trouble, and they lifted up their voices and continued to weep, and Jacob was yet lying upon the ground still as a stone.

34. And all his sons and his servants and his servants' children rose up and stood round him to comfort him, and he refused to be comforted.

35. And the whole household of Jacob rose up and mourned a great mourning on account of Joseph and their father's trouble, and the intelligence reached Isaac, the son of Abraham, the father of Jacob, and he wept bitterly on account of Joseph, he and all his household, and he went from the place where he dwelt in Hebron, and his men with him, and he comforted Jacob his son, and he refused to be comforted.

36. And after this, Jacob rose up from the ground, and his tears were running down his cheeks, and he said unto his sons, rise up and take your swords and your bows, and go forth into the field, and seek whether you can find my son's body and bring it unto me that I may bury it.

37. Seek *also*, I pray you, among the beasts and hunt them, and that which shall come the first before you seize and bring it unto me, perhaps the Lord will this day pity my affliction, and prepare before you that which did tear my son in *pieces*, and bring it unto me, and I will avenge the cause of my son.

38. And his sons did as their father had commanded them, and they rose up early in the morning, and each took his sword and his bow in his hand, and they went forth into the field to hunt the beasts.

39. And Jacob was still crying aloud and weeping and walking to and fro in the house, and smiting his hands together, saying, Joseph my son, Joseph my son.

40. And the sons of Jacob went into the wilderness to seize the beasts, and behold a wolf came to-ward them, and they seized him, and brought him unto their father, and they said unto him, this is the first we have found, and we have brought him unto thee as thou didst command us, and thy son's body we could not find.

41. And Jacob took the beast from the hands of his sons, and he cried out with a loud and weeping voice, holding the beast in his hand, and he spoke with a bitter heart unto the beast, why didst thou devour my son Joseph, and how didst thou have no fear of the God of the earth, or of my trouble for my son Joseph?

42. And thou didst devour my son for naught, because he committed no violence, and didst *thereby* render me* culpable on his account, therefore God will require him that is persecuted.

43. And the Lord opened the mouth of the beast in order to comfort Jacob with its words, and it answered Jacob and spoke these words unto him.

44. As God liveth who created us in the earth, and as thy soul liveth, my lord, I did not see thy son, neither did I tear him to pieces, but from a distant land I also came to seek my son who went from me this day, and I know not whether he be living or dead.

45. And I came this day into the field to seek my son, and your sons found me, and seized me and increased my grief, and have this day brought me before thee, and I have now spoken all my words to thee.

46. And now therefore, O son of man, I am in thy hands, and do unto me this day as it may seem good in

* In Jacob's lamentation, he blames himself for having sent him, and having been the cause of his death.

thy sight, but by the life of God who created me, I did not see thy son, nor did I tear him to pieces, neither has the flesh of man entered my mouth all the days of my life.

47. And when Jacob heard the words of the beast he was greatly astonished, and sent forth the beast from his hand, and she went her way.

48. And Jacob was still crying aloud and weeping for Joseph day after day, and he mourned for his son many days.

CHAPTER XLIV.

1. And the sons of Ishmael who had bought Joseph from the Midianites, who had bought him from his brethren, went to Egypt with Joseph, and they came upon the borders of Egypt, and when they came near unto Egypt, they met four men of the sons of Medan the son of Abraham, who had gone forth from the land of Egypt on their journey.

2. And the Ishmaelites said unto them, do you desire to purchase this slave from us? and they said, deliver him over to us, and they delivered Joseph over to them, and they beheld him, that he was a very comely youth and they purchased him for twenty shekels.

3. And the Ishmaelites continued their journey to Egypt, and the Medanim also returned that day to Egypt, and the Medanim said to each other, behold we have heard that Potiphar, an officer of Pharaoh, captain of the guard, seeketh a good servant who shall stand before him to attend him, and to make him overseer over his house and all belonging to him.

4. Now therefore come let us sell him to him for what we may desire, if he be able to give unto us that which we shall require for him.

5. And these Medanim went and came to the house of Potiphar, and said unto him, we have heard that thou seekest a good servant to attend thee, behold we have a servant that will please thee, if thou canst give unto us that which we may desire, and we will sell him unto thee.

6. And Potiphar said, bring him before me, and I will see him, and if he please me I will give unto you that which you may require for him.

7. And the Medanim went and brought Joseph and placed him before Potiphar, and he saw him, and he pleased him exceedingly, and Potiphar said unto them, tell me what you require for this youth?

8. And they said, four hundred pieces of silver we desire for him, and Potiphar said, I will give it you if you bring me the record of his sale to you, and will tell me his history, for perhaps he may be stolen, for this youth is neither a slave, nor the son of a slave, but I observe in him the appearance of a goodly and handsome person.

9. And the Medanim went and brought unto him the Ishmaelites who had sold him to them, and they told him, saying, he is a slave and we sold him to them.

10. And Potiphar heard the words of the Ishmaelites in his giving the silver unto the Medanim, and the Medanim took the silver and went on their journey, and the Ishmaelites also returned home.

11. And Potiphar took Joseph and brought him to his house that he might serve him, and Joseph found favor in the sight of Potiphar, and he placed confidence in him, and made

him overseer over his house, and all that belonged to him he delivered over into his hand.

12. And the Lord was with Joseph and he became a prosperous man, and the Lord blessed the house of Potiphar for the sake of Joseph.

13. And Potiphar left all that he had in the hand of Joseph, and Joseph was one that caused things to come in and go out, and every thing was regulated by his wish in the house of Potiphar.

14. And Joseph was eighteen years old, a youth with beautiful eyes and of comely appearance, and like unto him was not in the whole land of Egypt.

15. At that time whilst he was in his master's house, going in and out of the house and attending his master, Zelicah his master's wife lifted up her eyes toward Joseph and she looked at him, and behold he was a youth comely and well favored.

16. And she coveted his beauty in her heart, and her soul was fixed upon Joseph, and she enticed him day after day, and Zelicah persuaded Joseph daily, but Joseph did not lift up his eyes to behold his master's wife.

17. And Zelicah said unto him, how goodly are thy appearance and form, truly I have looked at all the slaves, and have not seen so beautiful a slave as thou art; and Joseph said unto her, surely he who created me in my mother's womb created all mankind.

18. And she said unto him, how beautiful are thine eyes, with which thou hast dazzled* all the inhabitants

* The Hebrew word רהב is generally rendered, to make sure or firm, to strengthen ; but in Canticles, ch. 6, v. 5, it is translated, to overcome, and according to some commentators, to comfort.

of Egypt, men and women ; and he said unto her, how beautiful they are whilst we are alive, but shouldst thou behold them in the grave, surely thou wouldst move away from them.

19. And she said unto him, how beautiful and pleasing are all thy words ; take *now* I pray thee, the harp which is in the house, and play with thy hands and let us hear thy words.

20. And he said unto her, how beautiful and pleasing are my words when I speak the praise of my God and his glory ; and she said unto him how very beautiful is the hair of thy head, behold the golden comb which is in the house, take it I pray thee and curl the hair of thy head.

21. And he said unto her, how long wilt thou speak these words ? cease to utter these words to me, and rise and attend to thy domestic affairs.

22. And she said unto him, there is no one in my house, and there is nothing to attend to but to thy words and to thy wish ; yet notwithstanding all this she could not bring Joseph unto her, neither did he place his eye upon her, but directed his eyes below to the ground.

23. And Zelicah desired Joseph in her heart, that he should lie with her, and at the time that Joseph was sitting in the house doing his work, Zelicah came and sat before him, and she enticed him daily with *her* discourse to lie with her, or *even* to look at her, but Joseph would not hearken to her.

24. And she said unto him, if thou wilt not do *according* to my words, I will chastise thee with the punishment of death, and put an iron yoke upon thee.

25. And Joseph said unto her,

surely God who created man looseth the fetters of prisoners, and it is he who will deliver me from thy prison and from thy judgment.

26. And when she could not prevail over him, to persuade him, and her soul *being still* fixed upon him, her desire threw her into a grievous sickness.

27. And all the women of Egypt came to visit her, and they said unto her, why art thou in this declining state? thou that lackest nothing; surely thy husband is a great and esteemed prince in the sight of the king, shouldst thou lack any thing of what thy heart desireth?

28. And Zelicah answered them, saying, this day it shall be made known to you, whence this *disorder* springs in which you see me, and she commanded her maid servants to prepare food for all the women, and she made a banquet for them, and all the women ate in the house of Zelicah.

29. And she gave them knives to peel the citrons to eat them, and she commanded that they should dress Joseph in costly garments, and that he should appear before them, and Joseph came before their eyes and all the women looked on Joseph, and could not take their eyes from off him, and they all cut their hands with the knives that they had in their hands, and all the citrons that were in their hands were filled with blood.

30. And they knew not what they had done but they continued to look at the beauty of Joseph, and did not turn their eyelids from him.

31. And Zelicah saw what they had done, and she said unto them, what is this work that you have done? behold I gave you citrons to eat and you have all cut your hands.

32. And all the women saw their hands, and behold they were full of blood, and their blood flowed down upon their garments, and they said unto her, this slave in your house has overcome us, and we could not turn our eyelids from him on account of his beauty.

33. And she said unto them, surely this happened to you in the moment that you looked at him, and you could not contain yourselves from him; how then can I refrain when he is constantly in my house, and I see him day after day going in and out of my house? how *then* can I keep from declining or even from perishing on account of this?

34. And they said unto her, the words are true, for who can see this *beautiful* form in the house and refrain from him, and is he not thy slave and attendant in thy house, and why dost thou not tell him that which is in thy heart, and sufferest thy soul to perish through this matter?

35. And she said unto them, I am daily endeavoring to persuade him, and he will not consent to my wishes, and I promised him every thing that is good, and yet I could meet* with no return from him; I am therefore in a declining state as you see.

36. And Zelicah became very ill on account of *her* desire toward Joseph, and she was desperately love-sick on account of him, and all the people of the house of Zelicah and her husband knew nothing of this matter, that Zelicah was ill on account of her love to Joseph.

37. And all the people of her house asked her, saying, why art thou ill and declining, and lackest nothing?

* Hebrew, I could not find anything in him.

and she said unto them, I know not this thing which is daily increasing upon me.

38. And all the women and her friends came daily to see her, and they spoke with her, and she said unto them, this can only be through the love of Joseph; and they said unto her, entice him and seize him secretly, perhaps he may hearken to thee, and put off this death from thee.

39. And Zelicah became worse from her love to Joseph, and she continued to decline, till she had scarce strength to stand.

40. And on a certain day Joseph was doing his master's work in the house, and Zelicah came secretly and fell suddenly upon him, and Joseph rose up against her, and he was more powerful than she, and he brought her down to the ground.

41. And Zelicah wept on account of the desire of her heart toward him, and she supplicated him with weeping, and her tears flowed down her cheeks, and she spoke unto him in a voice of supplication and in bitterness of soul, saying,

42. Hast thou ever heard, seen or known of so beautiful a woman as I am, or better than myself, who speak daily unto thee, fall into a decline through love for thee, confer all this honor upon thee, and still thou wilt not hearken to my voice?

43. And if it be through fear of thy master lest he punish thee, as the king liveth no harm shall come to thee from thy master through this thing; now therefore pray listen to me, and consent for the sake of the honor which I have conferred upon thee, and put off this death from me, and why should I die for thy sake? and she ceased to speak.

44. And Joseph answered her, saying, refrain from me, and leave this matter to my master; behold my master knoweth not what there is with me in the house, for all that belongeth to him he has delivered into my hand, and how shall I do these things in my master's house?

45. For he hath also greatly honored me in his house, and he hath also made me overseer over his house, and he hath exalted me, and there is no one greater in this house than I am, and my master hath refrained nothing from me, excepting thee who art his wife, how then canst thou speak these words unto me, and how can I do this great evil and sin to God and to thy husband?

46. Now therefore refrain from me, and speak no more such words as these, for I will not hearken to thy words. But Zelicah would not hearken to Joseph when he spoke these words unto her, but she daily enticed him to listen to her.

47. And it was after this that the brook of Egypt was filled above all its sides, and all the inhabitants of Egypt went forth, and also the king and princes went forth with timbrels and dances, for it was a great rejoicing in Egypt, and a holiday at the time of the inundation of the sea Sihor, and they went there to rejoice all the day.

48. And when the Egyptians went out to the river to rejoice, as was their custom, all the people of the house of Potiphar went with them, but Zelicah would not go with them, for she said, I am indisposed, and she remained alone in the house, and no other person was with her in the house.

49. And she rose up and ascended to her temple in the house, and dress-

ed herself in princely garments, and she placed upon her head precious stones of onyx stones, inlaid with silver and gold, and she beautified her face and skin with all sorts of women's purifying liquids, and she perfumed the temple and the house with cassia and frankincense, and she spread myrrh and aloes, and she afterward sat in the entrance of the temple, in the passage of the house, through which Joseph passed to do his work, and behold Joseph came from the field, and entered the house to do his master's work.

50. And he came to the place *through which* he had to pass, and he saw all the work of Zelicah, and he turned back.

51. And Zelicah saw Joseph turning back from her, and she called out to him, saying, what aileth thee Joseph? come to thy work, and behold I will make room for thee until thou shalt have passed to thy seat.

52. And Joseph returned and came to the house, and passed from thence to the place of his seat, and he sat down to do his master's work as usual, and behold Zelicah came to him and stood before him in princely garments, and the scent from her clothes was spread to a distance.

53. And she hastened and caught hold of Joseph and his garments, and she said unto him, as the king liveth if thou wilt not perform my request thou shalt die this day, and she hastened and stretched forth her other hand and drew a sword from beneath her garments, and she placed it upon Joseph's neck, and she said, rise and perform my request, and if not thou diest this day.

54. And Joseph was afraid of her at her doing this thing, and he rose up to flee from her, and she seized the front of his garments, and in the terror of his flight the garment which Zelicah seized was torn, and Joseph left the garment in the hand of Zelicah, and he fled and got out, for he was in fear.

55. And when Zelicah saw that Joseph's garment was torn, and that he had left it in her hand, and had fled, she was afraid of her life, lest the report should spread concerning her, and she rose up and acted with cunning, and put off the garments in which she was dressed, and she put on her *other* garments.

56. And she took Joseph's garment and she laid it beside her, and she went and seated herself in the place where she had sat in her illness, before the people of her house had gone out to the river, and she called a young lad who was *then* in the house, and she ordered him to call the people of the house to her.

57. And when she saw them she said unto them with a loud voice and lamentation see what a Hebrew your master has brought to me in the house, for he came this day to lie with me.

58. For when you had gone out he came to the house, and seeing that there was no person in the house, he came unto me, and caught hold of me, *with intent* to lie with me.

59. And I seized his garments and tore them and called out against him with a loud voice, and when I had lifted up my voice he was afraid of his life and left his garment before me, and fled.

60. And the people of her house spoke nothing, but their wrath was very much kindled against Joseph, and they went to his master and told him the words of his wife.

61. And Potiphar came home enraged, and his wife cried out to him, saying, what is *this* thing that thou hast done unto me in bringing a Hebrew servant into my house, for he came unto me this day to sport with me ; thus did he do unto me this day.

62. And Potiphar heard the words of his wife, and he ordered Joseph to be punished with severe stripes, and they did so to him.

63. And whilst they were smiting him, Joseph called out with a loud voice, and he lifted up his eyes to heaven, and he said, O Lord God, thou knowest that I am innocent of all these things, and why shall I die this day through falsehood, by the hand of these uncircumcised wicked men, whom thou knowest ?

64. And whilst Potiphar's men were beating Joseph he continued to cry out and weep, and there was a child there eleven months old, and the Lord opened the mouth of the child, and he spake these words before Potiphar's men, who were smiting Joseph, saying,

65. What do you want of this man, and why do you do this evil unto him ? my mother speaketh falsely and uttereth lies ; thus was the transaction.

66. And the child told them accurately all that happened, and all the words of Zelicah to Joseph day after day did he declare unto them.

67. And all the men heard the words of the child and they wondered greatly at the child's words, and the child ceased to speak and became still.

68. And Potiphar was very much ashamed at the words of his son, and he commanded his men not to beat Joseph any more, and the men ceased beating Joseph.

69. And Potiphar took Joseph and ordered him to be brought to justice before the priests, who were judges belonging to the king, in order to judge him concerning this affair.

70. And Potiphar and Joseph came before the priests *who were* the king's judges, and he said unto them, decide I pray you what judgment is due to a servant, for thus has he done.

71. And the priests said unto Joseph, why didst thou do this thing to thy master ? and Joseph answered them, saying, not so my lords, thus was the matter ; and Potiphar said unto Joseph, surely I entrusted in thy hands all that belonged to me, and I withheld nothing from thee but my wife, and how couldst thou do this evil ?

72. And Joseph answered, saying, not so my lord, as the Lord liveth, and as thy soul liveth, my lord, the word which thou didst hear from thy wife is untrue, for thus was the affair this day.

73. A year has elapsed to me since I have been in thy house; hast thou seen any iniquity in me, or any thing which might cause thee to demand my life?

74. And the priests said unto Potiphar, send, we pray thee, and let them bring before us Joseph's torn garment, and let us see the tear in it, and if it shall be that the tear is in front of the garment, then his face must have been opposite to her and she must have caught hold of him, to come to her, and with deceit did thy wife do all that she has spoken.

75. And they brought Joseph's garment before the priests *who were* judges, and they saw and behold the

tear was in front of Joseph, and all the judging priests knew that she had pressed him, and they said, the judgment of death is not due to this slave for he has done nothing, but his judgment is, that he be placed in the prison house on account of the report, which through him has gone forth against thy wife.

76. And Potiphar heard their words, and he placed him in the prison house, the place where the king's prisoners are confined, and Joseph was in the house of confinement twelve years.

77. And notwithstanding this, his master's wife did not turn from him, and she did not cease from speaking to him day after day to hearken to her, and at the end of three months Zelicah continued going to Joseph to the house of confinement day by day, and she enticed him to hearken to her, and Zelicah said unto Joseph, how long wilt thou remain in this house? but hearken now to my voice and I will bring thee out of this house.

78. And Joseph answered her, saying, it is better for me to remain in this house than to hearken to thy words, to sin against God; and she said unto him, if thou wilt not perform my wish, I will pluck out thine eyes, add fetters to thy feet, and will deliver thee into the hands of them whom thou didst not know before.

79. And Joseph answered her and said, behold the God of the whole earth is able to deliver me from all that thou canst do unto me, for he openeth *the eyes* of the blind, and looseth those that are bound, and preserveth all strangers who are unacquainted with the land.

80. And when Zelicah was unable to persuade Joseph to hearken to her, she left off going to entice him; and Joseph was still confined in the house of confinement. And Jacob the father of Joseph, and all his brethren who were in the land of Canaan still mourned and wept in those days on account of Joseph, for Jacob refused to be comforted for his son Joseph, and Jacob cried aloud, and wept and mourned all *those* days.

CHAPTER XLV.

1. And it was at that time in that year, which is the year of Joseph's going down to Egypt after his brothers had sold him, that Reuben the son of Jacob went to Timnah and took unto him for a wife Eliuram, the daughter of Avi the Canaanite, and he came to her.

2. And Eliuram the wife of Reuben conceived and bare him Hanoch, Palu, Chetzron and Carmi, four sons; and Simeon his brother took his sister Dinah for a wife, and she bare unto him Memuel, Yamin, Ohad, Jachin and Zochar, five sons.

3. And he afterward came to Bunah the Canaanitish *woman*, the same is Bunah whom Simeon took captive from the city of Shechem, and Bunah was before Dinah and attended upon her, and Simeon came to her, and she bare unto him Saul,

4. And Judah went at that time to Adulam, and he came to a man of Adulam, and his name was Hirah, and Judah saw there the daughter of a man from Canaan, and her name was Aliyath, the daughter of Shua, and he took her, and came to her, and Aliyath bare unto Judah, Er, Onan and Shiloh; three sons.

5. And Levi and Issachar went

to the land of the east, and they took unto themselves for wives the daughters of Jobab the son of Yoktan, the son of Eber; and Jobab the son of Yoktan had two daughters; the name of the elder was Adinah, and the name of the younger was Aridah.

6. And Levi took Adina, and Issachar took Aridah, and they came to the land of Canaan, to their father's house, and Adinah bare unto Levi, Gershon, Kehath and Merari; three sons.

7. And Aridah bare unto Issachar Tola, Puvah, Job and Shomron, four sons; and Dan went to the land of Moab and took for a wife Aphlaleth, the daughter of Chamudan the Moabite, and he brought her to the land of Canaan.

8. And Aphlaleth was barren, she had no offspring, and God afterward remembered Aphlaleth the wife of Dan, and she conceived and bare a son, and she called his name Chushim.

9. And Gad and Naphtali went to Haran and took from thence the daughters of Amuram the son of Uz, the son of Nahor, for wives.

10. And these are the names of the daughters of Amuram; the name of the elder was Merimah, and the name of the younger Uzith; and Naphtali took Merimah, and Gad took Uzith; and brought them to the land of Canaan, to their father's house.

11. And Merimah bare unto Naphtali Yachzeel, Guni, Jazer and Shalem, four sons; and Uzith bare unto Gad Zephion, Chagi, Shuni, Ezbon, Eri, Arodi and Arali, seven sons.

12. And Asher went forth and took Adon the daughter of Aphlal,

the son of Hadad, the son of Ishmael, for a wife, and he brought her to the land of Canaan.

13. And Adon the wife of Asher died in those days; she had no offspring; and it was after the death of Adon that Asher went to the other side of the river and took for a wife Hadurah the daughter of Abimael, the son of Eber, the son of Shem.

14. And the young woman was of a comely appearance, and a woman of sense, and she had been the wife of Malkiel the son of Elam, the son of Shem.

15. And Hadurah bare a daughter unto Malkiel, and he called her name Serach, and Malkiel died after this, and Hadurah went and remained in her father's house.

16. And after the death of the wife of Asher he went and took Hadurah for a wife, and brought her to the land of Canaan, and Serach her daughter he also brought with them, and she was three years old, and the damsel was brought up in Jacob's house.

17. And the damsel was of a comely appearance, and she went in the sanctified ways of the children of Jacob; she lacked nothing, and the Lord gave her wisdom and understanding.

18. And Hadurah the wife of Asher conceived and bare unto him Yimnah, Yishvah, Yishvi and Beriah; four sons.

19. And Zebulun went to Midian, and took for a wife Merishah the daughter of Molad, the son of Abida, the son of Midian, and brought her to the land of Canaan.

20. And Merushah bare unto Zebulun Sered; Elon and Yachleel; three sons.

21. And Jacob sent to Aram, the

son of Zoba, the son of Terah, and he took for his son Benjamin Mechalia the daughter of Aram, and she came to the land of Canaan to the house of Jacob; and Benjamin was ten years old when he took Mechalia the daughter of Aram for a wife.

22. And Mechalia conceived and bare unto Benjamin Bela, Becher, Ashbel, Gera and Naaman, five sons; and Benjamin went afterward and took for a wife Aribath, the daughter of Shomron, the son of Abraham, in addition to his *first* wife, and he was eighteen years old; and Aribath bare unto Benjamin Achi, Vosh, Mupim, Chupim, and Ord; five sons.

23. And in those days Judah went to the house of Shem and took Tamar the daughter of Elam, the son of Shem, for a wife for his first born Er.

24. And Er came to his wife Tamar, and she became his wife, and when he came to her he outwardly destroyed his seed, and his work was evil in the sight of the Lord, and the Lord slew him.

25. And it was after the death of Er, Judah's first born, that Judah said unto Onan, go to thy brother's wife and marry her as the next of kin, and raise up seed to thy brother.

26. And Onan took Tamar for a wife and he came to her, and Onan also did like unto the work of his brother, and his work was evil in the sight of the Lord, and he slew him also.

27. And when Onan died, Judah said unto Tamar, remain in thy father's house until my son Shiloh shall have grown up, and Judah did no more delight in Tamar, to give her unto Shiloh, for he said, peradventure he will also die like his brothers.

28. And Tamar rose up and went and remained in her father's house, and Tamar was in her father's house for some time.

29. And at the revolution of the year, Aliyath the wife of Judah died; and Judah was comforted for his wife, and after the death of Aliyath, Judah went up with his friend Hirah to Timnah to shear their sheep.

30. And Tamar heard that Judah had gone up to Timnah to shear the sheep, and that Shiloh was grown up, and Judah did not delight in her.

31. And Tamar rose up and put off the garments of her widowhood, and she put a vail upon her, and she entirely covered herself, and she went and sat in the public thoroughfare, which is upon the road to Timnah.

32. And Judah passed and saw her and took her and he came to her, and she conceived by him, and at the time of being delivered, behold, there were twins in her womb, and he called the name of the first Perez, and the name of the second Zarah.

CHAPTER XLVI.

1. In those days Joseph was still confined in the prison house in the land of Egypt.

2. At that time the attendants of Pharaoh were standing before him, the chief of the butlers and the chief of the bakers which belonged to the king of Egypt.

3. And the butler took wine and placed it before the king to drink, and the baker placed bread before the king to eat, and the king drank of the wine and ate of the bread, he and his servants and ministers that ate at the king's table.

4. And whilst they were eating and

drinking, the butler and the baker remained there, and Pharaoh's ministers found many flies in the wine, which the butler had brought, and stones of nitre were found in the baker's bread.

5. And the captain of the guard placed Joseph as an attendant on Pharaoh's officers, and Pharaoh's officers were in confinement one year.

6. And at the end of the year, they both dreamed dreams in one night, in the place of confinement where they were, and in the morning Joseph came to them to attend upon them as usual, and he saw them, and behold their countenances were dejected and sad.

7. And Joseph asked them, why are your countenances sad and dejected this day? and they said unto him we dreamed a dream, and there is no one to interpret it; and Joseph said unto them, relate, I pray you, your dream unto me, and God shall give you an answer of peace as you desire.

8. And the butler related his dream unto Joseph, and he said, I saw in my dream, and behold a large vine was before me, and upon that vine I saw three branches, and *the vine* speedily blossomed and reached a great height, and its clusters were ripened and became grapes.

9. And I took the grapes and pressed them in a cup, and placed it in Pharaoh's hand and he drank; and Joseph said unto him, the three branches that were upon the vine are three days.

10. Yet within three days, the king will order thee to be brought out and he will restore thee to thy office, and thou shalt give the king his wine to drink as at first when thou wast his butler; but let me find favor in thy sight, that thou shalt remember me to Pharaoh when it will be well with thee, and do kindness unto me, and get me brought forth from this prison, for I was stolen away from the land of Canaan and was sold for a slave in this place.

11. And also that which was told thee concerning my master's wife is false, for they placed me in this dungeon for naught; and the butler answered Joseph, saying, if the king deal well with me as at first, as thou hast interpreted to me, I will do all that thou desirest, and get thee brought out of this dungeon.

12. And the baker, seeing that Joseph had accurately interpreted the butler's dream, also approached, and related the whole of his dream to Joseph.

13. And he said unto him, in my dream I saw and behold three white baskets upon my head, and I looked, and behold there were in the uppermost basket all manner of baked meats for Pharaoh, and behold the birds were eating them from off my head.

14. And Joseph said unto him, the three baskets which thou didst see are three days, yet within three days Pharaoh will take off thy head, and hang thee upon a tree, and the birds will eat thy flesh from off thee, as thou sawest in thy dream.

15. In those days the queen was about to be delivered, and upon that day she bare a son unto the king of Egypt, and they proclaimed that the king had gotten *his* first born son and all the *people of* Egypt together with the officers and servants of Pharaoh rejoiced greatly.

16. And upon the third day of his birth Pharaoh made a feast for his officers and servants, for the hosts of

10

the land of Zoar and of the land of Egypt.

17. And all *the people of* Egypt and the servants of Pharaoh came to eat and drink with the king at the feast of his son, and to rejoice at the king's rejoicing.

18. And all the officers of the king and his servants were rejoicing at that time for eight days at the feast, and they made merry with all sorts of musical instruments, with timbrels and with dances in the king's house for eight days.

19. And the butler, to whom Joseph had interpreted his dream, forgot Joseph, and he did not mention him to the king as he had promised, for this thing was from the Lord in order to punish Joseph because he had trusted in man.

20. And Joseph remained after this in the prison house two years, until he had completed twelve years.

CHAPTER XLVII.

1. And Isaac the son of Abraham was still living in those days in the land of Canaan; *he was* very aged, one hundred and eighty years old, and Esau his son, the brother of Jacob, was in the land of Edom, and he and his sons had possessions in it amongst the children of Seir.

2. And Esau heard that his father's time was drawing nigh to die, and he and his sons and household came unto the land of Canaan, unto his father's house, and Jacob and his sons went forth from the place where they dwelt in Hebron, and they all came to their father Isaac, and they found Esau and his sons in the tent.

3. And Jacob and his sons sat before his father Isaac, and Jacob was still mourning for his son Joseph.

4. And Isaac said unto Jacob, bring me hither thy sons and I will bless them; and Jacob brought his eleven children before his father Isaac.

5. And Isaac placed his hands upon all the sons of Jacob, and he took hold of them and embraced them, and kissed them one by one, and Isaac blessed them on that day, and he said unto them, may the God of your fathers bless you and increase your seed like the stars of heaven for number.

6. And Isaac also blessed the sons of Esau, saying, may God cause you to be a dread and a terror to all that will behold you, and to all your enemies.

7. And Isaac called Jacob and his sons, and they all came and sat before Isaac, and Isaac said unto Jacob, the Lord God of the whole earth said unto me, unto thy seed will I give this land for an inheritance if thy children keep my statutes and my ways, and I will perform unto them the oath which I swore unto thy father Abraham.

8. Now therefore my son, teach thy children and thy children's children to fear the Lord, and to go in the good way which will please the Lord thy God, for if you keep the ways of the Lord and his statutes the Lord will also keep unto you his covenant with Abraham, and will do well with you and your seed all the days.

9. And when Isaac had finished commanding Jacob and his children, he gave up the ghost and died, and was gathered unto his people.

10. And Jacob and Esau fell upon the face of their father Isaac, and they wept, and Isaac was one hundred and eighty years old when he

died in the land of Canaan, in Hebron, and his sons carried him to the
cave of Machpelah, which Abraham
had bought from the children of Heth
for a possession of a burial place.

11. And all the kings of the land
of Canaan went with Jacob and Esau
to bury Isaac, and all the kings of
Canaan showed Isaac great honor at
his death.

12. And the sons of Jacob and the
sons of Esau went barefooted round
about, walking and lamenting until
they reached Kireath-arba.

13. And Jacob and Esau buried
their father Isaac in the cave of Machpelah, which is in Kireath-arba in
Hebron, and they buried him with very
great honor, as at the funeral of kings.

14. And Jacob and his sons, and
Esau and his sons, and all the kings
of Canaan made a great and heavy
mourning, and they buried him and
mourned for him many days.

15. And at the death of Isaac, he
left his cattle and his possessions and
all belonging to him to his sons; and
Esau said unto Jacob, behold I pray
thee, all that our father has left we
will divide it in two parts, and I will
have the choice, and Jacob said we
will do so.

16. And Jacob took all that Isaac
had left in the land of Canaan, the
cattle and the property, and he placed
them in two *parts* before Esau and
his sons, and he said unto E: m, behold all this is before thee choose
thou unto thyself the half which thou
wilt take.

17. And Jacob said unto Esau,
hear thou I pray thee what I will
speak unto thee, saying, the Lord
God of heaven and earth spoke unto
our fathers Abraham and Isaac, saying, unto thy seed will I give this
land for an inheritance forever.

18. Now therefore all that our father has left is before thee, and behold all the land is before thee;
choose thou from them what thou
desirest.

19. If thou desirest the whole land
take it for thee and thy children forever, and I will take this riches, and
if thou desirest the riches take it unto
thee, and I will take this land for me
and for my children to inherit it forever.

20. And Nebayoth, the son of Ishmael, was then in the land with his
children, and Esau went on that day
and consulted with him, saying,

21. Thus has Jacob spoken unto
me, and thus has he answered me,
now give thy advice and we will
hear.

22. And Nebayoth said, what is
this that Jacob hath spoken unto
thee? behold all the children of Canaan are dwelling securely in their
land, and Jacob sayeth he will inherit it with his seed all the days.

23. Go now *therefore* and take all
thy father's riches and leave Jacob
thy brother in the land, as he has
spoken.

24. And Esau rose up and returned to Jacob, and did all that Nebayoth the son of Ishma :l had advised;
and Esau took all the riches that
Isaac had left, the souls, the beasts,
the cattle and the property, and all
the riches; he gave nothing to his
brother Jacob; and Jacob took all
the land of Canaan, from the brook
of Egypt unto the river Euphrates,
and he took it for an everlasting possession, and for his children and for
his seed after him forever.

25. Jacob also took from his brother Esau the cave of Machpelah,
which is in Hebron, which Abraham
had bought from Ephron for a pos-

session of a burial place for him and his seed for ever.

26. And Jacob wrote all these things in the book of purchase, and he signed it, and he testified all this with four faithful witnesses.

27. And these are the words which Jacob wrote in the book, saying: The land of Canaan and all the cities of the Hittites, the Hivites, the Jebusites, the Amorites, the Perizzites, and the Gergashites, all the seven nations from the river of Egypt unto the river Euphrates;

28. And the city of Hebron Kireath-arba and the cave which is in it, the whole did Jacob buy from his brother Esau for value, for a possession and for an inheritance for his seed after him forever.

29. And Jacob took the book of purchase and the signature, the command and the statutes and the revealed book, and he placed them in an earthen vessel in order that they should remain for a long time, and he delivered them into the hands of his children.

30. Esau took all that his father had left him after his death from his brother Jacob, and he took all the property, from man and beast, camel and ass, ox and lamb, silver and gold, stones and bdellium, and all the riches which had belonged to Isaac the son of Abraham ; there was nothing left which Esau did not take unto himself, from all that Isaac had left after his death.

31. And Esau took all this, and he and his children went home to the land of Seir the Horite, away from his brother Jacob and his children.

32. And Esau had possessions amongst the children of Seir, and Esau returned not to the land of Canaan from that day forward.

33. And the whole land of Canaan became an inheritance to the children of Israel for an everlasting inheritance, and Esau with all his children inherited the mountain of Seir.

CHAPTER XLVIII.

1. In those days, after the death of Isaac, the Lord commanded and caused a famine upon the whole earth.

2. At that time Pharaoh king of Egypt was sitting upon his throne in the land of Egypt, and lay in his bed and dreamed dreams, and Pharaoh saw in his dream that he was standing by the side of the river of Egypt.

3. And whilst he was standing he saw and behold seven fat fleshed and well favored kine came up out of the river.

4. And seven other kine, lean fleshed and ill favored, came up after them, and the seven ill favored ones swallowed up the well favored ones, and still their appearance was ill as at first.

5. And he awoke, and he slept *again* and he dreamed a second time, and he saw and behold seven ears of corn came up upon one stalk, rank and good, and seven thin ears blasted with the east wind sprang up after them, and the thin ears swallowed up the full ones, and Pharaoh awoke out of his dream.

6. And in the morning the king remembered his dreams, and his spirit was sadly troubled on account of his dreams, and the king hastened and sent and called for all the magicians of Egypt, and the wise men, and they came and stood before Pharaoh.

7. And the king said unto them, I have dreamed dreams, and there is none to interpret them; and they said unto the king, relate thy dreams to thy servants and let us hear them.

8. And the king related his dreams to them, and they all answered and said with one voice to the king, may the king live for ever; and this is the interpretation of thy dreams.

9. The seven good kine which thou didst see *denote* seven daughters that will be born unto thee in the latter days, and the seven kine which thou sawest come up after them, and swallowed them up, are for a sign that the daughters which will be born unto thee will all die in the life-time of the king.

10. And that which thou didst see in the second dream *of* seven full and good ears of corn coming up upon one stalk, this is their interpretation, that thou wilt build unto thyself in the latter days seven cities throughout the land of Egypt; and that which thou sawest of the seven blasted ears of corn springing up after them and swallowing them up whilst thou didst behold them with thine eyes, is for a sign that the cities which thou wilt build will all be destroyed in the latter days, in the life-time of the king.

11. And when they spoke these words the king did not incline his ear to their words, neither did he fix his heart upon them, for the king knew in his wisdom that they did not give a proper interpretation of the dreams; and when they had finished speaking before the king, the king answered them, saying, what is this thing that you have spoken unto me? surely you have uttered falsehood and *spoken* lies; *therefore* now give the proper inter-pretation of my dreams, that you may not die.

12. And the king commanded after this, and he sent and called again for other wise men, and they came and stood before the king, and the king related his dreams to them, and they all answered him according to the first interpretation, and the king's anger was kindled and he was very wroth, and the king said unto them, surely you speak lies and utter falsehood in what you have said.

13. And the king commanded that a proclamation should be issued throughout the land of Egpt, saying, it is resolved by the king and his great men, that any wise man who knoweth and understandeth the interpretation of dreams, and will not come this day before the king, *he* shall die.

14. And the man that will declare unto the king the proper interpretation of his dreams, there shall be given unto him all that he will require from the king. And all the wise men of the land of Egypt came before the king, together with all the magicians and sorcerers that were in Egypt and in Goshen, in Raamses, in Tachpanches, in Zoar, and in all the *places* on the borders of Egypt, and they all stood before the king.

15. And all the nobles and the princes, and the attendants belonging to the king, came together from all the cities of Egypt, and they all sat before the king, and the king related his dreams before the wise men, and the princes and all that sat before the king were astonished at the vision.

16. And all the wise men who were before the king were greatly divided in their interpretation of his dreams; some of them interpreted

them to the king, saying, the seven good kine *are* seven kings, who from the king's issue will be raised over Egypt.

17. And the seven bad kine *are* seven princes, who will stand up against them in the latter days and destroy them ; and the seven ears of corn are the seven great princes belonging to Egypt, who will fall in the hands of the seven less powerful princes of their enemies, in the wars of *our* lord the king.

18. And some of them interpreted to the king in this manner, saying, the seven good kine are the strong cities of Egypt, and the seven bad kine are the seven nations of the land of Canaan, who will come against the seven cities of Egypt in the latter days and destroy them.

19. And that which thou sawest in the second dream, of seven good and bad ears of corn, is a sign that the government of Egypt will again return to thy seed as at first.

20. And in his reign the people of the cities of Egypt will turn against the seven cities of Canaan who are stronger than they are, and will destroy them, and the government of Egypt will return to thy seed.

21. And some of them said unto the king, this is the interpretation of thy dreams ; the seven good kine are seven queens, whom thou wilt take for wives in the latter days, and the seven bad kine denote that those women will all die in the lifetime of the king.

22. And the seven good and bad ears of corn which thou didst see in the second dream are fourteen children, and it will be in the latter days that they will stand up and fight amongst themselves, and seven of them will smite the seven that are more powerful.

23. And some of them said these words unto the king, saying, the seven good kine *denote* that seven children will be born to thee, and they will slay seven of thy children's children in the latter days ; and the seven good ears of corn which thou didst see in the second dream, are those princes against whom seven other less powerful princes will fight and destroy them in the latter days, and avenge thy children's cause, and the government will again return to thy seed.

24. And the king heard all the words of the wise men of Egypt and their interpretation of his dreams, and none of them pleased the king.

25. And the king knew in his wisdom that they did not altogether speak correctly in all these words, for this was from the Lord to frustrate the words of the wise men of Egypt, in order that Joseph might go forth from the house of confinement, and in order that he should become great in Egypt.

26. And the king saw that none amongst all the wise men and magicians of Egypt spoke correctly to him, and the king's wrath was kindled, and his anger burned within him.

27. And the king commanded that all the wise men and magicians should go out from before him, and they all went out from before the king with shame and disgrace.

28. And the king commanded that a proclamation be sent throughout Egypt to slay all the magicians that were in Egypt, *and* not one of them should be suffered to live.

29. And the captains of the guards belonging to the king rose up, and each man drew his sword, and they began to smite the magicians of Egypt, and the wise men.

30. And after this Merod, chief butler to the king, came and bowed down before the king and sat before him;

31. And the butler said unto the king, may the king live forever, and his government be exalted in the land.

32. Thou wast angry with thy servant in those days, now two years past, and didst place me in the ward, and I was for some time in the ward, I and the chief of the bakers.

33. And there was with us a Hebrew servant belonging to the captain of the guard, his name was Joseph, for his master had been angry with him and placed him in the house of confinement, and he attended us there.

34. And in some time after when we were in the ward, we dreamed dreams in one night, I and the chief of the bakers; we dreamed, each man according to the interpretation of his dream.

35. And we came in the morning and told *them* to that servant, and he interpreted to us our dreams, to each man according to his dream, did he correctly interpret.

36. And it came to pass as he interpreted to us, so was the event; there fell not to the ground any of his words.

37. And now therefore my lord and king do not slay the people of Egypt for naught; behold that slave is still confined in the house by the captain of the guard his master, in the house of confinement.

38. If it pleaseth the king let him send for him that he may come before thee and he will make known to thee, the correct interpretation of the dream which thou didst dream.

39. And the king heard the words of the chief butler, and the king ordered that the wise men of Egypt should not be slain.

40. And the king ordered his servants to bring Joseph before him, and the king said unto them, go to him and do not terrify him lest he be confused and will not know to speak properly.

41. And the servants of the king went to Joseph, and they brought him hastily out of the dungeon, and the king's servants shaved him, and he changed his prison garment and he came before the king.

42. And the king was sitting upon his royal throne in a princely dress girt round with a golden ephod, and the fine gold which was upon it sparkled, and the carbuncle and the ruby and the emerald, together with all the precious stones that were upon the king's head, dazzled *the eye*, and Joseph wondered greatly at the king.

43. And the throne upon which the king sat was covered with gold and silver, and with onyx stones, and it had seventy steps.

44. And it was their custom throughout the land of Egypt, that every man who came to speak to the king, if he was a prince or one that was estimable in the sight of the king, he ascended to the king's throne as far as the thirty first step, and the king would descend to the thirty sixth step, and speak with him.

45. If he was one of the *common* people, he ascended to the third step, and the king would descend to the fourth* and speak to him, and their custom was, moreover, that any man who understood to speak in all the seventy languages, he ascended *the*

* From his throne, leaving in this instance a space of sixty three steps, but in the former there was only the space of three steps intervening between the king and his favorites.

seventy steps, and went up and spoke till he reached the king.

46. And any man who could not complete the seventy, he ascended as many steps as the languages which he knew to speak *in*.

47. And it was customary in those days in Egypt that no one should reign over them, but who understood to speak in the seventy languages.

48. And when Joseph came before the king he bowed down to the ground before the king, and he ascended to the third step, and the king sat upon the fourth step and spoke with Joseph.

49. And the king said unto Joseph, I dreamed a dream, and there is no interpreter to interpret it properly, and I commanded this day that all the magicians of Egypt and the wise men thereof, should come before me, and I related my dreams to them, and no one has properly interpreted them to me.

50. And after this I this day heard concerning thee, that thou art a wise man, and canst correctly interpret every dream that thou hearest.

51. And Joseph answered Pharaoh, saying, let Pharoah relate his dreams that he dreamed; surely the interpretations belong to God; and Pharaoh related his dreams to Joseph, the dream of the kine, and the dream of the ears of corn, and the king left off speaking.

52. And Joseph was then clothed with the spirit of God before the king, and he knew all the things that would befall the king from that day forward, and he knew the proper interpretation of the king's dream, and he spoke before the king.

53. And Joseph found favor in the sight of the king, and the king inclined his ears and his heart, and he heard all the words of Joseph. And Joseph said unto the king, do not imagine that they are two dreams, for it is only one dream, for that which God has chosen to do throughout the land he has shown to the king in his dream, and this is the proper interpretation of thy dream.

54. The seven good kine and ears of corn are seven years, and the seven bad kine and ears of corn are *also* seven years; it is one dream.

55. Behold the seven years that are coming there will be a great plenty throughout the land, and after that the seven years of famine will follow them, a very grievous famine, and all the plenty will be forgotten from the land, and the famine will consume all the inhabitants of the land.

56. The king dreamed one dream, and the dream was therefore repeated unto Pharaoh because the thing *is* established by God, and God will shortly bring it to pass.

57. Now *therefore* I will give thee counsel and deliver thy soul and the souls of the inhabitants of the land from the evil of the famine, that thou seek throughout thy kingdom *for* a man very discreet and wise, who knoweth all the affairs of government, and appoint him to superintend* over the land of Egypt.

58. And let the man whom thou placest over Egypt appoint officers under him, that they gather in all the food of the good years that are coming, and let them lay up corn and deposit it in thy appointed stores.

59. And let them keep that food for the seven years of famine, that it may be found for thee and thy people and thy whole land, and that thou and thy land be not cut off by the famine.

* Hebrew, to go out and come in.

60. Let all the inhabitants of the land be also ordered that they gather in, every man the produce of his field, of all sorts of food, during the seven good years, and that they place it in their stores, that it may be found for them in the days of the famine and that they may live upon it.

61. This is the proper interpretation of thy dream, and this is the counsel given to save thy soul and the souls of all thy subjects.

62. And the king answered and said unto Joseph, who sayeth and who knoweth that thy words are correct? And he said unto the king, this shall be a sign for thee respecting all my words, that they are true and that my advice is good for thee.

63. Behold thy wife sitteth this day upon the stool of delivery, and she will bear thee a son and thou wilt rejoice with him; when thy child shall have gone forth from his mother's womb, thy first born son that has been born these two years back shall die, and thou wilt be comforted in the child that will be born unto thee this day.

64. And Joseph finished speaking these words to the king, and he bowed down to the king and he went out, and when Joseph had gone out from the king's presence, those signs which Joseph had spoken unto the king came to pass on that day.

65. And the queen bare a son on that day and the king heard the glad tidings about his son, and he rejoiced, and when the reporter had gone forth from the king's presence, the king's servants found the first born son of the king fallen dead upon the ground.

66. And there was great lamentation and noise in the king's house, and the king heard it, and he said, what is the noise and lamentation that I have heard in the house? and they told the king that his first born son had died; then the king knew that all Joseph's words that he had spoken were correct, and the king was consoled for his son by the child that was born to him on that day as Joseph had spoken.

CHAPTER XLIX.

1. After these things the king sent and assembled all his officers and servants, and all the princes and nobles belonging to the king, and they all came before the king.

2. And the king said unto them, behold you have seen and heard all the words of this Hebrew man, and all the signs which he declared would come to pass, and not any of his words have fallen to the ground.

3. You know that he has given a proper interpretation of the dream, and it will surely come to pass, now therefore take counsel and know what you will do and how the land will be delivered from the famine.

4. Seek now and see whether the like can be found in whose heart there is wisdom and knowledge, and I will appoint him over the land.

5. For you have heard what the Hebrew man has advised concerning this to save the land therewith from the famine, and I know that the land will not be delivered from the famine but with the advice of the Hebrew man, him that advised me.

6. And they all answered the king and said, the counsel which the Hebrew has given concerning this is good; now therefore, our lord and king, behold the whole land is in thy hand, do that which seemeth good in thy sight.

7. Him whom thou choosest, and whom thou in thy wisdom knowest to be wise and *capable* of delivering the land with his wisdom, him shall the king appoint to be under him over the land.

8. And the king said to all the officers, I have thought that since God has made known to the Hebrew man all that he has spoken, there is none so discreet and wise in the whole land as he is ; if it seem good in your sight I will place him over the land, for he will save the land with his wisdom.

9. And all the officers answered the king and said, but surely it is written in the laws of Egypt, and it should not be violated, that no man shall reign over Egypt, nor be the second to the king, but one who has knowledge in all the languages of the sons of men.

10. Now therefore our lord and king, behold this Hebrew man can only speak the Hebrew language, and how then can he be over us the second *under government*, a man who not even knoweth our language ?

11. Now we pray thee send for him, and let him come before thee, and prove him in all things, and do as thou seest *fit*.

12. And the king said, it shall be done so to-morrow, and the thing that you have spoken is good ; and all the officers came on that day before the king.

13. And on that night the Lord sent one of his ministering angels, and he came unto the land of Egypt unto Joseph, and the angel of the Lord stood over Joseph, and behold Joseph was lying in the bed at night in his master's house in the dungeon, for his master had put him back into the dungeon on account of his wife.

14. And the angel roused him from his sleep, and Joseph rose up and stood upon his legs, and behold the angel of the Lord was standing opposite to him ; and the angel of the Lord spoke with Joseph, and he taught him all the languages of man in that night, and he called his name Jehoseph.

15. And the angel of the Lord went from him, and Joseph returned and lay upon his bed, and Joseph was astonished at the vision which he saw.

16. And it came to pass in the morning that the king sent for all his officers and servants, and they all came and sat before the king, and the king ordered Joseph to be brought, and the king's servants went and brought Joseph before Pharaoh.

17. And the king came forth and ascended the steps of the throne, and Joseph spoke unto the king in all languages, and Joseph went up to him and spoke unto the king until he arrived before the king in the seventieth step, and he sat before the king.

18. And the king greatly rejoiced on account of Joseph, and all the king's officers rejoiced greatly with the king when they heard all the words of Joseph.

19. And the thing seemed good in the sight of the king and the officers, to appoint Joseph to be second to the king over the whole land of Egypt, and the king spoke to Joseph, saying,

20. Now thou didst give me counsel to appoint a wise man over the land of Egypt, in order with his wisdom to save the land from the famine ; now therefore, since God has made all this known to thee, and all the words which thou hast spoken, there

is not throughout the land a discreet and wise man like unto thee.

21. And thy name no more shall be called Joseph, but Zaphnath Paaneah shall be thy name; thou shalt be second to me, and according to thy word shall be all the affairs of my government, and at thy word shall my people go out and come in.

22. Also from under thy hand shall my servants and officers receive their salary which is given to them monthly, and to thee shall all the people of the land bow down; only in my throne will I be greater than thou.

23. And the king took off his ring from his hand and put it upon the hand of Joseph, and the king dressed Joseph in a princely garment, and he put a golden crown upon his head, and he put a golden chain upon his neck.

24. And the king commanded his servants, and they made him ride in the second chariot belonging to the king, that went opposite to the king's chariot, and he caused him to ride upon a great and strong horse from the king's horses, and to be conducted through the streets of the land of Egypt.

25. And the king commanded that all those that played upon timbrels, harps and other musical instruments should go forth with Joseph; one thousand timbrels, one thousand Mecholoth, and one thousand Nebalim went after him.

26. And five thousand men, with drawn swords glittering in their hands, and they went marching and playing before Joseph, and twenty thousand of the great men of the king girt with girdles of skin covered with gold, marched at the right hand of Joseph, and twenty thousand at his left, and all the women and damsels went upon the roofs or stood in the streets playing and rejoicing at Joseph, and gazed at the appearance of Joseph and at his beauty.

27. And the king's people went before him and behind him, perfuming the road with frankincense and with cassia, and with all sorts of fine perfume, and scattered myrrh and aloes along the road, and twenty men proclaimed these words before him throughout the land in a loud voice;

28. Do you see this man whom the king has chosen to be his second? all the affairs of government shall be regulated by him, and he that transgresses his orders, or that does not bow down before him to the ground, shall die, for he rebels against the king and his second.

29. And when the heralds had ceased proclaiming, all *the people of* Egypt bowed down to the ground before Joseph and said, may the king live, also may his second live; and all the inhabitants of Egypt bowed down along the road, *and* when the heralds approached them, they bowed down, and they rejoiced with all sorts of timbrels, mechol and nebal before Joseph.

30. And Joseph upon his horse lifted up his eyes to heaven, and called out and said, He raiseth the poor man from the dust, He lifteth up the needy from the dunghill. O Lord of hosts, happy is the man who trusteth in thee.

31. And Joseph passed throughout the land of Egypt with Pharaoh's servants and officers, and they showed him the whole land of Egypt and all the king's treasures.

32. And Joseph returned and came on that day before Pharaoh, and the king gave unto Joseph a

possession in the land of Egypt, a possession of fields and vineyards, and the king gave unto Joseph three thousand talents of silver and one thousand talents of gold, and onyx stones and bdellium and many gifts.

33. And on the next day the king commanded all *the people* of Egypt to bring unto Joseph offerings and gifts, and that he that violated the command of the king should die; and they made a high place in the street of the city, and they spread out garments there, and whoever brought anything to Joseph put it into the high place.

34. And all *the people of* Egypt cast *something* into the high place, one man a golden ear-ring, and the other rings and ear-rings, and different vessels of gold and silver work, and onyx stones and bdellium did he cast upon the high place; every one gave something of what he possessed.

35. And Joseph took all these and placed them in his treasures, and all the officers and nobles belonging to the king exalted Joseph, and they gave him many gifts, seeing that the king had chosen him to be his second.

36. And the king sent to Potiphera, the son of Ahiram priest of On, and he took his young daughter Osnath and gave her unto Joseph for a wife.

37. And the damsel was very comely, a virgin, *one* whom man had not known, and Joseph took her for a wife; and the king said unto Joseph, I am Pharaoh, and beside thee none shall *dare to* lift up his hand or his foot to regulate* my people throughout the land of Egypt.

38. And Joseph was thirty years

Hebrew, to go out and come in.

old when he stood before Pharaoh, and Joseph went out from before the king, and he became the king's second in Egypt.

39. And the king gave Joseph a hundred servants to attend him in his house, and Joseph also sent and purchased many servants and they remained in the house of Joseph.

40. Joseph then built for himself a very magnificent house like unto the houses of kings, before the court of the king's palace, and he made in the house a large temple, very elegant in appearance and convenient for his residence; three years was Joseph in erecting his house.

41. And Joseph made unto himself a very elegant throne of abundance of gold and silver, and he covered it with onyx stones and bdellium, and he made upon it the likeness of the whole land of Egypt, and the likeness of the river of Egypt that watereth the whole land of Egypt; and Joseph sat securely upon his throne in his house and the Lord increased Joseph's wisdom.

42. And all the inhabitants of Egypt and Pharaoh's servants and his princes loved Joseph exceedingly, for this thing was from the Lord to Joseph.

43. And Joseph had an army that made war, going out in hosts and troops to the number of forty thousand six hundred men, capable of bearing arms to assist the king and Joseph against the enemy, besides the king's officers and his servants and inhabitants of Egypt without number.

44. And Joseph gave unto his mighty men, and to all his host, shields and javelins, and caps and coats of mail and stones for slinging.

CHAPTER L.

1. At that time the children of Tarshish came against the sons of Ishmael, and made war with them, and the children of Tarshish spoiled the Ishmaelites for a long time.

2. And the children of Ishmael were small in number in those days, and they could not prevail over the children of Tarshish, and they were sorely oppressed.

3. And the old men of the Ishmaelites sent a record to the king of Egypt, saying, send I pray thee unto thy servants officers and hosts to help us to fight against the children of Tarshish, for we have been consuming away for a long time.

4. And Pharaoh sent Joseph with the mighty men and host which were with him, and *also* his mighty men from the king's house.

5. And they went to the land of Havilah to the children of Ishmael, to assist them against the children of Tarshish, and the children of Ishmael fought with the children of Tarshish, and Joseph smote the Tarshishites and he subdued all their land, and the children of Ishmael dwelt therein unto this day.

6. And when the land of Tarshish was subdued, all the Tarshishites ran away and came on the border of their brethren the children of Javan, and Joseph with all his mighty men and host returned to Egypt, not one man of them was missing.

7. And at the revolution of the year, in the second year of Joseph's reigning over Egypt, the Lord gave great plenty throughout the land for seven years as Joseph had spoken, for the Lord blessed all the produce of the earth in those days for seven years, and they ate and were greatly satisfied.

8. And Joseph at that time had officers under him, and they collected all the food of the good years, and heaped corn year by year, and they placed it in the treasuries of Joseph.

9. And at any time when they gathered the food Joseph commanded that they should bring the corn in the ears, and also bring with it some of the soil of the field, that it should not spoil.

10. And Joseph did according to this year by year, and he heaped up corn like the sand of the sea for abundance, for his stores were immense and could not be numbered for abundance.

11. And also all the inhabitants of Egypt gathered all sorts of food in their stores in great abundance *during* the seven good years, but they did not do unto it as Joseph did.

12. And all the food which Joseph and the Egyptians had gathered *during* the seven years of plenty, was secured for the land in stores for the seven years of famine, for the support of the whole land.

13. And the inhabitants of Egypt filled each man his store and his concealed place with corn, to be for *support* during the famine.

14. And Joseph placed all the food that he had gathered in all the cities of Egypt, and he closed all the stores and placed sentinels over them.

15. And Joseph's wife Osnath the daughter of Potiphera bare him two sons, Manasseh and Ephraim, and Joseph was thirty four years old when he begat them.

16. And the lads grew up and they went in his ways and in his instructions, they did not deviate from

the way which their father taught them, either to the right or left.

17. And the Lord was with the lads, and they grew up and had understanding and skill in all wisdom and in all the affairs of government, and all the king's officers and his great men of the inhabitants of Egypt exalted the lads, and they were brought up amongst the king's children.

18. And the seven years of plenty that were throughout the land were at an end, and the seven years of famine came after them as Joseph had spoken, and the famine was throughout the land.

19. And all *the people of* Egypt saw that the famine had commenced in the land of Egypt, and all *the people of* Egypt opened their stores of corn for the famine prevailed over them.

20. And they found all the food that was in their stores, full of vermin and not fit to eat, and the famine prevailed throughout the land, and all the inhabitants of Egypt came and cried before Pharaoh, for the famine was heavy upon them.

21. And they said unto Pharaoh, give food unto thy servants, and wherefore shall we die through hunger before thy eyes, even we and our little ones?

22. And Pharaoh answered them, saying, and wherefore do you cry unto me? did not Joseph command that the corn should be laid up during the seven years of plenty for the years of famine? and wherefore did you not hearken to his voice?

23. And *the people* of Egypt answered the king, *saying*, as thy soul liveth, our lord, thy servants have done all that Joseph ordered, for thy servants also gathered in all the pro-duce of their fields during the seven years of plenty and laid it in the stores unto this day.

24. And when the famine prevailed over thy servants we opened our stores, and behold all our produce was filled with vermin and was not fit for food.

25. And when the king heard all that had befallen to the inhabitants of Egypt, the king was greatly afraid on account of the famine, and he was much terrified; and the king answered the people of Egypt, saying, since all this has happened unto you, go unto Joseph, do whatever he shall say unto you, transgress not his commands.

26. And all *the people* of Egypt went forth and came unto Joseph, and said unto him, give unto us food and wherefore shall we die before thee through hunger? for we gathered in our produce during the seven years as thou didst command, and we put it in store, and thus has it befallen us.

27. And when Joseph heard all the words of *the people of* Egypt and what had befallen them, Joseph opened all his stores of the produce and he sold it unto *the people* of Egypt.

28. And the famine prevailed throughout the land, and the famine was in all countries, but in the land of Egypt there was produce for sale.

29. And all the inhabitants of Egypt came unto Joseph to buy corn, for the famine prevailed over them, and all their corn was spoiled, and Joseph daily sold it to all the people of Egypt.

30. And all the inhabitants of the land of Canaan and the Philistines, and *those* beyond the Jordan, and the children of the east and all the cities

of the lands far and nigh heard that there was corn in Egypt, and they all came to Egypt to buy corn, for the famine prevailed over them.

31. And Joseph opened the stores of corn and placed officers over them, and they daily stood and sold to all that came.

32. And Joseph knew that his brethren also would come to Egypt to buy corn, for the famine prevailed throughout the earth. And Joseph commanded all his people that they should cause it to be proclaimed throughout the land of Egypt, saying,

33. It is the pleasure of the king, of his second and of their great men, that any person who wishes to buy corn in Egypt shall not send his servants to Egypt to purchase, but his sons, and also any Egyptian or Canaanite, who shall come from any of the stores from buying corn in Egypt, and shall go and sell it throughout the land, he shall die, for no one shall buy but *for* the support of his household.

34. And any man leading two or three beasts shall die, for a man shall only lead his own beast.

35. And Joseph placed sentinels at the gates of Egypt, and commanded them, saying, any person who may come to buy corn, suffer him not to enter until his name, and the name of his father, and the name of his father's father be written down, and whatever is written by day, send their names unto me in the evening that I may know their names.

36. And Joseph placed officers throughout the land of Egypt, and he commanded them to do all these things.

37. And Joseph did all these things, and *made* these statutes, in order that he might know when his brethren should come to Egypt to buy corn ; and Joseph's people caused it daily to be proclaimed in Egypt according to these words and statutes which Joseph had commanded.

38. And all the inhabitants of the east and west country, and of all the earth, heard of the statutes and regulations which Joseph had enacted in Egypt, and the inhabitants of the extreme parts of the earth came and they bought corn in Egypt day after day, and then went away.

39. And all the officers of Egypt did as Joseph had commanded, and all that came to Egypt to buy corn, the gate keepers would write their names, and their fathers' names, and daily bring them in the evening before Joseph.

CHAPTER LI.

1. And Jacob afterward heard that there was corn in Egypt, and he called unto his sons to go to Egypt to buy corn, for upon them also did the famine prevail, and he called unto his sons, saying,

2. Behold I hear that there is corn in Egypt and all the *people of the* earth go there to purchase, now *therefore* why will you show yourselves satisfied before the whole earth ? go you also down to Egypt and buy us a little corn amongst those that come *there*, that we may not die.

3. And the sons of Jacob hearkened to the voice of their father, and they rose up to go down to Egypt in order to buy corn amongst *the rest* that came *there*.

4. And Jacob their father commanded them, saying, when you come into the city do not enter together in one gate, on account of the inhabitants of the land.

5. And the sons of Jacob went forth and they went to Egypt, and the sons of Jacob did all as their father had commanded them, and Jacob did not send Benjamin, for he said, lest an accident might befall him on the road like his brother ; and ten of Jacob's sons went forth.

6. And whilst the sons of Jacob were going on the road, they repented of what they had done to Joseph, and they spoke to each other, saying, we know that our brother Joseph went down to Egypt, and now we will seek him where we go, and if we find him we will take him from his master for a ransom, and if not, by force, and we will die for him.

7. And the sons of Jacob agreed to this thing and strengthened themselves on account of Joseph, to deliver him from the hand of his master, and the sons of Jacob went to Egypt ; and when they came near to Egypt they separated from each other and they came through ten gates of Egypt, and the gate keepers wrote their names on that day, and brought them to Joseph in the evening.

8. And Joseph read the names from the hand of the gate-keepers of the city, and he found that his brethren had entered at the ten gates of the city, and Joseph at that time commanded that it should be proclaimed throughout the land of Egypt, saying,

9. Go forth all ye store guards, close all the corn stores and let only one remain open, that those who come may purchase from it.

10. And all the officers of Joseph did so at that time, and they closed all the stores and left only one open.

11. And Joseph gave the written names of his brethren to him that was set over the open store, and he said unto him, whosoever shall come to thee to buy corn, ask his name, and when men of these names shall come before thee, seize them and send them, and they did so.

12. And when the sons of Jacob came into the city, they joined together in the city to seek Joseph before they bought themselves corn.

13. And they went to the walls of the harlots, and they sought Joseph in the walls of the harlots for three days, for they thought that Joseph would come in the walls of the harlots, for Joseph was very comely and well favored, and the sons of Jacob sought Joseph for three days, and they could not find him.

14. And the man who was set over the open store sought for those names which Joseph had given him, and he did not find them.

15. And he sent to Joseph, saying, these three days have passed, and those men whose names thou didst give unto me have not come ; and Joseph sent servants to seek the men in all Egypt, and to bring them before Joseph.

16. And Joseph's servants went and came into Egypt and could not find them, and went to Goshen and they were not there, and then went to the city of Raamses and could not find them.

17. And Joseph continued to send sixteen servants to seek his brothers, and they went and spread themselves in the four corners of the city, and four of the servants went into the house of the harlots, and they found the ten men there seeking their brother.

18. And those four men took them and brought them before him, and they bowed down to him to the ground, and Joseph was sitting upon his throne in his temple, clothed with

princely garments, and upon his head was a large crown of gold, and all the mighty men were sitting around him.

19. And the sons of Jacob saw Joseph, and his figure and comeliness and dignity of countenance seemed wonderful in their eyes, and they again bowed down to him to the ground.

20. And Joseph saw his brethren, and he knew them, but they knew him not, for Joseph was very great in their eyes, therefore they knew him not.

21. And Joseph spoke to them, saying, from whence come ye? and they all answered and said, thy servants have come from the land of Canaan to buy corn, for the famine prevails throughout the earth, and thy servants heard that there was corn in Egypt, so they have come amongst the *other* comers to buy corn for their support.

22. And Joseph answered them, saying, if you have come to purchase as you say, why do you come through ten gates of the city? it can only be that you have come to spy through the land.

23. And they all together answered Joseph, and said, not so my lord, we are right, thy servants are not spies, but we have come to buy corn, for thy servants are all brothers, the sons of one man in the land of Canaan, and our father commanded us, saying, when you come to the city do not enter together at one gate on account of the inhabitants of the land.

24. And Joseph again answered them and said, that is the thing which I spoke unto you, you have come to spy through the land, therefore you all came through ten gates of the city; you have come to see the nakedness of the land.

25. Surely every one that cometh to buy corn goeth his way, and you are *already* three days in the land, and what do you do in the walls of harlots in which you have been for these three days? surely spies do like unto these *things*.

26. And they said unto Joseph, far be it from our lord to speak thus, for we are twelve brothers, the sons of our father Jacob, in the land of Canaan, the son of Isaac, the son of Abraham, the Hebrew, and behold the youngest is with our father this day in the land of Canaan, and one is not, for he was lost from us, and we thought perhaps he might be in this land, so we are seeking him throughout the land, and have come even to the houses of harlots to seek him there.

27. And Joseph said unto them, and have you then sought him throughout the earth, that there only remained Egypt for you to seek him in? And what also should your brother do in the houses of harlots, although he were in Egypt? have you not said that you are from the sons of Isaac, the son of Abraham, and what shall the sons of Jacob do *then* in the houses of harlots?

28. And they said unto him, because we heard that Ishmaelites stole him from us, and it was told unto us that they sold him in Egypt, and thy servant, our brother, is very comely and well favored, so we thought he would surely be in the houses of harlots, therefore thy servants went there to seek him and give ransom for him.

29. And Joseph still answered them, saying, surely you speak falsely and utter lies, to say of yourselves

11

that you are the sons of Abraham ; as Pharaoh liveth you are spies, therefore have you come to the houses of harlots that you should not be known.

30. And Joseph said unto them, and now if you find him, and his master requireth of you a great price, will you give it for him? and they said, it shall be given.

31. And he said unto them, and if his master will not consent to part with him for a great price, what will you do unto him on his account? and they answered him, saying, if he will not give him unto us we will slay him, and take our brother and go away.

32. And Joseph said unto them, that is the thing which I have spoken to you; you are spies, for you are come to slay the inhabitants of the land, for we heard that two of your brethren smote all the inhabitants of Shechem, in the land of Canaan, on account of your sister, and you *now* come to do the like in Egypt on account of your brother.

33. Only hereby shall I know that you are true *men ;* if you will send *home* one from amongst you to fetch your youngest brother from your father, and to bring him here unto me, and by doing this thing I will know that you are right.

34. And Joseph called to seventy of his mighty men, and he said unto them, take these men and bring them into the ward.

35. And the mighty men took the ten men, they laid hold of them and put them into the ward, and they were in the ward three days.

36. And on the third day Joseph had them brought out of the ward, and he said unto them, do this for yourselves if you be *true men,* so that you may live, one of your breth-ren shall be confined in the ward whilst you go and take home the corn for your household to the land of Canaan, and fetch your youngest brother and bring him here unto me, that I may know that you are true *men* when you do this thing.

37. And Joseph went out from them and came into the chamber, and wept a great weeping, for his pity was excited for them, and he washed his face, and returned to them again, and he took Simeon from them and ordered him to be bound, but Simeon was not willing to be done so, for he was a very powerful man and they could not bind him.

38. And Joseph called unto his mighty men and seventy valiant men came before him with drawn swords in their hands, and the sons of Jacob were terrified at them.

39. And Joseph said unto them, seize this man and confine him in prison until his brethren come to him, and Joseph's valiant men hastened and they all laid hold of Simeon to bind *him,* and Simeon gave a loud and terrible shriek and the cry was heard at a distance.

40. And all the valiant men of Joseph were terrified at the sound of the shriek, that they fell upon their faces, and they were greatly afraid and fled.

41. And all the men that were with Joseph fled, for they were greatly afraid of their lives, and only Joseph Manasseh his son remained there, and Manasseh the son of Joseph saw the strength of Simeon, and he was exceedingly wroth.

42. And Manasseh the son of Joseph rose up to Simeon, and Manasseh smote Simeon a heavy blow with his fist against the back of his neck, and Simeon was stilled of his rage.

43. And Manasseh laid hold of Simeon and he seized him violently and he bound him and brought him into the house of confinement, and all the sons of Jacob were astonished at the act of the youth.

44. And Simeon said unto his brethren, none of you must say that *this is* the smiting of an Egyptian, but *it is* the smiting of the house of my father.

45. And after this Joseph ordered him to be called who was set over the storehouse, to fill their sacks with corn as much as they could carry, and to restore every man's money into his sack, and to give them provision for the road, and thus did he unto them.

46. And Joseph commanded them, *saying*, take heed less you transgress my orders to bring your brother as I have told you, and it shall be when you bring your brother hither unto me, then will I know that you are true men, and you shall traffick in the land, and I will restore unto you your brother and you shall return in peace to your father.

47. And they all answered and said, according as our lord speaketh so will we do, and they bowed down to him to the ground.

48. And every man lifted his corn upon his ass, and they went out to go *to* the land of Canaan to their father, and they came to the inn and Levi spread his sack to give provender to his ass, when he saw and behold his money in full weight was still in his sack.

49. And the man was greatly afraid, and he said unto his brethren, my money is restored and lo, it is even in my sack, and the men were greatly afraid, and they said, what is this that God hath done unto us?

50. And they all said, and where is the Lord's kindness with our fathers, with Abraham, Isaac and Jacob, that the Lord has this day delivered us into the hands of the king of Egypt to contrive against us?

51. And Judah said unto them, surely we are guilty sinners before the Lord our God in having sold our brother, our own flesh, and wherefore do you say, where is the Lord's kindness with our fathers?

52. And Reuben said unto them, said I not unto you, do not sin against the lad, and you would not listen to me? now God requireth him from us, and how dare you say, where is the Lord's kindness with our fathers, whilst you have sinned unto the Lord?

53. And they tarried over night in that place, and they rose up early in the morning and laded their asses with their corn, and they led them and went on and came to their father's house in the land of Canaan.

54. And Jacob and his household went out to meet his sons, and Jacob saw and behold their brother Simeon was not with them, and Jacob said unto his sons, where is your brother Simeon, whom I do not see? and his sons told him all that had befallen them in Egypt.

CHAPTER LII.

1. And they entered their house, and every man opened his sack and they saw and behold every man's bundle of money *was there*, at which they and their father were greatly terrified.

2. And Jacob said unto them, what is this that you have done to me? I sent your brother Joseph to inquire after your welfare and you

said unto me, a wild beast did devour him.

3. And Simeon went with you to buy food and you say the king of Egypt hath confined him in prison, and you wish to take Benjamin to cause his death also, and bring down my grey hairs with sorrow to the grave on account of Benjamin and his brother Joseph.

4. Now *therefore* my son shall not go down with you, for his brother is dead and he is left alone, and mischief may befall him by the way in which you go, as it befel his brother.

5. And Reuben said unto his father, thou shalt slay my two sons if I do not bring thy son and place him before thee ; and Jacob said unto his sons, abide ye *here* and do not go down to Egypt, for my son shall not go down with you to Egypt, nor die like his brother.

6. And Judah said unto them, refrain ye from him until the corn is finished, and he will then say, take down your brother, when he will find his *own* life and the life of his household in danger from the famine.

7. And in those days the famine was sore throughout the land, and all the people of the earth went and came to Egypt to buy food, for the famine prevailed greatly amongst them, and the sons of Jacob remained in Canaan a year and two months until their corn was finished.

8. And it came to pass after their corn was finished, the whole household of Jacob was pinched with hunger, and all the infants of the sons of Jacob came together and they all approached Jacob, and they said unto him, give unto us bread and wherefore shall we all perish through hunger in thy presence ?

9. Jacob heard the words of his sons' and children, and he wept a great weeping, and his pity was roused for them, and Jacob called unto his sons and they all came and sat before him.

10. And Jacob said unto them, and have you not seen how your children have been weeping over me this day, *saying*, give unto us bread, and there is none ? now *therefore* return *and* buy for us a little food.

11. And Judah answered and said unto his father, if thou wilt send our brother with us we will go down and buy corn for thee, and if thou wilt not send *him then* we will not go down, for surely the king of Egypt particularly enjoined us, *saying*, you shall not see my face unless your brother be with you, for the king of Egypt is a strong and mighty king, and behold if we shall go to him without our brother we shall all be put to death.

12. Dost thou not know *and* hast thou not heard that this king is very powerful and wise, and there is not like unto him in all the earth ? behold we have seen all the kings of the earth and we have not seen one like that king, the king of Egypt; surely amongst all the kings of the earth there is none greater than Abimelech king of the Philistines, yet the king of Egypt is greater and mightier than he, and Abimelech can only be *compared* to one of his officers.

13. Father, thou hast not seen his palace and his throne, and all his servants standing before him ; thou hast not seen that king upon his throne in his pomp and royal appearance, dressed in his kingly robes with a large golden crown upon his head ; thou hast not seen the honor and glory which God has given unto him,

for there is not like unto him in all the earth.

14. Father, thou hast not seen the wisdom, the understanding and the knowledge which God has given in his heart, nor heard his sweet voice when he spake unto us.

15. We know not, father, who made him acquainted with our names and all that befel us, *yet* he asked also after thee, saying, is your father still living, *and* is it well with him?

16. Thou hast not seen the affairs of the government of Egypt regulated by him, without inquiring of Pharaoh his lord; thou hast not seen the awe and fear which he impressed upon all the Egyptians.

17. And also when we went from him, we threatened to do unto Egypt like unto the rest of the cities of the Amorites, and we were exceedingly wroth against all his words which he spoke considering us as spies, and *now* when we shall again come before him his terror will fall upon us all, and not *one of us* will be able to speak to him either a little or great thing.

18. Now therefore, father, send we pray thee the lad with us, and we will go down and buy thee food for our support, and not die through hunger; and Jacob said, why have you dealt so ill with me to tell the king you had a brother? what is this thing that you have done unto me?

19. And Judah said unto Jacob his father, give the lad into my care and we will rise up and go down to Egypt and buy corn, and *then* return, and it shall be when we return if the lad be not with us, then let me bear thy blame forever.

20. Hast thou seen all our infants weeping over thee through hunger and there is no power in thy hand *to* satisfy them? now let thy pity be roused for them and send our brother with us and we will go.

21. For how will the Lord's kindness to our ancestors be *manifested* to thee when thou sayest that the king of Egypt will take away thy son? as the Lord liveth I will not leave him until I bring him and place him before thee; but pray for us unto the Lord, that he may deal kindly with us, to cause us to be received favorably and kindly before the king of Egypt and his men, for had we not delayed surely now we had returned a second time with thy son.

22. And Jacob said unto his sons, I trust in the Lord God that he may deliver you and give you favor in the sight of the king of Egypt, and in the sight of all his men.

23. Now therefore rise up and go to the man, and take for him in your hands a present from what can be obtained in the land and bring it before him, and may the Almighty God give you mercy before him that he may send Benjamin and Simeon your brethren with you.

24. And all the men rose up, and they took their brother Benjamin, and they took in their hands a large present of the best of the land, and they also took a double portion of silver.

25. And Jacob strictly commanded his sons concerning Benjamin, *saying*, take heed of him in the way in which you are going, and do not separate yourselves from him in the road, neither in Egypt.

26. And Jacob rose up from his sons and spread forth his hands and he prayed unto the Lord on account of his sons, saying, O Lord God of heaven and earth, remember thy covenant with our father Abraham, re-

member *it* with my father Isaac and deal kindly with my sons and deliver them not into the hands of the king of Egypt; do it I pray thee O God for the sake of thy mercies and redeem all my children and rescue them from Egyptian power, and send them their two brothers.

27. And all the wives of the sons of Jacob and their children lifted up their eyes to heaven and they all wept before the Lord, and cried *unto him* to deliver their fathers from the hand of the king of Egypt.

28. And Jacob wrote a record to the king of Egypt and gave it into the hand of Judah and into the hands of his sons for the king of Egypt, saying,

29. From thy servant Jacob, son of Isaac, son of Abraham the Hebrew, the prince of God, to the powerful and wise king, the revealer of secrets, king of Egypt, greeting.

30. Be it known to my lord *the* king of Egypt, the famine was sore upon us in the land of Canaan, and I sent my sons to thee to buy us a little food from thee for our support.

31. For my sons surrounded me and I being very old cannot see with my eyes, for my eyes have become very heavy through age, as well as with daily weeping for my son, for Joseph who was lost from before me, and I commanded my sons that they should not enter together the gates of the city when they came to Egypt, on account of the inhabitants of the land.

32. And I also commanded them to go about Egypt to seek for my son Joseph, perhaps they might find him there, and they did so, and thou didst consider them as spies of the land.

33. Have we not heard concerning thee that thou didst interpret Pha·raoh's dream and didst speak truly unto him? how *then* dost thou not know in thy wisdom whether my sons are spies or not?

34. Now *therefore*, my lord *and* king, behold I have sent my son before thee, as thou didst speak unto my sons; I beseech thee to put thy eyes upon him until he is returned to me in peace with his brethren.

35. For dost thou not know, or hast thou not heard that which our God did unto Pharaoh when he took my mother Sarah, and what he did unto Abimelech king of the Philistines on account of her, and also what our father Abraham did unto the nine kings of Elam, how he smote them all with a few men that were with him?

36. And also what my two sons Simeon and Levi did unto the eight cities of the Amorites, how they destroyed them on account of their sister Dinah?

37. And also on account of their brother Benjamin they consoled themselves for *the loss of his* brother Joseph; what will they *then* do for him when they see the hand of any people prevailing over them, for his sake?

38. Dost thou not know, O king of Egypt, that the power of God is with us, and that also God ever heareth our prayers and forsaketh us not all the days?

39. And when my sons told me of thy dealings with them, I called not unto the Lord on account of thee, for then thou wouldst have perished with thy men before my son Benjamin came before thee, but I thought that *as* Simeon my son was in thy house, perhaps thou mightest deal kindly with him, therefore I did not this thing unto thee.

40. Now *therefore* behold Benjamin my son cometh unto thee with my sons, take heed of him and put thy eyes upon him, and then will God place his eyes over thee *and* throughout thy kingdom.

41. Now I have told thee all that is in my heart, and behold my sons are coming to thee with their brother, examine the face of the whole earth for their sake and send them back in peace with their brethren.

42. And Jacob gave the record to his sons into the care of Judah to give it unto the king of Egypt.

CHAPTER LIII.

1. And the sons of Jacob rose up and took Benjamin and the whole of the presents, and they went and came to Egypt and they stood before Joseph.

2. And Joseph beheld his brother Benjamin with them and he saluted them, and these men came to Joseph's house.

3. And Joseph commanded the superintendant of his house to give to his brethren to eat, and he did so unto them.

4. And at noon time Joseph sent for the men to come before him with Benjamin, and the men told the superintendant of Joseph's house concerning the silver that was returned in their sacks, and he said unto them, it will be well with you, fear not, and he brought their brother Simeon unto them.

5. And Simeon said unto his brethren, the lord of the Egyptians has acted very kindly unto me, he did not keep me bound, as you saw with your eyes, for when you went out from the city he let me free and dealt kindly with me in his house.

6. And Judah took Benjamin by the hand, and they came before Joseph, and they bowed down to him to the ground.

7. And the men gave the present unto Joseph and they all sat before him, and Joseph said unto them, is it well with you, is it well with your children, is it well with your aged father? and they said it is well, and Judah took the record which Jacob had sent and gave it into the hand of Joseph.

8. And Joseph read the letter and knew his father's writing, and he wished to weep and he went into an inner room and he wept a great weeping; and he went out.

9. And he lifted up his eyes and beheld his brother Benjamin, and he said, is this your brother of whom you spoke unto me? and Benjamin approached Joseph, and Joseph placed *his* hand upon his head and he said unto him, may God be gracious unto thee my son.

10. And when Joseph saw his brother, the son of his mother, he again wished to weep, and he entered the chamber, and he wept there, and he washed his face, and went out and refrained *from weeping*, and he said, prepare food.

11. And Joseph had a cup from which he drank, and it was of silver beautifully inlaid with onyx stones and bdellium, and Joseph struck the cup in the sight of his brethren whilst they were sitting to eat with him.

12. And Joseph said unto the men, I know by this cup that Reuben the first born, Simeon and Levi and Judah, Issachar and Zebulun are children from one mother, seat yourselves to eat according to your births.

13. And he also placed the others

according to their births, and he said, I know that this your youngest brother has no brother, and I, like him, have no brother, he shall *therefore* sit down to eat with me.

14. And Benjamin went up before Joseph and sat upon the throne, and the men beheld the acts of Joseph, and they were astonished at them; and the men ate and drank at that time with Joseph, and he then gave presents unto them, and Joseph gave one gift unto Benjamin, and Manasseh and Ephraim saw the acts of their father, and they also gave presents unto him, and Osnath gave him one present, and they were five presents in the hand of Benjamin.

15. And Joseph brought them out wine to drink, and they would not drink, and they said, from the day on which Joseph was lost we have not drunk wine, nor eaten any delicacies.

16. And Joseph swore unto them, and he pressed them hard, and they drank plentifully with him on that day, and Joseph afterward turned to his brother Benjamin to speak with him, and Benjamin was still sitting upon the throne before Joseph.

17. And Joseph said unto him, hast thou begotten any children? and he said, thy servant has ten sons, and these are their names, Bela, Becher, Ashbal, Gera, Naaman, Achi, Rosh, Mupim, Chupim and Ord, and I called their names after my brother whom I have not seen.

18. And he ordered them to bring before him his map of the stars, whereby Joseph knew all the times, and Joseph said unto Benjamin, I have heard that the Hebrews are acquainted with all wisdom, dost thou know any thing of this?

19. And Benjamin said, thy servant is knowing also in all the wisdom which my father taught me, and Joseph said unto Benjamin, look now at this instrument and understand where thy brother Joseph is in Egypt, who you said went down to Egypt.

20. And Benjamin beheld that instrument with the map of the stars of heaven, and he was wise and looked therein to know where his brother was, and Benjamin divided the whole land of Egypt into four divisions, and he found that he who was sitting upon the throne before him was his brother Joseph, and Benjamin wondered greatly, and when Joseph saw that his brother Benjamin was so much astonished, he said unto Benjamin, what hast thou seen, and why art thou astonished?

21. And Benjamin said unto Joseph, I can see by this that Joseph my brother sitteth here with me upon the throne, and Joseph said unto him, I am Joseph thy brother, reveal not this thing unto thy brethren; behold I will send thee with them when they go away, and I will command them to be brought back again into the city, and I will take thee away from them.

22. And if they dare their lives and fight for thee, then shall I know that they have repented of what they did unto me, and I will make myself known to them, and if they forsake thee when I take thee, then shalt thou remain with me, and I will wrangle with them, and they shall go away, and I will not become known to them.

23. At that time Joseph commanded his officer to fill their sacks with food, and to put each man's money into his sack, and to put the cup in the sack of Benjamin, and to give

them provision for the road, and they did so unto them.

24. And on the next day the men rose up early in the morning, and they loaded their asses with their corn, and they went forth with Benjamin, and they went to the land of Canaan with their brother Benjamin.

25. They had not gone far from Egypt when Joseph commanded him that was set over his house, saying, rise, pursue these men before they get too far from Egypt, and say unto them, why have you stolen my master's cup?

26. And Joseph's officer rose up and he reached them, and he spoke unto them all the words of Joseph; and when they heard this thing they became exceedingly wroth, and they said, he with whom thy master's cup shall be found shall die, and we will also become slaves.

27. And they hastened and each man brought down his sack from his ass, and they looked in their bags and the cup was found in Benjamin's bag, and they all tore their garments and they returned to the city, and they smote Benjamin in the road, continually smiting him until he came into the city, and they stood before Joseph.

28. And Judah's anger was kindled, and he said, this man has only brought me back to destroy Egypt this day.

29. And the men came to Joseph's house, and they found Joseph sitting upon his throne, and all the mighty men standing at his right and left.

30. And Joseph said unto them, what is this act that you have done, that you took away my silver cup and went away? but I know that you took my cup in order to know thereby in what part of the land your brother was.

31. And Judah said, what shall we say to our lord, what shall we speak and how shall we justify *ourselves?* God has this day found the iniquity of all thy servants, therefore has he done this thing to us this day.

32. And Joseph rose up and caught hold of Benjamin and took him from his brethren with violence, and he came to the house and locked the door at them, and Joseph commanded him that was set over his house that he should say unto them, thus saith the king, go in peace to your father, behold I have taken the man in whose hand my cup was found.

CHAPTER LIV.

1. And when Judah saw the dealings of Joseph with them, Judah approached him and broke open the door, and came with his brethren before Joseph.

2. And Judah said unto Joseph, let it not seem grievous in the sight of my lord, may thy servant I pray thee speak a word before thee? and Joseph said unto him, speak.

3. And Judah spoke before Joseph, and his brethren were there standing before them; and Judah said unto Joseph, surely when we first came to our lord to buy food, thou didst consider us as spies of the land, and we brought Benjamin before thee, and thou still makest sport of us this day.

4. Now *therefore* let the king hear my words, and send I pray thee our brother that he may go along with us to our father, lest thy soul perish this day with all the souls of the inhabitants of Egypt.

5. Dost thou not know what two

of my brethren, Simeon and Levi, did unto the city of Shechem, and unto seven cities of the Amorites, on account of our sister Dinah, and also what they would do for the sake of their brother Benjamin?

6. And I with my strength, who am greater and mightier than both of them, come this day upon thee and thy land if thou art unwilling to send our brother.

7. Hast thou not heard what our God who made choice of us did unto Pharaoh on account of Sarah our mother, whom he took away from our father, that he smote him and his household with heavy plagues, that even unto this day the Egyptians relate this wonder to each other? so will our God do unto thee on account of Benjamin whom thou hast this day taken from his father, and on account of the evils which thou this day heapest over us in thy land; for our God will remember his covenant with our father Abraham and bring evil upon thee, because thou hast grieved the soul of our father this day.

8. Now *therefore* hear my words that I have this day spoken unto thee, and send our brother that he may go away lest thou and the people of thy land die by the sword, for you cannot all prevail over me.

9. And Joseph answered Judah, saying, why hast thou opened wide thy mouth and why dost thou boast over us, saying, strength is with thee? as Pharaoh liveth, if I command all my valiant men to fight with you, surely thou and these thy brethren would sink in the mire.

10. And Judah said unto Joseph, surely it becometh thee and thy people to fear me; as the Lord liveth if I once draw my sword I shall not sheathe it again until I shall this day have slain all Egypt, and I will commence with thee and finish with Pharaoh thy master.

11. And Joseph answered and said unto him, surely strength belongeth not alone to thee; I am stronger and mightier than thou; surely if thou drawest thy sword I will put it to thy neck and the necks of all thy brethren.

12. And Judah said unto him, surely if I this day open my mouth against thee I would swallow thee up that thou be destroyed from off the earth and perish this day from thy kingdom. And Joseph said, surely if thou openest thy mouth I have power and might to close thy mouth with a stone until thou shalt not be able to utter a word; see how many stones are before us, truly I can take a stone, and force it into thy mouth and break thy jaws.

13. And Judah said, God is witness between us, that we have not hitherto desired to battle with thee, only give us our brother and we will go from thee; and Joseph answered and said, as Pharaoh liveth, if all the kings of Canaan came together with you, you should not take him from my hand.

14. Now therefore go your way to your father, and your brother shall be unto me for a slave, for he has robbed the king's house. And Judah said, what is it to thee or to the character of the king, surely the king sendeth forth from his house, throughout the land, silver and gold either in gifts or expenses, and thou still talkest about thy cup which thou didst place in our brother's bag and sayest that he has stolen it from thee?

15. God forbid that our brother Benjamin or any of the seed of Abra-

ham should do this thing to steal from thee, or from any one else, whether king, prince, or any man.

16. Now therefore cease this accusation lest the whole earth hear thy words, saying, for a little silver the king of Egypt wrangled with the men, and he accused them and took their brother for a slave.

17. And Joseph answered and said, take unto you this cup and go from me and leave your brother for a slave, for it is the judgment of a thief to be a slave.

18. And Judah said, why art thou not ashamed of thy words, to leave our brother and to take thy cup? Surely if thou givest us thy cup, or a thousand times as much, we will not leave our brother for the silver which is found in the hand of any man, that we will not die over him.

19. And Joseph answered, and why did you forsake your brother and sell* him for twenty pieces of silver unto this day, and why then will you not do the same to this your brother?

20. And Judah said, the Lord is witness between me and thee that we desire not thy battles ; now *therefore* give us our brother and we will go from thee without quarreling.

21. And Joseph answered and said, if all the kings of the land should assemble they will not be able to take your brother from my hand ;

* It may seem strange that they were not surprised at hearing this declaration from Joseph, how he should become acquainted with what was only known to themselves, but it must be remembered that they knew that Joseph was an interpreter of dreams and a noted magician ; this may be corroborated by Jacob's letter to Joseph, ch. 52, v. 33. "Have we not heard concerning thee, that thou didst interpret Pharaoh's dream, and didst make this famine known to him before it came, and didst speak truly unto him, how *then* dost thou not know in thy wisdom whether my sons are spies or not?"

and Judah said, what shall we say unto our father, when he seeth that our brother cometh not with us, and will grieve over him ?

22. And Joseph answered and said, this is the thing which you shall tell unto your father, saying, the rope has gone after the bucket.

23. And Judah said, surely thou art a king, and why speakest thou these things, giving a false judgment? woe unto the king who is like unto thee.

24. And Joseph answered and said, there is no false judgment in the word that I spoke on account of your brother Joseph, for all of you sold him to the Midianites for twenty pieces of silver, and you all denied it to your father and said unto him, an evil beast has devoured him, Joseph has been torn to pieces.

25. And Judah said, behold the fire of Shem burneth in my heart, now I will burn all your land with fire ; and Joseph answered and said, surely thy sister-in-law Tamar, who killed your sons, extinguished the fire of Shechem.

26. And Judah said, if I pluck out a single hair from my flesh, I will fill all Egypt with its blood.

27. And Joseph answered and said, such is your custom to do as you did to your brother whom you sold, and you dipped his coat in blood and brought it to your father in order that he might say an evil beast devoured him and here is his blood.

28. And when Judah heard this thing he was exceedingly wroth and his anger burned within him, and there was before him in that place a stone, the weight of which was about four hundred shekels, and Judah's anger was kindled and he took the stone in one hand and cast it to the

heavens and caught it with his left hand.

29. And he placed it afterward under his legs, and he sat upon it with all his strength and the stone was turned into dust from the force of Judah.

30. And Joseph saw the act of Judah and he was very much afraid, but he commanded Manasseh his son and he also did with another stone like unto the act of Judah, and Judah said unto his brethren, let not any of you say, this man is an Egyptian, but by his doing this thing he is of our father's family.

31. And Joseph said, not to you only is strength given, for we are also powerful men, and why will you boast over us all? and Judah said unto Joseph, send I pray thee our brother and ruin not thy country this day.

32. And Joseph answered and said unto them, go and tell your father, an evil beast hath devoured him as you said concerning your brother Joseph.

33. And Judah spoke to his brother Naphtali, and he said unto him, make haste, go now and number all the streets of Egypt and come and tell me; and Simeon said unto him, let not this thing be a trouble to thee; now I will go to the mount and take up one large stone from the mount and level it at every one in Egypt and kill all that are in it.

34. And Joseph heard all these words that his brethren spoke before him, and they did not know that Joseph understood them, for they imagined that he knew not to speak Hebrew.

35. And Joseph was greatly afraid at the words of his brethren lest they should destroy Egypt, and he commanded his son Manasseh, saying,

go now make haste and gather unto me all the inhabitants of Egypt and all the valiant men together, and let them come to me now upon horseback and on foot and with all sorts of musical instruments, and Manasseh went and did so.

36. And Naphtali went as Judah had commanded him, for Naphtali was light-footed as one of the swift stags, and he would go upon the ears of corn and they would not break under him.

37. And he went and numbered all the streets of Egypt, and found them to be twelve, and he came hastily and told Judah, and Judah said unto his brethren, hasten you and put on every man his sword upon his loins and we will come over Egypt, and smite them all, and let not a remnant remain.

38. And Judah said, behold, I will destroy three of the streets with my strength, and you shall each destroy one street ; and when Judah was speaking this thing, behold the inhabitants of Egypt and all the mighty men came toward them with all sorts of musical instruments and with loud shouting.

39. And their number was five hundred cavalry and ten thousand infantry, and four hundred men who could fight without sword or spear, only with their hands and strength.

40. And all the mighty men came with great storming and shouting, and they all surrounded the sons of Jacob and terrified them, and the ground quaked at the sound of their shouting.

41. And when the sons of Jacob saw these troops they were greatly afraid of their lives, and Joseph did so in order to terrify the sons of Jacob to become tranquilized.

42. And Judah, seeing some of his brethren terrified, said unto them, why are you afraid whilst the grace of God is with us? and when Judah saw all the people of Egypt surrounding them at the command of Joseph to terrify them, only Joseph commanded them, saying, do not touch any of them;

43. Then Judah hastened and drew his sword, and uttered a loud and bitter scream, and he smote with his sword, and he sprang upon the ground, and he still continued to shout against all the people.

44. And when he did this thing the Lord caused the terror of Judah and his brethren to fall upon the valiant men and all the people that surrounded them.

45. And they all fled at the sound of the shouting, and they were terrified and fell one upon the other, and many of them died as they fell, and they all fled from before Judah and his brethren and from before Joseph.

46. And whilst they were fleeing Judah and his brethren pursued them unto the house of Pharaoh, and they all escaped, and Judah again sat before Joseph and roared at him like a lion, and gave a great and tremendous shriek at him.

47. And the shriek was heard at a distance, and all the inhabitants of Succoth heard *it*, and all Egypt quaked at the sound of the shriek, and also the walls of Egypt and of the land of Goshen fell in from the shaking of the earth, and Pharaoh also fell from his throne upon the ground, and also all the pregnant women of Egypt and Goshen miscarried when they heard the noise of the shaking, for they were terribly afraid.

48. And Pharaoh sent word, saying, what is this thing that has this day happened in the land of Egypt? and they came and told him all the things from beginning to end, and Pharaoh was alarmed and he wondered and was greatly afraid.

49. And his fright increased when he heard all these things, and he sent unto Joseph, saying, thou hast brought unto me the Hebrews to destroy all Egypt; what wilt thou do with that thievish slave? send him away and let him go with his brethren, and let us not perish through their evil, even we, you and all Egypt.

50. And if thou desirest not to do this thing, cast off from thee all my valuable things, and go with them to their land, if thou delightest in it, for they will this day destroy my whole country and slay all my people; *even* all the women of Egypt have miscarried through their screams; see what they have done *merely* by their shouting and speaking, moreover if they fight with the sword, they will destroy the land; now therefore choose that which thou desirest, whether me or the Hebrews, whether Egypt or the land of the Hebrews.

51. And they came and told Joseph all the words of Pharaoh that he had said concerning him, and Joseph was greatly afraid at the words of Pharaoh, and Judah and his brethren were still standing before Joseph indignant and enraged, and all the sons of Jacob roared at Joseph, like the roaring of the sea and its waves.

52. And Joseph was greatly afraid of his brethren and on account of Pharaoh, and Joseph sought a pretext to make *himself* known unto his

brethren, lest they should destroy all Egypt.

53. And Joseph commanded his son Manasseh, and Manasseh went and approached Judah, and placed his hand upon his shoulder, and the anger of Judah was stilled.

54. And Judah said unto his brethren, let no one of you say that this is the act of an Egyptian youth for this is the work of my father's house.

55. And Joseph seeing and knowing that Judah's anger was stilled, he approached to speak unto Judah in the language of mildness.

56. And Joseph said unto Judah, surely you speak truth and have this day verified your assertions concerning your strength, and may your God who delighteth in you, increase your welfare; but tell me truly why from amongst all thy brethren dost thou wrangle with me on account of the lad, as none of them had spoken one word to me concerning him.

57. And Judah answered Joseph, saying, surely thou must know that I was security for the lad to his father, saying, if I brought him not unto him I should bear his blame forever.

58. Therefore have I approached thee from amongst all my brethren, for I saw that thou wast unwilling to suffer him to go from thee; now therefore may I find grace in thy sight that thou shalt send him to go with us, and behold I will remain as a substitute for him, to serve thee in whatever thou desirest, for wheresoever thou shalt send me I will go to serve thee with great energy.

59. Send me now to a mighty king who has rebelled against thee and thou shalt know what I will do unto him and unto his land; although

he may have cavalry and infantry or an exceeding mighty people, I will slay them all and bring the king's head before thee.

60. Dost thou not know or hast thou not heard that our father Abraham with his servant Eliezer smote all the kings of Elam with their hosts in one night, they left not one remaining? and ever since that day our father's strength was given unto us for an inheritance, for us and our seed forever.

61. And Joseph answered and said, you speak truth and falsehood is not in your mouth, for it was also told unto us that the Hebrews have power and that the Lord their God delighteth much in them, and who *then* can stand before them?

62. However on this condition will I send your brother, if you will bring before me his brother the son of his mother, of whom you said that he had gone from you down to Egypt; and it shall come to pass when you bring unto me his brother I will take him in his stead, because not one of you was security for him to your father, and when he shall come unto me, I will then send with you his brother for whom you have been security.

63. And Judah's anger was kindled against Joseph when he spoke this thing, and his eyes dropped blood with anger, and he said unto his brethren, how doth this man this day seek his own destruction and that of all Egypt!

64. And Simeon answered Joseph, saying, did we not tell thee at first that we knew not the *particular** spot to which he went, and whether

* Although they knew he went down to Egypt, they could not tell to what part or what town of Egypt he went.

he be dead or alive, and wherefore speaketh my lord like unto these things?

65. And Joseph observing the countenance of Judah discerned that his anger began to kindle when he spoke unto him, saying bring unto me your other brother instead of this brother.

66. And Joseph said unto his brethren, surely you said that your brother was either dead or lost, now if I should call him this day and he should come before you, would you give him unto me instead of his brother?

67. And Joseph began to speak and call out, Joseph, Joseph, come this day before me, and appear to thy brethren and sit before them.

68. And when Joseph spoke this thing before them, they looked each a different way to see from whence Joseph would come before them.

69. And Joseph observed all their acts, and said unto them, why do you look here and there? I am Joseph whom you sold to Egypt, now therefore let it not grieve you that you sold me, for as a support during the famine did God send me before you.

70. And his brethren were terrified at him when they heard the words of Joseph, and Judah was exceedingly terrified at him.

71. And when Benjamin heard the words of Joseph he was before them in the inner part of the house, and Benjamin ran unto Joseph his brother and embraced him and fell upon his neck, and they wept.

72. And when Joseph's brethren saw that Benjamin had fallen upon his brother's *neck* and wept with him, they also fell upon Joseph and embraced him, and they wept a great weeping with Joseph.

73. And the voice was heard in the house of Joseph that they were Joseph's brethren, and it pleased Pharaoh exceedingly, for he was afraid of them lest they should destroy Egypt.

74. And Pharaoh sent his servants unto Joseph to congratulate him concerning his brethren who had come to him, and all the captains of the armies and troops that were in Egypt came to rejoice with Joseph, and all Egypt rejoiced greatly about Joseph's brethren.

75. And Pharaoh sent his servants to Joseph, saying, tell thy brethren to fetch all belonging to them and let them come unto me and I will place them in the best part of the land of Egypt, and they did so.

76. And Joseph commanded him that was set over his house to bring out to his brethren gifts and garments, and he brought out to them many garments *being* robes of royalty and many gifts, and Joseph divided them amongst his brethren.

77. And he gave unto each of his brethren a change of garments of gold and silver, and three hundred *pieces of* silver, and Joseph commanded them all to be dressed in these garments and to be brought before Pharaoh.

78. And Pharaoh seeing that all Joseph's brethren were valiant men, and of beautiful appearance, he greatly rejoiced.

79. And they afterward went out from the presence of Pharaoh to go to the land of Canaan, to their father, and their brother Benjamin was with them.

80. And Joseph rose up and gave unto them eleven chariots from Pharaoh, and Joseph gave unto them his chariot, upon which he rode on the

day of his being crowned in Egypt, to fetch his father to Egypt; and Joseph sent to all his brothers' children, garments according to their numbers, and a hundred *pieces* of silver to each of them, and he also sent garments to the wives of his brethren from the garments of the king's wives, and he sent them.

81. And he gave unto each of his brethren ten men to go with them to the land of Canaan to serve them, to serve their children and all belonging to them in coming to Egypt.

82. And Joseph sent by the hand of his brother Benjamin ten *suits of* garments for his ten sons, a portion above the rest of the children of the sons of Jacob.

83. And he sent to each fifty pieces of silver, and ten chariots on the account of Pharaoh, and he sent to his father ten asses laden with all the luxuries of Egypt, and ten she-asses laden with corn and bread and nourishment for his father, and to all that were with him as provision for the road.

84. And he sent to his sister Dinah garments of silver and gold, and frankincense and myrrh, and aloes and women's ornaments in great plenty, and he sent the same from the wives of Pharaoh to the wives of Benjamin.

85. And he gave unto all his brethren, also to their wives, all sorts of onyx stones and bdellium, and from all the valuable things amongst the great people of Egypt, nothing of all the costly things was left but what Joseph sent of to his father's household.

86. And he sent his brethren away, and they went, and he sent his brother Benjamin with them.

87. And Joseph went out with them to accompany them on the road unto the borders of Egypt, and he commanded them concerning his father and his household, to come to Egypt.

88. And he said unto them, do not quarrel on the road, for this thing was from the Lord to keep a great people from starvation, for there *will be* yet five years of famine in the land.

89. And he commanded them, saying, when you come unto the land of Canaan, do not come suddenly before my father in this affair, but act in your wisdom.

90. And Joseph ceased to command them, and he turned and went back to Egypt, and the sons of Jacob went to the land of Canaan with joy and cheerfulness to their father Jacob.

91. And they came unto the borders of the land, and they said to each other, what shall we do in this matter before our father, for if we come suddenly to him and tell him the matter, he will be greatly alarmed at our words and will not believe us.

92. And they went along until they came nigh unto their houses, and they found Serach, the daughter of Asher, going forth to meet them, and the damsel was very good and subtle, and knew how to play upon the harp.

93. And they called unto her and she came before them, and she kissed them, and they took her and gave unto her a harp, saying, go now before our father, and sit before him, and strike upon the harp, and speak these words.

94. And they commanded her to go to their house, and she took the harp and hastened before them, and she came and sat near Jacob.

95. And she played well and sang, and uttered in the sweetness of her words, Joseph my uncle is living, and he ruleth throughout the land of Egypt, and is not dead.

96. And she continued to repeat and utter these words, and Jacob heard her words and they were agreeable to him.

97. He listened whilst she repeated them twice and thrice, and joy entered the heart of Jacob at the sweetness of her words, and the spirit of God was upon him, and he knew all her words to be true.

98. And Jacob blessed Serach when she spoke these words before him, and he said unto her, my daughter, may death never prevail over thee, for thou hast revived my spirit; only speak yet before me as thou hast spoken, for thou hast gladdened me with all thy words.

99. And she continued to sing these words, and Jacob listened and it pleased him, and he rejoiced, and the spirit of God was upon him.

100. Whilst he was yet speaking with her, behold his sons came to him with horses and chariots and royal garments and servants running before them.

101. And Jacob rose up to meet them, and saw his sons dressed in royal garments and he saw all the treasures that Joseph had sent to them.

102. And they said unto him, be informed that our brother Joseph is living, and it is he who ruleth throughout the land of Egypt, and it is he who spoke unto us as we told thee.

103. And Jacob heard all the words of his sons, and his heart palpitated at their words, for he could not believe them until he saw all that Joseph had given them and what he had sent him, and all the signs which Joseph had spoken unto them.

104. And they opened out before him, and showed him all that Joseph had sent, they gave unto each what Joseph had sent him, and he knew that they had spoken the truth, and he rejoiced exceedingly on account of his son.

105. And Jacob said, it is enough for me that my son Joseph is still living, I will go and see him before I die.

106. And his sons told him all that had befallen them, and Jacob said, I will go down to Egypt to see my son and his offspring.

107. And Jacob rose up and put on the garments which Joseph had sent him, and after he had washed, and shaved his hair, he put upon his head the turban which Joseph had sent him.

108. And all the people of Jacob's house and their wives put on *the garments* which Joseph had sent to them, and they greatly rejoiced at Joseph that he was still living and that he was ruling in Egypt.

109. And all the inhabitants of Canaan heard *of* this thing, and they came and rejoiced much with Jacob that he was still living.

110. And Jacob made a feast for them for three days, and all the kings of Canaan and nobles of the land ate and drank and rejoiced in the house of Jacob.

CHAPTER LV.

1. And it came to pass after this that Jacob said, I will go and see my son in Egypt and will then come back to the land of Canaan of which God had spoken unto Abraham, for I cannot leave the land of my birthplace.

12

2. Behold the word of the Lord *came* unto him, saying, go down to Egypt with all thy household and remain there, fear not to go down to Egypt for I will there make thee a great nation.

3. And Jacob said within himself, I will go and see my son whether the fear of his God is yet in his heart amidst all the inhabitants of Egypt.

4. And the Lord said unto Jacob, fear not about Joseph, for he still retaineth his integrity to serve me, as will seem good in thy sight, and Jacob rejoiced exceedingly concerning his son.

5. At that time Jacob commanded his sons and household to go to Egypt according to the word of the Lord unto him ; and Jacob rose up with his sons and all his household, and he went out from the land of Canaan from Beer-sheba, with joy and gladness of heart, and they went to the land of Egypt.

6. And it came to pass when they came near Egypt, Jacob sent Judah before him to Joseph that he might show him a situation in Egypt, and Judah did according to the word of his father, and he hastened and ran and came to Joseph, and they assigned for them a place in the land of Goshen for all his household, and Judah returned and came along the road to his father.

7. And Joseph harnessed the chariot, and he assembled all his mighty men and his servants and all the officers of Egypt in order to go and meet his father Jacob, and Joseph's mandate was proclaimed in Egypt, saying, all that do not go to meet Jacob shall die.

8. And on the next day Joseph went forth with all Egypt a great and mighty host, all dressed in garments of fine linen and purple and *with* instruments of silver and gold and with their instruments of war with them.

9. And they all went to meet Jacob with all sorts of musical instruments, with drums and timbrels, strewing myrrh and aloes all along the road, and they all went after this fashion, and the earth shook at their shouting.

10. And all the women of Egypt went upon the roofs of Egypt and upon the walls to meet Jacob, and upon the head of Joseph was Pharaoh's regal crown, for Pharaoh had sent it unto him to put on at the time of his going to meet his father.

11. And when Joseph came within fifty cubits of his father, he alighted from the chariot and he walked toward his father, and when all the officers of Egypt and her nobles saw that Joseph had gone on foot toward his father, they also alighted and walked on foot toward Jacob.

12. And when Jacob approached the camp of Joseph, Jacob observed the camp that was coming toward him with Joseph, and it gratified him and Jacob was astonished at it.

13. And Jacob said unto Judah, who is *that* man whom I see in the camp of Egypt dressed in kingly robes with a very red garment upon him and a royal crown upon his head, who has alighted from his chariot and is coming toward us ? and Judah answered his father, saying, he is thy son Joseph the king ; and Jacob rejoiced in seeing the glory of his son.

14. And Joseph came nigh unto his father and he bowed to his father, and all the men of the camp bowed to the ground with him before Jacob.

15. And behold Jacob ran and hastened to his son Joseph and fell

upon his neck and kissed him, and they wept, and Joseph also embraced his father and kissed him, and they wept and all the people of Egypt wept with them.

16. And Jacob said unto Joseph, now I will die cheerfully after I have seen thy face, that thou art still living and with glory.

17. And the sons of Jacob and their wives and their children and their servants, and all the household of Jacob wept exceedingly with Joseph, and they kissed him and wept greatly with him.

18. And Joseph and all his people returned afterward home to Egypt, and Jacob and his sons and all the children of his household came with Joseph to Egypt, and Joseph placed them in the best part of Egypt, in the land of Goshen.

19. And Joseph said unto his father and unto his brethren, I will go up and tell Pharaoh, saying, my brethren and my father's household and all belonging to them have come unto me, and behold they are in the land of Goshen.

20. And Joseph did so and took from his brethren Reuben, Issachar Zebulun and his brother Benjamin, and he placed them before Pharaoh.

21. And Joseph spoke unto Pharaoh, saying, my brethren and my father's household and all belonging to them together with their flocks and cattle have come unto me from the land of Canaan, to sojourn in Egypt; for the famine was sore upon them.

22. And Pharaoh said unto Joseph, place thy father and brethren in the best part of the land, withhold not from them all that is good, and cause them to eat of the fat of the land.

23. And Joseph answered, saying, behold I have stationed them in the land of Goshen, for they are shepherds, therefore let them remain in Goshen to feed their flocks apart from the Egyptians.

24. And Pharaoh said unto Joseph, do with thy brethren all that they shall say unto thee; and the sons of Jacob bowed down to Pharaoh, and they went forth from him in peace, and Joseph afterward brought his father before Pharaoh.

25. And Jacob came and bowed down to Pharaoh, and Jacob blessed Pharaoh, and he then went out; and Jacob and all his sons, and all his household dwelt in the land of Goshen.

26. In the second year, that is in the hundred and thirtieth year of the life of Jacob, Joseph maintained his father and his brethren, and all his father's household, with bread according to their little ones, all the days of the famine; they lacked nothing.

27. And Joseph gave unto them the best part of the whole land; the best of Egypt had they all the days of Joseph; and Joseph also gave unto them and unto the whole of his father's household, clothes and garments year by year; and the sons of Jacob remained securely in Egypt all the days of their brother.

28. And Jacob always ate at Joseph's table, Jacob and his sons did not leave Joseph's table day or night, besides what Jacob's children consumed in their houses.

29. And all Egypt ate bread during the days of the famine from the house of Joseph, for all the Egyptians sold all belonging to them on account of the famine.

30. And Joseph purchased all the lands and fields of Eygpt for bread

on the account of Pharaoh, and Joseph supplied all Egypt with bread all the days of the famine, and Joseph collected all the silver and gold that came unto him for the corn which they bought throughout the land, and he accumulated much gold and silver, besides an immense quantity of onyx stones, bdellium and valuable garments which they brought unto Joseph from every part of the land when their money was spent.

31. And Joseph took of all the silver and gold that came into his hand, about seventy two talents of gold and silver, and also onyx stones and bdellium in great abundance, and Joseph went and concealed them in four parts, and he concealed one *part* in the wilderness near the Red sea, and one *part* by the river Perath, and the third and fourth part he concealed in the desert opposite to the wilderness of Persia and Media.

32. And he took part of the gold and silver that was left, and gave it unto all his brothers and unto all his father's household, and unto all the women of his father's household, and the rest he brought to the house of Pharaoh, about twenty talents of gold and silver.

33. And Joseph gave all the gold and silver that was left unto Pharaoh, and Pharaoh placed it in the treasury, and the days of the famine ceased after that in the land, and they sowed and reaped in the whole land, and they obtained their usual quantity year by year ; they lacked nothing.

34. And Joseph dwelt securely in Egypt, and the whole land was under his advice, and his father and all his brethren dwelt in the land of Goshen and took possession of it.

35. And Joseph was very aged, advanced in days, and his two sons, Ephraim and Manasseh, remained constantly in the house of Jacob, together with the children of the sons of Jacob their brethren, to learn the ways of the Lord and his law.

36. And Jacob and his sons dwelt in the land of Egypt in the land of Goshen, and they took possession in it, and they were fruitful and multiplied in it.

CHAPTER LVI.

1. And Jacob lived in the land of Egypt seventeen years, and the days of Jacob, *and* the years of his life were a hundred and forty seven years.

2. At that time Jacob was attacked with that illness of which he died, and he sent and called for his son Joseph from Egypt, and Joseph his son came from Egypt, and Joseph came unto his father.

3. And Jacob said unto Joseph and unto his sons, behold I die, and the God of your ancestors will visit you, and bring you back to the land, which the Lord sware to give unto you and unto your children after you; now therefore when I am dead, bury me in the cave which is in Machpelah in Hebron in the land of Canaan, near my ancestors.

4. And Jacob made his sons swear to bury him in Machpelah, in Hebron, and his sons swore unto him concerning this thing.

5. And he commanded them, saying, serve the Lord your God, for he who delivered your fathers will *also* deliver you from all trouble.

6. And Jacob said, call all your children unto me, and all the children of Jacob's sons came and sat be-

fore him, and Jacob blessed them, and he said unto them, the Lord God of your fathers shall grant you a thousand times as much and bless you, and may he give you the blessing of your father Abraham ; and all the children of Jacob's sons went forth on that day after he had blessed them.

7. And on the next day Jacob again called for his sons, and they all assembled and came to him and sat before him, and Jacob on that day blessed his sons before his death, each man did he bless according to his blessing ; behold it is written in the book of the law of the Lord *appertaining* to Israel.

8. And Jacob said unto Judah, I know my son that thou art a mighty *man* for thy brethren ; reign over them, and thy sons shall reign over their sons forever.

9. Only teach thy sons the bow and all weapons of war, in order that they may fight the battles of their brother who will rule over his enemies.*

10. And Jacob again commanded his sons on that day, saying, behold I shall be this day gathered unto my people ; carry me up from Egypt, and bury me in the cave of Machpelah as I have commanded you.

11. Howbeit take heed I pray you that none of your sons carry me, only yourselves, and this is the manner you shall do unto me, when you carry my body to go with it to the land of Canaan to bury me.

12. Judah, Issachar and Zebulun shall carry my bier at the eastern side ; Reuben, Simeon and Gad at the south, Ephraim, Manasseh and Benjamin at the west, Dan, Asher and Naphtali at the north.

* See II Samuel, ch. 1, v. 18.

13. Let not Levi carry with you, for he and his sons will carry the ark of the covenant of the Lord with the Israelites in the camp, neither let Joseph my son carry, for as a king so let his glory be ; howbeit, Ephraim and Manasseh shall be in their stead.*

14. Thus shall you do unto me when you carry me away ; do not neglect any thing of all that I command you ; and it shall come to pass when you do this unto me, that the Lord will remember you favorably and your children after you forever.

15. And you my sons, honor each his brother and his relative, and command your children and your children's children after you to serve the Lord God of your ancestors all the days,

16. In order that you may prolong *your* days in the land, you and your children and your children's children for ever, when you do what is good and upright in the sight of the Lord your God, to go in all his ways.

17. And thou, Joseph my son, forgive I pray thee the wrongs of thy brethren and all their misdeeds in the injury that they heaped upon thee, for God intended it for thine and thy children's benefit.

18. And O my son leave not thy brethren to the inhabitants of Egypt, neither hurt their feelings, for behold I consign them to the hand of God and in thy hand to guard them from the Egyptians ; and the sons of Jacob answered their father saying, O, our father, all that thou hast commanded us, so will we do ; may God only be with us.

19. And Jacob said unto his sons, so may God be with you when you

* Instead of Levi and Joseph.

keep all his ways; turn not from his ways either to the right or the left in performing what is good and upright in his sight.

20. For I know that many and grievous troubles will befall you in the latter days in the land, *yea* your children and children's children; only serve the Lord and he will save you from all trouble.

21. And it shall come to pass when you shall go after God to serve him and will teach your children after you, and your children's children, to know the Lord, then will the Lord raise up unto you and your children a servant from amongst your children, and the Lord will deliver you through his hand from all affliction, and bring you out of Egypt and bring you back to the land of your fathers to inherit it securely.

22. And Jacob ceased commanding his sons, and he drew his feet into the bed, he died and was gathered to his people.

23. And Joseph fell upon his father and he cried out and wept over him and he kissed him, and he called out in a bitter voice, and he said, O my father, my father.

24. And his sons' wives and all his household came and fell upon Jacob, and they wept over him, and cried in a very loud voice concerning Jacob.

25. And all the sons of Jacob rose up together, and they tore their garments, and they all put sackcloth upon their loins, and they fell upon their faces, and they cast dust upon their heads toward the heavens.

26. And the thing was told unto Osnath Joseph's wife, and she rose up and put on a sack and she with all the Egyptian women with her came and mourned and wept for Jacob.

27. And also all the people of Egypt who knew Jacob came all on that day when they heard this thing, and all Egypt wept for many days.

28. And also from the land of Canaan did the women come unto Egypt when they heard that Jacob was dead, and they wept for him in Egypt for seventy days.

29. And it came to pass after this that Joseph commanded his servants the doctors to embalm his father with myrrh and frankincense and all manner of incense and perfume, and the doctors embalmed Jacob as Joseph had commanded them.

30. And all the *people of* Egypt and the elders and all the inhabitants of the land of Goshen wept and mourned over Jacob, and all his sons and the children of his household lamented and mourned over their father Jacob many days.

31. And after the days of his weeping had passed away, at the end of seventy days, Joseph said unto Pharaoh, I will go up and bury my father in the land of Canaan as he made me swear, and then I will return.

32. And Pharaoh sent Joseph, saying, go up and bury thy father as he said, and as he made thee swear; and Joseph rose up with all his brethren to go to the land of Canaan to bury their father Jacob as he had commanded them.

33. And Pharaoh commanded that it should be proclaimed throughout Egypt, saying, whoever goeth not up with Joseph and his brethren to the land of Canaan to bury Jacob, shall die.

34. And all Egypt heard of Pharaoh's proclamation, and they all rose up together, and all the servants of Pharaoh, and the elders of his house,

and all the elders of the land of Egypt went up with Joseph, and all the officers and nobles of Pharaoh went up *as* the servants of Joseph, and they went to bury Jacob in the land of Canaan.

35. And the sons of Jacob carried the bier upon which he lay; according to all that their father commanded them, so did his sons unto him.

36. And the bier was of pure gold, and it was inlaid round about with onyx stones and bdellium; and the covering of the bier was gold woven work, joined with threads, and over them were hooks of onyx stones and bdellium.

37. And Joseph placed upon the head of his father Jacob a large golden crown, and he put a golden sceptre in his hand, and they surrounded the bier as was the custom of kings during their lives.

38. And all the troops of Egypt went before him in this array, at first all the mighty men of Pharaoh and the mighty men of Joseph, and after them the rest of the inhabitants of Egypt, and they were all girded with swords and equipped with coats of mail, and the trappings of war were upon them.

39. And all the weepers and mourners went at a distance opposite to the bier, going and weeping and lamenting, and the rest of the people went after the bier.

40. And Joseph and his household went together near the bier barefooted and weeping, and the rest of Joseph's servants went around him; each man had his ornaments upon him, and they were all armed with their weapons of war.

41. And fifty of Jacob's servants went in front of the bier, and they strewed along the road myrrh and aloes, and all manner of perfume, and all the sons of Jacob that carried the bier walked upon the perfumery, and the servants of Jacob went before them strewing the perfume along the road.

42. And Joseph went up with a heavy camp, and they did after this manner every day until they reached the land of Canaan, and they came to the threshing floor of Atad, which was on the other side of Jordan, and they mourned an exceeding great and heavy mourning in that place.

43. And all the kings of Canaan heard of this thing and they all went forth, each man from his house, thirty-one kings of Canaan, and they all came with their men to mourn and weep over Jacob.

44. And all these kings beheld Jacob's bier, and behold Joseph's crown was upon it, and they also put their crowns upon the bier, and encircled it with crowns.

45. And all these kings made in that place a great and heavy mourning with the sons of Jacob and Egypt over Jacob, for all the kings of Canaan knew the valor of Jacob and his sons.

46. And the report reached Esau, saying, Jacob died in Egypt, and his sons and all Egypt are conveying him to the land of Canaan to bury him.

47. And Esau heard this thing, and he was dwelling in mount Seir, and he rose up with his sons and all his people and all his household, a people exceedingly great, and they came to mourn and weep over Jacob.

48. And it came to pass, when Esau came he mourned for his brother Jacob, and all Egypt and all Canaan again rose up and mourned a great mourning with Esau over Jacob in that place.

49. And Joseph and his brethren brought their father Jacob from that place, and they went to Hebron to bury Jacob in the cave by his fathers.

50. And they came unto Kireath-arba, to the cave, and as they came Esau stood with his sons against Joseph and his brethren as an hindrance in the cave, saying, Jacob shall not be buried therein, for it belongeth to us and to our father.

51. And Joseph and his brethren heard the words of Esau's sons, and they were exceedingly wroth, and Joseph approached unto Esau, saying, what is this thing which they have spoken? surely my father Jacob bought it from thee for great riches after the death of Isaac, now* five and twenty years ago, and also all the land of Canaan he bought from thee and from thy sons, and thy seed after thee.

52. And Jacob bought it for his sons and his seed after him for an inheritance for ever, and why speakest thou these things this day?

53. And Esau answered, saying, thou speakest falsely and utterest lies, for I sold not anything belonging to me in all this land, as thou sayest, neither did my brother Jacob buy aught belonging to me in this land.

* From this it appears that the sale did not take place until two years after Isaac's death, because there were twenty seven years between Isaac's and Jacob's deaths, for when Isaac died at the age of one hundred and eighty, Jacob was one hundred and twenty, and Jacob died aged one hundred and forty seven, consequently twenty seven years elapsed; the purchase of the cave of Machpelah is also mentioned in the book of Jasher when Jacob bought Esau's birthright, see ch. 27, but it was all inserted afresh in the new contract mentioned in ch. 47; and this is corroborated in the 57th verse of this chapter, where Joseph tells Naphtali to bring "all the records, the records of the purchase, the sealed up one and the open one, also all the *first books* in which are written all the words of the birthright."

54. And Esau spoke these things in order to deceive Joseph with his words, for Esau knew that Joseph was not *present* in those days when Esau sold all belonging to him in the land of Canaan to Jacob.

55. And Joseph said unto Esau, surely my father inserted these things with thee in the record of purchase, and testified the record with witnesses, and behold it is with us in Egypt.

56. And Esau answered, saying unto him, bring the record, all that thou wilt find in the record, so will we do.

57. And Joseph called unto Naphtali his brother, and he said, hasten quickly, stay not, and run I pray thee to Egypt and bring all the records; the record of the purchase, the sealed record and the open record, and also all the first records in which all the transactions of the birth-right are written, fetch thou.

58. And thou shalt bring *them* unto us hither, that we may know from them all the words of Esau and his sons which they spoke this day.

59. And Naphtali hearkened to the voice of Joseph and he hastened and ran to go down to Egypt, and Naphtali was lighter on foot than any of the stags that were upon the wilderness, for he would go upon ears of corn without crushing them.

60. And when Esau saw that Naphtali had gone to fetch the records he and his sons increased their resistance against the cave, and Esau and all his people rose up against Joseph and his brethren to battle.

61. And all the sons of Jacob and the *people of* Egypt fought with Esau and his men, and the sons of Esau and his people were smitten before the sons of Jacob, and the

sons of Jacob slew of Esau's people forty men.

62. And Chushim the son of Dan, the son of Jacob, was at that time with Jacob's sons, but he was about a hundred cubits distant from the place of battle, for he remained with the children of Jacob's sons by Jacob's bier to guard it.

63. And Chushim was dumb and deaf, still he understood the voice of consternation *amongst* the men.

64. And he asked, saying, why do you not bury the dead and what is this great consternation? and they answered him the words of Esau and his sons; and he ran to Esau in the midst of the battle, and he slew Esau with a sword, and he cut off his head, and it sprang to a distance, and Esau fell amongst the people of the battle.

65. And when Chushim did this thing the sons of Jacob prevailed over the sons of Esau, and the sons of Jacob buried their father Jacob by force in the cave, and the sons of Esau beheld *it*.

66. And Jacob was buried in Hebron, in the cave of Machpelah which Abraham had bought from the sons of Heth for the possession of a burial place, and he was buried in very costly garments.

67. And no king had such honor paid him as Joseph paid unto his father at his death, for he buried him with great honor like unto the burial of kings.

68. And Joseph and his brethren made a mourning of seven days for their father.

CHAPTER LVII.

1. And it was after this that the sons of Esau waged war with the sons of Jacob, and the sons of Esau fought with the sons of Jacob in Hebron, and Esau was still *lying* dead, and not buried.

2. And the battle was heavy between them, and the sons of Esau were smitten before the sons of Jacob, and the sons of Jacob slew of the sons of Esau eighty men, and not one died of the people of the sons of Jacob ; and the hand of Joseph prevailed over all the people of the sons of Esau, and he took Zepho, the son of Eliphaz, the son of Esau, and fifty of his men captive, and he bound them with chains of iron, and gave them into the hand of his servants to bring them to Egypt.

3. And it came to pass when the sons of Jacob had taken Zepho and his people captive, all those that remained were greatly afraid of their lives from the house of Esau, lest they should also be taken captive, and they all fled with Eliphaz the son of Esau and his people, with Esau's body, and they went on their road to mount Seir.

4. And they came unto mount Seir and they buried Esau in Seir, but they had not brought his head with them to Seir, for it was buried in that place where the battle had been in Hebron.

5. And it came to pass when the sons of Esau had fled from before the sons of Jacob, the sons of Jacob pursued them unto the borders of Seir, but they did not slay a single man from amongst them when they pursued them, for Esau's body which they carried with them *excited* their confusion, so they fled and the sons of Jacob turned back from them and came up to the place where their brethren were in Hebron, and they remained there on that day, and on

the next day until they rested from the battle.

6. And it came to pass on the third day they assembled all the sons of Seir the Horite, and they assembled all the children of the east, a multitude of people like the sand of the sea, and they went and came down to Egypt to fight with Joseph and his brethren, *in order* to deliver their brethren.

7. And Joseph and all the sons of Jacob heard that the sons of Esau and the children of the east had come upon them to battle *in order* to deliver their brethren.

8. And Joseph and his brethren and the strong men of Egypt went forth and fought in the city of Raamses, and Joseph and his brethren dealt out a tremendous blow amongst the sons of Esau and the children of the east.

9. And they slew of them six hundred thousand men, and they slew amongst them all the mighty *men* of the children of Seir the Horite ; there were only a few of them left, and they slew *also* a great many of the children of the east, and of the children of Esau ; and Eliphaz the son of Esau and the children of the east all fled before Joseph and his brethren.

10. And Joseph and his brethren pursued them until they came unto Succoth, and they yet slew of them in Succoth thirty men, and the rest escaped and they fled each to his city.

11. And Joseph and his brethren and the mighty men of Egypt turned back from them with joy and cheerfulness of heart, for they had smitten all their enemies.

12. And Zepho the son of Eliphaz and his men were still slaves in Egypt to the sons of Jacob, and their pains increased.

13. And when the sons of Esau and the sons of Seir returned to their land, the sons of Seir saw that they had all fallen into the hand of the sons of Jacob, and *the people of* Egypt, on account of the battle of the sons of Esau.

14. And the sons of Seir said unto the sons of Esau, you have seen and *therefore* you know that this camp was on your account, and not one mighty man or an adept in war remaineth.

15. Now therefore go forth from our land, go from us to the land of Canaan to the land of the dwelling of your fathers ; wherefore shall your children inherit *the effects* of our children in latter days ?

16. And the children of Esau would not listen to the children of Seir, and the children of Seir considered to make war with them.

17. And the children of Esau sent secretly to Angeas king of Africa, the same is Dinhabah, saying,

18. Send unto us some of thy men and let them come unto us, and we will fight together with the children of Seir the Horite, for they have resolved to fight with us to drive us away from the land.

19. And Angeas king of Dinhabah did so, for he was in those days friendly to the children of Esau, and Angeas sent five hundred valiant infantry to the children of Esau, and eight hundred cavalry.

20. And the children of Seir sent unto the children of the east and unto *the children of* Midian, saying, you have seen what the children of Esau have done unto us, upon whose account we are *almost* all destroyed, in their battle with the sons of Jacob.

21. Now *therefore* come unto us and assist us, and we will fight them together, and we will drive them from the land and be avenged of the cause of our brethren who died for their sakes in their battle with their brethren the sons of Jacob.

22. And all the children of the east listened to the children of Seir, and they came unto them about eight hundred men with drawn swords, and the children of Esau fought with the children of Seir at that time in the wilderness of Paran.

23. And the children of Seir prevailed then over the sons of Esau, and the children of Seir slew on that day of the children of Esau in that battle about two hundred men of the people of Angeas king of Dinhabah.

24. And on the second day the children of Esau came again to fight a second time with the children of Seir, and the battle was sore upon the children of Esau this second time, and it troubled them greatly on account of the children of Seir.

25. And when the children of Esau saw that the children of Seir were more powerful than they were, some men of the children of Esau turned and assisted the children of Seir their enemies.

26. And there fell yet of the people of the children of Esau in the second battle fifty eight men of the people of Angeas king of Dinhabah.

27. And on the third day the children of Esau heard that some of their brethren had turned from them to fight against them in the second battle ; and the children of Esau mourned when they heard this thing.

28. And they said, what shall we do unto our brethren who turned from us to assist the children of Seir our enemies? and the children of

Esau again sent to Angeas king of Dinhabah, saying,

29. Send unto us again other men that with them we may fight with the children of Seir, for they have already twice been heavier than we were.

30. And Angeas again sent to the children of Esau about six hundred valiant men, and they came to assist the children of Esau.

31. And in ten days' time the children of Esau again waged war with the children of Seir in the wilderness of Paran, and the battle was very severe upon the children of Seir, and the children of Esau prevailed at this time over the children of Seir, and the children of Seir were smitten before the children of Esau, and the children of Esau slew from them about two thousand men.

32. And all the mighty men of the children of Seir died in this battle, and there only remained their young children that were left in their cities.

33. And all Midian and the children of the east betook themselves to flight from the battle, and they left the children of Seir and fled when they saw that the battle was severe upon them, and the children of Esau pursued all the children of the east until they reached their land.

34. And the children of Esau slew yet of them about two hundred and fifty men and from the people of the children of Esau there fell in that battle about thirty men, but this evil came upon them through their brethren turning from them to assist the children of Seir the Horite, and the children of Esau again heard of the evil doings of their brethren, and they again mourned on account of this thing.

35. And it came to pass after the

battle, the children of Esau turned back and came home unto Seir, and the children of Esau slew those who had remained in the land of the children of Seir; they slew also their wives and little ones, they left not a soul alive excepting fifty young lads and damsels whom they suffered to live, and the children of Esau did not put them to death, and the lads became their slaves, and the damsels they took for wives.

36. And the children of Esau dwelt in Seir in the place of the children of Seir, and they inherited their land and took possession of it.

37. And the children of Esau took all belonging in the land to the children of Seir, also their flocks, their bullocks and their goods, and all belonging to the children of Seir, did the children of Esau take, and the children of Esau dwelt in Seir in the place of the children of Seir unto this day, and the children of Esau divided the land into divisions to the five sons of Esau, according to their families.

38. And it came to pass in those days, that the children of Esau resolved to crown a king over them in *the land* of which they became possessed. And they said to each other, not so, for he shall reign over us in *our land*, and we shall be under his counsel and he shall fight our battles, against our enemies, and they did so.

39. And all the children of Esau swore, saying that none of their brethren should ever reign over them, but a strange man who is not of their brethren, for the souls of all the children of Esau were embittered every man against his son, brother and friend, on account of the evil *they sustained* from their brethren when they fought with the children of Seir.

40. Therefore the sons of Esau swore, saying, from that day forward they would not choose a king from their brethren, but one from a strange *land* unto this day.

41. And there was a man there from the people of Angeas king of Dinhabah; his name was Bela the son of Beor, who was a very valiant man, beautiful and comely and wise in all wisdom and a man of sense and counsel; and there was none of the people of Angeas like unto him.

42. And all the children of Esau took him and anointed him and they crowned him for a king, and they bowed down to him, and they said unto him, may the king live, may the king live.

43. And they spread out the sheet, and they brought him each man ear rings of gold and silver or rings or bracelets, and they made him very rich in silver and in gold, in onyx stones and bdellium, and they made him a royal throne, and they placed a regal crown upon his head, and they built a palace for him and he dwelt therein and he became king over all the children of Esau.

44. And the people of Angeas took their hire for their battle from the children of Esau, and they went and returned at that time to their master in Dinhabah.

45. And Bela reigned over the children of Esau thirty years, and the children of Esau dwelt in the land instead of the children of Seir, and they dwelt securely in their stead unto this day.

CHAPTER LVIII.

1. And it came to pass in the thirty second year of the Israelites going down to Egypt, that is *in the*

seventy first year of the life of Joseph, in that year died Pharaoh king of Egypt, and Magron his son reigned in his stead.

2. And Pharaoh commanded Joseph before his death to be a father to his son Magron, and that Magron should be under the care of Joseph and under his counsel.

3. And all Egypt consented to this thing that Joseph should be king over them, for all the Egyptians loved Joseph as of heretofore, only Magron the son of Pharaoh sat upon his father's throne, and he became king in those days in his father's stead.

4. Magron was forty one years old when he *began* to reign, and forty years he reigned in Egypt, and all Egypt called his name Pharaoh after the name of his father, as it was their custom to do in Egypt to every king that reigned over them.

5. And it came to pass when Pharaoh reigned in his father's stead, he placed the laws of Egypt and all the affairs of government in the hand of Joseph, as his father had commanded him.

6. And Joseph became king over Egypt, for he superintended over all Egypt, and all Egypt was under his care and under his counsel, for all Egypt inclined to Joseph after the death of Pharaoh, and they loved him exceedingly to reign over them.

7. But there were some people amongst them, who did not like him, saying, no stranger shall reign over us; still the whole government of Egypt devolved in those days upon Joseph, after the death of Pharaoh, he being the regulator, doing as he liked throughout the land without any one interfering.

8. And all Egypt was under the care of Joseph, and Joseph made war with all his surrounding enemies, and he subdued them; also all the land and all the Philistines, unto the borders of Canaan, did Joseph subdue, and they were all under his power and they gave a yearly tax unto Joseph.

9. And Pharaoh king of Egypt sat upon his throne in his father's stead, but he was under the control and counsel of Joseph, as he was at first under the control of his father.

10. Neither did he reign but in the land of Egypt only, under the counsel of Joseph, but Joseph reigned over the whole country at that time, from Egypt unto the great river Perath.

11. And Joseph was successful in all his ways, and the Lord was with him, and the Lord gave Joseph additional wisdom, and honor, and glory and love *toward him* in the hearts of the Egyptians and throughout the land, and Joseph reigned over the whole country forty years.

12. And all the countries of the Philistines and Canaan and Zidon, and on the other side of Jordan, brought presents unto Joseph all his days, and the whole country was in the hand of Joseph, and they brought unto him a yearly tribute as it was regulated, for Joseph had fought against all his surrounding enemies and subdued them, and the whole country was in the hand of Joseph, and Joseph sat securely upon his throne in Egypt.

13. And also all his brethren the sons of Jacob dwelt securely in the land, all the days of Joseph, and they were fruitful and multiplied exceedingly in the land, and they served the Lord all their days, as their father Jacob had commanded them.

14. And it came to pass at the end of many days and years, when the children of Esau were dwelling quietly in their land with Bela their king, that the children of Esau were fruitful and multiplied in the land, and they resolved to go and fight with the sons of Jacob and all Egypt, and to deliver their brother Zepho, the son of Eliphaz, and his men, for they were yet in those days slaves to Joseph.

15. And the children of Esau sent unto all the children of the east, and they made peace with them, and all the children of the east came unto them to go with the children of Esau to Egypt to battle.

16. And there came also unto them of the people of Angeas, king of Dinhabah, and they also sent unto the children of Ishmael and they also came unto them.

17. And all this people assembled and came unto Seir to assist the children of Esau in their battle, and this camp was very large and heavy with people, numerous as the sand of the sea, about eight hundred thousand men, infantry and cavalry, and all these troops went down to Egypt to fight with the sons of Jacob, and they encamped by Raamses.

18. And Joseph went forth with his brethren with the mighty men of Egypt, about six hundred men, and they fought with them in the land of Raamses ; and the sons of Jacob at that time again fought with the children of Esau, in the fiftieth year of the sons of Jacob going down to Egypt, that is the thirtieth year of the reign of Bela over the children of Esau in Seir.

19. And the Lord gave all the mighty men of Esau and the children of the east into the hand of Joseph and his brethren, and the people of the children of Esau and the children of the east were smitten before Joseph.

20. And of the people of Esau and the children of the east that were slain, there fell before the sons of Jacob about two hundred thousand men, and their king Bela the son of Beor fell with them in the battle, and when the children of Esau saw that their king had fallen in battle and was dead, their hands became weak in the combat.

21. And Joseph and his brethren and all Egypt were still smiting the people of the house of Esau, and all Esau's people were afraid of the sons of Jacob and fled from before them.

22. And Joseph and his brethren and all Egypt pursued them a day's journey, and they slew yet from them about three hundred men, continuing to smite them in the road ; and they afterward turned back from them.

23. And Joseph and all his brethren returned to Egypt, not one man was missing from them, but of the Egyptians there fell twelve men.

24. And when Joseph returned to Egypt he ordered Zepho and his men to be additionally bound, and they bound them in irons and they increased their grief.

25. And all the people of the children of Esau, and the children of the east, returned in shame each unto his city, for all the mighty men that were with them had fallen in battle.

26. And when the children of Esau saw that their king had died in battle they hastened and took a man from the people of the children of the east ; his name was Jobab the son of Zarach, from the land of Botzrah, and they caused him to

reign over them instead of Bela their king.

27. And Jobab sat upon the throne of Bela as king in his stead, and Jobab reigned in Edom over all the children of Esau ten years, and the children of Esau went no more to fight with the sons of Jacob from that day forward, for the sons of Esau knew the valor of the sons of Jacob, and they were greatly afraid of them.

28. But from that day forward the children of Esau hated the sons of Jacob, and the hatred and enmity were very strong between them all the days, unto this day.

29. And it came to pass after this, at the end of ten years, Jobab, the son of Zarach, from Botzrah, died, and the children of Esau took a man whose name was Chusham, from the land of Teman, and they made him king over them instead of Jobab, and Chusham reigned in Edom over all the children of Esau for twenty years.

30. And Joseph, king of Egypt, and his brethren, and all the children of Israel dwelt securely in Egypt in those days, together with all the children of Joseph and his brethren, *having* no hindrance or evil accident; and the land of Egypt was at that time at rest from war in the days of Joseph and his brethren.

CHAPTER LIX.

1. And these are the names of the sons of Israel who dwelt in Egypt, who had come with Jacob, all the sons of Jacob came unto Egypt, every man with his household.

2. The children of Leah *were* Reuben, Simeon, Levi, Judah, Issachar and Zebulun, and their sister Dinah.

3. And the sons of Rachel *were* Joseph and Benjamin.

4. And the sons of Zilpah, the handmaid of Leah, were Gad and Asher.

5. And the sons of Bilhah, the handmaid of Rachel, were Dan and Naphtali.

6. And these were their offspring that were born unto them in the land of Canaan, before they came unto Egypt with their father Jacob.

7. The sons of Reuben *were* Chanoch, Pallu, Chetzron and Carmi.

8. And the sons of Simeon *were* Jemuel, Jamin, Ohad, Jachin, Zochar and Saul, the son of the Canaanitish woman.

9. And the children of Levi *were* Gershon, Kehath and Merari, and their sister Jochebed, who was born unto them in *their* going down to Egypt.

10. And the sons of Judah *were* Er, Onan, Shelah, Perez and Zarach.

11. And Er and Onan died in the land of Canaan; and the sons of Perez *were* Chezron and Chamul.

12. And the sons of Issachar *were* Tola, Puvah, Job and Shomron.

13. And the sons of Zebulun *were* Sered, Elon and Jachleel, and the son of Dan *was* Chushim.

14. And the sons of Naphtali *were* Jachzeel, Guni, Jetzer and Shilam.

15. And the sons of Gad were Ziphion, Chaggi, Shuni, Ezbon, Eri, Arodi and Areli.

16. And the children of Asher *were* Jimnah, Jishvah, Jishvi, Beriah and their sister Serach; and the sons of Beriah *were* Cheber and Malchiel.

17. And the sons of Benjamin *were* Bela, Becher, Ashbel, Gera, Naaman, Achi, Rosh, Mupim, Chupim and Ord.

18. And the sons of Joseph, that

were born unto him in Egypt, *were* Manasseh and Ephraim.

19. And all the souls that went forth from the loins of Jacob, were seventy souls ; these are they who came with Jacob their father unto Egypt to dwell there ; and Joseph and all his brethren dwelt securely in Egypt, and they ate of the best of Egypt all the days of the life of Joseph.

20. And Joseph lived in the land of Egypt ninety-three years, and Joseph reigned over all Egypt eighty years.

21. And when the days of Joseph drew nigh that he should die, he sent and called for his brethren and all his father's household, and they all came together and sat before him.

22. And Joseph said unto his brethren and unto the whole of his father's household, behold I die, and God will surely visit you and bring you up from this land to the land which he swore to your fathers to give unto them.

23. And it shall be when God shall visit you to bring you up from here to the land of your fathers, *then* bring up my bones with you from here.

24. And Joseph made the sons of Israel to swear for their seed after them, saying, God will surely visit you and you shall bring up my bones with you from here.

25. And it came to pass after this that Joseph died in that year, the seventy-first year of the Israelites going down to Egypt.

26. And Joseph was one hundred and ten years old when he died in the land of Egypt, and all his brethren and all his servants rose up and they embalmed Joseph, as was their custom, and his brethren and all Egypt mourned over him for seventy days.

27. And they put Joseph in a coffin filled with spices and all sorts of perfume, and they buried him by the side of the river, that is Sihor, and his sons and all his brethren, and the whole of his father's household made a seven days' mourning for him.

28. And it came to pass after the death of Joseph, all the Egyptians began in those days to rule over the children of Israel, and Pharaoh, king of Egypt, who reigned in his father's stead, took all the laws of Egypt and conducted the whole government of Egypt under his counsel, and he reigned securely over his people.

CHAPTER LX.

1. And when the year came round, being the seventy-second year from the Israelites going down to Egypt, after the death of Joseph, Zepho, the son of Eliphaz, the son of Esau, fled from Egypt, he and his men, and they went away.

2. And he came to Africa, which is Dinhabah, to Angeas king of Africa, and Angeas received them with great honor, and he made Zepho the captain of his host.

3. And Zepho found favor in the sight of Angeas and in the sight of his people, and Zepho was captain of the host to Angeas king of Africa for many days.

4. And Zepho enticed Angeas king of Africa to collect all his army to go and fight with the Egyptians, and with the sons of Jacob, and to avenge of them the cause of his brethren.

5. But Angeas would not listen to Zepho to do this thing, for Angeas knew the strength of the sons of Jacob, and what they had done to his army in their warfare with the children of Esau.

6. And Zepho was in those days very great in the sight of Angeas and in the sight of all his people, and he continually enticed them to make war against Egypt, but they would not.

7. And it came to pass in those days there was in the land of Chittim a man in the city of Puzimna, whose name was Uzu, and he became degenerately deified by the children of Chittim, and the man died and had no son, only one daughter whose name was Jania.

8. And the damsel was exceedingly beautiful, comely and intelligent, there was none seen like unto her for beauty and wisdom throughout the land.

9. And the people of Angeas king of Africa saw her and they came and praised her unto him, and Angeas sent to the children of Chittim, and he requested to take her unto himself for a wife. And the people of Chittim consented to give her unto him for a wife.

10. And when the messengers of Angeas were going forth from the land of Chittim to take their journey, behold the messengers of Turnus king of Bibentu came unto Chittim, for Turnus king of Bibentu also sent his messengers to request Jania for him, to take unto himself for a wife, for all his men had also praised her to him, therefore he sent all his servants unto her.

11. And the servants of Turnus came to Chittim, and they asked for Jania, to be taken unto Turnus their king for a wife.

12. And the people of Chittim said unto them, we cannot give her, because Angeas king of Africa desired her to take her unto him for a wife before you came, and that we should give her unto him, and now *therefore* we cannot do this thing to deprive Angeas of the damsel in order to give her unto Turnus.

13. For we are greatly afraid of Angeas lest he come in battle against us and destroy us, and Turnus your master will not be able to deliver us from his hand.

14. And when the messengers of Turnus heard all the words of the children of Chittim, they turned back to their master and told him all the words of the children of Chittim.

15. And the children of Chittim sent a memorial to Angeas, saying, behold Turnus has sent for Jania to take her unto him for a wife, and thus have we answered him; and we heard that he has collected his whole army to go to war against thee, and he intends to pass by the road of Sardunia to fight against thy brother Lucus, and after that he will come to fight against thee.

16. And Angeas heard the words of the children of Chittim which they sent him in the record, and his anger was kindled and he rose up and assembled his whole army and came through the islands of the sea, the road to Sardunia, unto his brother Lucus king of Sardunia.

17. And Niblos, the son of Lucus, heard that his uncle Angeas was coming, and he went out to meet him with a heavy army, and he kissed him and embraced him, and Niblos said unto Angeas, when thou askest my father after *his* welfare, when I shall go with thee to fight with Turnus, ask of him to make me captain of his host, and Angeas did so, and he came unto his brother and his brother came to meet him, and he asked him after *his* welfare.

18. And Angeas asked his brother

13

Lucus after his welfare, and to *make* his son Niblos captain of his host, and Lucus did so, and Angeas and his brother Lucus rose up and they went toward Turnus to battle, and there was with them a great army and a heavy people.

19.. And he came in ships, and they came into the province of Ashtorash, and behold Turnus came toward them, for he went forth to Sardunia, and intended to destroy it and afterward to pass on from there to Angeas to fight with him.

20. And Angeas and Lucus his brother met Turnus in the valley of Canopia, and the battle was strong and mighty between them in that place.

21. And the battle was severe upon Lucus king of Sardunia, and all his army fell, and Niblos his son fell also in that battle.

22. And his uncle Angeas commanded his servants and they made a golden coffin for Niblos and they put him into it, and Angeas again waged battle toward Turnus, and Angeas was stronger than he, and he slew him, and he smote all his people with the edge of the sword, and Angeas avenged the cause of Niblos his brother's son and the cause of the army of his brother Lucus.

23. And when Turnus died, the hands of those that survived the battle became weak, and they fled from before Angeas and Lucus his brother.

24. And Angeas and his brother Lucus pursued them unto the highroad, which is between Alphanu and Romah, and they slew the whole army of Turnus with the edge of the sword.

25. And Lucus king of Sardunia commanded his servants that they should make a coffin of brass, and that they should place therein the body of his son Niblos, and they buried him in that place.

26. And they built upon it a high tower there upon the highroad, and they called its name after the name of Niblos unto this day, and they also buried Turnus king of Bibentu there in that place with Niblos.

27. And behold upon the highroad between Alphanu and Romah the grave of Niblos is on one side and the grave of Turnus on the other, and a pavement between them unto this day.

28. And when Niblos was buried Lucus his father returned with his army to his land Sardunia, and Angeas his brother king of Africa went with his people unto the city of Bibentu, that is the city of Turnus.

29. And the inhabitants of Bibentu heard of his fame and they were greatly afraid of him, and they went forth to meet him with weeping and supplication, and the inhabitants of Bibentu entreated of Angeas not to slay them nor to destroy their city; and he did so, for Bibentu was in those days reckoned as one of the cities of the children of Chittim; therefore he did not destroy the city.

30. But from that day forward the troops of the king of Africa would go to Chittim to spoil and plunder it, and whenever they went Zepho the captain of the host of Angeas would go with them.

31. And it was after this that Angeas turned with his army and they came to the city of Puzimna, and Angeas took thence Jania the daughter of Uzu for a wife and brought her unto his city unto Africa.

CHAPTER LXI.

1. And it came to pass at that time Pharaoh king of Egypt commanded all his people to make for him a strong palace in Egypt.

2. And he also commanded the sons of Jacob to assist the Egyptians in the building, and the Egyptians made a beautiful and elegant palace for a royal habitation, and he dwelt therein and he renewed his government and he reigned securely.

3. And Zebulun the son of Jacob died in that year, that is the seventy second year of the going down of the Israelites to Egypt, and Zebulun died a hundred and fourteen years old, and was put into a coffin and given into the hands of his children.

4. And in the seventy fifth year died his brother Simeon, he was a hundred and twenty years old at his death, and he was also put into a coffin and given into the hands of his children.

5. And Zepho the son of Eliphaz the son of Esau, captain of the host to Angeas king of Dinhabah, was still daily enticing Angeas to prepare for battle to fight with the sons of Jacob in Egypt, and Angeas was unwilling to do this thing, for his servants had related to him all the might of the sons of Jacob, what they had done unto them in their battle with the children of Esau.

6. And Zepho was in those days daily enticing Angeas to fight with the sons of Jacob in those days.

7. And after some time Angeas hearkened to the words of Zepho and consented to him to fight with the sons of Jacob in Egypt, and Angeas got all his people in order, a people numerous as the sand which is upon the sea shore, and he formed his resolution to go to Egypt to battle.

8. And amongst the servants of Angeas was a youth fifteen years old, Balaam the son of Beor was his name, and the youth was very wise and understood the art of witchcraft.

9. And Angeas said unto Balaam, conjure for us, I pray thee, with the witchcraft, that we may know who will prevail in this battle to which we are now proceeding.

10. And Balaam ordered that they should bring him wax, and he made thereof the likeness of chariots and horsemen representing the army of Angeas and the army of Egypt, and he put them in the cunningly prepared waters that he had for that purpose, and he took in his hand the boughs of myrtle trees, and he exercised his cunning, and he joined them over the water, and there appeared unto him in the water the resembling images of the hosts of Angeas falling before the resembling images of the Egyptians and the sons of Jacob.

11. And Balaam told this thing to Angeas and Angeas despaired and did not arm himself to go down to Egypt to battle, and he remained in his city.

12. And when Zepho the son of Eliphaz saw that Angeas despaired of going forth to battle with the Egyptians, Zepho fled from Angeas from Africa, and he went and came unto Chittim.

13. And all the people of Chittim received him with great honor, and they hired him to fight their battles all the days, and Zepho became exceedingly rich in those days, and the troops of the king of Africa still spread themselves in those days, and the children of Chittim assembled

and went to Mount Cuptizia on account of the troops of Angeas king of Africa, who were advancing upon them.

14. And it was one day that Zepho lost a young heifer, and he went to seek it, and he heard it lowing round about the mountain.

15. And Zepho went and he saw and behold there was a large cave at the bottom of the mountain, and there was a great stone there at the entrance of the cave, and Zepho split the stone and he came unto the cave and he looked and behold, a large animal was devouring the ox; from the middle upward it resembled a man, and from the middle downward it resembled an animal, and Zepho rose up against the animal and slew it with his sword.

16. And the inhabitants of Chittim heard of this thing, and they rejoiced exceedingly, and they said, what shall we do unto this man who has slain this animal that devoured our cattle?

17. And they all assembled to consecrate one day in the year to him, and they called the name thereof Zepho after his name, and they brought unto him drink offerings year after year on that day, and they brought unto him gifts.

18. At that time Jania the daughter of Uzu wife of king Angeas became ill, and her illness was heavily felt by Angeas and his officers, and Angeas said unto his wise men, what shall I do to Jania and how shall I heal her *from her* illness? and his wise men said unto him, because the air of our country is not like the air of the land of Chittim, and our water is not like their water, therefore from this has the queen become ill.

19. For through the change of air and water she became ill, and also because in her country she drank only the water which came from Purmah, which her ancestors had brought up with bridges.

20. And Angeas commanded his servants, and they brought unto him in vessels of the waters of Purmah belonging to Chittim, and they weighed those waters with all the waters of the land of Africa and they found those waters lighter than the waters of Africa.

21. And Angeas saw this thing and he commanded all his officers to assemble the hewers of stone in thousands and tens of thousands, and they hewed stones without number, and the builders came and they built an exceedingly strong bridge, and they conveyed the spring of water from the land of Chittim unto Africa, and those waters were for Jania the queen and for all her concerns, to drink from and to bake, wash and bathe therewith, and also to water *therewith* all seed from which food can be obtained, and all fruit of the ground.

22. And the king commanded that they should bring of the soil of Chittim in large ships, and they also brought stones to build therewith, and the builders built palaces for Jania the queen, and the queen became healed of her illness.

23. And at the revolution of the year the troops of Africa continued coming to the land of Chittim to plunder as usual, and Zepho son of Eliphaz heard their report, and he gave orders concerning them and he fought with them, and they fled before him, and he delivered the land of Chittim from them.

24. And the children of Chittim saw the valor of Zepho, and the chil-

dren of Chittim resolved and they made Zepho king over them, and he became king over them, and whilst he reigned they went to subdue the children of Tubal, and all the surrounding islands.

25. And their king Zepho went at their head and they made war with Tubal and the islands, and they subdued them, and when they returned from the battle they renewed his government for him, and they built for him a very large palace for his royal habitation and seat, and they made a large throne for him, and Zepho reigned over the whole land of Chittim and over the land of Italia fifty years.

CHAPTER LXII.

1. In that year, being the seventy-ninth year of the Israelites going down to Egypt, died Reuben the son of Jacob, in the land of Egypt; Reuben was a hundred and twenty-five years old when he died, and they put him into a coffin, and he was given into the hands of his children.

2. And in the eightieth year died his brother Dan; he was a hundred and twenty years old at his death, and he was also put into a coffin and given into the hands of his children.

3. And in that year died Chusham king of Edom, and after him reigned Hadad the son of Bedad, for thirty-five years; and in the eighty-first year died Issachar the son of Jacob, in Egypt, and Issachar was a hundred and twenty-two years old at his death, and he was put into a coffin in Egypt, and given into the hands of his children.

4. And in the eighty-second year died Asher his brother, he was a hundred and twenty-three years old at his death, and he was placed in a coffin in Egypt, and given into the hands of his children.

5. And in the eighty-third year died Gad, he was a hundred and twenty-five years old at his death, and he was put into a coffin in Egypt, and given into the hands of his children.

6. And it came to pass in the eighty-fourth year, that is the fiftieth year of the reign of Hadad, son of Bedad, king of Edom, that Hadad assembled all the children of Esau, and he got his whole army in readiness, about four hundred thousand men, and he directed his way to the land of Moab, and he went to fight with Moab and to make them tributary to him.

7. And the children of Moab heard this thing, and they were very much afraid, and they sent to the children of Midian to assist them in fighting with Hadad, son of Bedad, king of Edom.

8. And Hadad came unto the land of Moab, and Moab and the children of Midian went out to meet him, and they placed themselves in battle array against him in the field of Moab.

9. And Hadad fought with Moab, and there fell of the children of Moab and the children of Midian many slain ones, about two hundred thousand men.

10. And the battle was very severe upon Moab, and when the children of Moab saw that the battle was sore upon them, they weakened their hands and turned their backs, and left the children of Midian to carry on the battle.

11. And the children of Midian knew not the intentions of Moab, but they strengthened themselves in battle and fought with Hadad and all

his host, and all Midian fell before him.

12. And Hadad smote all Midian with a heavy smiting, and he slew them with the edge of the sword, he left none remaining of those who came to assist Moab.

13. And when all the children of Midian had perished in battle, and the children of Moab had escaped, Hadad made all Moab at that time tributary to him, and they became under his hand, and they gave a yearly tax as it was ordered, and Hadad turned and went back to his land.

14. And at the revolution of the year, when the rest of the *people* of Midian that were in the land heard that all their brethren had fallen in battle *with* Hadad for the sake of Moab, because the children of Moab had turned their backs in battle and left Midian to fight, *then* five of the princes of Midian resolved with the rest of their brethren who remained in their land, to fight with Moab to avenge the cause of their brethren.

15. And the children of Midian sent to all their brethren the children of the east, and all their brethren, all the children of Keturah came to assist Midian to fight with Moab.

16. And the children of Moab heard this thing, and they were greatly afraid that all the children of the east had assembled together against them for battle, and they the children of Moab sent a memorial to the land of Edom to Hadad the son of Bedad, saying,

17. Come now unto us and assist us and we will smite Midian, for they all assembled together and have come against us with all their brethren the children of the east to battle, to avenge the cause of Midian that fell in battle.

18. And Hadad, son of Bedad, king of Edom, went forth with his whole army and went to the land of Moab to fight with Midian, and Midian and the children of the east fought with Moab in the field of Moab, and the battle was very fierce between them.

19. And Hadad smote all the children of Midian and the children of the east with the edge of the sword, and Hadad at that time delivered Moab from the hand of Midian, and those that remained of Midian and of the children of the east fled before Hadad and his army, and Hadad pursued them to their land, and smote them with a very heavy slaughter, and the slain fell in the road.

20. And Hadad delivered Moab from the hand of Midian, for all the children of Midian had fallen by the edge of the sword, and Hadad turned and went back to his land.

21. And from that day forth, the children of Midian hated the children of Moab, because they had fallen in battle for their sake, and there was a great and mighty enmity between them all the days.

22. And all that were found of Midian in the road of the land of Moab perished by the sword of Moab, and all that were found of Moab in the road of the land of Midian, perished by the sword of Midian; thus did Midian unto Moab and Moab unto Midian for many days.

23. And it came to pass at that time that Judah the son of Jacob died in Egypt, in the eighty sixth year of Jacob's going down to Egypt, and Judah was a hundred and twenty nine years old at his death, and they embalmed him and put him into a coffin and he was given into the hands of his children.

24. And in the eighty ninth year died Naphtali, he was a hundred and thirty two years old, and he was put into a coffin and given into the hands of his children.

25. And it came to pass in the ninety first year of the Israelites going down to Egypt, that *is* in the thirtieth year of the reign of Zepho the son of Eliphaz, the son of Esau, over the children of Chittim, the children of Africa came upon the children of Chittim to plunder them as usual, but they had not come upon them for these thirteen years.

26. And they came to them in that year, and Zepho the son of Eliphaz went out to them with some of his men and smote them desperately, and the troops of Africa fled from before Zepho and the slain fell before him, and Zepho and his men pursued them, going on and smiting them until *they were* near unto Africa.

27. And Angeas king of Africa heard the thing which Zepho had done, and it vexed him exceedingly, and Angeas was afraid of Zepho all the days.

CHAPTER LXIII.

1. And in the ninety third year died Levi the son of Jacob in Egypt, and Levi was a hundred and thirty seven years old when he died, and they put him into a coffin and he was given into the hands of his children.

2. And it came to pass after the death of Levi, when all Egypt saw that the sons of Jacob the brethren of Joseph were dead, all the Egyptians began to afflict the children of Jacob, and to embitter their lives from that day unto the day of their going forth from Egypt, and they took from their hands all the vine-yards and fields which Joseph had given unto them, and all the elegant houses in which the people of Israel lived, and all the fat of Egypt, the Egyptians took all from the sons of Jacob in those days.

3. And the hand of all Egypt became more grievous in those days against the children of Israel, and the Egyptians injured the Israelites until the children of Israel were wearied of their lives on account of the Egyptians.

4. And it came to pass in those days, in the hundred and second year of Israel's going down to Egypt, that Pharaoh king of Egypt died, and Melol his son reigned in his stead, and all the mighty men of Egypt and all that generation which knew Joseph and his brethren died in those days.

5. And another generation rose up in their stead, which had not known the sons of Jacob and all the good which they had done to them, and all their might in Egypt.

6. Therefore all Egypt began from that day forth to embitter the lives of the sons of Jacob, and to afflict them with all manner of hard labor, because they had not known their ancestors who had delivered them in the days of the famine.

7. And this was also from the Lord, for the children of Israel, to benefit them in their latter days, in order that all the children of Israel might know the Lord their God.

8. And in order to know the signs and mighty wonders which the Lord would do in Egypt on account of his people Israel, in order that the children of Israel might fear the Lord God of their ancestors, and walk in all his ways, they and their seed after them all the days.

9. Melol was twenty years old when he began to reign, and he reigned ninety four years, and all Egypt called his name Pharaoh after the name of his father, as it was their custom to do to every king who reigned over them in Egypt.

10. At that time all the troops of Angeas king of Africa went forth to spread along the land of Chittim as usual for plunder.

11. And Zepho the son of Eliphaz the son of Esau heard their report, and he went forth to meet them with his army, and he fought them there in the road.

12. And Zepho smote the troops of the king of Africa with the edge of the sword, and left none remaining of them, and not even one returned to his master in Africa.

13. And Angeas heard of this which Zepho the son of Eliphaz had done to all his troops, that he had destroyed them, and Angeas assembled all his troops, all the men of the land of Africa, a people numerous like the sand by the sea shore.

14. And Angeas sent to Lucus his brother, saying, come to me with all thy men and help me to smite Zepho and all the children of Chittim who have destroyed my men, and Lucus came with his whole army, a very great force, to assist Angeas his brother to fight with Zepho and the children of Chittim.

15. And Zepho and the children of Chittim heard this thing, and they were greatly afraid and a great terror fell upon their hearts.

16. And Zepho also sent a letter to the land of Edom to Hadad the son of Bedad king of Edom and to all the children of Esau, saying,

17. I have heard that Angeas king of Africa is coming to us with his brother for battle against us, and we are greatly afraid of him, for his army is very great, particularly as he comes against us with his brother and his army likewise.

18. Now therefore come you also up with me and help me, and we will fight together against Angeas and his brother Lucus, and you will save us out of their hands, but if not, know ye that we shall all die.

19. And the children of Esau sent a letter to the children of Chittim and to Zepho their king, saying, we cannot fight against Angeas and his people for a covenant of peace has been between us these many years, from the days of Bela the first king, and from the days of Joseph the son of Jacob king of Egypt, with whom we fought on the other side of Jordan when he buried his father.

20. And when Zepho heard the words of his brethren the children of Esau he refrained from them, and Zepho was greatly afraid of Angeas.

21. And Angeas and Lucus his brother arrayed all their forces, about eight hundred thousand men, against the children of Chittim.

22. And all the children of Chittim said unto Zepho, pray for us to the God of thy ancestors, peradventure he may deliver us from the hand of Angeas and his army, for we have heard that he is a great God and that he delivers all who trust in him.

23. And Zepho heard their words, and Zepho sought the Lord and he said,

24. O Lord God of Abraham and Isaac my ancestors, this day I know that thou art a true God, and all the gods of the nations are vain and useless.

25 Remember now this day un-

to me thy covenant with Abraham our father, which our ancestors related unto us, and do graciously with me this day for the sake of Abraham and Isaac our fathers, and save me and the children of Chittim from the hand of the king of Africa who comes against us for battle.

26. And the Lord hearkened to the voice of Zepho, and he had regard for him on account of Abraham and Isaac, and the Lord delivered Zepho and the children of Chittim from the hand of Angeas and his people.

27. And Zepho fought Angeas king of Africa and all his people on that day, and the Lord gave all the people of Angeas into the hands of the children of Chittim.

28. And the battle was severe upon Angeas, and Zepho smote all the men of Angeas and Lucus his brother, with the edge of the sword, and there fell from them until the evening of that day about four hundred thousand men.

29. And when Angeas saw that all his men perished, he sent a letter to all the inhabitants of Africa to come to him in the battle, and he wrote in the letter, saying, all who are found in Africa let them come unto me from ten years old and upward; let them all come unto me, and behold if he comes ·not he shall die, and all that he has, with his whole household, the king will take.

30. And all the *rest* of the inhabitants of Africa were terrified at the words of Angeas, and there went out of the city about three hundred thousand men and boys, from ten years upward, and they came to Angeas.

31. And at the end of ten days Angeas renewed the battle against Zepho and the children of Chittim,

and the battle was very great and strong between them.

32. And from the army of Angeas and Lucus Zepho sent many of the wounded unto *his* land, about two thousand men, and Sosiphtar the captain of the host of Angeas fell in that battle.

33. And when Sosiphtar had fallen the African troops turned their backs to flee, and they fled, and Angeas and Lucus his brother were with them.

34. And Zepho and the children of Chittim pursued them, and they smote them still heavily on the road, about two hundred men, and they pursued Azdrubal the son of Angeas who had fled with his father, and they smote twenty of his men in the road, and Azdrubal escaped from the children of Chittim, and they did not slay him.

35. And Angeas and Lucus his brother fled with the rest of their men, and they escaped and came into Africa with terror ·and consternation, and Angeas feared all the days lest Zepho the son of Eliphaz should go to war with him.

CHAPTER LXIV.

1. And Balaam the son of Beor was at that time with Angeas in the battle, and when he saw that Zepho prevailed over Angeas, he fled from there and came to Chittim.

2. And Zepho and the children of Chittim received ·him with great honor, for Zepho knew Balaam's wisdom, and Zepho gave unto Balaam many gifts and he remained with him.

3. And when Zepho had returned from the war, he commanded all the children of Chittim to be numbered

who had gone into battle with him, and behold not one was missed.

4. And Zepho rejoiced at this thing, and he renewed his kingdom,* and he made a feast to all his subjects.

5. But Zepho remembered not the Lord and considered not that the Lord had helped him in battle, and that he had delivered him and his people from the hand of the king of Africa, but still walked in the ways of the children of Chittim and the wicked children of Esau, to serve other gods which his brethren the children of Esau had taught him; it is therefore said, from the wicked goes forth wickedness.

6. And Zepho reigned over all the children of Chittim securely, but knew not the Lord who had delivered him and all his people from the hand of the king of Africa; and the troops of Africa came no more to Chittim to plunder as usual, for they knew of the power of Zepho who had smitten them all at the edge of the sword, so Angeas was afraid of Zepho the son of Eliphaz, and of the children of Chittim all the days.

7. At that time when Zepho had returned from the war, and when Zepho had seen how he prevailed over all the people of Africa and had smitten them in battle at the edge of the sword, then Zepho advised with the children of Chittim, to go to Egypt to fight with the sons of Jacob and with Pharaoh king of Egypt.

8. For Zepho heard that the mighty men of Egypt were dead and that Joseph and his brethren the sons of Jacob were dead, and that all their children the children of Israel remained in Egypt.

9. And Zepho considered to go to

* i. e. After the fatigues of war, to attend again to domestic government.

fight against them and all Egypt, to avenge the cause of his brethren the children of Esau, whom Joseph with his brethren and all Egypt had smitten in the land of Canaan, when they went up to bury Jacob in Hebron.

10. And Zepho sent messengers to Hadad, son of Bedad, king of Edom, and to all his brethren the children of Esau, saying,

11. Did you not say that you would not fight against the king of Africa for he is a member of your covenant? behold I fought with him and smote him and all his people.

12. Now therefore I have resolved to fight against Egypt and the children of Jacob who are there, and I will be revenged of them for what Joseph, his brethren and ancestors did to us in the land of Canaan when they went up to bury their father in Hebron.

13. Now then if you are willing to come to me to assist me in fighting against them and Egypt, then shall we avenge the cause of our brethren.

14. And the children of Esau hearkened to the words of Zepho, and the children of Esau gathered themselves together, a very great people, and they went to assist Zepho and the children of Chittim in battle.

15. And Zepho sent to all the children of the east and to all the children of Ishmael with words like unto these, and they gathered themselves and came to the assistance of Zepho and the children of Chittim in the war upon Egypt.

16. And all these kings, the king of Edom and the children of the east, and all the children of Ishmael, and Zepho the king of Chittim went forth and arrayed all their hosts in Hebron.

17. And the camp was very heavy, extending *in length a distance* of three days' journey, a people numerous as the sand upon the sea shore which cannot be counted.

18. And all these kings and their hosts went down and came against all Egypt in battle, and encamped together in the valley of Pathros.

19. And all Egypt heard their report, and they also gathered themselves together, all the people of the land of Egypt, and of all the cities belonging to Egypt, about three hundred thousand men.

20. And the men of Egypt sent also to the children of Israel who were in those days in the land of Goshen, to come to them in order to go and fight with these kings.

21. And the men of Israel assembled and were about* one hundred and fifty men, and they went into battle to assist the Egyptians.

22. And the men of Israel and of Egypt went forth, about three hundred thousand men and one hundred and fifty men, and they went toward these kings to battle, and they placed themselves from without the land of Goshen opposite Pathros.

23. And the Egyptians believed not in Israel to go with them in their camps together for battle, for all the Egyptians said, perhaps the children of Israel will deliver us into the hand of the children of Esau and Ishmael, for they are their brethren.

24. And all the Egyptians said unto the children of Israel, remain you here together in your stand and we will go and fight against the children of Esau and Ishmael, and if these kings should prevail over us,

* *i. e.* Those who were willing to go amounted to 150 men, who were nothing in such a great army : see the 23d verse for the cause.

then come you altogether upon them and assist us, and the children of Israel did so.

25. And Zepho the son of Eliphaz the son of Esau king of Chittim, and Hadad the son of Bedad king of Edom, and all their camps, and all the children of the east, and children of Ishmael, a people numerous as sand, encamped together in the valley of Pathros opposite Tachpanches.

26. And Balaam the son of Beor the Syrian was there in the camp of Zepho, for he came with the children of Chittim to the battle, and Balaam was a man highly honored in the eyes of Zepho and his men.

27. And Zepho said unto Balaam, try by divination for us that we may know who will prevail in the battle, we or the Egyptians.

28. And Balaam rose up and tried the art of divination, and he was skilful in the knowledge *of it*, but he was confused and the work was destroyed in his hand.

29. And he tried it again but it did not succeed, and Balaam despaired of it and left it and did not complete it, for this was from the Lord, in order to cause Zepho and his people to fall into the hand of the children of Israel, who had trusted in the Lord, the God of their ancestors, in their war.

30. And Zepho and Hadad put their forces in battle array, and all the Egyptians went alone against them, about three hundred thousand men, and not one man of Israel was with them.

31. And all the Egyptians fought with these kings opposite Pathros and Tachpanches, and the battle was severe against the Egyptians.

32. And the kings were stronger than the Egyptians in that battle, and

about one hundred and eighty men of Egypt fell on that day, and about thirty men of the forces of the kings, and all the men of Egypt fled from before the kings, so the children of Esau and Ishmael pursued the Egyptians, continuing to smite them unto the place where was the camp of the children of Israel.

33. And all the Egyptians cried unto the children of Israel, saying, hasten to us and assist us and save us from the hand of Esau, Ishmael and the children of Chittim.

34. And the hundred and fifty men of the children of Israel ran from their station to the camps of these kings, and the children of Israel cried unto the Lord their God to deliver them.

35. And the Lord hearkened to Israel, and the Lord gave all the men of the kings into their hand, and the children of Israel fought against these kings, and the children of Israel smote about four thousand of the kings' men.

36. And the Lord threw a great consternation in the camp of the kings, so that the fear of the children of Israel fell upon them.

37. And all the hosts of the kings fled from before the children of Israel, and the children of Israel pursued them continuing to smite them unto the borders of the land of Cush.

38. And the children of Israel slew of them in the road yet two thousand men, and of the children of Israel not one fell.

39. And when the Egyptians saw that the children of Israel had fought with such few men with the kings, and that the battle was so very severe against them,

40. All the Egyptians were greatly afraid of their lives on account of the strong battle, and all Egypt fled, every man hiding himself from the arrayed forces, and they hid themselves in the road, and they left the Israelites to fight.

41. And the children of Israel inflicted a terrible blow upon the kings' men, and they returned from them after they had driven them to the border of the land of Cush.

42. And all Israel knew the thing which the men of Egypt had done to them, that they had fled from them in battle, and had left them to fight *alone.*

43. So the children of Israel also acted with cunning, and as the children of Israel returned from battle, they found some of the Egyptians in the road and smote them there.

44. And whilst they slew them, they said unto them these words,

45. Wherefore did you go from us and leave us, being a few people, to fight against these kings who had a great people to smite us, that you might thereby deliver your own souls?

46. And of some which the Israelites met on the road, they the children of Israel spoke to each other, saying, smite, smite, for he is an Ishmaelite, or an Edomite, or from the children of Chittim, and they stood over him and slew him, and they knew that he was an Egyptian.

47. And the children of Israel did these things cunningly against the Egyptians, because they had deserted them in battle and had fled from them.

48. And the children of Israel slew of the men of Egypt in the road in this manner, about two hundred men.

49. And all the men of Egypt saw the evil which the children of Israel had done to them, so all Egypt fear-

ed greatly the children of Israel, for they had seen their great power, and that not one man of them had fallen.

50. So all the children of Israel returned with joy on their road to Goshen, and the rest of Egypt returned each man to his place.

CHAPTER LXV.

1. And it came to pass after these things, that all the counsellors of Pharaoh, king of Egypt, and all the elders of Egypt assembled and came before the king and bowed down to the ground, and they sat before him.

2. And the counsellors and elders of Egypt spoke unto the king, saying,

3. Behold the people of the children of Israel is greater and mightier than we are, and thou knowest all the evil which they did to us in the road when we returned from battle.

4. And thou hast also seen their strong power, for this power is unto them from their fathers, for but a few men stood up against a people numerous as the sand, and smote them at the edge of the sword, and of themselves not one has fallen, so that if they had been numerous they would then have utterly destroyed them.

5. Now therefore give us counsel what to do with them, until we gradually destroy them from amongst us, lest they become too numerous for us in the land.

6. For if the children of Israel should increase in the land, they will become an obstacle to us, and if any war should happen to take place, they with their great strength will join our enemy against us, and fight against us, destroy us from the land and go away from it.

7. So the king answered the elders of Egypt and said unto them, this is the plan advised against Israel, from which we will not depart.

8. Behold in the land are Pithom and Rameses, cities unfortified against battle, *it behoves* you and us to build them, and to fortify them.

9. Now therefore go you also and act cunningly toward them, and proclaim a voice in Egypt and in Goshen at the command of the king, saying,

10. All ye men of Egypt, Goshen, Pathros and all their inhabitants ! the king has commanded us to build Pithom and Rameses, and to fortify them for battle ; who amongst you of all Egypt, of the children of Israel and of all the inhabitants of the cities, *are willing* to build with us, shall each have his wages given to him daily at the king's order ; so go you first and do cunningly, and gather yourselves and come to Pithom and Rameses to build.

11. And whilst you are building, cause a proclamation of this kind to be made throughout Egypt every day at the command of the king.

12. And when some of the children of Israel shall come to build with you, you shall give them their wages daily for a few days.

13. And after they shall have built with you for their daily hire, draw yourselves away from them daily one by one in secret, and then you shall rise up and become their task-masters and officers, and you shall leave them afterward to build without wages, and should they refuse, then force them with all your might to build.

14. And if you do this it will be well with us to strengthen our land against the children of Israel, for on account of the fatigue of the building and the work, the children of Israel

will decrease, because you will deprive them from their wives day by day.

15. And all the elders of Egypt heard the counsel of the king, and the counsel seemed good in their eyes and in the eyes of the servants of Pharaoh, and in the eyes of all Egypt, and they did according to the word of the king.

16. And all the servants went away from the king, and they caused a proclamation to be made in all Egypt, in Tachpanches and in Goshen, and in all the cities which surrounded Egypt, saying,

17. You have seen what the children of Esau and Ishmael did to us, who came to war against us and wished to destroy us;

18. Now therefore the king commanded us to fortify the land, to build the cities Pithom and Rameses, and to fortify them for battle, if they should *again* come against us.

19. Whosoever of you from all Egypt and from the children of Israel will come to build with us, he shall have his daily wages given by the king, as his command is unto us.

20. And when Egypt and all the children of Israel heard all that the servants of Pharaoh had spoken, there came from the Egyptians and the children of Israel to build with the servants of Pharaoh, Pithom and Rameses, but none of the children of Levi came with their brethren to build.

21. And all the servants of Pharaoh and his princes came at first with deceit to build with all Israel as daily hired *laborers*, and they gave to Israel their daily hire at the beginning.

22. And the servants of Pharaoh built with all Israel, and were employed in that work with Israel for a month.

23. And at the end of the month, all the servants of Pharaoh began to withdraw secretly from the people of Israel daily.

24. And Israel went on with the work at that time, but they then received their daily hire, because some of the men of Egypt were yet carrying on the work with Israel at that time; therefore the Egyptians gave Israel their hire in those days, in order that they, the Egyptians their fellow workmen, might also take the pay for their labour.

25. And at the end of a year and four months all the Egyptians had withdrawn from the children of Israel, so that the children of Israel were left alone engaged in the work.

26. And after all the Egyptians had withdrawn from the children of Israel they returned and became oppressors and officers over them, and some of them stood over the children of Israel as task masters, to receive from them all that they gave them for the pay of their labour.

27. And the Egyptians did in this manner to the children of Israel day by day, in order to afflict the Israelites in their work.

28. And all the children of Israel were alone engaged in the labor, and the Egyptians refrained from giving any pay to the children of Israel from that time forward.

29. And when some of the men of Israel refused to work on account of the wages not being given to them, then the exactors and the servants of Pharaoh oppressed them and smote them with heavy blows, and made them return by force, to labor with their brethren; thus did all the

Egyptians unto the children of Israel all the days.

30. And all the children of Israel were greatly afraid of the Egyptians in this matter, and all the children of Israel returned and worked alone without pay.

31. And the children of Israel built Pithom and Rameses, and all the children of Israel did the work, some making bricks, and some building, and the children of Israel built and fortified all the land of Egypt and its walls, and the children of Israel were engaged in work for many years, until the time came when the Lord remembered them and brought them out of Egypt.

32. But the children of Levi were not employed in the work with their brethren of Israel, from the beginning unto the day of their going forth from Egypt.

33. For all the children of Levi knew that the Egyptians had spoken all these words with deceit to the Israelites, therefore the children of Levi refrained from approaching to the work with their brethren.

34. And the Egyptians did not direct their attention to make the children of Levi work afterward, since they had not been with their brethren at the beginning, therefore the Egyptians left them alone.

35. And the hands of the men of Egypt were directed with continued severity against the children of Israel in that work, and the Egyptians made the children of Israel work with rigor.

36. And the Egyptians embittered the lives of the children of Israel with hard work, in mortar and bricks, and also in all manner of work in the field.

37. And the children of Israel

called Melol the king of Egypt "Meror,* king of Egypt," because in his days the Egyptians had embittered their lives with all manner of work.

38. And all the work wherein the Egyptians made the children of Israel labor, they exacted with rigor, in order to afflict the children of Israel, but the more they afflicted them, the more they increased and grew, and the Egyptians were grieved because of the children of Israel.

CHAPTER LXVI.

1. At that time died Hadad the son of Bedad king of Edom, and Samlah from Mesrekah, from the country of the children of the east, reigned in his place.

2. In the thirteenth year *of the reign* of Pharaoh king of Egypt, which was the hundred and twenty fifth year of the Israelites going down into Egypt, Samlah had reigned over Edom eighteen years.

3. And when he reigned, he drew forth his hosts to go and fight against Zepho the son of Eliphaz and the children of Chittim, because they had made war against Angeas king of Africa, and they destroyed his whole army.

4. But he did not engage with him, for the children of Esau prevented him, saying he was their brother, so Samlah listened to the voice of the children of Esau, and turned back with all his forces to the land of Edom, and did not proceed to fight against Zepho the son of Eliphaz.

5. And Pharaoh king of Egypt heard this thing, saying, Samlah king of Edom has resolved to fight the children of Chittim, and after-

* מרור from מרר to embitter.

ward he will come to fight against Egypt.

6. And when the Egyptians heard this matter, they increased the labor upon the children of Israel, lest the Israelites should do unto them as they did unto them in their war with the children of Esau in the days of Hadad.

7. So the Egyptians said unto the children of Israel, hasten and do your work, and finish your task, and strengthen the land, lest the children of Esau your brethren should come to fight against us, for on your account will they come against us.

8. And the children of Israel did the work of the men of Egypt day by day, and the Egyptians afflicted the children of Israel in order to lessen them in the land.

9. But as the Egyptians increased the labor upon the children of Israel, so did the children of Israel increase and multiply, and all Egypt was filled with the children of Israel.

10. And in the hundred and twenty fifth year of Israel's going down into Egypt, all the Egyptians saw that their counsel did not succeed against Israel, but that they increased and grew, and the land of Egypt and the land of Goshen were filled with the children of Israel.

11. So all the elders of Egypt and its wise men came before the king and bowed down to him and sat before him.

12. And all the elders of Egypt and the wise men thereof said unto the king, may the king live forever; thou didst counsel us the counsel against the children of Israel, and we did unto them according to the word of the king.

13. But in proportion to the increase of the labor so do they increase and grow in the land, and behold the whole country is filled with them.

14. Now therefore our lord and king, the eyes of all Egypt are upon thee to give them advice with thy wisdom, by which they may prevail over Israel to destroy them, or to diminish them from the land; and the king answered them, saying, give you counsel in this mattter that we may know what to do unto them.

15. And an officer, one of the king's counsellors, whose name was Job, from Mesopotamia, in the land of Uz, answered the king, saying,

16. If it please the king, let him hear the counsel of his servant; and the king said unto him, speak.

17. And Job spoke before the king, the princes, and before all the elders of Egypt, saying,

18. Behold the counsel of the king which he advised formerly respecting the labor of the children of Israel is very good, and you must not remove from them that labor forever.

19. But this is the advice counselled by which you may lessen them, if it seems good to the king to afflict them.

20. Behold we have feared war for a long time, and we said, when Israel becomes fruitful in the land, they will drive us from the land if a war should take place.

21. If it please the king, let a royal decree go forth, and let it be written in the laws of Egypt which shall not be revoked, that every male child born to the Israelites, his blood shall be spilled upon the ground.

22. And by your doing this, when all the male children of Israel shall have died, the evil of their wars will cease; let the king do so

and send for all the Hebrew mid-wives and order them in this matter to execute it; so the thing pleased the king and the princes, and the king did according to the word of Job.

23. And the king sent for the Hebrew midwives to be called, of which the name of one was Shephrah, and the name of the other Puah.

24. And the midwives came before the king, and stood in his presence.

25. And the king said unto them, when you do the office of a midwife to the Hebrew women, and see them upon the stools, if it be a son, then you shall kill him, but if it be a daughter, then she shall live.

26. But if you will not do this thing, then will I burn you up and all your houses with fire.

27. But the midwives feared God and did not hearken to the king of Egypt nor to his words, and when the Hebrew women brought forth to the midwife son or daughter, then did the midwife do all that was necessary to the child and let it live; thus did the midwives all the days.

28. And this thing was told to the king, and he sent and called for the midwives and he said to them, why have you done this thing and have saved the children alive?

29. And the midwives answered, and spoke together before the king, saying,

30. Let not the king think that the Hebrew women are as the Egyptian women, for all the children of Israel are hale,* and before the midwife comes to them they are delivered, and as for us thy handmaids, for

*כי חיות הנה same as in Exodus, ch. 1, v. 19, where the English version is "for they are lively." I prefer my translation.

14

many days no Hebrew woman has brought forth upon us, for all the Hebrew women are their own midwives, because they are hale.

31. And Pharaoh heard their words and believed them in this matter, and the midwives went away from the king, and God dealt well with them, and the people multiplied and waxed exceedingly.

CHAPTER LXVII.

1. There was a man in the land of Egypt of the seed of Levi, whose name was Amram, the son of Kehath, the son of Levi, the son of Israel.

2. And this man went and took a wife, namely Jochebed the daughter of Levi his father's sister, and she was one hundred and twenty six years old, and he came unto her.

3. And the woman conceived and bare a daughter, and she called her name Miriam, because in those days the Egyptians had embittered the lives of the children of Israel.

4. And she conceived again and bare a son and she called his name Aaron, for in the days of her conception, Pharaoh began to spill the blood of the male children of Israel.

5. In those days died Zepho the son of Eliphaz, son of Esau, king of Chittim, and Janeas reigned in his stead.

6. And the time that Zepho reigned over the children of Chittim was fifty years, and he died and was buried in the city of Nabna in the land of Chittim.

7. And Janeas, one of the mighty men of the children of Chittim, reigned after him and he reigned fifty years.

8. And it was after the death of

the king of Chittim that Balaam the son of Beor fled from the land of Chittim, and he went and came to Egypt to Pharaoh king of Egypt.

9. And Pharaoh received him with great honor, for he had heard of his wisdom, and he gave him presents and made him for a counsellor, and aggrandized him.

10. And Balaam dwelt in Egypt, in honor with all the nobles of the king, and the nobles exalted him, because they all coveted to learn his wisdom.

11. And in the hundred and thirtieth year of Israel's going down to Egypt, Pharaoh dreamed that he was sitting upon his kingly throne, and lifted up his eyes and saw an old man standing before him, and there were scales in the hands of the old man, such scales as are used by merchants.

12. And the old man took the scales and hung them before Pharaoh.

13. And the old man took all the elders of Egypt and all its nobles and great men, and he tied them together and put them in one scale.

14. And he took a milk kid and put it into the other scale, and the kid preponderated over all.

15. And Pharaoh was astonished at this dreadful vision, why the kid should preponderate over all, and Pharaoh woke and behold it was a dream.

16. And Pharaoh rose up early in the morning and called all his servants and related to them the dream, and the men were greatly afraid.

17. And the king said to all his wise men, interpret I pray you the dream which I dreamed, that I may know it.

18. And Balaam the son of Beor

answered the king and said unto him, this means nothing else but a great evil that will spring up against Egypt in the latter days.

19. For a son will be born to Israel who will destroy all Egypt and its inhabitants, and bring forth the Israelites from Egypt with a mighty hand.

20. Now therefore O king, take counsel upon this matter, that you may destroy the hope of the children of Israel and their expectation, before this evil arise against Egypt.

21. And the king said unto Balaam, and what shall we do unto Israel? surely after a certain manner did we at first counsel against them and could not prevail over them.

22. Now therefore give you also advice against them by which we may prevail over them.

23. And Balaam answered the king, saying, send now and call thy two counsellors, and we will see what their advice is upon this matter and afterward thy servant will speak.

24. And the king sent and called his two counsellors Reuel the Midianite and Job the Uzite, and they came and sat before the king.

25. And the king said to them, behold you have both heard the dream which I have dreamed, and the interpretation thereof; now therefore give counsel and know and see what is to be done to the children of Israel, whereby we may prevail over them, before their evil shall spring up against us.

26. And Reuel the Midianite answered the king and said, may the king live, may the king live forever.

27. If it seem good to the king, let him desist from the Hebrews and leave them, and let him not stretch forth his hand against them.

28. For these are they whom the Lord chose in days of old, and took as the lot of his inheritance from amongst all the nations of the earth and the kings of the earth; and who is there that stretched his hand against them with impunity, of whom their God was not avenged?

29. Surely thou knowest that when Abraham went down to Egypt, Pharaoh, the former king of Egypt, saw Sarah his wife, and took her for a wife, because Abraham said, she is my sister, for he was afraid, lest the men of Egypt should slay him on account of his wife.

30. And when the king of Egypt had taken Sarah then God smote him and his household with heavy plagues, until he restored unto Abraham his wife Sarah, then was he healed.

31. And Abimelech the Gerarite, king of the Philistines, God punished on account of Sarah wife of Abraham, in stopping up every womb from man to beast.

32. When their God came to Abimelech in the dream of night and terrified him, in order that he might restore to Abraham Sarah whom he had taken, and afterward all the people of Gerar were punished on account of Sarah, and Abraham prayed to his God for them, and he was intreated of him, and he healed them.

33. And Abimelech feared all this evil that came upon him and his people, and he returned to Abraham his wife Sarah, and gave him with her many gifts.

34. He did so also to Isaac when he had driven him from Gerar, and God had done wonderful things to him, that all the water courses of Gerar were dried up, and their productive trees did not bring forth.

35. Until Abimelech of Gerar, and Ahuzzath one of his friends, and Pichol the captain of his host, went to him and they bent and bowed down before him to the ground,

36. And they requested of him to supplicate for them, and he prayed to the Lord for them, and the Lord was intreated of him and he healed them.

37. Jacob also, the plain man, was delivered through his integrity from the hand of his brother Esau, and the hand of Laban the Syrian his mother's brother, who had sought his life; likewise from the hand of all the kings of Canaan who had come together against him and his children to destroy them, and the Lord delivered them out of their hands, that they turned upon them and smote them, for who had ever stretched forth his hand against them with impunity?

38. Surely Pharaoh the former, thy father's father, raised Joseph the son of Jacob above all the princes of the land of Egypt, when he saw his wisdom, for through his wisdom he rescued all the inhabitants of the land from the famine.

39. After which he ordered Jacob and his children to come down to Egypt, in order that through their virtue, the land of Egypt and the land of Goshen might be delivered from the famine.

40. Now therefore if it seem good in thine eyes, cease from destroying the children of Israel, but if it be not thy will that they shall dwell in Egypt, send them forth from here, that they may go to the land of Canaan, the land where their ancestors sojourned.

41. And when Pharaoh heard the words of Jethro he was very angry with him, so that he rose with shame

from the king's presence, and went to Midian, his land, and took Joseph's stick with him.

42. And the king said to Job the Uzite, what sayest thou Job, and what is thy advice respecting the Hebrews?

43. So Job said to the king, behold all the inhabitants of the land are in thy power, let the king do as it seems good in his eyes.

44. And the king said unto Balaam, what dost thou say, Balaam, speak thy word that we may hear it.

45. And Balaam said to the king, of all that the king has counselled against the Hebrews will they be delivered, and the king will not be able to prevail over them with any counsel.

46. For if thou thinkest to lessen them by the flaming fire, thou canst not prevail over them, for surely their God delivered Abraham their father from Ur* of the Chaldeans; and if thou thinkest to destroy them with a sword, surely Isaac their father was delivered from it, and a ram was placed in his stead.

47. And if with hard and rigorous labor thou thinkest to lessen them, thou wilt not prevail even in this, for their father Jacob served Laban in all manner of hard work, and prospered.

48. Now therefore, O King, hear my words, for this is the counsel which is counselled against them, by which thou wilt prevail over them, and from which thou shouldst not depart.

49. If it please the king let him order all their children which shall be born from this day forward, to be

* It was stated before that אור was a fire in which Abraham was put, and from which God delivered ..im.

thrown into the water, for by this canst thou wipe away their name, for none of them, nor of their fathers, were* tried in this manner.

50. And the king heard the words of Balaam, and the thing pleased the king and the princes, and the king did according to the word of Balaam.

51. And the king ordered a proclamation to be issued and a law to be made throughout the land of Egypt, saying, every male child born to the Hebrews from this day forward shall be thrown into the water.

52. And Pharaoh called unto all his servants, saying, go now and seek throughout the land of Goshen where the children of Israel are, and see that every son born to the Hebrews shall be cast into the river, but every daughter you shall let live.

53. And when the children of Israel heard this thing which Pharaoh had commanded, to cast their male children into the river, some of the people separated from their wives and others adhered to them.

54. And from that day forward, when the time of delivery arrived to those women of Israel who had remained *with their husbands*, they went to the field to bring forth there, and they brought forth in the field, and left their children upon the field and returned home.

55. And the Lord who had sworn to their ancestors to multiply them, sent one of his ministering angels which are in heaven to wash *each child* in water, to anoint and swathe it and to put into its hands two smooth stones from one of which it sucked milk and from the other honey, and he caused its hair to grow to his knees, by which it might

* Had any miraculous escape from water.

cover itself, to* comfort it and to
cleave to it, through his compassion
for it.

56. And when God had compassion over them and had desired to
multiply them upon the face of the
land, he ordered his earth to receive
them to be preserved therein till the
time of their growing up, after which
the earth opened its mouth and
vomited them forth and† they sprouted forth from the city like the herb
of the earth and the grass of the
forest, and they returned each to his
family and to his father's house, and
they remained with them.

57. And the babes of the children
of Israel were upon the earth like
the herb of the field, through God's
grace to them.

58. And when all the Egyptians
saw this thing, they went forth, each
to his field with his yoke of oxen and
his ploughshare, and they ploughed
it up as one ploughs the earth at seed
time.

59. And when they ploughed they
were unable to hurt the infants of the
children of Israel, so the people increased and waxed exceedingly

60. And Pharaoh ordered his
officers daily to go to Goshen to
seek for the babes of the children of
Israel.

61. And when they had sought
and found one, they took it from its
mother's bosom by force, and threw
it into the river, but the female child
they left with its mother ; thus did
the Egyptians do to the Israelites
all the days.

---

* i. c. That the angel was to comfort it and
cleave to it.

† ויציצו מעיר כעשב הארץ; the same sentence is
to be found in Psalm 2. v 16, upon which the
Rabbins formed this fable, and which has no
connexion with it.

CHAPTER LXVIII.

1. And it was at that time the spirit
of God was upon Miriam the daughter of Amram the sister of Aaron,
and she went forth and prophecied
about the house, saying, behold a
son will be born unto us from my
father and mother this time, and he
will save Israel from the hands of
Egypt.

2. And when Amram heard the
words of his daughter, he went and
took his wife back to the house, after
he had driven her away at the time
when Pharaoh ordered every male
child of the house of Jacob to be
thrown into the water.

3. So Amram took Jochebed his
wife, three years after he had driven
her away, and he came to her and
she conceived.

4. And at the end of seven months
from her conception she brought
forth a son, and the whole house was
filled with great light as of the light
of the sun and moon at the time of
their shining.

5. And when the woman saw the
child that it was good and pleasing
to the sight, she hid it for three
months in an inner room.

6. In those days the Egyptians
conspired to destroy all the Hebrews
there.

7. And the Egyptian women went
to Goshen where the children of
Israel were, and they carried their
young ones upon their shoulders,
their babes who could not yet speak.

8. And in those days, when the
women of the children of Israel
brought forth, each woman had hidden her son from before the Egyptians, that the Egyptians might not
know of their bringing forth, and
might not destroy them from the land.

9. And the Egyptian women came to Goshen and their children who could not speak were upon their shoulders, and when an Egyptian *woman* came into the house of a Hebrew *woman* her babe began to cry.

10. And when it cried the child that was in the inner room answered it, so the Egyptian women went and told it at the house of Pharaoh.

11. And Pharaoh sent his officers to take the children and slay them; thus did the Egyptians to the Hebrew women all the days.

12. And it was at that time, about three months from Jochebed's concealment of her son, that the thing was known in Pharaoh's house.

13. And the woman hastened to take away her son before the officers came, and she took for him an ark of bulrushes, and daubed it with slime and with pitch, and put the child therein, and she laid it in the flags by the river's brink.

14. And his sister Miriam stood afar off to know what would be done to him, and what would become of her words.*

15. And God sent forth at that time a terrible heat in the land of Egypt, which burned up the flesh of man like the sun in his circuit, and it greatly oppressed the Egyptians.

16. And all the Egyptians went down to bathe in the river, on account of the consuming heat which burned up their flesh.

17. And Bathia, the daughter of Pharaoh, went also to bathe in the river, owing to the consuming heat, and her maidens walked at the river side, and all the women of Egypt† as well.

18. And Bathia lifted up her eyes to the river, and she saw the ark upon the water, and sent her maid to fetch it.

19. And she opened it and saw the child, and behold the babe wept, and she had compassion on him, and she said, this is one of the Hebrew children.

20. And all the women of Egypt walking on the river side desired to give him suck, but he would not suck, for this thing was from the Lord, in order to restore him to his mother's breast.

21. And Miriam his sister was at that time amongst the Egyptian women at the river *side*, and she saw this thing and she said to Pharaoh's daughter, shall I go and fetch a nurse of the Hebrew women, that she may nurse the child for thee?

22. And Pharaoh's daughter said to her, go, and the young woman went and called the child's mother.

23. And Pharaoh's daughter said to Jochebed, take this child away and suckle it for me, and I will pay thee thy wages, two bits of silver daily; and the woman took the child and nursed it.

24. And at the end of two years, when the child grew up, she brought him to the daughter of Pharaoh, and he was unto her as a son, and she called his name Moses, for she said, because I drew him out of the water

25. And* Amram his father called his name Chabar, for he said, it was

* Her prophecy, mentioned in v. 1.
† Walked about in respectful attendance on Bathia.

*These different names arise from a Rabbinical torture of a genealogical account in 1 Chronicles. ch. 4. v. 18. which has nothing to do with the birth of Moses, only a woman's name, Bathia, daughter of Pharaoh, whom Mered took, and by a similarity of name to the great Pharaoh king of Egypt, as if no private person could be called so, they imagined it must have been Moses the adopted son of king Pharaoh's daughter. The same story is in the Talmud.

for him that he associated with his wife whom he had turned away.

26. And Jochebed his mother called his name Jekuthiel, because, she said, I have hoped for him to the Almighty, and God restored him unto me.

27. And Miriam his sister called him Jered, for she descended after him to the river to know what his end would be.

28. And Aaron his brother called his name Abi Zanuch, saying, my father left my mother and returned to her on his account.

29. And Kehath the father of Amram called his name Abigdor, because on his account did God repair the breach of the house of Jacob, that they could no longer throw their male children into the water.

30. And their nurse called him Abi Socho, saying, in his tabernacle was he hidden for three months, on account of the children of Ham.*

31. And all† Israel called his name Shemaiah, son of Nethanel, for they said, in his days has God heard their cries and rescued them from their oppressors.

32. And Moses was in Pharaoh's house, and was unto Bathia, Pharaoh's daughter, as a son, and Moses grew up amongst the king's children.

CHAPTER LXIX.

1. And the king of Edom died in those days, in the eighteenth year of his reign, and was buried in his temple which he had built for himself as his royal residence in the land of Edom.

* The Egyptians.
† They must have called him so after the exodus, or about the time ; but I conjecture the whole of this part a spurious addition, extracted from the Rabbinical works.

2. And the children of Esau sent to Pethor, which is upon the river, and they fetched from there a young man of beautiful eyes and comely aspect, whose name was Saul, and they made him king over them in the place of Samlah.

3. And Saul reigned over all the children of Esau in the land of Edom for forty years.

4. And when Pharaoh king of Egypt saw that the counsel which Balaam had advised respecting the children of Israel did not succeed, but that still they were fruitful, multiplied and increased throughout the land of Egypt,

5. Then Pharaoh commanded in those days that a proclamation should be issued throughout Egypt to the children of Israel, saying, no man shall diminish any thing of his daily labor.

6. And the man who shall be found deficient in his labor which he performs daily, whether in mortar or in bricks, then his youngest son shall be put in their place.

7. And the labor of Egypt strengthened upon the children of Israel in those days, and behold if one brick was deficient in any man's daily labor, the Egyptians took his youngest boy by force from his mother, and put him into the building in the place of the brick which his father had left wanting.

8. And the men of Egypt did so to all the children of Israel day by day, all the days for a long period.

9. But the tribe of Levi did not at that time work with the Israelites their brethren, from the beginning, for the children of Levi knew the cunning of the Egyptians which they exercised at first toward the Israelites.

CHAPTER LXX.

1. And in the third year from the birth of Moses, Pharaoh was sitting at a banquet, when Alparanith the queen was sitting at his right and Bathia at his left, and the lad Moses was lying upon her bosom, and Balaam the son of Beor with his two sons, and all the princes of the kingdom were sitting at table in the king's presence.

2. And the lad stretched forth his hand upon the king's head, and took the crown from the king's head and placed it on his own head.

3. And when the king and princes saw the work which the boy had done, the king and princes were terrified, and one man to his neighbor expressed astonishment.

4. And the king said unto the princes who were before him at table, what speak you and what say you, O ye princes, in this matter, and what is to be judgment against the boy on account of this act?

5. And Balaam the son of Beor the magician answered before the king and princes, and he said, remember now, O my lord and king, the dream which thou didst dream many days since, and that which thy servant interpreted unto thee.

6. Now therefore this is a child from the Hebrew children, in whom is the spirit of God, and let not my lord the king imagine that this youngster did this thing without knowledge.

7. For he is a Hebrew boy, and wisdom and understanding are with him, although he is yet a child, and with wisdom has he done this and chosen unto himself the kingdom of Egypt.

8. For this is the manner of all the Hebrews to deceive kings and their nobles, to do all these things cunningly, in order to make the kings of the earth and their men tremble.

9. Surely thou knowest that Abraham their father acted thus, who deceived the army of Nimrod king of Babel, and Abimelech king of Gerar, and that he possessed *himself* of the land of the children of Heth and all the kingdoms of Canaan.

10. And that he descended into Egypt and said of Sarah his wife, she is my sister, in order to mislead Egypt and her king.

11. His son Isaac also did so when he went to Gerar and dwelt there, and his strength prevailed over the army of Abimelech king of the Philistines.

12. He also thought of making the kingdom of the Philistines stumble, in saying that Rebecca his wife was his sister.

13. Jacob also dealt treacherously with his brother, and took from his hand his birthright and his blessing.

14. He went then to Padan-aram to the house of Laban his mother's brother, and cunningly obtained from him his daughter, his cattle, and all belonging to him, and fled away and returned to the land of Canaan to his father.

15. His sons sold their brother Joseph, who went down into Egypt and became a slave, and was placed in the prison house for twelve years.

16. Until the former Pharaoh dreamed dreams, and withdrew him from the prison house, and magnified him above all the princes in Egypt on account of his interpreting his dreams to him.

17. And when God caused a famine throughout the land he sent for

and brought his father and all his brothers, and the whole of his father's household, and supported them without price or reward, and bought the Egyptians for slaves.

18. Now therefore my lord king behold this child has risen up in their stead in Egypt, to do according to their deeds and to trifle with every king, prince and judge.

19. If it please the king, let us now spill his blood upon the ground, lest he grow up and take away the government from thy hand, and the hope of Egypt perish after he shall have reigned.

20. And Balaam said to the king, let us moreover call for all the judges of Egypt and the wise men thereof, and let us know if the judgment of death is due to this boy as thou didst say, and then we will slay him.

21. And Pharaoh sent and called for all the wise men of Egypt and they came before the king, and an angel of the Lord came amongst them, and he was like one of the wise men of Egypt.

22. And the king said to the wise men, surely you have heard what this Hebrew boy who is in the house has done, and thus has Balaam judged in the matter.

23. Now judge you also and see what is due to the boy for the act which he has committed.

24. And the angel, who seemed like one of the wise men of Pharaoh, answered and said as follows, before all the wise men of Egypt and before the king and the princes.

25. If it please the king let the king send for *men* who shall bring before him an onyx stone and a coal of fire, and place them before the child, and if the child shall stretch forth his hand and take the onyx

stone, then shall we know that with wisdom has the youth done all that he has done, and we must slay him.

26. But if he stretch forth his hand upon the coal, then shall we know that it was not with knowledge that he did this thing, and he shall live.

27. And the thing seemed good in the eyes of the king and the princes, so the king did according to the word of the angel of the Lord.

28. And the king ordered the onyx stone and coal to be brought and placed before Moses.

29. And they placed the boy before them, and the lad endeavored to stretch forth his hand to the onyx stone, but the angel of the Lord took his hand and placed it upon the coal, and the coal became extinguished in his hand, and he lifted it up and put it into his mouth, and burned part of his lips and part of his tongue, and he became heavy in mouth and tongue.

30. And when the king and princes saw this, they knew that Moses had not acted with wisdom in taking off the crown from the king's head.

31. So the king and princes refrained from slaying the child, so Moses remained in Pharaoh's house, growing up, and the Lord was with him.

32. And whilst the boy was in the king's house, he was robed in purple and he grew amongst the children of the king.

33. And when Moses grew up in the king's house, Bathia the daughter of Pharaoh considered him as a son, and all the household of Pharaoh honored him, and all the men of Egypt were afraid of him.

34. And he daily went forth and came into the land of Goshen, where

his brethren the children of Israel were, and Moses saw them daily in shortness of breath and hard labor.

35. And Moses asked them, saying, wherefore is this labor meted out unto you day by day?

36. And they told him all that had befallen them, and all the injunctions which Pharaoh had put upon them before his birth.

37. And they told him all the counsels which Balaam the son of Beor had counselled against them, and what he had also counselled against him in order to slay him when he had taken the king's crown from off his head.

38. And when Moses heard these things his anger was kindled against Balaam, and he sought to kill him, and he was in ambush for him day by day.

39. And Balaam was afraid of Moses, and he and his two sons rose up and went forth from Egypt, and they fled and delivered their souls and betook themselves to the land of Cush to Kikianus, king of Cush.

40. And Moses was in the king's house going out and coming in, the Lord gave him favor in the eyes of Pharaoh, and in the eyes of all his servants, and in the eyes of all the people of Egypt, and they loved Moses exceedingly.

41. And the day arrived when Moses went to Goshen to see his brethren, that he saw the children of Israel in their burdens and hard labor, and Moses was grieved on their account.

42. And Moses returned to Egypt and came to the house of Pharaoh, and came before the king, and Moses bowed down before the king.

43. And Moses said unto Pharaoh, I pray thee my lord, I have come to seek a small request from thee, turn not away my face empty; and Pharaoh said unto him, speak.

44. And Moses said unto Pharaoh, let there be given unto thy servants the children of Israel who are in Goshen, one day to rest therein from their labor.

45. And the king answered Moses and said, behold I have lifted up thy face in this thing to grant thy request.

46. And Pharaoh ordered a proclamation to be issued throughout Egypt and Goshen, saying,

47. To you, all the children of Israel, thus says the king, for six days you shall do your work and labor but on the seventh day you shall rest, and shall not perform any work, thus shall you do all the days, as the king and Moses the son of Bathia have commanded.

48. And Moses rejoiced at this thing which the king had granted to him, and all the children of Israel did as Moses ordered them.

49. For this thing was from the Lord to the children of Israel, for the Lord had begun to remember the children of Israel to save them for the sake of their fathers.

50. And the Lord was with Moses and his fame went throughout Egypt.

51. And Moses became great in the eyes of all the Egyptians, and in the eyes of all the children of Israel, seeking good for his people Israel and speaking words of peace regarding them to the king.

CHAPTER LXXI.

1. And when Moses was eighteen years old, he desired to see his father and mother and he went to them to

Goshen, and when Moses had come near Goshen, he came to the place where the children of Israel were engaged in work, and he observed their burdens, and he saw an Egyptian smiting one of his Hebrew brethren.

2. And when the man who was beaten saw Moses he ran to him for help, for the man Moses was greatly respected in the house of Pharaoh, and he said to him, my lord attend to me, this Egyptian came to my house in the night, bound me, and came to my wife in my presence, and now he seeks to take my life away.

3. And when Moses heard this wicked thing, his anger was kindled against the Egyptian, and he turned this way and the other, and when he saw there was no man there he smote the Egyptian and hid him in the sand, and delivered the Hebrew from the hand of him that smote him.

4. And the Hebrew went to his house, and Moses returned to his home, and went forth and came back to the king's house.

5. And when the man had returned home, he thought of repudiating his wife, for it was not right in the house of Jacob, for any man to come to his wife after she had been defiled.

6. And the woman went and told her brothers, and the woman's brothers sought to slay him, and he fled to his house and escaped.

7. And on the second day Moses went forth to his brethren, and saw, and behold two men were quarreling, and he said to the wicked one, why dost thou smite thy neighbor?

8. And he answered him and said to him, who has set thee for a prince and judge over us? dost thou think to slay me as thou didst slay the Egyptian? and Moses was afraid and he said, surely the thing is known!

9. And Pharaoh heard of this affair, and he ordered Moses to be slain, so God sent his angel, and he appeared unto Pharaoh in the likeness of a captain of the guard.

10. And the angel of the Lord took the sword from the hand of the captain of the guard, and took his head off with it, for the likeness of the captain of the guard was turned into the likeness of Moses.

11. And the angel of the Lord took hold of the right hand of Moses, and brought him forth from Egypt, and placed him from without the borders of Egypt, *a distance of* forty days' journey.

12. And Aaron his brother alone remained in the land of Egypt, and he prophecied to the children of Israel, saying,

13. Thus says the Lord God of your ancestors, throw* away, each man, the abominations of his eyes, and do not defile yourselves with the idols of Egypt.

14. And the children of Israel rebelled and would not hearken to Aaron at that time.

15. And the Lord thought to destroy them, were it not that the Lord remembered the covenant which he had made with Abraham, Isaac and Jacob.

16. In those days the hand of Pharaoh continued to be severe against the children of Israel, and he crushed and oppressed them until the time when God sent forth his word and took notice of them.

CHAPTER LXXII.

1. And it was in those days that there was a great war between the children of Cush and the children of

*This is demonstrated in Ezekiel, ch. 20, v. 30.

the east and Aram, and they rebelled against the king of Cush in whose hands they were.

2. So Kikianus king of Cush went forth with all the children of Cush, a people numerous as the sand, and he went to fight against Aram and the children of the east, to bring them under subjection.

3. And when Kikianus went out, he left Balaam the magician, with his two sons, to guard the city, and the lowest sort of the people of the land.

4. So Kikianus went forth to Aram and the children of the east, and he fought against them and smote them, and they all fell down wounded before Kikianus and his people.

5. And he took many of them captives and he brought them under subjection as at first, and he encamped upon their land to take tribute from them as usual.

6. And Balaam the son of Beor, when the king of Cush had left him to guard the city and the poor of the city, he rose up and advised with the people of the land to rebel against king Kikianus, not to let him enter the city when he should come home.

7. And the people of the land hearkened to him, and they swore to him and made him king over them, and his two sons for captains of the army.

8. So they rose up and raised the walls of the city at the two corners, and they built an exceeding strong building.

9. And at the third corner they dug ditches without number, between the city and the river which surrounded the whole land of Cush, and they made the waters of the river burst forth there.

10. At the fourth corner they collected numerous serpents by their incantations and enchantments, and they fortified the city and dwelt therein, and no one went out or in before them.

11. And Kikianus fought against Aram and the children of the east and he subdued them as before, and they gave him their usual tribute, and he went and returned to his land.

12. And when Kikianus the king of Cush approached his city and all the captains of the forces with him, they lifted up their eyes and saw that the walls of the city were built up and greatly elevated, so the men were astonished at this.

13. And they said one to the other, it is because they saw that we were delayed, in the battle, and were greatly afraid of us, therefore have they done this thing and raised the city walls and fortified them so that the kings of Canaan might not come in battle against them.

14. So the king and the troops approached the city door and they looked up and behold, all the gates of the city were closed, and they called out to the sentinels, saying, open unto us, that we may enter the city.

15. But the sentinels refused to open to them by the order of Balaam the magician their king, they suffered them not to enter their city.

16. So they raised a battle with them opposite the city gate, and one hundred and thirty men of the army of Kikianus fell on that day.

17. And on the next day they continued to fight and they fought at the side of the river; they endeavored to pass but were not able, so some of them sank in the pits and died.

18. So the king ordered *them* to cut down trees to make rafts, upon which they might pass to them, and they did so.

19. And when they came to the place of the ditches, the waters revolved* by mills, and two hundred men upon ten rafts were drowned.

20. And on the third day they came to fight at the side where the serpents were, but they could not approach there, so the serpents slew of them one hundred and seventy men, and they ceased fighting against Cush, and they besieged Cush for nine years, no person came out or in.

21. At that time that the war and the siege were against Cush, Moses fled from Egypt from Pharaoh who sought to kill him for having slain the Egyptian.

22. And Moses was eighteen years old when he fled from Egypt from the presence of Pharaoh, and he fled and escaped to the camp of Kikianus, which at that time was besieging Cush.

23. And Moses was nine years in the camp of Kikianus king of Cush, all the time that they were besieging Cush, and Moses went out and came in with them.

24. And the king and princes and all the fighting men loved Moses, for he was great and worthy, his stature was like a noble lion, his face was like the sun, and his strength was like that of a lion, and he was counsellor to the king.

25. And at the end of nine years Kikianus was seized with a mortal disease, and his illness prevailed over him, and he died on the seventh day.

26. So his servants embalmed him and carried him and buried him opposite the city gate to the north of the land of Egypt.

27. And they built over him an elegant strong and high building, and they placed great stones below.

28. And the king's scribes engraved upon those stones all the might of their king Kikianus, and all his battles which he had fought, behold they are written there at this day.

29. Now after the death of Kikianus king of Cush it grieved his men and troops greatly on account of the war.

30. So they said one to the other, give us counsel what we are to do at this time, as we have resided in the wilderness nine years away from our homes.

31. If we say we will fight against the city many of us will fall wounded or killed, and if we remain here in the siege we shall also die.

32. For now all the kings of Aram and of the children of the east will hear that our king is dead, and they will attack us suddenly in a hostile manner, and they will fight against us and leave no remnant of us.

33. Now therefore let us go and make a king over us, and let us remain in the siege until the city is delivered up to us.

34. And they wished to choose on that day a man for king from the army of Kikianus, and they found no object* of their choice like Moses to reign over them.

35. And they hastened and stripped off each man his garments and cast them upon the ground, and they made a great heap and placed Moses thereon.

36. And they rose up and blew with trumpets and called out before him, and said, may the king live, may the king live!

---

* These water mills must have been erected with a design of setting the water going if the enemy should attempt a passage, but רחים in scripture is only applied to mill stones for grinding corn.

* בחור besides a young man, denotes also a choice man, see 1 Samuel, ch. 8, v. 16, and ch. 9, v. 2; Proverbs, ch. 20, v. 29.

37. And all the people and nobles swore unto him to give him for a wife Adoniah the queen, the Cushite, wife of Kikianus, and they made Moses king over them on that day.

38. And all the people of Cush issued a proclamation on that day, saying, every man must give something to Moses of what is in his possession.

39. And they spread out a sheet upon the heap, and every man cast into it something of what he had, one a gold ear ring and the other a coin.

40. Also of onyx stones, bdellium, pearls and marble did the children of Cush cast unto Moses upon the heap, also silver and gold in great abundance.

41. And Moses took all the silver and gold, all the vessels, and the bdellium and onyx stones, which all the children of Cush had given to him, and he placed them amongst his treasures.

42. And Moses reigned over the children of Cush on that day, in the place of Kikianus king of Cush.

CHAPTER LXXIII.

1. In the fifty fifth year of *the reign of* Pharaoh king of Egypt, that is in the hundred and fifty seventh year of the Israelites going down into Egypt, reigned Moses in Cush.

2. Moses was twenty seven years old when he began to reign over Cush, and forty years did he reign.

3. And the Lord granted Moses favor and grace in the eyes of all the children of Cush, and the children of Cush loved him exceedingly, so Moses was favored by the Lord and by men.

4. And in the seventh day of his reign, all the children of Cush assembled and came before Moses and bowed down to him to the ground.

5. And all the children spoke together in the presence of the king, saying, give us counsel that we may see what is to be done to this city.

6. For it is now nine years that we have been besieging round about the city, and have not seen our children and our wives.

7. So the king answered them, saying, if you will hearken to my voice in all that I shall command you, then will the Lord give the city into our hands and we shall subdue it.

8. For if we fight with them as in the former battle which we had with them before the death of Kikianus, many of us will fall down wounded as before.

9. Now therefore behold here is counsel for you in this matter; if you will hearken to my voice, then will the city be delivered into our hands.

10. So all the forces answered the king, saying, all that our lord shall command that will we do.

11. And Moses said unto them, pass through and proclaim a voice in the whole camp unto all the people, saying,

12. Thus says the king, go into the forest and bring with you of the young ones of the stork, each man a young one in his hand.

13. And any person transgressing the word of the king, who shall not bring his young one, he shall die, and the king will take all belonging to him.

14. And when you shall bring them they shall be in your keeping, you shall rear them until they grow up, and you shall teach them to dart upon, as is the way of the young ones of the hawk.

15. So all the children of Cush heard the words of Moses, and they rose up and caused a proclamation to be issued throughout the camp, saying,

16. Unto you, all the children of Cush, the king's order is, that you go all together to the forest, and catch there the young storks each man his young one in his hand, and you shall bring them home.

17. And any person violating the order of the king shall die, and the king will take all that belongs to him.

18. And all the people did so, and they went out to the wood and they climbed the fir trees and caught, each man a young one in his hand, all the young of the storks, and they brought them *into the desert* and reared them by order of the king, and they taught them to dart upon, similar to the young hawks.

19. And after the young storks were reared, the king ordered them to be hungered for three days, and all the people did so.

20. And on the third day, the king said unto them, strengthen yourselves and become valiant men, and put on each man his armour and gird on his sword upon him, and ride each man his horse and take each his young *stork* in his hand.

21. And we will rise up and fight against the city at the place where the serpents are ; and all the people did as the king had ordered.

22. And they took each man his young one in his hand, and they went away, and when they came to the place of the serpents the king said to them, send forth each man his young *stork* upon the serpents.

23. And they sent forth each man his young stork at the king's order, and the young storks ran upon the serpents and they devoured them all and destroyed them out of that place.

24. And when the king and people had seen that all the serpents were destroyed in that place, all the people set up a great shout.

25. And they approached and fought against the city and took it and subdued it, and they entered the city.

26. And there died on that day one thousand and one hundred men of the people of the city, all that inhabited the city, but of the people besieging not one died.

27. So all the children of Cush went each to his home, to his wife and children and to all belonging to him.

28. And Balaam the magician, when he saw that the city was taken, he opened the gate and he and his two sons and eight brothers fled and returned to Egypt to Pharaoh king of Egypt.

29. They are the sorcerers and magicians who are mentioned in the book of the law, standing against Moses when the Lord brought the plagues upon Egypt.

30. So Moses took the city by his wisdom, and the children of Cush placed him on the throne instead of Kikianus king of Cush.

31. And they placed the royal crown upon his head, and they gave him for a wife Adoniah the Cushite queen, wife of Kikianus.

32. And Moses feared the Lord God of his fathers, so that he came not to her, nor did he turn his eyes to her.

33. For Moses remembered how Abraham had made his servant Eliezer swear, saying *unto him*, thou shalt not take a woman from the

daughters of Canaan for my son Isaac.

34. Also what Isaac did when Jacob had fled from his brother, when he commanded him, saying, thou shalt not take a wife from the daughters of Canaan, nor make alliance with any of the children of Ham.

35. For the Lord our God gave Ham the son of Noah, and his children and all his seed, as slaves to the children of Shem and to the children of Japheth, and unto their seed after them for slaves, forever.

36. Therefore Moses turned not his heart nor his eyes to the wife of Kikianus all the days that he reigned over Cush.

37. And Moses feared the Lord his God all his life, and Moses walked before the Lord in truth, with all his heart and soul, he turned not from the right way all the days of his life ; he declined not from the way either to the right or to the left, in which Abraham, Isaac and Jacob had walked.

38. And Moses strengthened himself in the kingdom of the children of Cush, and he guided the children of Cush with his usual wisdom, and Moses prospered in his kingdom.

39. And at that time Aram and the children of the east heard that Kikianus king of Cush had died, so Aram and the children of the east rebelled against Cush in those days.

40. And Moses gathered all the children of Cush, a people very mighty, about thirty thousand men, and he went forth to fight with Aram and the children of the east.

41. And they went at first to the children of the east, and when the children of the east heard their report, they went to meet them, and engaged in battle with them.

42. And the war was severe against the children of the east, so the Lord gave all the children of the east into the hand of Moses, and about three hundred men fell down slain.

43. And all the children of the east turned back and retreated, so Moses and the children of Cush followed them and subdued them and put a tax upon them, as was their custom.

44. So Moses and all the people with him passed from there to the land of Aram for battle.

45. And the people of Aram also went to meet them, and they fought against them, and the Lord delivered them into the hand of Moses, and many of the men of Aram fell down wounded.

46. And Aram also were subdued by Moses and *the people of Cush*, and also gave their usual tax.

47. And Moses brought Aram and the children of the east under subjection to the children of Cush, and Moses and all the people who were with him, turned to the land of Cush.

48. And Moses strengthened himself in the kingdom of the children of Cush, and the Lord was with him, and all the children of Cush were afraid of him.

CHAPTER LXXIV.

1. In the end of years died Saul king of Edom, and Baal Chanan the son of Achbor reigned in his place.

2. In the sixteenth year of the reign of Moses over Cush, Baal Chanan the son of Achbor reigned in the land of Edom over all the children of Edom for thirty eight years. ·

3. In his days Moab rebelled

against the power of Edom, having been under Edom since the days of Hadad the son of Bedad, who smote them and Midian, and brought Moab under subjection to Edom.

4. And when Baal Chanan the son of Achbor reigned over Edom, all the children of Moab withdrew their allegiance from Edom.

5. And Angeas king of Africa died in those days, and Azdrubal his son reigned in his stead.

6. And in those days died Janeas king of the children of Chittim, and they buried him in his temple which he had built for himself in the plain of Canopia for a residence, and Latinus reigned in his stead.

7. In the twenty-second year of the reign of Moses over the children of Cush, Latinus reigned over the children of Chittim forty-five years.

8. And he also built for himself a great and mighty tower, and he built therein an elegant temple for his residence, to conduct his government, as was the custom.

9. In the third year of his reign he caused a proclamation to be made to all his skilful men, who made many ships for him.

10. And Latinus assembled all his forces, and they came in ships, and went therein to fight with Azdrubal son of Angeas king of Africa, and they came to Africa and engaged in battle with Azdrubal and his army.

11. And Latinus prevailed over Azdrubal, and Latinus took from Azdrubal the aqueduct which his father had brought from the children of Chittim, when he took Janiah the daughter of Uzi for a wife, so Latinus overthrew the bridge of the aqueduct, and smote the whole army of Azdrubal a severe blow.

12. And the remaining strong men of Azdrubal strengthened themselves, and their hearts were filled with envy, and they courted death, and again engaged in battle with Latinus king of Chittim.

13. And the battle was severe upon all the men of Africa, and they all fell wounded before Latinus and his people, and Azdrubal the king also fell in that battle.

14. And the king Azdrubal had a very beautiful daughter, whose name was Ushpezena, and all the men of Africa embroidered her likeness on their garments, on account of her great beauty and comely appearance.

15. And the men of Latinus saw Ushpezena, the daughter of Azdrubal, and praised her unto Latinus their king.

16. And Latinus ordered her to be brought to him, and Latinus took Ushpezena for a wife, and he turned back on his way to Chittim.

17. And it was after the death of Azdrubal son of Angeas, when Latinus had turned back to his land from the battle, that all the inhabitants of Africa rose up and took Anibal the son of Angeas, the younger brother of Azdrubal, and made him king instead of his brother over the whole land of Africa.

18. And when he reigned, he resolved to go to Chittim to fight with the children of Chittim, to avenge the cause of Azdrubal his brother, and the cause of the inhabitants of Africa, and he did so.

19. And he made many ships, and he came therein with his whole army, and he went to Chittim.

20. So Anibal fought with the children of Chittim, and the children of Chittim fell wounded before Anibal and his army, and Anibal avenged his brother's cause.

15

21. And Anibal continued the war for eighteen years with the children of Chittim, and Anibal dwelt in the land of Chittim and encamped there for a long time.

22. And Anibal smote the children of Chittim very severely, and he slew their great men and princes, and of the rest of the people he smote about eighty thousand men.

23. And at the end of days and years, Anibal returned to his land of Africa, and he reigned securely in the place of Azdrubal his brother.

CHAPTER LXXV.

1. At that time, in the hundred and eightieth year of the Israelites going down into Egypt, there went forth from Egypt valiant men, thirty thousand on foot, from the children of Israel, who were all of the tribe of Joseph, of the children of Ephraim the son of Joseph.

2. For they said the period was completed which the Lord had appointed to the children of Israel in the times of old, which he had spoken to Abraham.

3. And these men girded themselves, and they put each man his sword at his side, and every man his armour upon him, and they trusted to their strength, and they went out together from Egypt with a mighty hand.

4. But they brought no provision for the road, only silver and gold, not even bread for that day did they bring in their hands, for they thought of getting their provision for pay from the Philistines, and if not they would take it by force.

5. And these men were very mighty and valiant men, one man could pursue a thousand and two could rout ten thousand, so they trusted to their strength and went together as they were.

6. And they directed their course toward the land of Gath, and they went down and found the shepherds of Gath feeding the cattle of the children of Gath.

7. And they said to the shepherds, give us some of the sheep for pay, that we may eat, for we are hungry, for we have eaten no bread this day.

8. And the shepherds said, are they our sheep or cattle that we should give them to you even for pay? so the children of Ephraim approached to take them by force.

9. And the shepherds of Gath shouted over them that their cry was heard at a distance, so all the children of Gath went out to them.

10. And when the children of Gath saw the evil doings of the children of Ephraim, they returned and assembled the men of Gath, and they put on each man his armour, and came forth to the children of Ephraim for battle.

11. And they engaged with them in the valley of Gath, and the battle was severe, and they smote from each other a great many on that day.

12. And on the second day the children of Gath sent to all the cities of the Philistines that they should come to their help, saying,

13. Come up unto us and help us, that we may smite the children of Ephraim who have come forth from Egypt to take our cattle, and to fight against us without cause.

14. Now the souls of the children of Ephraim were exhausted with hunger and thirst, for they had eaten no bread for three days. And forty thousand men went forth from the

cities of the Philistines to the assistance of the men of Gath.

15. And these men were engaged in battle with the children of Ephraim, and the Lord delivered the children of Ephraim into the hands of the Philistines.

16. And they smote all the children of Ephraim, all who had gone forth from Egypt, none were remaining but ten men who had run away from the engagement.

17. For this evil was from the Lord against the children of Ephraim, for they transgressed the word of the Lord in going forth from Egypt, before the period had arrived which the Lord in the days of old had appointed to Israel.

18. And of the Philistines also there fell a great many, about twenty thousand men, and their brethren carried them and buried them in their cities.

19. And the slain of the children of Ephraim remained forsaken in the valley of Gath for many days and years, and were not brought to burial, and the valley was filled with men's bones.

20. And the men who had escaped from the battle came to Egypt, and told all the children of Israel all that had befallen them.

21. And their father Ephraim mourned over them for many days, and his brethren came to console him.

22. And he came unto his wife and she bare a son, and he called his name Beriah, for she was unfortunate in his house.

CHAPTER LXXVI.

1. And Moses the son of Amram was still king in the land of Cush in those days, and he prospered in his kingdom, and he conducted the government of the children of Cush in justice, in righteousness and integrity.

2. And all the children of Cush loved Moses all the days that he reigned over them, and all the inhabitants of the land of Cush were greatly afraid of him.

3. And in the fortieth year of the reign of Moses over Cush, Moses was sitting on the royal throne whilst Adoniah the queen was before him, and all the nobles were sitting around him.

4. And Adoniah the queen said before the king and the princes, what is this thing which you, the children of Cush, have done for this long time?

5. Surely you know that for forty years that this *man* has reigned over Cush he has not approached me, nor has he served the gods of the children of Cush.

6. Now therefore hear, O ye children of Cush, and let this *man* no more reign over you as he is not of our flesh.

7. Behold Menacrus my son is grown up, let him reign over you, for it is better for you to serve the son of your lord, than to serve a stranger, a slave of the king of Egypt.

8. And all the people and nobles of the children of Cush heard the words which Adoniah the queen had spoken in their ears.

9. And all the people were preparing until the evening, and in the morning they rose up early and made Menacrus son of Kikianus king over them.

10. And all the children of Cush were afraid to stretch forth their hand against Moses, for the Lord

was with Moses, and the children of Cush remembered the oath which they swore unto Moses, therefore they did no harm to him.

11. But the children of Cush gave many presents to Moses, and sent him from them with great honor.

12. So Moses went forth from the land of Cush, and went home and ceased to reign over Cush, and Moses was sixty six years old when he went out of the land of Cush, for the thing was from the Lord, for the period had arrived which he had appointed in the days of old, to bring forth Israel from the affliction of the children of Ham.

13. So Moses went to Midian, for he was afraid to return to Egypt on account of Pharaoh, and he went and sat at a well of water in Midian.

14. And the seven daughters of Reuel the Midianite went out to feed their father's flock.

15. And they came to the well and drew water to water their father's flock.

16. So the shepherds of Midian came and drove them away, and Moses rose up and helped them and watered the flock.

17. And they came home to their father Reuel, and told him what Moses did for them.

18. And they said, an Egyptian man has delivered us from the hands of the shepherds, he drew up *water* for us and watered the flock.

19. And Reuel said to his daughters, and where is he? wherefore have you left the man?

20. And Reuel sent for him and fetched him and brought him home, and he ate bread with him.

21. And Moses related to Reuel that he had fled from Egypt and that he reigned forty years over Cush, and that they afterward had taken the government from him, and had sent him away in peace with honor and with presents.

22. And when Reuel had heard the words of Moses, Reuel said within himself, I will put this man into the prison house, whereby I shall conciliate the children of Cush, for he has fled from them.

23. And they took and put him into the prison house, and Moses was in prison ten years, and whilst Moses was in the prison house, Zipporah the daughter of Reuel took pity over him, and supported him with bread and water all the time.

24. And all the children of Israel were yet in the land of Egypt serving the Egyptians in all manner of hard work, and the hand of Egypt continued in severity over the children of Israel in those days.

25. At that time the Lord smote Pharaoh king of Egypt, and he afflicted him with the plague of leprosy from the sole of his foot to the crown of his head; owing to the cruel treatment of the children of Israel was this plague at that time from the Lord upon Pharaoh king of Egypt.

26. For the Lord had hearkened to the prayer of his people the children of Israel, and their cry reached them on account of their hard work.

27. Still his anger did not turn from them, and the hand of Pharaoh was still stretched out against the children of Israel, and Pharaoh hardened his neck before the Lord, and he increased his yoke over the children of Israel, and embittered their lives with all manner of hard work.

28. And when the Lord had inflicted the plague upon Pharaoh king

of Egypt, he asked his wise men and sorcerers to cure him.

29. And his wise men and sorcerers said unto him, that if the blood of little children were put into the wounds he would be healed.

30. And Pharaoh hearkened to them, and sent his ministers to Goshen to the children of Israel to take their little children.

31. And Pharaoh's ministers went and took the infants of the children of Israel from the bosoms of their mothers by force, and they brought them to Pharaoh daily, a child each day, and the physicians killed them and applied them * to the plague; thus did they all the days.

32. And the number of the children which Pharaoh slew was three hundred and seventy five.

33. But the Lord hearkened not to the physicians of the king of Egypt, and the plague went on increasing mightily.

34. And Pharaoh was ten years afflicted with that plague, *still* the heart of Pharaoh was more hardened against the children of Israel.

35. And at the end of ten years the Lord continued to afflict Pharaoh with destructive plagues.

36. And the Lord smote him with a bad tumor and sickness at the stomach, and that plague turned to a severe boil.

37. At that time the two ministers of Pharaoh came from the land of Goshen where all the children of Israel were, and went to the house of Pharaoh and said to him, we have seen the children of Israel slacken in their work and negligent in their labor.

38. And when Pharaoh heard the words of his ministers, his anger was

* *i. e.* Their blood.

kindled against the children of Israel exceedingly, for he was greatly grieved at his bodily pain.

39. And he answered and said, now that the children of Israel know that I am ill, they turn and scoff at us, now therefore harness my chariot for me, and I will betake myself to Goshen and will see the scoff of the children of Israel with which they are deriding me ; so his servants harnessed the chariot for him.

40. And they took and made him ride upon a horse, for he was not able to ride *of himself.*

41. And he took with him ten horsemen and ten footmen, and went to the children of Israel to Goshen.

42. And when they had come to the border of Egypt, the king's horse passed into a narrow place, elevated in the hollow part of the vineyard, fenced on both sides, the low, plain country being on the other side.

43. And the horses ran rapidly in that place and pressed each other, and the other horses pressed the king's horse.

44. And the king's horse fell into the low plain whilst the king was riding upon it, and when he fell the chariot turned over the king's face and the horse lay upon the king, and the king cried out, for his flesh was very sore.

45. And the flesh of the king was torn from him, and his bones were broken and he could not ride, for this thing was from the Lord to him, for the Lord had heard the cries of his people the children of Israel and their affliction.

46. And his servants carried him upon their shoulders, a little at a time, and they brought him back to Egypt, and the horsemen who were with him came also back to Egypt.

47. And they placed him in his bed, and the king knew that his end was come to die, so Aparanith the queen his wife came and cr.ed before the king, and the king wept a great weeping with her.

48. And all his nobles and servants came on that day and saw the king in that affliction, and wept a great weeping with him.

49. And the princes of the king and all his counsellors advised the king to cause one to reign in his stead in the land, whomsoever he should choose from his sons.

50. And the king had three sons and two daughters which Aparanith the queen his wife had borne to him, besides the king's children of concubines.

51. And these were their names, the first born Othri, the second Adikam and the third Morion, and their sisters, the name of the elder Bathia and of the other Acuzi.

52. And Othri the first born of the king was an idiot, precipitate and hurried in his words.

53. But Adikam was a cunning and a wise man and knowing in all the wisdom of Egypt, but of unseemly aspect, thick in flesh, and very short in stature ; his height was one cubit.

54. And when the king saw Adikam his son intelligent and wise in all things, the king resolved that he should be king in his stead after his death.

55. And he took for him a wife Gedudah daughter of Abilot, and he was ten years old, and she bare unto him four sons.

56. And he afterward went and took three wives and begat eight sons and three daughters.

57. And the disorder greatly pre-vailed over the king, and his flesh stank like the flesh of a carcase cast upon the field in summer time, during the heat of the sun.

58. And when the king saw that his sickness had greatly strengthened itself over him, he ordered his son Adikam to be brought to him, and they made him king over the land in his place.

59. And at the end of three years, the king died, in shame, disgrace and disgust, and his servants carried him and buried him in the sepulchre of the kings of Egypt in Zoan Mizraim.

60. But they embalmed him not as was usual with kings, for his flesh was putrid, and they could not approach to embalm him on account of the stench, so they buried him in haste.

61. For this evil was from the Lord to him, for the Lord had requited him evil for the evil which in his days he had done to Israel.

62. And he died with terror and with shame, and his son Adikam reigned in his place.

CHAPTER LXXVII.

1. Adikam was twenty years old when he reigned over Egypt, he reigned four years.

2. In the two hundred and sixth year of Israel's going down to Egypt did Adikam reign over Egypt, but he continued not so long in his reign over Egypt as his fathers had continued in their reigns.

3. For Melol his father reigned ninety four years in Egypt, but he was ten years sick and died, for he had been wicked before the Lord.

4. And all the Egyptians called the name of Adikam Pharaoh like

the name of his fathers, as was their custom to do in Egypt.

5. And all the wise men of Pharaoh called the name of Adikam Ahuz, for short is called Ahuz in the Egyptian language.

6. And Adikam was exceedingly ugly, and he was a cubit and a span and he had a great beard which reached to the soles of his feet.

7. And Pharaoh sat upon his father's throne to reign over Egypt, and he conducted the government of Egypt in his wisdom.

8. And whilst he reigned he exceeded his father and all the preceding kings in wickedness, and he increased his yoke over the children of Israel.

9. And he went with his servants to Goshen to the children of Israel, and he strengthened the labor over them and he said unto them, complete your work, each day's task, and let not your hands slacken from our work from this day forward as you did in the days of my father.

10. And he placed officers over them from amongst the children of Israel, and over these officers he placed taskmasters from amongst his servants.

11. And he placed over them a measure of bricks for them to do according to that number, day by day, and he turned back and went to Egypt.

12. At that time the taskmasters of Pharaoh ordered the officers of the children of Israel according to the command of Pharaoh, saying,

13. Thus says Pharaoh, do your work each day, and finish your task, and observe the daily measure of bricks; diminish not any thing.

14. And it shall come to pass that if you are deficient in your daily bricks, I will put your young children in their stead.

15. And the task masters of Egypt did so in those days as Pharaoh had ordered them.

16. And whenever any deficiency was found in the children of Israel's measure of their daily bricks, the task masters of Pharaoh would go to the wives of the children of Israel and take infants of the children of Israel to the number of bricks deficient, they would take them by force from their mother's laps, and put them in the building instead of the bricks;

17. Whilst their fathers and mothers were crying over them and weeping when they heard the weeping voices of their infants in the wall of the building.

18. And the task masters prevailed over Israel, that the Israelites should place their children in the building, so that a man placed his son in the wall and put mortar over him, whilst his eyes wept over him, and his tears ran down upon his child.

19. And the task masters of Egypt did so to the babes of Israel for many days, and no one pitied or had compassion over the babes of the children of Israel.

20. And the number of all the children killed in the building was two hundred and seventy, some whom they had built upon instead of the bricks which had been left deficient by their fathers, and some whom they had drawn out dead from the building.

21. And the labor imposed upon the children of Israel in the days of Adikam exceeded in hardship that which they performed in the days of his father.

22. And the children of Israel sighed every day on account of their heavy work, for they had said *to themselves*, behold, when Pharaoh shall die, his son will rise up and lighten our work!

23. But they increased the latter work more than the former, and the children of Israel sighed at this and their cry ascended to God on account of their labor.

24. And God heard the voice of the children of Israel and their cry, in those days, and God remembered to them his covenant which he had made with Abraham, Isaac and Jacob

25. And God saw the burden of the children of Israel, and their heavy work in those days, and he determined to deliver them.

26. And Moses the son of Amram was still confined in the dungeon in those days, in the house of Reuel the Midianite, and Zipporah the daughter of Reuel did support him with food secretly day by day.

27. And Moses was confined in the dungeon in the house of Reuel for ten years.

28. And at the end of ten years, which was the first year of the reign of Pharaoh* over Egypt, in the place of his father,

29. Zipporah said to her father Reuel, no person inquires or seeks after the Hebrew man, whom thou didst bind in prison now ten years.

30. Now therefore, if it seem good in thy sight, let us send and see whether he is living or dead, but her father knew not that she had supported him.

31. And Reuel her father answered and said to her, has ever such a thing happened that a man should be

shut up in a prison without food for ten years, and that he should live?

32. And Zipporah answered her father, saying, surely thou hast heard that the God of the Hebrews is great and awful, and does wonders for them at all times.

33. He it was who delivered Abraham from Ur* of the Chaldeans, and Isaac from the sword of his father, and Jacob from the angel of the Lord who wrestled with him at the ford of Jabbuk.

34. Also with this man has he done many things, he delivered him from the river in Egypt and from the sword of Pharaoh, and from the children of Cush, so also can he deliver him from famine and make him live.

35. And the thing seemed good in the sight of Reuel, and he did according to the word of his daughter, and sent to the dungeon to ascertain what became of Moses.

36. And he saw, and behold the man Moses was living in the dungeon, standing upon his feet, praising and praying to the God of his ancestors.

37. And Reuel commanded Moses to be brought out of the dungeon, so they shaved him and he changed his prison garments and ate bread.

38. And afterward Moses went into the garden of Reuel which was behind the house, and he there prayed to the Lord his God, who had done mighty wonders for him.

39. And it was that whilst he prayed he looked opposite to him, and behold a sapphire stick was placed in the ground, which was planted in the midst of the garden.

* אור means also a fire and this alludes (according to a story in this book) to the oven in which Abraham was put.

* Adikam.

40. And he approached the stick and he looked, and behold the name of the Lord God of hosts* was engraved thereon, written and developed upon the stick.

41. And he read it and stretched forth his hand and he plucked it like a forest tree from the thicket, and the stick was in his hand.

42. And this was the stick with which all the works† of our God were performed, after he had created heaven and earth, and all the host of them, seas, rivers and all their fishes.

43. And when God had driven Adam from the garden of Eden, he took the stick in his hand and went and tilled the ground from which he was taken.

44. And the stick came down to Noah and was given to Shem and his descendants, until it came into the hand of Abraham the Hebrew.

45. And when Abraham had given all he had to his son Isaac, he also gave to him this stick.

46. And when Jacob had fled to Padan-aram, he took it into his hand, and when he returned to his father he had not left it *behind him*.

47. Also when he went down to Egypt he took it into his hand and gave it to Joseph, one portion above his brethren, for Jacob had taken it by force from his brother Esau.‡

48. And after the death of Joseph,

* Meaning that the full name, what the Hebrews call the ineffable name of Jehovah, was written upon the stick. (See Talmud.) In one edition I find שם יי אלהי צבאות and in another שם אלהים צבאות.

† Meaning the works of man influenced by God, as he enumerates.

‡ The author of this book wishes here to explain that obscure part in the Bible, Genesis, ch. 48, v. 22, "Moreover I have given to thee a portion above thy brethren which I took out of the hands of the Amorite, &c." calling Esau, from his conduct, an Amorite; but it never alluded to this tale.

the nobles of Egypt came into the house of Joseph, and the stick came into the hand of Reuel the Midianite, and when he went out of Egypt, he took it in his hand and planted it in his garden.

49. And all the mighty men of the Kinites tried to pluck it when they endeavored to get Zipporah his daughter, but they were unsuccessful.

50. So that stick remained planted in the garden of Reuel, until he came who had a right to it and took it.

51. And when Reuel saw the stick in the hand of Moses, he wondered at it, and he gave him his daughter Zipporah for a wife.

CHAPTER LXXVIII.

1. At that time died Balchannan son of Achbor, king of Edom, and was buried in his house in the land of Edom.

2. And after his death the children of Esau sent to the land of Edom, and took from there a man who was in Edom, whose name was Hadad, and they made him king over them in the place of Balchannan, their king.

3. And Hadad reigned over the children of Edom forty eight years.

4. And when he reigned he resolved to fight against the children of Moab, to bring them under the power of the children of Esau as *they were* before, but he was not able, because the children of Moab heard this thing, and they rose up and hastened to elect a king over them from amongst their brethren.

5. And they afterward gathered together a great people, and sent to the children of Ammon their brethren

for help to fight against Hadad king of Edom.

6. And Hadad heard the thing which the children of Moab had done, and was greatly afraid of them, and refrained from fighting against them.

7. In those days Moses, the son of Amram, in Midian, took Zipporah, the daughter of Reuel the Midianite, for a wife.

8. And Zipporah walked in the ways of the daughters of Jacob, she was nothing short of the righteousness of Sarah, Rebecca, Rachel and Leah.

9. And Zipporah conceived and bare a son and he called his name Gershom, for he said, I was a stranger in a foreign land ; but he circumcised not his foreskin, at the command of Reuel his father-in-law.

10. And she conceived again and bare a son, but circumcised *his* foreskin, and called his name Eliezer, for Moses said, because the God of my fathers was my help, and delivered me from the sword of Pharaoh.

11. And Pharaoh king of Egypt greatly increased the labor of the children of Israel in those days, and continued to make his yoke heavier upon the children of Israel.

12. And he ordered a proclamation to be made in Egypt, saying, give no more straw to the people to make bricks with, let them go and gather themselves straw as they can find it.

13. Also the tale of bricks which they shall make let them give each day, and diminish nothing from them, for they are idle in their work.

14. And the children of Israel heard this, and they mourned and sighed, and they cried unto the Lord on account of the bitterness of their souls.

15. And the Lord heard the cries of the children of Israel, and saw the oppression with which the Egyptians oppressed them.

16. And the Lord was jealous of his people and his inheritance,* and heard their voice, and he resolved to take them out of the affliction of Egypt, to give them the land of Canaan for a possession.

CHAPTER LXXIX.

1. And in those days Moses was feeding the flock of Reuel the Midianite his father-in-law, beyond the wilderness of Sin, and the stick which he took from his father-in-law was in his hand.

2. And it came to pass one day that a kid of goats strayed from the flock, and Moses pursued it and came to the mountain of God to Horeb.

3. And when he came to Horeb, the Lord appeared there unto him in the bush, and he found the bush burning with fire, but the fire had no power over the bush to consume it.

4. And Moses was greatly astonished at this sight, wherefore the bush was not consumed, and he approached to see this mighty thing, and the Lord called unto Moses out of the fire and commanded him to go down to Egypt, to Pharaoh king of Egypt, to send the children of Israel from his service.

5. And the Lord said unto Moses, go return to Egypt, for all those men who sought thy life are dead, and thou shalt speak unto Pharaoh to send forth the children of Israel from his land.

6. And the Lord showed him to do signs and wonders in Egypt before the eyes of Pharaoh and the eyes

* Israel was called God's inheritance.

of his subjects, in order that they might believe that the Lord had sent him.

7. And Moses hearkened to all that the Lord had commanded him, and he returned to his father-in-law and told him the thing, and Reuel said to him, go in peace.

8. And Moses rose up to go to Egypt, and he took his wife and sons with him, and he was at an inn in the road, and an angel of God came down, and sought an occasion against him.

9. And he wished to kill him on account of his first born son, because he had not circumcised him, and had transgressed the covenant which the Lord had made with Abraham.

10. For Moses had hearkened to the words of his father-in-law which he had spoken to him, not to circumcise his first born son, therefore he circumcised him not.

11. And Zipporah saw the angel of the Lord seeking an occasion against Moses, and she knew that this thing was owing to his not having circumcised her son Gershom.

12. And Zipporah hastened and took of the sharp rock stones that were there, and she circumcised her son, and delivered her husband and her son from the hand of the angel of the Lord.

13. And Aaron the son of Amram, the brother of Moses, was in Egypt walking at the river side on that day.

14. And the Lord appeared to him in that place, and he said to him, go now toward Moses in the wilderness, and he went and met him in the mountain of God, and he kissed him.

15. And Aaron lifted up his eyes, and saw Zipporah the wife of Moses and her children, and he said unto Moses, who are these unto thee?

16. And Moses said to him, they are my wife and sons, which God gave to me in Midian; and the thing grieved Aaron on account of the woman and her children.

17. And Aaron said to Moses, send away the woman and her children that *they may* go to her father's house, and Moses hearkened to the words of Aaron, and did so.

18. And Zipporah returned with her children, and they went to the house of Reuel, and remained there until the time arrived when the Lord had visited his people, and brought them forth from Egypt from the hand of Pharaoh.

19. And Moses and Aaron came to Egypt to the community of the children of Israel, and they spoke to them all the words of the Lord, and the people rejoiced an exceeding great rejoicing.

20. And Moses and Aaron rose up early on the next day, and they went to the house of Pharaoh and they took in their hands the stick of God.

21. And when they came to the king's gate, two young lions were confined there with iron instruments, and no person went out or came in from before them, unless those whom the king ordered to come, when the conjurors came and withdrew the lions by their incantations, and *thus* brought them to the king.

22. And Moses hastened and lifted up the stick upon the lions, and he loosed them, and Moses and Aaron came into the king's house.

23. The lions also came with them in joy, and they followed them and rejoiced as a dog rejoices over his master when he comes from the field.

24. And when Pharaoh saw this

thing he was astonished at it, and he was greatly terrified at the report, for their* appearance was like the appearance of the children† of God.

25. And Pharaoh said to Moses, what do you require? and they answered him, saying, the Lord God of the Hebrews has sent us to thee, to say, send forth my people that they may serve me.

26. And when Pharaoh heard their words he was greatly terrified before them, and he said to them, go to day and come back to me to-morrow, and they did according to the word of the king.

27. And when they had gone Pharaoh sent for Balaam the magician and to Jannes and Jambres his sons, and to all the magicians and conjurors and counsellors which belonged to the king, and they all came and sat before the king.

28. And the king told them all the words which Moses and his brother Aaron had spoken to him, and the magicians said to the king, but how came the men to thee, on account of the lions which were confined at the gate?

29. And the king said, because they lifted up their rod against the lions and loosed them, and came to me, and the lions also rejoiced at them as a dog rejoices to meet his master.

30. And Balaam the son of Beor the magician answered the king, saying, these are none else than magicians like ourselves.

31. Now therefore send for them, and let them come and we will try them, and the king did so.

32. And in the morning Pharaoh sent for Moses and Aaron to come before the king, and they took the

* Moses and Aaron.   † Angelic form.

rod of God, and came to the king and spoke to him, saying,

33. Thus said the Lord God of the Hebrews, send my people that they may serve me.

34. And the king said to them, but who will believe you that you are the messengers of God and that you come to me by his order?

35. Now therefore give a wonder or sign in this matter, and then the words which you speak will be believed.

36. And Aaron hastened and threw the rod out of his hand before Pharaoh and before his servants, and the rod turned into a serpent.

37. And the sorcerers saw this and they cast each man ... rod upon the ground and they bec... serpents.

38. And the serpent of Aaron's rod lifted up its head and opened its mouth to swallow the rods of the magicians.

39. And Balaam the magician answered and said, this thing has been from the days of old, that a serpent should swallow its fellow, and that living things devour each other.

40. Now therefore restore it to a rod as it was at first, and we will also restore our rods *as they were* at first, and if thy rod shall swallow our rods, then shall we know that the spirit of God is in thee, and if not, thou art *only* an artificer like unto ourselves.

41. And Aaron hastened and stretched forth his hand and caught hold of the serpent's tail and it became a rod in his hand, and the sorcerers did the like with their rods, and they got hold, each man of the tail of his serpent, and they became rods as at first.

42. And when they were restored

to rods, the rod of Aaron swallowed up their rods.

43. And when the king saw this thing, he ordered the book of records that related to the kings of Egypt, to be brought, and they brought the book of records, the chronicles of the kings of Egypt, in which all the idols of Egypt were inscribed, for they thought of finding therein the name of Jehovah, but they found it not.

44. And Pharaoh said to Moses and Aaron, behold I have not found the name of your God written in this book, and his name I know not.

45. And the counsellors and wise men answered the king, we have heard that the God of the Hebrews is a son of the wise,* the son of ancient kings.

46. And Pharaoh turned to Moses and Aaron and said to them, I know not the Lord whom you have declared, neither will I send his people.

47. And they answered and said to the king, the Lord God of Gods is his name, and he proclaimed his name over us from the days of our ancestors, and sent us, saying, go to Pharaoh and say unto him, send my people that they may serve me.

48. Now therefore send us, that we may take a journey for three days in the wilderness, and there may sacrifice to him, for from the days of our going down to Egypt, he has not taken from our hands, either burnt offering, oblation or sacrifice, and if thou wilt not send us, his anger will be kindled against thee, and he will smite Egypt either with the plague or with the sword.

49. And Pharaoh said to them, tell me now his power and his might; and they said to him, he created the

* See the same, Isaiah, ch. 19, v. 11.

heaven and the earth, the seas and all their fishes, he formed the light, created the darkness, caused rain upon the earth and watered it, and made the herbage and grass to sprout, he created man and beast and-the animals of the forest, the birds of the air and the fish of the sea, and by his mouth they live and die.

50. Surely he created thee in thy mother's womb, and put into thee the breath of life, and reared thee and placed thee upon the royal throne of Egypt, and he will take thy breath and soul from thee, and return thee to the ground whence thou wast taken.

51. And the anger of the king was kindled at their words, and he said to ·them, but who amongst all the Gods of nations can do this? my* river is mine own, and I have made it for myself.

52. And he drove them from him, and he ordered the labor upon Israel to be more severe than it was yester-day† and before.

53. And Moses and Aaron went out from the king's presence, and they saw the children of Israel in an evil condition for the task masters had made their labor exceedingly heavy.

54. And Moses returned to the Lord and said, why hast thou ill treated thy people? for since I came to speak to Pharaoh what thou didst send me for, he has exceedingly ill used the children of Israel.

55. And the Lord said to Moses, behold thou wilt see that with an outstretched hand and heavy plagues, Pharaoh will send the children of Israel from his land.

* See Ezekiel, ch. 29, v. 3.
†.Literally, from yesterday and the day before, i. e. lately.

56. And Moses and Aaron dwelt amongst their brethren the children of Israel in Egypt.

57. And as for the children of Israel the Egyptians embittered their lives, with the heavy work which they imposed upon them.

CHAPTER LXXX.

1. And at the end of two years, the Lord again sent Moses to Pharaoh to bring forth the children of Israel, and to send them out of the land of Egypt.

2. And Moses went and came to the house of Pharaoh, and he spoke to him the words of the Lord who had sent him, but Pharaoh would not hearken to the voice of the Lord, and God roused his might in Egypt upon Pharaoh and his subjects, and God smote Pharaoh and his people with very great and sore plagues.

3. And the Lord sent by the hand of Aaron and turned all the waters of Egypt into blood, with all their streams and rivers.

4. And when an Egyptian came to drink and draw water, he looked into his pitcher, and behold all the water was turned into blood; and when he came to drink from his cup the water in the cup became blood.

5. And when a woman kneaded her dough and cooked her victuals, their appearance was turned to that of blood.

6. And the Lord sent again and caused all their waters to bring forth frogs, and all the frogs came into the houses of the Egyptians.

7. And when the Egyptians drank, their bellies were filled with frogs and they danced in their bellies as they dance when in the river.

8. And all their drinking water and cooking water turned to frogs, also when they lay in their beds their perspiration bred frogs.

9. Notwithstanding all this the anger of the Lord did not turn from them, and his hand was stretched out against all the Egyptians to smite them with every heavy plague.

10. And he sent and smote their dust to lice, and the lice became in Egypt to the height of two cubits upon the earth.

11. The lice were also very numerous, in the flesh of man and beast, in all the inhabitants of Egypt, also upon the king and queen the Lord sent the lice, and it grieved Egypt exceedingly on account of the lice.

12. Notwithstanding this, the anger of the Lord did not turn away, and his hand was still stretched out over Egypt.

13. And the Lord sent all kinds of beasts of the field into Egypt, and they came and destroyed all Egypt, man and beast, and trees, and all things that were in Egypt.

14. And the Lord sent fiery serpents, scorpions, mice, weazles, toads, together with others creeping in dust.

15. Flies, hornets, fleas, bugs* and gnats, each swarm† according to its kind.

16. And all reptiles and winged animals according to their kind came to Egypt and grieved the Egyptians exceedingly.

17. And the fleas and flies came

* פשפש יתוש are not found in the Hebrew Bible, but in the Mishnah and Talmud mean a bug and a gnat. See Bux. Rabb. Lex.
† See Parkhurst's Hebrew Lexicon upon ערוב. In the Bible it is translated swarm of flies, but this book explains the swarm to be a mixture of all sorts of animals, birds and insects, as ערב means to mix.

into the eyes and ears of the Egyptians.

18. And the hornet came upon them and drove them away, and they removed from it into their inner rooms, and it pursued them.

19. And when the Egyptians hid themselves on account of the swarm of animals, they locked their doors after them, and God ordered the Sulanuth* which was in the sea, to come up and go into Egypt.

20. And she had long arms, ten cubits in length of the cubit of a man.

21. And she went upon the roofs and uncovered the raftering† and flooring and cut them. and stretched forth her arm into the house and removèd the lock and the bolt, and opened the houses of Egypt.

22. Afterward came the swarm of animals into the houses of Egypt, and the swarm of animals destroyed the Egyptians, and it grieved them exceedingly.

23. Notwithstanding this the anger of the Lord did not turn away from the Egyptians, and his hand was yet stretched forth against them.

24. And God sent the pestilence, and the pestilence pervaded Egypt, in the horses and asses, and in the camels, in herds of oxen and sheep and in man.

25. And when the Egyptians rose up early in the morning to take their cattle to pasture they found all their cattle dead.

26. And there remained of the cattle of the Egyptians only one in ten, and of the cattle belonging to Israel in Goshen not one died.

27. And God sent a burning inflammation in the flesh of the Egyptians, which burst their skins, and it became a severe itch in all the Egyptians from the soles of their feet to the crowns *of their heads.*

28. And many boils were in their flesh, that their flesh wasted away until they became rotten and putrid.

29. Notwithstanding this the anger of the Lord did not turn away, and his hand was still stretched out over all Egypt.

30. And the Lord sent a very heavy hail, which smote their vines and broke their fruit trees and dried them up that they* fell upon them.

31. Also every green herb became dry and perished, for a mingling† fire descended amidst the hail, therefore the hail and the fire consumed all things.

32. Also men and beasts that were found abroad perished of the flames of fire and of the hail, and all the young ‡ lions were exhausted.

33. And the Lord sent and brought numerous locusts into Egpyt, the Chasel, Salom Chargol, and Chagole,§ locusts each of its kind, which devoured all that the hail had left remaining.

* The trees became decayed and fell upon the Egyptians.

. † See Exodus, ch. 9, v. 24.

‡ וכל הכפירים נחשו it is thus in the modern edition, but in the Venice edition it is הכפרים which *may* mean villages, and the verb נחש means likewise to extirpate, root up, that all the villages were destroyed ; see Psalms, ch. 9, v. 7 ; Jeremiah, ch. 31, v. 40 ; but I prefer the first.

§ חסיל, סלעם, חרגל, חגב, four species of locusts mentioned in scripture and each translated locusts ; see Joel, 1, 4, and 2, 25. The סלעם is only found once. Levit. ch. 11, v. 22.

* סולנית the name of a sea monster, I cannot find it in any of the Hebrew books.

† את התקרה ומעזיבה, these two words are not found in the Bible, but are joined together in the Talmud, page 116, of Bava Metziah, where there is a rabbinical dispute what these words mean ; התקרה comes from קרה to contignate, and עזיבה comes from ויעזבו את ירושלים Nehemiah, ch. 3, v. 8, which some Jewish commentators give, to build up ; see Buxton, Gesenius and Parkhurst.

34. Then the Egyptians rejoiced at the locusts, although they consumed the produce of the field, and they caught them in abundance and salted them for food.*

35. And the Lord turned a mighty wind of the sea which took away all the locusts, even those that were salted, and thrust them into the Red Sea ; not one locust remained within the boundaries of Egypt.

36. And God sent darkness upon Egypt, that the whole land of Egypt and Pathros became dark for three days, so that a man could not see his hand when he lifted it to his mouth.

37. At that time died many of the people of Israel who had rebelled against the Lord and who would not hearken to Moses and Aaron, and believed not in them that God had sent them.

38. And who had said, we will not go forth from Egypt lest we perish with hunger in a desolate wilderness, and who would not hearken to the voice of Moses.

39. And the Lord plagued them in the three days of darkness, and the Israelites buried them in those days, without the Egyptians knowing of them or rejoicing over them.

40. And the darkness was very great in Egypt for three days, and any person who was standing when the darkness came, remained standing in his place, and he that was sitting, remained sitting, and he that was lying continued lying in the same state, and he that was walking remained sitting upon the ground in the same spot; and this thing happened to all the Egyptians, until the darkness had passed away.

41. And the days of darkness

‖ See Parkhurst upon ארבה locusts under the root רבה

passed away, and the Lord sent Moses and Aaron to the children of Israel, saying, celebrate your feast and make your passover, for behold I come in the midst of the night amongst all the Egyptians, and I will smite all their first born, from the first born of a man to the first born of a beast, and when I see your passover, I will pass over you.

42. And the children of Israel did according to all that the Lord had commanded Moses and Aaron, thus did they in that night.

43. And it came to pass in the middle of the night, that the Lord went forth in the midst of Egypt, and smote all the first born of the Egyptians, from the first born of man to the first born of beast.

44. And Pharaoh rose up in the night, he and all his servants and all the Egyptians, and there was a great cry throughout Egypt in that night, for there was not a house in which there was not a corpse.

45. Also the likenesses of the first born of Egypt, which were carved in the walls of their houses, were destroyed and fell to the ground.

46. Even the bones of their first born who had died before this and whom they had buried in their houses, were raked up by the dogs of Egypt on that night and dragged before the Egyptians and cast before them.

47. And all the Egyptians saw this evil which had suddenly come upon them, and all the Egyptians cried out with a loud voice.

48. And all the families of Egypt wept upon that night, each man for his son, and each man for his daughter, being the first born, and the tumult of Egypt was heard at a distance on that night.

49. And Bathia the daughter of

Pharaoh* went forth with the king on that night to seek Moses and Aaron in their houses, and they found them in their houses, eating and drinking and rejoicing with all Israel.

50. And Bathia said to Moses, is this the reward for the good which I have done to thee, who have reared thee and stretched thee out, and thou hast brought this evil upon me and my father's house?

51. And Moses said to her, surely ten plagues did the Lord bring upon Egypt; did any evil accrue to thee from any of them? did one of them affect thee? and she said, no.

52. And Moses said to her, although thou art the first born to thy mother, thou shalt not die, and no evil shall reach thee in the midst of Egypt.

53. And she said, what advantage is it to me, when I see the king, my brother, and all his household and subjects in this evil, whose first born perish with all the first born of Egypt?

54. And Moses said to her, surely thy brother and his household, and subjects, the families of Egypt, would not hearken to the words of the Lord, therefore did this evil come upon them.

55. And Pharaoh king of Egypt approached Moses and Aaron, and some of the children of Israel who were with them in that place, and he prayed to them, saying,

56. Rise up and take your brethren, all the children of Israel who are in the land, with their sheep and oxen, and all belonging to them, they shall leave nothing remaining, only pray for me to the Lord your God.

57. And Moses said to Pharaoh, behold though thou art thy mother's first born,* yet fear not, for thou wilt not die, for the Lord has commanded that thou shalt live, in order to show thee his great might and strong stretched out arm.

58. And Pharaoh ordered the children of Israel to be sent away, and all the Egyptians strengthened themselves to send them, for they said, we are all perishing.

59. And all the Egyptians sent the Israelites forth, with great riches, sheep and oxen and precious things, according to the oath of the Lord between him and our father Abraham.

60. And the children of Israel delayed going forth at night, and when the Egyptians came to them to bring them out, they said to them, are we thieves, that we should go forth at night?

61. And the children of Israel asked of the Egyptians, vessels of silver, and vessels of gold, and garments, and the children of Israel stripped the Egyptians.

62. And Moses hastened and rose up and went to the river of Egypt, and brought up from thence the coffin of Joseph and took it with him.

63. The children of Israel also brought up, each man his father's coffin with him, and each man the coffins† of his tribe.

CHAPTER LXXXI.

1. And the children of Israel journeyed from Raamses to Succoth, about six hundred thousand men on

* The former Pharaoh.

* In chapter 75, v. 50, we are told that Othri was the first born, but an idiot, I suppose therefore Adikam assumed the birth right with the crown.

†'I cannot understand this, only in the sense of all the Hebrew bodies being taken with them, unless it means the ark of his tribe.

foot, besides the little ones and their wives.

2. Also a mixed multitude went up with them, and flocks and herds, even much cattle.

3. And the sojourning of the children of Israel, who dwelt in the land of Egypt in hard labor, was two hundred and ten years.

4. And at the end of two hundred and ten years, the Lord brought forth the children of Israel from Egypt with a strong hand.

5. And the children of Israel travelled from Egypt and from Goshen and from Raamses, and encamped in Succoth on the fifteenth day of the first month.

6. And the Egyptians buried all their first born whom the Lord had smitten, and all the Egyptians buried their slain for three days.

7. And the children of Israel travelled from Succoth and encamped in Ethom, at the end of the wilderness.

8. And on the third day after the Egyptians had buried their first born, many men rose up from Egypt and went after Israel to make them return to Egypt, for they repented that they had sent the Israelites away from their servitude.

9. And one man said to his neighbor, surely Moses and Aaron spoke to Pharaoh, saying, we will go a three days' journey in the wilderness and sacrifice to the Lord our God.

10. Now therefore let us rise up early in the morning and cause them to return, and it shall be that if they return with us to Egypt to their masters, then shall we know that there is faith in them, but if they will not return, then will we fight with them, and make them come back with great power and a strong hand.

11. And all the nobles of Pharaoh rose up in the morning, and with them about seven hundred thousand men, and they went forth from Egypt on that day, and came to the place where the children of Israel were.

12. And all the Egyptians saw and behold Moses and Aaron and all the children of Israel were sitting before Pi-hahiroth, eating and drinking and celebrating the feast of the Lord.

13. And all the Egyptians said to the children of Israel, surely you said, we will go a journey for three days in the wilderness and sacrifice to our God, and return.

14. Now therefore this day makes five days since you went, why do you not return to your masters?

15. And Moses and Aaron answered them, saying, because the Lord our God has testified in us, saying, you shall no more return to Egypt, but we will betake ourselves to a land flowing with milk and honey, as the Lord our God had sworn to our ancestors to give to us.

16. And when the nobles of Egypt saw that the children of Israel did not hearken to them, to return to Egypt, they girded themselves to fight with Israel.

17. And the Lord strengthened the hearts of the children of Israel over the Egyptians, that they gave them a severe beating, and the battle was sore upon the Egyptians, and all the Egyptians fled from before the children of Israel, for many of them perished by the hand of Israel.

18. And the nobles of Pharaoh went to Egypt and told Pharaoh, saying, the children of Israel have fled, and will no more return to Egypt, and in this manner did Moses and Aaron speak to us.

19. And Pharaoh heard this thing, and his heart and the hearts of all his subjects were turned against Israel, and they repented that they had sent Israel; and all the Egyptians advised Pharaoh to pursue the children of Israel to make them come back to their burdens.

20. And they said each man to his brother, what is this which we have done, that we have sent Israel from our servitude?

21. And the Lord strengthened the hearts of all the Egyptians to pursue the Israelites, for the Lord desired to overthrow the Egyptians in the Red Sea.

22. And Pharaoh rose up and harnessed his chariot, and he ordered all the Egyptians to assemble, not one man was left excepting the little ones and the women.

23. And all the Egyptians went forth with Pharaoh to pursue the children of Israel, and the camp of Egypt was an exceedingly large and heavy camp, about ten hundred thousand men.

24. And the whole of this camp went and pursued the children of Israel to bring them back to Egypt, and they reached them encamping by the Red Sea.

25. And the children of Israel lifted up their eyes, and beheld all the Egyptians pursuing them, and the children of Israel were greatly terrified at them, and the children of Israel cried to the Lord.

26. And on account of the Egyptians, the children of Israel divided themselves into four divisions, and they were divided in their opinions, for they were afraid of the Egyptians, and Moses spoke to each of them.

27. The first division was of the children of Reuben, Simeon and Is-sachar, and they resolved to cast themselves into the sea, for they were exceedingly afraid of the Egyptians.

28. And Moses said to them, fear not, stand still and see the salvation of the Lord which he will effect this day for you.

29. The second division was of the children of Zebulun, Benjamin and Naphtali, and they resolved to go back to Egypt with the Egyptians.

30. And Moses said to them, fear not, for as you have seen the Egyptians this day, so shall you see them no more for ever.

31. The third division was of the children of Judah and Joseph, and they resolved to go to meet the Egyptians to fight with them.

32. And Moses said to them, stand in your places, for the Lord will fight for you, and you shall remain silent.

33. And the fourth division was of the children of Levi, Gad and Asher, and they resolved to go into the midst of the Egyptians to confound them, and Moses said to them, remain in your stations and fear not, only call unto the Lord that he may save you out of their hands.

34. After this Moses rose up from amidst the people, and he prayed to the Lord and said,

35. O Lord God of the whole earth, save now thy people whom thou didst bring forth from Egypt, and let not the Egyptians boast that power and might are theirs.

36. So the Lord said to Moses, why dost thou cry unto me? speak to the children of Israel that they shall proceed, and do thou stretch out thy rod upon the sea and divide it, and the children of Israel shall pass through it.

37. And Moses did so, and he lifted up his rod upon the sea and divided it.

38. And the waters of the sea were divided into twelve parts, and the children of Israel passed through on foot, with shoes, as a man would pass through a prepared road.

39. And the Lord manifested to the children of Israel his wonders in Egypt and in the sea by the hand of Moses and Aaron.

40. And when the children of Israel had entered the sea, the Egyptians came after them, and the waters of the sea returned upon them, and they all sank in the water, and not one man was left excepting Pharoah, who gave thanks to the Lord and believed in him, therefore the Lord did not cause him to perish at that time with the Egyptians.

41. And the Lord ordered an angel to take him from amongst the Egyptians, who cast him upon the land of Ninevah and he reigned over it for a long time.

42. And on that day the Lord saved Israel from the hand of Egypt, and all the children of Israel saw that the Egyptians had perished, and they beheld the great hand of the Lord, in what he had performed in Egypt and in the sea.

43. Then sang Moses and the children of Israel this song unto the Lord, on the day when the Lord caused the Egyptians to fall before them.

44. And all Israel sang in concert saying, I will sing to the Lord for he is greatly exalted, the horse and his rider has he cast into the sea ; behold it is written in the book of the law of God.

45. After this the children of Israel proceeded on their journey, and encamped in Marah, and the Lord gave to the children of Israel statutes and judgments in that place in Marah, and the Lord commanded the children of Israel to walk in all his ways and to serve him.

46. And they journeyed from Marah and came to Elim, and in Elim were twelve springs of water and seventy date trees, and the children encamped there by the waters.

47. And they journeyed from Elim and came to the wilderness of Sin, on the fifteenth day of the second month after their departure from Egypt.

48. At that time the Lord gave the manna to the children of Israel to eat, and the Lord caused food to rain from heaven for the children of Israel day by day.

49. And the children of Israel ate the manna for forty years, all the days that they were in the wilderness, until they came to the land of Canaan to possess it.

50. And they proceeded from the wilderness of Sin and encamped in Alush.

51. And they proceeded from Alush and encamped in Rephidim.

52. And when the children of Israel were in Rephidim, Amalek the son of Eliphaz, the son of Esau, the brother of Zepho, came to fight with Israel.

53. And he brought with him eight hundred and one thousand men, magicians and conjurers, and he prepared for battle with Israel in Rephidim.

54. And they carried on a great and severe battle against Israel, and the Lord delivered Amalek and his people into the hands of Moses and the children of Israel, and into the

hand of Joshua the son of Nun, the Ephrathite, the servant of Moses.

55. And the children of Israel smote Amalek and his people at the edge of the sword, but the battle was very sore upon the children of Israel.

56. And the Lord said to Moses, write this thing as a memorial for thee in a book, and place it in the hand of Joshua the son of Nun thy servant, and thou shalt command the children of Israel, saying, when thou shalt come to the land of Canaan, thou shalt utterly efface the remembrance of Amalek from under heaven.

57. And Moses did so, and he took the book and wrote upon it these words, saying,

58. Remember what Amalek has done to thee in the road when thou wentest forth from Egypt.

59. Who met thee in the road and smote thy rear, even those that were feeble behind thee when thou wast faint and weary.

60. Therefore it shall be when the Lord thy God shall have given thee rest from all thine enemies round about in the land which the Lord thy God giveth thee for an inheritance, to possess it, that thou shalt blot out the remembrance of Amalek from under heaven, thou shalt not forget it.

61. And the king who shall have pity on Amalek, or upon his memory or upon his seed, behold I will require it of him, and I will cut him off from amongst his people.

62. And Moses wrote all these things in a book, and he enjoined the children of Israel respecting all these matters.

CHAPTER LXXXII.

1. And the children of Israel proceeded from Rephidim and they encamped in the wilderness of Sinai, in the third month from their going forth from Egypt.

2. At that time came Reuel the Midianite, the father in law of Moses, with Zipporah his daughter and her two sons, for he had heard of the wonders of the Lord which he had done to Israel, that he had delivered them from the hand of Egypt.

3. And Reuel came to Moses to the wilderness where he was encamped, where was the mountain of God.

4. And Moses went forth to meet his father in law with great honor, and all Israel was with him.

5. And Reuel and his children remained amongst the Israelites for many days, and Reuel knew the Lord from that day forward.

6. And in the third month from the children of Israel's departure from Egypt, on the sixth day thereof, the Lord gave to Israel the ten commandments on mount Sinai.

7. And all Israel heard all these commandments, and all Israel rejoiced exceedingly in the Lord on that day.

8. And the glory of the Lord rested upon mount Sinai, and he called to Moses, and Moses came in the midst of a cloud and ascended the mountain.

9. And Moses was upon the mount forty days and forty nights; he ate no bread and drank no water, and the Lord instructed him in the statutes and judgments in order to teach the children of Israel.

10. And the Lord wrote the ten commandments which he had commanded the children of Israel upon two tablets of stone, which he gave to Moses to command the children of Israel.

11. And at the end of forty days

and forty nights, when the Lord had finished speaking to Moses on mount Sinai, then the Lord gave to Moses the tablets of stone, written with the finger of God.

12. And when the children of Israel saw that Moses tarried to come down from the mount, they gathered round Aaron, and said, as for this man Moses we know not what has become of him.

13. Now therefore rise up, make unto us a god who shall go before us, so that thou shalt not die.

14. And Aaron was greatly afraid of the people, and he ordered them to bring him gold and he made it into a molten calf for the people.

15. And the Lord said to Moses, before he had come down from the mount, get thee down for thy people whom thou didst bring forth from Egypt have corrupted themselves.

16. They have made to themselves a molten calf, and have bowed down to it, now therefore leave me, that I may consume them from off the earth, for they are a stiffnecked people.

17. And Moses besought the countenance of the Lord, and he prayed to the Lord for the people on account of the calf which they had made, and he afterward descended from the mount and in his hands were the two tablets of stone, which God had given him to command the Israelites.

18. And when Moses approached the camp and saw the calf which the people had made, the anger of Moses was kindled and he broke the tablets under the mount.

19. And Moses came to the camp and he took the calf and burned it with fire, and ground it till it became fine *dust*, and strewed it upon the water and gave it to the Israelites to drink.

20. And there died of the people by the swords of each other about three thousand men who had made the calf.

21. And on the morrow Moses said to the people, I will go up to the Lord, peradventure I may make atonement for your sins which you have sinned to the Lord.

22. And Moses again went up to the Lord, and he remained with the Lord forty days and forty nights.

23. And during the forty days did Moses intreat the Lord in behalf of the children of Israel, and the Lord hearkened to the prayer of Moses, and the Lord was intreated of him in behalf of Israel.

24. Then spake the Lord to Moses to hew two stone tablets and to bring them up to the Lord, who would write upon them the ten commandments.

25. Now Moses did so, and he came down and hewed the two tablets and went up to mount Sinai to the Lord, and the Lord wrote the ten commandments upon the tablets.

26. And Moses remained yet with the Lord forty days and forty nights, and the Lord instructed him in statutes and judgments *to impart* to Israel.

27. And the Lord commanded him respecting the children of Israel that they should make a sanctuary for the Lord, that his name might rest therein, and the Lord showed him the likeness of the sanctuary and the likeness of all its vessels.

28. And at the end of the forty days, Moses came down from the mount and the two tablets were in his hand.

29. And Moses came to the child-

ren of Israel and spoke to them all the words of the Lord, and he taught them laws, statutes and judgments which the Lord had taught him.

30. And Moses told the children of Israel the word of the Lord, that a sanctuary should be made for him, to dwell amongst the children of Israel.

31. And the people rejoiced greatly at all the good which the Lord had spoken to them, through Moses, and they said, we will do all that the Lord has spoken to thee.

32. And the people rose up like one man and they made generous offerings to the sanctuary of the Lord, and each man brought the offering of the Lord for the work of the sanctuary, and for all its service.

33. And all the children of Israel brought each man of all that was found in his possession for the work of the sanctuary of the Lord, gold, silver and brass, and every thing that was serviceable for the sanctuary.

34. And all the wise men who were practised in work came and made the sanctuary of the Lord, according to all that the Lord had commanded, every man in the work in which he had been practised; and all the wise men in heart made the sanctuary, and its furniture and all the vessels for the holy service, as the Lord had commanded Moses.

35. And the work of the sanctuary of the tabernacle was completed at the end of five months, and the children of Israel did all that the Lord had commanded Moses.

36. And they brought the sanctuary and all its furniture to Moses; like unto the representation which the Lord had shown to Moses, so did the children of Israel.

37. And Moses saw the work, and

behold they did it as the Lord had commanded him, so Moses blessed them.

CHAPTER LXXXIII.

1. And in the twelfth month, in the twenty third *day* of the month, Moses took Aaron and his sons, and he dressed them in their garments, and anointed them and did unto them as the Lord had commanded him, and Moses brought up all the offerings which the Lord had on that day commanded him.

2. Moses afterward took Aaron and his sons and said to them, for seven days shall you remain at the door of the tabernacle, for thus am I commanded.

3. And Aaron and his sons did all that the Lord had commanded them through Moses, and they remained for seven days at the door of the tabernacle.

4. And on the eighth day, being the first day of the first month, in the second year from the Israelites' departure from Egypt, Moses erected the sanctuary, and Moses put up all the furniture of the tabernacle and all the furniture of the sanctuary, and he did all that the Lord had commanded him.

5. And Moses called to Aaron and his sons, and they brought the burnt offering and the sin offering for themselves and the children of Israel, as the Lord had commanded Moses.

6. On that day the two sons of Aaron, Nadab and Abihu, took strange fire and brought it before the Lord who had not commanded them, and a fire went forth from before the Lord, and consumed them, and they died before the Lord on that day.

7. Then on the day when Moses

had completed to erect the sanctuary, the princes of the children of Israel began to bring their offerings before the Lord for the dedication of the altar.

8. And they brought up their offerings each prince for one day, a prince each day for twelve days.

9. And all the offerings which they brought, each man in his day, one silver charger weighing one hundred and thirty *shekels*, one silver bowl of seventy shekels after the shekel of the sanctuary, both of them full of fine flour, mingled with oil for a meat offering.

10. One spoon, weighing ten *shekels* of gold, full of incense.

11. One young bullock, one ram, one lamb of the first year for a burnt offering.

12. And one kid of the goats for a sin offering.

13. And for a sacrifice of peace offering, two oxen, five rams, five he-goats, five lambs of a year old.

14. Thus did the twelve princes of Israel day by day, each man *in* his day.

15. And it was after this, in the thirteenth day of the month, that Moses commanded the children of Israel to observe the Passover.

16. And the children of Israel kept the Passover in its season in the fourteenth day of the month, as the Lord had commanded Moses, so did the children of Israel.

17. And in the second month, on the first day thereof, the Lord spoke unto Moses, saying,

18. Number the heads of all the males of the children of Israel from twenty years old and upward, thou and thy brother Aaron and the twelve princes of Israel.

19. And Moses did so, and Aaron

came with the twelve princes of Israel, and they numbered the children of Israel in the wilderness of Sinai.

20. And the numbers of the children of Israel by the houses of their fathers, from twenty years old and upward, were six hundred and three thousand, five hundred and fifty.

21. But the children of Levi were not numbered amongst their brethren the children of Israel.

22. And the number of all the males of the children of Israel from one month old and upward, was twenty-two thousand, two hundred and seventy-three.

23. And the number of the children of Levi* from one month old and above, was twenty-two thousand.

24. And Moses placed the priests and the Levites each man to his service and to his burden to serve the sanctuary of the tabernacle, as the Lord had commanded Moses.

25. And on the twentieth day of the month, the cloud was taken away from the tabernacle of testimony.

26. At that time the children of Israel continued their journey from the wilderness of Sinai, and they took a journey of three days, and the cloud rested upon the wilderness of Paran; there the anger of the Lord was kindled against Israel, for they had provoked the Lord in asking him for meat, that they might eat.

27. And the Lord hearkened to their voice, and gave them meat which they ate for one month.

28. But after this the anger of the Lord was kindled against them, and he smote them with a great slaughter, and they were buried there in that place.

29. And the children of Israel called that place Kebroth Hattaavah,

* See Numbers, ch. 3, v. 39.

because there they buried the people that lusted flesh.

30. And they departed from Kebroth Hattaavah and pitched in Hazeroth, which is in the wilderness of Paran.

31. And whilst the children of Israel were in Hazeroth, the anger of the Lord was kindled against Miriam on account of Moses, and she became leprous, *white* as snow.

32. And she was confined without the camp for seven days, until she had been received again after her leprosy.

33. The children of Israel afterward departed from Hazeroth, and pitched in the end of the wilderness of Paran.

34. At that time, the Lord spoke to Moses to send twelve men from the children of Israel, one man to a tribe, to go and explore the land of Canaan.

35. And Moses sent the twelve men, and they came to the land of Canaan to search and examine it, and they explored the whole land from the wilderness of Sin to Rechob as thou comest to Chamoth.

36. And at the end of forty days they came to Moses and Aaron, and they brought him word as it was in their hearts, and ten of the men brought up an evil report to the children of Israel, of the land which they had explored, saying, it is better for us to return to Egypt than to go to this land, a land that consumes its inhabitants.

37. But Joshua the son of Nun, and Caleb the son of Jephuneh, who were of those that explored the land, said, the land is exceedingly good.

38. If the Lord delight in us, then he will bring us to this land and give it to us, for it is a land flowing with milk and honey.

39. But the children of Israel would not hearken to them, and they hearkened to the words of the ten men who had brought up an evil report of the land.

40. And the Lord heard the murmurings of the children of Israel and he was angry and swore, saying,

41. Surely not one man of this wicked generation shall see the land from twenty years old and upward excepting Caleb the son of Jephneh and Joshua the son of Nun.

42. But surely this wicked generation shall perish in this wilderness, and their children shall come to the land and they shall possess it; so the anger of the Lord was kindled against Israel, and he made them wander in the wilderness for forty years until the end of that wicked generation, because they did not follow the Lord.

43. And the people dwelt in the wilderness of Param a long time, and they afterward proceeded to the wilderness by the way of the Red Sea.

CHAPTER LXXXIV.

1. At that time Korah the son of Jetzer the son of Kehath the son of Levi, took many men of the children of Israel, and they rose up and quarrelled with Moses and Aaron and the whole congregation.

2. And the Lord was angry with them, and the earth opened its mouth, and swallowed them up, with their houses and all belonging to them, and all the men belongind to Korah.

3. And after this God made the people go round by the way of Mount Seir for a long time.

4. At that time the Lord said unto Moses, provoke not a war against the children of Esau, for I will not give

to you of any thing belonging to them, as much as the sole of the foot could tread upon, for I have given Mount Seir for an inheritance to Esau.

5. Therefore did the children of Esau fight against the children of Seir in former times, and the Lord had delivered the children of Seir into the hands of the children of Esau, and destroyed them from before them, and the children of Esau dwelt in their stead unto this day.

6. Therefore the Lord said to the children of Israel, fight not against the children of Esau your brethren, for nothing in their land belongs to you, but you may buy food of them for money and eat it, and you may buy water of them for money and drink it.

7. And the children of Israel did according to the word of the Lord.

8. And the children of Israel went about the wilderness, going round by the way of Mount Sinai for a long time, and touched not the children of Esau, and they continued in that district for nineteen years.

9. At that time died Latinus king of the children of Chittim, in the forty fifth year of his reign, which is the fourteenth year of the children of Israel's departure from Egypt.

10. And they buried him in his place which he had built for himself in the land of Chittim, and Abimnas reigned in his place for thirty eight years.

11. And the children of Israel passed the boundary of the children of Esau in those days, at the end of nineteen years, and they came and passed the road of the wilderness of Moab.

12. And the Lord said to Moses, besiege not Moab, and do not fight against them, for I will give you nothing of their land.

13. And the children of Israel passed the road of the wilderness of Moab for nineteen years, and they did not fight against them.

14. And in the thirty sixth year of the children of Israel's departure from Egypt the Lord smote the heart of Sihon, king of the Amorites, and he waged war, and went forth to fight against the children of Moab.

15. And Sihon sent messengers to Beor the son of Janeas, the son of Balaam, counsellor to the king of Egypt, and to Balaam his son, to curse Moab, in order that it might be delivered into the hand of Sihon.

16. And the messengers went and brought Beor the son of Janeas, and Balaam his son, from Pethor in Mesopotamia, so Beor and Balaam his son came to the city of Sihon and they cursed Moab and their king in the presence of Sihon king of the Amorites.

17. So Sihon went out with his whole army, and he went to Moab and fought against them, and he subdued them, and the Lord delivered them into his hands, and Sihon slew the king of Moab.

18. And Sihon took all the cities of Moab in the battle; he also took Heshbon from them, for Heshbon was one of the cities of Moab, and Sihon placed his princes and his nobles in Heshbon, and Heshbon belonged to Sihon in those days.

19. Therefore the parable speakers Beor and Balaam his son uttered these words, saying, come unto Heshbon, the city of Sihon will be built and established.

20. Woe unto thee Moab! thou art lost, O people of Kemosh! behold it is written upon the book of the law of God.

21. And when Sihon had conquered Moab, he placed guards in the cities which he had taken from Moab, and a considerable number of the children of Moab fell in battle into the hand of Sihon, and he made a great capture of them, sons and daughters, and he slew their king; so Sihon turned back to his own land.

22. And Sihon gave numerous presents of silver and gold to Beor and Balaam his son, and he dismissed them, and they went to Mesopotamia to their home and country.

23. At that time all the children of Israel passed from the road of the wilderness of Moab, and returned and surrounded the wilderness of Edom.

24. So the whole congregation came to the wilderness of Sin in the first month of the fortieth year from their departure from Egypt, and the children of Israel dwelt there in Kadesh, of the wilderness of Sin, and Miriam died there and she was buried there.

25. At that time Moses sent messengers to Hadad king of Edom, saying, thus says thy brother Israel, let me pass I pray thee through thy land, we will not pass through field or vineyard, we will not drink the water of the well; we will walk in the king's road.

26. And Edom said to him, thou shalt not pass through *my country*, and Edom went forth to meet the children of Israel with a mighty people.

27. And the children of Esau refused to let the children of Israel pass through their land, so the Israelites removed from them and fought not against them.

28. For before this the Lord had commanded the children of Israel,

saying, you shall not fight against the children of Esau, therefore the Israelites removed from them and did not fight against them.

29. So the children of Israel departed from Kadesh, and all the people came to mount Hor.

30. At that time the Lord said to Moses, tell thy brother Aaron that he shall die there, for he shall not come to the land which I have given to the children of Israel.

31. And Aaron went up, at the command of the Lord, to mount Hor, in the fortieth year, in the fifth month, in the first day of the month.

32. And Aaron was one hundred and twenty three years old when he died in mount Hor.

CHAPTER LXXXV.

1. And king Arad the Canaanite, who dwelt in the south, heard that the Israelites had come by the way of the spies, and he arranged his forces to fight against the Israelites.

2. And the children of Israel were greatly afraid of him, for he had a great and heavy army, so the children of Israel resolved to return to Egypt.

3. And the children of Israel turned back about the distance of three days' journey unto Maserath Beni Jaakon, for they were greatly afraid on account of the king Arad.

4. And the children of Israel would not get back to their places, so they remained in Beni Jaakon for thirty days.

5. And when the children of Levi saw that the children of Israel would not turn back, they were jealous for the sake of the Lord, and they rose up and fought against the Israelites their brethren, and slew of them a

great body, and forced them to turn back to their place, mount Hor.

6. And when they returned, king Arad was still arranging *his* host for battle against the Israelites.

7. And Israel vowed a vow, saying, if thou wilt deliver this people into my hand, then I will utterly destroy their cities.

8. And the Lord hearkened to the voice of Israel, and he delivered the Canaanites into their hand, and he utterly destroyed them and their cities, and he called the name of the place Hormah.

9. And the children of Israel journeyed from mount Hor and pitched in Oboth, and they journeyed from Oboth and they pitched at Ije-abarim, in the border of Moab.

10. And the children of Israel sent to Moab, saying, let us pass now through thy land into our place, but the children of Moab would not suffer the children of Israel to pass through their land, for the children of Moab were greatly afraid lest the children of Israel should do unto them as Sihon king of the Amorites had done to them, who had taken their land and had slain many of them.

11. Therefore Moab would not suffer the Israelites to pass through his land, and the Lord commanded the children of Israel, saying that they should not fight against Moab, so the Israelites removed from Moab.

12. And the children of Israel journeyed from the border of Moab and they came to the other side of Arnon, the border of Moab, between Moab and the Amorites, and they pitched in the border of Sihon, king of the Amorites, in the wilderness of Kedemoth.

13. And the children of Israel sent messengers to Sihon, king of the Amorites, saying,

14. Let us pass through thy land, we will not turn into the fields or into the vineyards, we will go along by the king's highway until we shall have passed thy border, but Sihon would not suffer the Israelites to pass.

15. So Sihon collected all the people of the Amorites and went forth into the wilderness to meet the children of Israel, and he fought against Israel in Jahaz.

16. And the Lord delivered Sihon king of the Amorites into the hand of the children of Israel, and Israel smote all the people of Sihon with the edge of the sword and avenged the cause of Moab.

17. And the children of Israel took possession of the land of Sihon from Aram unto Jabuk, unto the children of Ammon, and they took all the spoil of the cities.

18. And Israel took all these cities, and Israel dwelt in all the cities of the Amorites.

19. And all the children of Israel resolved to fight against the children of Ammon, to take their land also.

20. So the Lord said to the children of Israel, do not besiege the children of Ammon, neither stir up battle against them, for I will give nothing to you of their land, and the children of Israel hearkened to the word of the Lord, and did not fight against the children of Ammon.

21. And the children of Israel turned and went up by the way of Bashan to the land of Og, king of Bashan, and Og the king of Bashan went out to meet the Israelites in battle, and he had with him many valiant men, and a very strong force from the people of the Amorites.

22. And Og king of Bashan was a very powerful man, but Naaron his son was exceedingly powerful, even stronger than he was.

23. And Og said in his heart, behold now the whole camp of Israel takes up a space of three parsa,* now will I smite them at once without sword or spear.

24. And Og went up mount Jahaz and took therefrom one large stone, the length of which was three parsa, and he placed it on his head, and resolved to throw it upon the camp of the children of Israel, to smite all the Israëlites with that stone.

25. And the angel of the Lord came and pierced the stone upon the head of Og, and the stone fell upon the neck of Og that Og fell to the earth on account of the weight of the stone upon his neck.

26. At that time the Lord said to the children of Israel, be not afraid of him, for I have given him and all his people and all his land into your hand, and you shall do to him as you did to Sihon.

27. And Moses went down to him with a small number of the children of Israel, and Moses smote Og with a stick at the ankles of his feet and smote him.

28. The children of Israel afterward pursued the children of Og and all his people, and they beat and destroyed them till there was no remnant left of them.

29. Moses afterward sent some of the children of Israel to spy out Jaazer, for Jaazer was a very famous city.

30. And the spies went to Jaazer and explored it, and the spies trusted

*Talmudical term for four miles, each mile consisting of two thousand cubits.

in the Lord, and they fought against the men of Jaazer.

31. And these men took Jaazer and its villages, and the Lord delivered them into their hand, and they drove out the Amorites who had been there.

32. And the children of Israel took the land of the two kings of the Amorites, sixty cities which were on the other side of Jordan, from the brook of Arnon unto Mount Hermon.

33. And the children of Israel journeyed and came into the plain of Moab, which is on this side of Jordan, by Jericho.

34. And the children of Moab heard all the evil which the children of Israel had done to the two kings of the Amorites, to Sihon and Og, so all the men of Moab were greatly afraid of the Israelites.

35. And the elders of Moab said, behold the two kings of the Amorites, Sihon and Og, who were more powerful than all the kings of the earth, could not stand against the children of Israel, how then can we stand before them?

36. Surely they sent us a message before now to pass through our land on their way, and we would not suffer them, now they will turn upon us with their heavy swords and destroy us; and Moab was distressed on account of the children of Israel, and they were greatly afraid of them, and they counselled together what was to be done to the children of Israel.

37. And the elders of Moab resolved and took one of their men, Balak the son of Zippor the Moabite, and made him king over them at that time, and Balak was a very wise man.

38. And the elders of Moab rose up and sent to the children of Midian

to make peace with them, for a great battle and enmity had been in those days between Moab and Midian, from the days of Hadad the son of Bedad king of Edom, who smote Midian in the field of Moab, unto these days.

39. And the children of Moab sent to the children of Midian, and they made peace with them, and the elders of Midian came to the land of Moab *to make* peace *in behalf* of the children of Midian.

40. And the elders of Moab counselled with the elders of Midian what to do in order to save their lives from Israel.

41. And all the children of Moab said to the elders of Midian, now therefore the children of Israel lick up all that are round about us, as the ox licks up the grass of the field, for thus did they do to the two kings of the Amorites who are stronger than we are.

42. And the elders of Midian said to Moab, we have heard that at the time when Sihon king of the Amorites fought against you, when he prevailed over you and took your land, he had sent to Beor the son of Janeas and to Balaam his son from Mesopotamia, and they came and cursed you; therefore did the hand of Sihon prevail over you, that he took your land.

43. Now therefore send you also to Balaam his son, for he still remains in his land, and give him his hire, that he may come and curse all the people of whom you are afraid; so the elders of Moab heard this thing, and it pleased them to send to Balaam the son of Beor.

44. So Balak the son of Zippor king of Moab sent messengers to Balaam, saying,

45. Behold there is a people come out from Egypt, behold they cover the face of the earth, and they abide over against me.

46. Now therefore come and curse this people for me, for they are too mighty for me, peradventure I shall prevail to fight against them, and drive them out, for I heard that he whom thou blessest is blessed, and whom thou cursest is cursed.

47. So the messengers of Balak went to Balaam and brought Balaam to curse the people to fight against Moab.

48. And Balaam came to Balak to curse Israel, and the Lord said to Balaam, curse not this people for it is blessed.

49. And Balak urged Balaam day by day to curse Israel, but Balaam hearkened not to Balak on account of the word of the Lord which he had spoken to Balaam.

50. And when Balak saw that Balaam would not accede to his wish, he rose up and went home, and Balaam also returned to his land and he went from there to Midian.

51. And the children of Israel journeyed from the plain of Moab, and pitched by Jordan from Beth-jesimoth even unto Abel-shittim, at the end of the plains of Moab.

52. And when the children of Israel abode in the plain of Shittim, they began to commit whoredom with the daughters of Moab.

53. And the children of Israel approached Moab, and the children of Moab pitched their tents opposite to the camp of the children of Israel.

54. And the children of Moab were afraid of the children of Israel, and the children of Moab took all their daughters and their wives of beautiful aspect and comely appearance, and dressed them in gold and silver and costly garments.

55. And the children of Moab seated those women at the door of their tents, in order that the children of Israel might see them and turn to them, and not fight against Moab.

56. And all the children of Moab did this thing to the children of Israel, and every man placed his wife and daughter at the door of his tent, and all the children of Israel saw the act of the children of Moab, and the children of Israel turned to the daughters of Moab and coveted them, and they went to them.

57. And it came to pass that when a Hebrew came to the door of the tent of Moab, and saw a daughter of Moab and desired her in his heart, and spoke with her at the door of the tent that which he desired, whilst they were speaking together the men of the tent would come out and speak to the Hebrew like unto these words:

58. Surely you know that we are brethren, we are all the descendants of Lot and the descendants of Abraham his brother, wherefore then will you not remain with us, and wherefore will you not eat our bread and our sacrifice?

59. And when the children of Moab had thus overwhelmed him with their speeches, and enticed him by their flattering words, they seated him in the tent and cooked and sacrificed for him, and he ate of their sacrifice and of their bread.

60. They then gave him wine and he drank and became intoxicated, and they placed before him a beautiful damsel, and he did with her as he liked, for he knew not *what he was doing*, as he had drunk plentifully of wine.

61. Thus did the children of Moab to Israel in that place, in the plain of Shittim, and the anger of the Lord was kindled against Israel on account of this matter, and he sent a pestilence amongst them, and there died of the Israelites twenty-four thousand men.

62. Now there was a man of the children of Simeon whose name was Zimri, the son of Salu, who connected himself with the Midianite Cosbi, the daughter of Zur, king of Midian, in the sight of all the children of Israel.

63. And Phineas the son of Elazer, the son of Aaron the priest, saw this wicked thing which Zimri had done, and he took a spear and rose up and went after them, and pierced them both and slew them, and the pestilence ceased from the children of Israel.

CHAPTER LXXXVI.

1. At that time after the pestilence, the Lord said to Moses, and to Elazer the son of Aaron the priest, saying,

2. Number the heads of the whole community of the children of Israel, from twenty years old and upward, all that went forth in the army.

3. And Moses and Elazer numbered the children of Israel after their families, and the number of all Israel was seven hundred thousand, seven hundred and thirty.

4. And the number of the children of Levi, from one month old and upward, was twenty-three thousand, and amongst these there was not a man of those numbered by Moses and Aaron in the wilderness of Sinai.

5. For the Lord had told them that they would die in the wilderness, so they all died, and not one had been left of them excepting Caleb the son of Jephuneh, and Joshua the son of Nun.

6. And it was after this that the Lord said to Moses, say unto the children of Israel to avenge upon Midian the cause of their brethren the children of Israel.

7. And Moses did so, and the children of Israel chose from amongst them twelve thousand men, being one thousand to a tribe, and they went to Midian.

8. And the children of Israel warred against Midian, and they slew every male, also the five princes of Midian, and Balaam the son of Beor did they slay with the sword.

9. And the children of Israel took the wives of Midian captive, with their little ones and their cattle, and all belonging to them.

10. And they took all the spoil and all the prey, and they brought it to Moses and to Elazer to the plains of Moab.

11. And Moses and Elazer and all the princes of the congregation went forth to meet them with joy.

12. And they divided all the spoil of Midian, and the children of Israel had been revenged upon Midian for the cause of their brethren the children of Israel.

CHAPTER LXXXVII.

1. At that time the Lord said to Moses, behold thy days are approaching to an end, take now Joshua the son of Nun thy servant and place him in the tabernacle, and I will command him, and Moses did so.

2. And the Lord appeared in the tabernacle in a pillar of cloud, and the pillar of cloud stood at the entrance of the tabernacle.

3. And the Lord commanded Joshua the son of Nun and said unto him, be strong and courageous for thou shalt bring the children of Israel to the land which I swore to *give* them, and I will be with thee.

4. And Moses said to Joshua, be strong and courageous for thou wilt make the children of Israel inherit the land, and the Lord will be with thee, he will not leave thee nor forsake thee, be not afraid nor disheartened.

5. And Moses called to all the children of Israel and said to them, you have seen all the good which the Lord your God has done for you in the wilderness.

6. Now therefore observe all the words of this law, and walk in the way of the Lord your God, turn not from the way which the Lord has commanded you, either to the right or to the left.

7. And Moses taught the children of Israel statutes and judgments and laws to do in the land as the Lord had commanded him.

8. And he taught them the way of the Lord and his laws; behold they are written upon the book of the law of God which he gave to the children of Israel by the hand of Moses.

9. And Moses finished commanding the children of Israel, and the Lord said to him, saying, go up to the mount Abarim and die there, and be gathered unto thy people as Aaron thy brother was gathered.

10. And Moses went up as the Lord had commanded him, and he died there in the land of Moab by the order of the Lord, in the fortieth year from the Israelites going forth from the land of Egypt.

11. And the children of Israel wept for Moses in the plains of Moab for thirty days, and the days of weeping and mourning for Moses were completed.

CHAPTER LXXXVIII.

1. And it was after the death of Moses that the Lord said to Joshua the son of Nun, saying,

2. Rise up and pass the Jordan to the land which I have given to the children of Israel, and thou shalt make the children of Israel inherit the land.

3. Every place upon which the sole of your feet shall tread shall belong to you, 'from the wilderness of Lebanon unto the great river the river of Perath shall be your boundary.

4. No man shall stand up against thee all the days of thy life ; as I was with Moses, so will I be with thee, only be strong and of good courage to observe all the law which Moses commanded thee, turn not from the way either to the right or to the left, in order that thou mayst prosper in all that thou doest.

5. And Joshua commanded the officers of Israel, saying, pass through the camp and command the people, saying, prepare for yourselves provisions, for in three days more you will pass the Jordan to possess the land.

6. And the officers of the children of Israel did so, and they commanded the people and they did all that Joshua had commanded.

7. And Joshua sent two men to spy out the land of Jericho, and the men went and spied out Jericho.

8. And at the end of seven days they came to Joshua in the camp and said to him, the Lord has delivered the whole land into our hand, and the inhabitants thereof are melted *with fear* because of us.

9. And it came to pass after that, that Joshua rose up in the morning and all Israel with him, and they journeyed from Shittim. and Joshua and all Israel with him passed the Jordan ; and Joshua was eighty two years old when he passed the Jordan with Israel.

10. And the people went up from Jordan on the tenth *day* of the first month, and they encamped in Gilgal at the eastern corner of Jericho.

11. And the children of Israel kept the Passover in Gilgal, in the plains of Jericho, on the fourteenth *day* of the month, as it is written in the law of Moses.

12. And the manna ceased at that time on the morrow of the Passover, and there was no more manna for the children of Israel, and they ate of the produce of the land of Canaan.

13. And Jericho was entirely closed against the children of Israel, no one came out or went in.

14. And it was in the second month, on the first *day* of the month, that the Lord said to Joshua, rise up, behold I have given Jericho into thy hand with all the people thereof ; and all your fighting men shall go round the city, once each day, thus shall you do for six days.

15. And the priests shall blow upon trumpets, and when you shall hear the sound of the trumpet, all the people shall give a great shouting, that the walls of the city shall fall down ; all the people shall go up every man against his opponent.

16. And Joshua did so according to all that the Lord had commanded him.

17. And on the seventh day they went round the city seven times, and the priests blew upon trumpets.

18. And at the seventh *round*, Joshua said to the people, shout, for the Lord has delivered the whole city into our hands.

17

19. Only the city and all that it contains shall be accursed to the Lord, and keep yourselves from the accursed thing, lest you make the camp of Israel accursed and trouble it.

20. But all the silver and gold and brass and iron shall be consecrated to the Lord, they shall come into the treasury of the Lord.

21. And the people blew upon trumpets and made a great shouting, and the walls of Jericho fell down, and all the people went up, every man straight before him, and they took the city and utterly destroyed all that was in it, both man and woman, young and old, ox and sheep and ass, with the edge of the sword.

22. And they burned the whole city with fire; only the vessels of silver and gold, and brass and iron, they put into the treasury of the Lord.

23. And Joshua swore at that time, saying, cursed be the man who builds Jericho; he shall lay the foundation thereof in his first born, and in his youngest son shall he set up the gates thereof.

24. And Achan the son of Carmi, the son of Zabdi, the son of Zerah, son of Judah, dealt treacherously in the accursed thing, and he took of the accursed thing and hid it in the tent, and the anger of the Lord was kindled against Israel.

25. And it was after this when the children of Israel had returned from burning Jericho, Joshua sent men to spy out also Ai, and to fight against it.

26. And the men went up and spied out Ai, and they returned and said, let not all the people go up with thee to Ai, only let about three thousand men go up and smite the city, for the men thereof are but few.

27. And Joshua did so, and there went up with him of the children of Israel about three thousand men, and they fought against the men of Ai.

28. And the battle was severe against Israel, and the men of Ai smote thirty six men of Israel, and the children of Israel fled from before the men of Ai.

29. And when Joshua saw this thing, he tore his garments and fell upon his face to the ground before the Lord, he, with the elders of Israel, and they put dust upon their heads.

30. And Joshua said, why O Lord didst thou bring this people over the Jordan? what shall I say after the Israelites have turned their backs against their enemies?

31. Now therefore all the Canaanites, inhabitants of the land, will hear this thing, and surround us and cut off our name.

32. And the Lord said to Joshua, why dost thou fall upon thy face? rise, get thee off, for the Israelites have sinned, and taken of the accursed thing; I will no more be with them unless they destroy the accursed thing from amongst them.

33. And Joshua rose up and assembled the people, and brought the Urim by the order of the Lord, and the tribe of Judah was taken, and Achan the son of Carmi was taken.

34. And Joshua said to Achan, tell me my son, what hast thou done, and Achan said, I saw amongst the spoil a goodly garment of Shinar and two hundred shekels of silver, and a wedge of gold of fifty shekels weight; I coveted them and took them, and behold they are all hid in the earth in the midst of the tent.

35. And Joshua sent men who went and took them from the tent of Achan, and they brought them to Joshua.

36. And Joshua took Achan and these utensils, and his sons and daughters and all belonging to him, and they brought them into the valley of Achor.

37. And Joshua burned them there with fire, and all the Israelites stoned Achan with stones, and they raised over him a heap of stones; therefore did he call that place the valley of Achor, so the Lord's anger was appeased, and Joshua afterward came to the city and fought against it.

38. And the Lord said to Joshua, fear not, neither be thou dismayed, behold I have given into thy hand Ai, her king and her people, and thou shalt do unto them as thou didst to Jericho and her king, only the spoil thereof and the cattle thereof shall you take for a prey for yourselves; lay an ambush for the city behind it.

39. So Joshua did according to the word of the Lord, and he chose from amongst the sons of war thirty thousand valiant men, and he sent them, and they lay in ambush for the city.

40. And he commanded them, saying, when you shall see us we will flee before them with cunning, and they will pursue us, you shall then rise out of the ambush and take the city, and they did so.

41. And Joshua fought, and the men of the city went out toward Israel, not knowing that they were lying in ambush for them behind the city.

42. And Joshua and all the Israelites feigned themselves wearied out before them, and they fled by the way of the wilderness with cunning.

43. And the men of Ai gathered all the people who were in the city to pursue the Israelites, and they went out and were drawn away from the city, not one remained, and they left the city open and pursued the Israelites.

44. And those who were lying in ambush rose up out of their places, and hastened to come to the city and took it and set it on fire, and the men of Ai turned back, and behold the smoke of the city ascended to the skies, and they had no means of retreating either one way or the other.

45. And all the men of Ai were in the midst of Israel, some on this side and some on that side, and they smote them so that not one of them remained.

46. And the children of Israel took Melosh king of Ai alive, and they brought him to Joshua, and Joshua hanged him on a tree and he died.

47. And the children of Israel returned to the city after having burned it, and they smote all those that were in it with the edge of the sword.

48. And the number of those that had fallen of the men of Ai, both man and woman, was twelve thousand; only the cattle and the spoil of the city they took to themselves, according to the word of the Lord to Joshua.

49. And all the kings on this side Jordan, all the kings of Canaan, heard of the evil which the children of Israel had done to Jericho and to Ai, and they gathered themselves together to fight against Israel.

50. Only the inhabitants of Gibeon were greatly afraid of fighting against the Israelites lest they should perish, so they acted cunningly, and they came to Joshua and to all Israel, and said unto them, we have come from a distant land, now therefore make a covenant with us.

51. And the inhabitants of Gibeon over-reached the children of Israel, and the children of Israel made a covenant with them, and they made

peace with them, and the princes of the congregation swore unto them, but afterward the children of Israel knew that they were neighbors to them and were dwelling amongst them.

52. But the children of Israel slew them not; for they had sworn to them by the Lord, and they became hewers of wood and drawers of water.

53. And Joshua said to them, why did you deceive me, to do this thing to us? and they answered him, saying, because it was told to thy servants all that you had done to all the kings of the Amorites, and we were greatly afraid of our lives, and we did this thing.

54. And Joshua appointed them on that day to hew wood and to draw water, and he divided them for slaves to all the tribes of Israel.

55. And when Adonizedek king of Jerusalem heard all that the children of Israel had done to Jericho and to Ai, he sent to Hoham king of Hebron and to Piram king of Jarmuth, and to Japhia king of Lachish and to Deber king of Eglon, saying,

56. Come up to me and help me, that we may smite the children of Israel and the inhabitants of Gibeon who have made peace with the children of Israel.

57. And they gathered themselves together and the five kings of the Amorites went up with all their camps, a mighty people numerous as the sand of the sea shore.

58. And all these kings came and encamped before Gibeon, and they began to fight against the inhabitants of Gibeon, and all the men of Gibeon sent to Joshua, saying, come up quickly to us and help us, for all the kings of the Amorites have gathered together to fight against us.

59. And Joshua and all the fighting people went up from Gilgal, and Joshua came suddenly to them, and smote these five kings with a great slaughter.

60. And the Lord confounded them before the children of Israel, who smote them with a terrible slaughter in Gibeon, and pursued them along the way that goes up to Beth Horon unto Makkedah, and they fled from before the children of Israel.

61. And whilst they were fleeing, the Lord sent upon them hail stones from heaven, and more of them died by the hail-stones, than by the slaughter of the children of Israel.

62. And the children of Israel pursued them, and they still smote them in the road, going on and smiting them.

63. And when they were smiting, the day was declining toward evening, and Joshua said in the sight of all the people, sun, stand thou still upon Gibeon, and thou moon in the valley of Ajalon, until the nation shall have revenged *itself* upon its enemies.

64. And the Lord hearkened to the voice of Joshua, and the sun stood still in the midst of the heavens, and it stood still six and thirty moments,* and the moon also stood still and hastened not to go down a whole day.

65. And there was no day like that, before it or after it, that the Lord hearkened to the voice of a man, for the Lord fought for Israel.

CHAPTER LXXXIX.

1. Then spoke Joshua this song, on the day that the Lord had given

* עתים, literally *times;* what proportion of time, I cannot understand by this term, never used in scripture to express any division of time, so I have translated it *"moments."*

the Amorites into the hand of Joshua and the children of Israel, and he said in the sight of all Israel,

2. Thou hast done mighty things, O Lord, thou hast performed great deeds ; who is like unto thee ? my lips shall sing to thy name.

3. My goodness and my fortress, my high tower, I will sing a new song unto thee, with thanksgiving will I sing to thee, thou art the strength of my salvation.

4. All the kings of the earth shall praise thee, the princes of the world shall sing to thee, the children of Israel shall rejoice in thy salvation, they shall sing and praise thy power.

5. To thee, O Lord, did we confide ; we said thou art our God, for thou wast our shelter and strong tower against our enemies.

6. To thee we cried and were not ashamed, in thee we trusted and were delivered ; when we cried unto thee, thou didst hear our voice, thou didst deliver our souls from the sword, thou didst show unto us thy grace, thou didst give unto us thy salvation, thou didst rejoice our hearts with thy strength.

7. Thou didst go forth for our salvation, with thine arm thou didst redeem thy people ; thou didst answer us from the heavens of thy holiness, thou didst save us from ten thousands of people.

8. The sun and moon stood still in heaven, and thou didst stand in thy wrath against our oppressors and didst command thy judgments over them.

9. All the princes of the earth stood up, the kings of the nations had gathered themselves together, they were not moved at thy presence, they desired thy battles.

10. Thou didst rise against them in thine anger, and didst bring down thy wrath upon them ; thou didst destroy them in thine anger, and cut them off in thine heart.

11. Nations have been consumed with thy fury, kingdoms have declined because of thy wrath, thou didst wound kings in the day of thine anger.

12. Thou didst pour out thy fury upon them, thy wrathful anger took hold of them, thou didst turn their iniquity upon them, and didst cut them off in their wickedness.

13. They did spread a trap, they fell therein, in the net they hid their foot was caught.

14. Thine hand was ready for all thine enemies who said, through their sword they possessed the land, through their arm they dwelt in the city ; thou didst fill their faces with shame, thou didst bring their horns down to the ground, thou didst terrify them in thy wrath, and didst destroy them in thine anger.

15. The earth trembled and shook at the sound of thy storm over them, thou didst not withhold their souls from death, and didst bring down their lives to the grave.

16. Thou didst pursue them in thy storm, thou didst consume them in thy whirlwind, thou didst turn their rain into hail, they fell in deep pits so that they could not rise.

17. Their carcasses were like rubbish cast out in the middle of the streets.

18. They were consumed and destroyed in thine anger, thou didst save thy people with thy might.

19. Therefore our hearts rejoice in thee, our souls exult in thy salvation.

20. Our tongues shall relate thy might, we will sing and praise thy wondrous works.

21. For thou didst save us from our enemies, thou didst deliver us from those who rose up against us, thou didst destroy them from before us and depress them beneath our feet.

22. Thus shall all thine enemies perish O Lord, and the wicked shall be like chaff driven by the wind, and thy beloved shall be like trees planted by the waters.

23. So Joshua and all Israel with him returned to the camp in Gilgal, after having smitten all the kings, so that not a remnant was left of them.

24. And the five kings fled alone on foot from battle, and hid themselves in a cave, and Joshua sought for them in the field of battle, and did not find them.

25. And it was afterward told to Joshua, saying, the kings are found and behold they are hidden in a cave.

26. And Joshua said, appoint men to be at the mouth of the cave, to guard them, lest they take themselves away; and the children of Israel did so.

27. And Joshua called to all Israel and said to the officers of battle, place your feet upon the necks of these kings, and Joshua said, so shall the Lord do to all your enemies.

28. And Joshua commanded afterward that they should slay the kings and cast them into the cave, and to put great stones at the mouth of the cave.

29. And Joshua went afterward with all the people that were with him on that day to Makkedah, and he smote it with the edge of the sword.

30. And he utterly destroyed the souls and all belonging to *the city*, and he did to the king and people thereof as he had done to Jericho.

31. And he passed from there to Libnah and he fought against it, and the Lord delivered it into his hand, and Joshua smote it with the edge of the sword and all the souls thereof, and he did to it and to the king thereof as he had done to Jericho.

32. And from there he passed on to Lachish to fight against it, and Horam king of Gaza went up to assist the men of Lachish, and Joshua smote him and his people until there was none left to him.

33. And Joshua took Lachish and all the people thereof, and he did to it as he had done to Libnah.

34. And Joshua passed from there to Eglon, and he took that also, and he smote it and all the people thereof with the edge of the sword.

35. And from there he passed to Hebron and fought against it and took it and utterly destroyed it, and he returned from there with all Israel to Debir and fought against it and smote it with the edge of the sword.

36. And he destroyed every soul in it, he left none remaining, and he did to it and the king thereof as he had done to Jericho.

37. And Joshua smote all the kings of the Amorites from Kadesh-barnea to Azah, and he took their country at once, for the Lord had fought for Israel.

38. And Joshua with all Israel came to the camp to Gilgal.

39. When at that time Jabin king of Chazor heard all that Joshua had done to the kings of the Amorites, Jabin sent to Jobat king of Midian, and to Laban king of Shimron, to Jephal king of Achshaph, and to all the kings of the Amorites, saying,

40. Come quickly to us and help us, that we may smite the children of Israel, before they come upon us and do unto us as they have done to the other kings of the Amorites.

41. And all these kings hearkened to the words of Jabin, king of Chazor, and they went forth with all their camps, seventeen kings, and their people were as numerous as the sand on the sea shore, together with horses and chariots innumerable, and they came and pitched together at the waters of Merom, and they were met together to fight against Israel.

42. And the Lord said to Joshua, fear them not, for to morrow about this time I will deliver them up all slain before you, thou shalt hough their horses and burn their chariots with fire.

43. And Joshua with all the men of war came suddenly upon them and smote them, and they fell into their hands, for the Lord had delivered them into the hand of the children of Israel.

44. So the children of Israel pursued all these kings with their camps, and smote them until there was none left of them, and Joshua did to them as the Lord had spoken to him.

45. And Joshua returned at that time to Chazor and smote it with the sword and destroyed every soul in it, and burned it with fire, and from Chazor, Joshua passed to Shimron and smote it and utterly destroyed it.

46. From there he passed to Achshaph and he did to it as he had done to Shimron.

47. From there he passed to Adulam and he smote all the people in it, and he did to Adulam as he had done to Achshaph and to Shimron.

48. And he passed from them to all the cities of the kings which he had smitten, and he smote all the people that were left of them and he utterly destroyed them.

49. Only their booty and cattle the Israelites took to themselves as a prey, but every human being they smote, they suffered not a soul to live.

50. As the Lord had commanded Moses so did Joshua and all Israel, they failed not in any thing.

51. So Joshua and all the children of Israel smote the whole land of Canaan as the Lord had commanded them, and smote all their kings, being thirty and one kings, and the children of Israel took their whole country.

52. Besides the kingdoms of Sihon and Og which are on the other side Jordan, of which Moses had smitten many cities, and Moses gave them to the Reubenites and the Gadites and to half the tribe of Manasseh.

53. And Joshua smote all the kings that were on this side Jordan to the west, and gave them for an inheritance to the nine tribes and to the half tribe of Israel.

54. For five years did Joshua carry on the war with these kings, and he gave their cities to the Israelites, and the land became tranquil from battle throughout the cities of the Amorites and the Canaanites.

CHAPTER XC.

1. At that time in the fifth year after the children of Israel had passed over Jordan, after the children of Israel had rested from their war with the Canaanites, at that time great and severe battles arose between Edom and the children of Chittim, and the children of Chittim fought against Edom.

2. And Abianus king of Chittim went forth in that year, that is in the thirty first year of his reign, and a great force with him of the mighty men of the children of Chittim, and he went to Seir to fight against the children of Esau.

3. And Hadad the king of Edom

heard of his report, and he went forth to meet him with a heavy people and strong force, and engaged in battle with him in the field of Edom.

4. And the hand of Chittim prevailed over the children of Esau, and the children of Chittim slew of ,the children of Esau two and twenty thousand *men*, and all the children of Esau fled from before them.

5. And the children of Chittim pursued them and they reached Hadad king of Edom, who was running before them, and they caught him alive, and brought him to Abianus king of Chittim.

6. And Abianus ordered him to be slain, and Hadad king of Edom died in the forty eighth year of his reign.

7. And the children of Chittim continued their pursuit of Edom, and they smote them with a great slaughter and Edom became subject to the children of Chittim.

8. And the children of Chittim ruled over Edom, and Edom became under the hand of the children of Chittim and became one kingdom from that day.

9. And from that time they could no more lift up their heads, and their kingdom became one with the children of Chittim.

10. And Abianus placed officers in Edom and all the children of Edom became subject and tributary to Abianus, and Abianus turned back to his own land, Chittim.

11. And when he returned · he renewed his government and built for himself a spacious and fortified palace for a royal residence, and reigned securely over the children of Chittim and over Edom.

12. In those days, after the children of Israel had driven away all the Canaanites and Amorites, Joshua was old and advanced in years.

13. And the Lord said to Joshua, thou art old, advanced in life, and a great part of the land remains to be possessed.

14. Now therefore divide this land for an inheritance to the nine tribes and to the half tribe of Manasseh, and Joshua rose up and did as the Lord had spoken to him.

15. And he divided the whole land to the tribes of Israel as an inheritance, according to their divisions.

16. But to the tribe of Levi he gave no inheritance, the offerings of the Lord are their inheritance as the Lord had spoken of them by the hand of Moses.

17. And Joshua gave Mount Hebron to Galeb the son of Jephuneh, one portion above his brethren, as the Lord had spoken through Moses.

18. Therefore Hebron became an inheritance to Caleb and his children unto this day.

19. And Joshua divided the whole land by lots to all Israel for an inheritance, as the Lord had commanded him.

20. And the children of Israel gave cities to the Levites from their own inheritance, and suburbs for their cattle, and property, as the Lord had commanded Moses so did the children of Israel, and they divided the land by lot whether great or small.

21. And they went to inherit the land according to their boundaries, and the children of Israel gave to Joshua the son of Nun an inheritance amongst them.

22. By the word of the Lord did they give to him the city which he required, Timnath-serach in mount

Ephraim, and he built the city and dwelt therein.

23. These are the inheritances which Elazer the priest and Joshua the son of Nun and the heads of the fathers of the tribes portioned out to the children of Israel by lot in Shiloh, before the Lord, at the door of the tabernacle, and they left off dividing the land.

24. And the Lord gave the land to the Israelites, and they possessed it as the Lord had spoken to them, and as the Lord had sworn to their ancestors.

25. And the Lord gave to the Israelites rest from all their enemies around them, and no man stood up against them, and the Lord delivered all their enemies into their hands, and not one thing failed of all the good which the Lord had spoken to the children of Israel, yea the Lord performed every thing.

26. And Joshua called to all the children of Israel and he blessed them, and commanded them to serve the Lord, and he afterward sent them away, and they went each man to his city, and each man to his inheritance.

27. And the children of Israel served the Lord all the days of Joshua, and the Lord gave them rest from all around *them*, and they dwelt securely in their cities.

28. And it came to pass in those days, that Abianus king of Chittim died, in the thirty eighth year of his reign, that is the seventh year of his reign over Edom, and they buried him in his place which he had built for himself, and Latinus reigned in his stead fifty years.

29. And during his reign he brought forth an army, and he went and fought against the inhabitants of Britannia

and Kernania,* the children of Elisha son of Javan, and he prevailed over them and made them tributary.

30. He then heard that Edom had revolted from under the hand of Chittim, and Latinus went to them and smote them and subdued them, and placed them under the hand of the children of Chittim, and Edom became one kingdom with the children of Chittim all the days.

31. And for many years there was no king in Edom, and their government was with the children of Chittim and their king.

32. And it was in the twenty sixth year after the children of Israel had passed the Jordan, that is the sixty sixth year after the children of Israel had departed from Egypt, that Joshua was old, advanced in years, being one hundred and eight years old in those days.

33. And Joshua called to all Israel, to their elders, their judges and officers, after the Lord had given to all the Israelites rest from all their enemies round about, and Joshua said to the elders of Israel, and to their judges, behold I am old, advanced in years, and you have seen what the Lord has done to all the nations whom he has driven away from before you, for it is the Lord who has fought for you.

34. Now therefore strengthen yourselves to keep and to do all the words of the law of Moses, not to deviate from it to the right or to the left, and not to come amongst those nations who are left in the land; neither shall you make mention of the name of their gods, but you shall cleave to the Lord your God, as you have done to this day.

* ברטניא וכסביא, probably names of places in ancient Greece.

35. And Joshua greatly exhorted the children of Israel to serve the Lord all their days.

36. And all the Israelites said, we will serve the Lord our God all our days, we and our children, and our children's children, and our seed for ever.

37. And Joshua made a covenant with the people on that day, and he sent away the children of Israel, and they went each man to his inheritance and to his city.

38. And it was in those days, when the children of Israel were dwelling securely in their cities, that they buried the coffins of the tribes of their ancestors, which they had brought up from Egypt, each man in the inheritance of his children, the twelve sons of Jacob did the children of Israel bury, each man in the possession of his children.

39. And these are the names of the cities wherein they buried the twelve sons of Jacob, whom the children of Israel had brought up from Egypt.

40. And they buried Reuben and Gad on this side Jordan, in Romia, which Moses had given to their children.

41. And Simeon and Levi they buried in the city Mauda, which he had given to the children of Simeon, and the suburb of the city was for the children of Levi.

42. And Judah they buried in the city of Benjamin opposite Bethlehem.

43. And the bones of Issachar and Zebulun they buried in Zidon, in the portion which fell to their children.

44. And Dan was buried in the city of his children in Eshtael, and Naphtali and Asher they buried in Kadesh-naphtali, each man in his place which he had given to his children.

45. And the bones of Joseph they buried in Shechem, in the part of the field which Jacob had purchased from Hamor, and which became to Joseph for an inheritance.

46. And they buried Benjamin in Jerusalem opposite the Jebusite, which was given to the children of Benjamin; the children of Israel buried their fathers each man in the city of his children.

47. And at the end of two years, Joshua the son of Nun died, one hundred and ten years old, and the time which Joshua judged Israel was twenty eight years, and Israel served the Lord all the days of his life.

48. And the other affairs of Joshua and his battles and his reproofs with which he reproved Israel, and all which he had commanded them, and the names of the cities which the children of Israel possessed in his days, behold they are written in the book of the words of Joshua to the children of Israel, and in the book of the wars of the Lord, which Moses and Joshua and the children of Israel had written.

49. And the children of Israel buried Joshua in the border of his inheritance, in Timnath-serach, which was given to him in mount Ephraim.

50. And Elazer the son of Aaron died in those days, and they buried him in a hill *belonging to* Phineas his son, which was given him in mount Ephraim.

CHAPTER XCI.

1. At that time, after the death of Joshua, the children of the Canaanites were still in the land, and the Israelites resolved to drive them out.

2. And the children of Israel asked of the Lord, saying, who shall first go up for us to the Canaanites to fight against them? and the Lord said, Judah shall go up.

3. And the children of Judah said to Simeon, go up with us into our lot, and we will fight against the Canaanites and we likewise will go up with you, in *your* lot, so the children of Simeon went with the children of Judah.

4. And the children of Judah went up and fought against the Canaanites, so the Lord delivered the Canaanites into the hands of the children of Judah, and they smote them in Bezek, ten thousand men.

5. And they fought with Adoni-bezek in Bezek, and he fled from before them, and they pursued him and caught him, and they took hold of him and cut off his thumbs and great toes.

6. And Adoni-bezek said, three score and ten kings having their thumbs and great toes cut off, gathered *their meat* under my table, as I have done, so God has requited me, and they brought him to Jerusalem and he died there.

7. And the children of Simeon went with the children of Judah, and they smote the Canaanites with the edge of the sword.

8. And the Lord was with the children of Judah, and they possessed the mountain, and the children of Joseph went up to Bethel, the same is Luz, and the Lord was with them.

9. And the children of Joseph spied out Bethel, and the watchmen saw a man going forth from the city, and they caught him and said unto him, show us now the entrance of the city and we will show kindness to thee.

10. And that man showed them the entrance of the city, and the children of Joseph came and smote the city with the edge of the sword.

11. And the man with his family they sent away, and he went to the Hittites and he built a city, and he called the name thereof Luz, so all the Israelites dwelt in their cities, and the children of Israel dwelt in their cities, and the children of Israel served the Lord all the days of Joshua, and all the days of the elders, who had lengthened their days after Joshua, and saw the great work of the Lord, which he had performed for Israel.

12. And the elders judged Israel after the death of Joshua for seventeen years.

13. And all the elders also fought the battles of Israel against the Canaanites, and the Lord drove the Canaanites from before the children of Israel, *in order* to place the Israelites in their land.

14. And he accomplished all the words which he had spoken to Abraham, Isaac and Jacob, and the oath which he had sworn, to give to them and to their children, the land of the Canaanites.

15. And the Lord gave to the children of Israel the whole land of Canaan, as he had sworn to their ancestors, and the Lord gave them rest from *those* around *them*, and the children of Israel dwelt securely in their cities.

16. Blessed be the Lord for ever, amen, and amen.

17. Strengthen yourselves, and let the hearts of all you that trust in the Lord be of good courage.

THE END

The Book of Enoch: Translated from the Editor's Ethiopic Text and Edited with an Enlarged Introduction, Notes and Indexes, Together with a Reprint of the Greek Fragments edited by R. H. Charles. *The Book of Enoch* was considered one of the most important books in early  Christianity and was used widely. It seems to have predated everything in the New Testament, having been written, for the most part, in the second century BC (the first 36 chapters have been dated to approximately 175 BC). R. H. Charles, who translated the book, said, "the influence of *I Enoch* on the New Testament has been greater than that of all the other apocryphal and pseudepigraphical books put together." This book is undoubtedly the most important book left out of the Bible. This fact was acknowledged by editor R. H. Charles, so he researched the text with amazing detail. All his notes are included here, along with a list of every known translation of the texts and how they contributed to our knowledge. This is by far the most complete, thorough and scholarly edition which every serious researcher and student should have. In the early 1900s, after the book was first released, a number of Greek fragments were discovered. R. H. Charles used these newly discovered fragments along with Dillmann's earlier translation to create this invaluable, updated version in 1912. Five years later, in 1917, the slimmer edited version (ISBN 1-58509-019-0) replaced this thicker book, making it virtually impossible to find—until now. **ISBN 1-58509-080-8 • 448 pages • 6 x 9 • trade paper • $34.95**

The Book of the Secrets of Enoch, translated from the Slavonic by W.R. Morfill. Edited, with Introduction and Notes by R. H. Charles. For 1200 years this book was known to only a few people in Russia. When it was finally revealed to the world in 1892, it was announced that it was a Slavonic version of The Book of Enoch. This was wrong. Once translated, it was found that we have an entirely different book on and about Enoch, described, by the editor, as having no less value than the other book. This is a completely new and valuable pseudepigraph, one which every person should read who is interested in apocalyptic literature and the origins of Christianity. This particular book was read extensively by many separate Christian groups during the first three centuries, and it has left us today with many traces of its influence. It is now time to bring this book back into print so we may relearn its value to the world. This work was written in Egypt and we have determined that its author or original editor was a Hellenistic Jew. The Greek original has been lost to history, but the Slavonic text somehow survived. In its original Greek form it had a direct influence on the writers of the New Testament. This book was also referred to by Origen and used by the Church father, Irenaeus. It was read and considered valuable by the heretics of the day in addition to mainstream Christians. This may be one reason why it was excluded from the Bible. We hope this book will enlighten and inform those who are seeking the truth. **ISBN 1-58509-020-4 • 148 pages • 5 1/2 x 8 1/2 • trade paper • $13.95**

Enuma Elish: The Seven Tablets of Creation (in two volumes), by **L. W. King.** Subtitled: The Babylonian and Assyrian Legends  Concerning the Creation of the World and of Mankind. The *Enuma Elish* is one of the oldest stories known to mankind. It is a story first written down by the ancient Sumerians thousands of years ago. As a one-time assistant in the Department of Egyptian and Assyrian Antiquities at the British Museum, L. W. King provides us with a qualified translation of the tablets that were originally written in cuneiform script. The *Enuma Elish* is receiving renewed interest from modern researchers delving into the origins of mankind, the earth, and the solar system. Over the centuries a copy ended up in the library at Nineveh in the 7th century BC, and was uncovered by archaeologists in the late 1800s. Written in cuneiform text and preserved on seven clay tablets, the entire story was called *The Seven Tablets of Creation*. After being translated the story revealed how the planets became aligned, how a cosmic catastrophe affected the earth, how mankind came upon the scene, and how the "gods" played a role in all of it. *The Seven Tablets of Creation* have had many profound implications since they were first discovered and published. They predate many parts of the Book of Genesis as well as other worldwide creation myths. Volume One includes this epic poem's English translation. It also includes information on parallels in Hebrew literature, the date and origin of the Babylonian creation legends, and more. **Vo 1: ISBN 1-58509-041-7 • 236 pages • 6 x 9 • trade paper • illustrated • $18.95. Vo 2: ISBN 1-58509-042-5 • 260 pages • 6 x 9 • trade paper • illustrated • $19.95**

Of Heaven and Earth: Essays Presented at the First Sitchin Studies Day, edited by Zecharia Sitchin. ISBN 1-885395-17-5 • 164 pages • 5 1/2 x 8 1/2 • trade paper • illustrated • $14.95

God Games: What Do You Do Forever?, by Neil Freer. ISBN 1-885395-39-6 • 312 pages • 6 x 9 • trade paper • $19.95

Space Travelers and the Genesis of the Human Form: Evidence of Intelligent Contact in the Solar System, by Joan d'Arc. ISBN 1-58509-127-8 • 208 pages • 6 x 9 • trade paper • illustrated • $18.95

Humanity's Extraterrestrial Origins: ET Influences on Humankind's Biological and Cultural Evolution, by Dr. Arthur David Horn with Lynette Mallory-Horn. ISBN 3-931652-31-9 • 373 pages • 6 x 9 • trade paper • $17.00

Past Shock: The Origin of Religion and Its Impact on the Human Soul, by Jack Barranger. ISBN 1-885395-08-6 • 126 pages • 6 x 9 • trade paper • illustrated • $12.95

Flying Serpents and Dragons: The Story of Mankind's Reptilian Past, by R.A. Boulay. ISBN 1-885395-38-8 • 276 pages • 6 x 9 • trade paper • illustrated • $19.95

Triumph of the Human Spirit: The Greatest Achievements of the Human Soul and How Its Power Can Change Your Life, by Paul Tice. ISBN 1-885395-57-4 • 295 pages • 6 x 9 • trade paper • illustrated • $19.95

Mysteries Explored: The Search for Human Origins, UFOs, and Religious Beginnings, by Jack Barranger and Paul Tice. ISBN 1-58509-101-4 • 104 pages • 6 x 9 • trade paper • $12.95

Mushrooms and Mankind: The Impact of Mushrooms on Human Consciousness and Religion, by James Arthur. ISBN 1-58509-151-0 • 180 pages • 6 x 9 • trade paper • $16.95

Vril or Vital Magnetism, with an Introduction by Paul Tice. ISBN 1-58509-030-1 • 124 pages • 5 1/2 x 8 1/2 • trade paper • $12.95

The Odic Force: Letters on Od and Magnetism, by Karl von Reichenbach. ISBN 1-58509-001-8 • 192 pages • 6 x 9 • trade paper • $15.95

The New Revelation: The Coming of a New Spiritual Paradigm, by Arthur Conan Doyle. ISBN 1-58509-220-7 • 124 pages • 6 x 9 • trade paper • $12.95

The Astral World: Its Scenes, Dwellers, and Phenomena, by Swami Panchadasi. ISBN 1-58509-071-9 • 104 pages • 6 x 9 • trade paper • $11.95

Reason and Belief: The Impact of Scientific Discovery on Religious and Spiritual Faith, by Sir Oliver Lodge. ISBN 1-58509-226-6 • 180 pages • 6 x 9 • trade paper • $17.95

William Blake: A Biography, by Basil De Selincourt. ISBN 1-58509-225-8 • 384 pages • 6 x 9 • trade paper • $28.95

The Divine Pymander: And Other Writings of Hermes Trismegistus, translated by John D. Chambers. ISBN 1-58509-046-8 • 196 pages • 6 x 9 • trade paper • $16.95

Theosophy and The Secret Doctrine, by Harriet L. Henderson. Includes **H.P. Blavatsky: An Outline of Her Life,** by Herbert Whyte, ISBN 1-58509-075-1 • 132 pages • 6 x 9 • trade paper • $13.95

The Light of Egypt, Volume One: The Science of the Soul and the Stars, by Thomas H. Burgoyne. ISBN 1-58509-051-4 • 320 pages • 6 x 9 • trade paper • illustrated • $24.95

The Light of Egypt, Volume Two: The Science of the Soul and the Stars, by Thomas H. Burgoyne. ISBN 1-58509-052-2 • 224 pages • 6 x 9 • trade paper • illustrated • $17.95

The Jumping Frog and 18 Other Stories: 19 Unforgettable Mark Twain Stories, by Mark Twain. ISBN 1-58509-200-2 • 128 pages • 6 x 9 • trade paper • $12.95

The Devil's Dictionary: A Guidebook for Cynics, by Ambrose Bierce. ISBN 1-58509-016-6 • 144 pages • 6 x 9 • trade paper • $12.95

The Smoky God: Or The Voyage to the Inner World, by Willis George Emerson. ISBN 1-58509-067-0 • 184 pages • 6 x 9 • trade paper • illustrated • $15.95

A Short History of the World, by H.G. Wells. ISBN 1-58509-211-8 • 320 pages • 6 x 9 • trade paper • $24.95

The Voyages and Discoveries of the Companions of Columbus, by Washington Irving. ISBN 1-58509-500-1 • 352 pages • 6 x 9 • hard cover • $39.95

History of Baalbek, by Michel Alouf. ISBN 1-58509-063-8 • 196 pages • 5 x 8 • trade paper • illustrated • $15.95

Ancient Egyptian Masonry: The Building Craft, by Sommers Clarke and R. Engelback. ISBN 1-58509-059-X • 350 pages • 6 x 9 • trade paper • illustrated • $26.95

That Old Time Religion: The Story of Religious Foundations, by Jordan Maxwell and Paul Tice. ISBN 1-58509-100-6 • 220 pages • 6 x 9 • trade paper • $19.95

Jumpin' Jehovah: Exposing the Atrocities of the Old Testament God, by Paul Tice. ISBN 1-58509-102-2 • 104 pages • 6 x 9 • trade paper • $12.95

The Book of Enoch: A Work of Visionary Revelation and Prophecy, Revealing Divine Secrets and Fantastic Information about Creation, Salvation, Heaven and Hell, translated by R. H. Charles. ISBN 1-58509-019-0 • 152 pages • 5 1/2 x 8 1/2 • trade paper • $13.95

The Book of Enoch: Translated from the Editor's Ethiopic Text and Edited with an Enlarged Introduction, Notes and Indexes, Together with a Reprint of the Greek Fragments, edited by R. H. Charles. ISBN 1-58509-080-5 • 448 pages • 6 x 9 • trade paper • $34.95

The Book of the Secrets of Enoch, translated from the Slavonic by W. R. Morfill. Edited, with Introduction and Notes by R. H. Charles. ISBN 1-58509-020-4 • 148 pages • 5 1/2 x 8 1/2 • trade paper • $13.95

Enuma Elish: The Seven Tablets of Creation, Volume One, by L. W. King. ISBN 1-58509-041-7 • 236 pages • 6 x 9 • trade paper • illustrated • $18.95

Enuma Elish: The Seven Tablets of Creation, Volume Two, by L. W. King. ISBN 1-58509-042-5 • 260 pages • 6 x 9 • trade paper • illustrated • $19.95

Enuma Elish, Volumes One and Two: The Seven Tablets of Creation, by L. W. King. Two volumes from above bound as one. ISBN 1-58509-043-3 • 496 pages • 6 x 9 • trade paper • illustrated • $38.90

The Archko Volume: Documents that Claim Proof to the Life, Death, and Resurrection of Christ, by Drs. McIntosh and Twyman. ISBN 1-58509-082-4 • 248 pages • 6 x 9 • trade paper • $20.95

The Lost Language of Symbolism: An Inquiry into the Origin of Certain Letters, Words, Names, Fairy-Tales, Folklore, and Mythologies, by Harold Bayley. ISBN 1-58509-070-0 • 384 pages • 6 x 9 • trade paper • $27.95

The Book of Jasher: A Suppressed Book that was Removed from the Bible, Referred to in Joshua and Second Samuel, translated by Albinus Alcuin (800 AD). ISBN 1-58509-081-6 • 304 pages • 6 x 9 • trade paper • $24.95

The Bible's Most Embarrassing Moments, with an Introduction by Paul Tice. ISBN 1-58509-025-5 • 172 pages • 5 x 8 • trade paper • $14.95

History of the Cross: The Pagan Origin and Idolatrous Adoption and Worship of the Image, by Henry Dana Ward. ISBN 1-58509-056-5 • 104 pages • 6 x 9 • trade paper • illustrated • $11.95

Was Jesus Influenced by Buddhism? A Comparative Study of the Lives and Thoughts of Gautama and Jesus, by Dwight Goddard. ISBN 1-58509-027-1 • 252 pages • 6 x 9 • trade paper • $19.95

History of the Christian Religion to the Year Two Hundred, by Charles B. Waite. ISBN 1-885395-15-9 • 556 pages. • 6 x 9 • hard cover • $25.00

Symbols, Sex, and the Stars, by Ernest Busenbark. ISBN 1-885395-19-1 • 396 pages • 5 1/2 x 8 1/2 • trade paper • $22.95

History of the First Council of Nice: A World's Christian Convention, A.D. 325, by Dean Dudley. ISBN 1-58509-023-9 • 132 pages • 5 1/2 x 8 1/2 • trade paper • $12.95

The World's Sixteen Crucified Saviors, by Kersey Graves. ISBN 1-58509-018-2 • 436 pages 5 1/2 x 8 1/2 • trade paper • $29.95

Babylonian Influence on the Bible and Popular Beliefs: A Comparative Study of Genesis I.2 by A. Smythe Palmer. ISBN 1-58509-000-X • 124 pages • 6 x 9 • trade paper • $12.95

Biography of Satan: Exposing the Origins of the Devil, by Kersey Graves. ISBN 1-885395-11-6 • 168 pages • 5 1/2 x 8 1/2 • trade paper • $13.95

The Malleus Maleficarum: The Notorious Handbook Once Used to Condemn and Punish "Witches", by Heinrich Kramer and James Sprenger. ISBN 1-58509-098-0 • 332 pages • 6 x 9 • trade paper • $25.95

Crux Ansata: An Indictment of the Roman Catholic Church, by H. G. Wells. ISBN 1-58509-210-X • 160 pages • 6 x 9 • trade paper • $14.95

Emanuel Swedenborg: The Spiritual Columbus, by U.S.E. (William Spear). ISBN 1-58509-096-4 • 208 pages • 6 x 9 • trade paper • $17.95

Dragons and Dragon Lore, by Ernest Ingersoll. ISBN 1-58509-021-2 • 228 pages • 6 x 9 • trade paper • illustrated • $17.95

The Vision of God, by Nicholas of Cusa. ISBN 1-58509-004-2 • 160 pages • 5 x 8 • trade paper $13.95

The Historical Jesus and the Mythical Christ: Separating Fact From Fiction, by Gerald Massey. ISBN 1-58509-073-5 • 244 pages • 6 x 9 • trade paper • $18.95

Gog and Magog: The Giants in Guildhall; Their Real and Legendary History, with a Account of Other Giants at Home and Abroad, by F.W. Fairholt. ISBN 1-58509-084-0 • 17 pages • 6 x 9 • trade paper • $16.95

The Origin and Evolution of Religion, by Albert Churchward. ISBN 1-58509-078-6 • 504 page • 6 x 9 • trade paper • $39.95

The Origin of Biblical Traditions, by Albert T. Clay. ISBN 1-58509-065-4 • 220 pages • 5 1/2 8 1/2 • trade paper • $17.95

Aryan Sun Myths, by Sarah Elizabeth Titcomb, Introduction by Charles Morris. ISBN 1-58509-069-7 • 192 pages • 6 x 9 • trade paper • $15.95

The Social Record of Christianity, by Joseph McCabe. Includes *The Lies and Fallacies of the Encyclopedia Britannica,* ISBN 1-58509-215-0 • 204 pages • 6 x 9 • trade paper • $17.95

The History of the Christian Religion and Church During the First Three Centuries, by Dr Augustus Neander. ISBN 1-58509-077-8 • 112 pages • 6 x 9 • trade paper • $12.95

Ancient Symbol Worship: Influence of the Phallic Idea in the Religions of Antiquity, by Hodder M. Westropp and C. Staniland Wake. ISBN 1-58509-048-4 • 120 pages • 6 x 9 • trade paper • illustrated • $12.95

The Gnosis: Or Ancient Wisdom in the Christian Scriptures, by William Kingsland. ISBN 1-58509-047-6 • 232 pages • 6 x 9 • trade paper • $18.95

The Evolution of the Idea of God: An Inquiry into the Origin of Religions, by Grant Allen. ISBN 1-58509-074-3 • 160 pages • 6 x 9 • trade paper • $14.95

Sun Lore of All Ages: A Survey of Solar Mythology, Folklore, Customs, Worship, Festivals, and Superstition, by William Tyler Olcott. ISBN 1-58509-044-1 • 316 pages • 6 x 9 • trade paper • $24.95

Nature Worship: An Account of Phallic Faiths and Practices Ancient and Modern, by the Author of Phallicism with an Introduction by Tedd St. Rain. ISBN 1-58509-049-2 • 112 pages • 6 x 9 • trade paper • illustrated • $12.95

Life and Religion, by Max Muller. ISBN 1-885395-10-8 • 237 pages • 5 1/2 x 8 1/2 • trade paper • $14.95

Jesus: God, Man, or Myth? An Examination of the Evidence, by Herbert Cutner. ISBN 1-58509-072-7 • 304 pages • 6 x 9 • trade paper • $23.95

Pagan and Christian Creeds: Their Origin and Meaning, by Edward Carpenter. ISBN 1-58509-024-7 • 316 pages • 5 1/2 x 8 1/2 • trade paper • $24.95

The Christ Myth: A Study, by Elizabeth Evans. ISBN 1-58509-037-9 • 136 pages • 6 x 9 • trade paper • $13.95

Popery: Foe of the Church and the Republic, by Joseph F. Van Dyke. ISBN 1-58509-058-1 • 336 pages • 6 x 9 • trade paper • illustrated • $25.95

Career of Religious Ideas, by Hudson Tuttle. ISBN 1-58509-066-2 • 172 pages • 5 x 8 • trade paper • $15.95

Buddhist Suttas: Major Scriptural Writings from Early Buddhism, by T.W. Rhys Davids. ISBN 1-58509-079-4 • 376 pages • 6 x 9 • trade paper • $27.95

Early Buddhism, by T. W. Rhys Davids. Includes *Buddhist Ethics: The Way to Salvation?,* by Paul Tice. ISBN 1-58509-076-X • 112 pages • 6 x 9 • trade paper • $12.95

The Fountain-Head of Religion: A Comparative Study of the Principal Religions of the World and a Manifestation of their Common Origin from the Vedas, by Ganga Prasad. ISBN 1-58509-054-9 • 276 pages • 6 x 9 • trade paper • $22.95

India: What Can It Teach Us?, by Max Muller. ISBN 1-58509-064-6 • 284 pages • 5 1/2 x 8 1/2 • trade paper • $22.95

Matrix of Power: How the World has Been Controlled by Powerful People Without Your Knowledge, by Jordan Maxwell. ISBN 1-58509-120-0 • 104 pages • 6 x 9 • trade paper • $12.95

Cyberculture Counterconspiracy: A Steamshovel Web Reader, Volume One, edited by Kenn Thomas. ISBN 1-58509-125-1 • 180 pages • 6 x 9 • trade paper • illustrated • $16.95

Cyberculture Counterconspiracy: A Steamshovel Web Reader, Volume Two, edited by Kenn Thomas. ISBN 1-58509-126-X • 132 pages • 6 x 9 • trade paper • illustrated • $13.95

Oklahoma City Bombing: The Suppressed Truth, by Jon Rappoport. ISBN 1-885395-22-1 • 112 pages • 5 1/2 x 8 1/2 • trade paper • $12.95

The Protocols of the Learned Elders of Zion, by Victor Marsden. ISBN 1-58509-015-8 • 312 pages • 6 x 9 • trade paper • $24.95

Secret Societies and Subversive Movements, by Nesta H. Webster. ISBN 1-58509-092-1 • 432 pages • 6 x 9 • trade paper • $29.95

The Secret Doctrine of the Rosicrucians, by Magus Incognito. ISBN 1-58509-091-3 • 256 pages • 6 x 9 • trade paper • $20.95

The Origin and Evolution of Freemasonry: Connected with the Origin and Evolution of the Human Race, by Albert Churchward. ISBN 1-58509-029-8 • 240 pages • 6 x 9 • trade paper • $18.95

The Lost Key: An Explanation and Application of Masonic Symbols, by Prentiss Tucker. ISBN 1-58509-050-6 • 192 pages • 6 x 9 • trade paper • illustrated • $15.95

The Character, Claims, and Practical Workings of Freemasonry, by Rev. C.G. Finney. ISBN 1-58509-094-8 • 288 pages • 6 x 9 • trade paper • $22.95

The Secret World Government or "The Hidden Hand": The Unrevealed in History, by Maj.-Gen., Count Cherep-Spiridovich. ISBN 1-58509-093-X • 270 pages • 6 x 9 • trade paper • $21.95

The Magus, Book One: A Complete System of Occult Philosophy, by Francis Barrett. ISBN 1-58509-031-X • 200 pages • 6 x 9 • trade paper • illustrated • $16.95

The Magus, Book Two: A Complete System of Occult Philosophy, by Francis Barrett. ISBN 1-58509-032-8 • 220 pages • 6 x 9 • trade paper • illustrated • $17.95

The Magus, Book One and Two: A Complete System of Occult Philosophy, by Francis Barrett. ISBN 1-58509-033-6 • 420 pages • 6 x 9 • trade paper • illustrated • $34.90

The Key of Solomon The King, by S. Liddell MacGregor Mathers. ISBN 1-58509-022-0 • 152 pages • 6 x 9 • trade paper • illustrated • $12.95

Magic and Mystery in Tibet, by Alexandra David-Neel. ISBN 1-58509-097-2 • 352 pages • 6 x 9 • trade paper • $26.95

The Comte de St. Germain, by I. Cooper Oakley. ISBN 1-58509-068-9 • 280 pages • 6 x 9 • trade paper • illustrated • $22.95

Alchemy Rediscovered and Restored, by A. Cockren. ISBN 1-58509-028-X • 156 pages • 5 1/2 x 8 1/2 • trade paper • $13.95

The 6th and 7th Books of Moses, with an Introduction by Paul Tice. ISBN 1-58509-045-X • 188 pages • 6 x 9 • trade paper • illustrated • $16.95

Printed in the United States
6690